GERMAN CRUISERS
OF WORLD WAR TWO

M. J. WHITLEY

NAVAL INSTITUTE PRESS

Published and distributed
in the United States of America
by the Naval Institute Press, Annapolis, Maryland 21402.

Library of Congress Catalog Card No. 85-72222
ISBN 0-87021-217-6

This edition is authorized for sale only in
the United States and its territories and possessions.

Designed by David Gibbons; layout, maps and diagrams
by Anthony A. Evans; edited by Michael Boxall; typeset by
Typesetters (Birmingham) Limited; printed and bound by
R. J. Acford, Chichester, England.

CONTENTS

PREFACE

This book is a design and operational history of German cruisers during the period 1920 to 1945 and thus is not a complete history of German cruiser development. Chapter 1 is, therefore, merely included as a background piece, setting the scene for the main events of the book. Together with my previous work, *Destroyer!*, this book covers a wide range of actions and events, some of which have not so far received detailed attention. The technical sections have been based both on original German documents and handbooks, as well as upon post-war Allied analyses and reports. Operational chapters have been compiled mainly from the contemporary war diaries of the various ships and commands, cross-referenced where appropriate with the relevant British log-books and reports for the same actions. In common with my *modus operandi* for *Destroyer!*, I have not attempted to use comment and opinion of the original participants for, rightly or wrongly, I believe that memory is fallible and after all, forty years have passed since the events described herein.

In determining the scope of the classes of ship to be covered, I have decided to include the overgrown destroyers that were the 'Spähkreuzer' if only briefly, but omit the larger and much more famous 'Panzerschiffen', despite their being later reclassified as 'Schwerekreuzer' or Heavy Cruisers. These ships were designed as capital ships and not cruisers, their size and power being dictated by the limits of the Treaty of Versailles. It was because Germany's rivals, unfettered by such tight restrictions, produced ships which so obviously outclassed them (and possibly also to reduce enemy propaganda value in the event of a loss) that the ships were reclassified as heavy cruisers at the beginning of the Second World War.

In the text, all times are German time unless otherwise stated, and all measurements metric. Thus ranges are quoted in metres (although contemporary German practice was to use hectometres). Similarly, it will be noted that gun calibres are quoted in centimetres and not millimetres, as was the practice at the time.

Written sources are listed at the end of the book, but in any work of this nature, the assistance of many organizations and individuals is necessary if an accurate and factual account is to result. In consequence I should like to express my grateful thanks to the following:

R. M. Coppock and his colleague, M. R. Wilson, of the Naval Historical Branch, London, for patiently answering my many questions: E. R. Coffee of the Modern Military Branch of the US National Records and Archives Service and his opposite number at the US Navy Historical Center in Washington, Mr D. C. Allard for much help and assistance; M. Furget of the Centre D'Archives De L'Armament, France and S. W. Hackmann of the RN Ordnance Museum, Priddy's Hard, for details of French and British guns and armour; Paul Schmalenbach, former gunnery officer of *Prinz Eugen* for some useful gunnery data; Dip.Ing. R. Brencke, Chief Hull Designer at A.G. Weser; Commander R. F. James, RN College Manadon; Commander P. Siedenburg, Federal German Navy; N. Kelling, Archive Gröner; R. Erikson of Phoenix, Arizona; J. Meister in Australia; Dr J. Rowher of Marine Rundschau; Dr Maierhöfer at the Bundesarchiv in Freiburg and Dr Trumpp at Köblenz; Frank Abelson of Norway; A. M. Sinclair of Y.A.R.D.; David Ennor; Capt C. Haun in France; Gerd-Dietrich Schneider in Germany; Jak Mallmann Showell; Michael Bullen; and Valery Rowley for typing help with the appendices.

All of these have helped in many and various ways. Once again, special thanks are due to my long-suffering wife Rita, both for the vast amount of typing involved and also for putting up with my long periods of hibernation in my den while putting it all together!

1: CRUISER DEVELOPMENT 1887–1918

The cruiser of the twentieth century is generally accepted as being the lineal descendant of the frigate in the days of the 'wooden walls' and was expected to perform similar duties, such as scouting and detached commerce raiding. The path from the single-decked sail frigate to the First and Second World war cruiser, however, is rather tortuous, because of the considerable advances in technology which took place between the middle years of the nineteenth century and the beginning of the twentieth century. Thus, the advent of steam power, iron and then steel construction, the development of more powerful guns, the introduction of the torpedo and mine, all helped to throw the established order of battle into complete confusion. In almost all the major navies, ship construction degenerated into a succession of single ship classes as each new idea was cautiously adopted, with the result that by late Victorian times, all semblance of a balanced fleet had disappeared and the navies of many of the major powers were motley collections of slow, big-gunned ironclads.

As the turn of the century approached, however, a pattern was beginning to emerge, with three distinct types of warship becoming evident. These were the Battleship (descendant of the old wooden, sail 1st Rate), the Cruiser, and a totally new category, spawned solely by advancing technology, the torpedo-boat. As far as the cruiser was concerned, there were several different ideas as to what constituted such, ranging from the 'poor man's battleship' to little more than an overgrown sloop, depending upon the nation concerned. By 1900, such terms as 'Armoured', 'Protected', 'Scout' and 'Small' were used to distinguish various designs of cruiser whose sizes ranged from 2,500 tonnes to about 15,000 tonnes. Armaments too, were equally varied from 10.5cm up to 25.4cm depending upon the particular category concerned and the national preferences of the country in question.

The 1890s saw the beginnings of the cruiser as we know it today, with the major powers, France, Great Britain, the USA and Russia all laying down classes of this type, while the newly emergent naval power, Germany, also began the construction of cruisers, albeit with less diversification than her contemporaries. The reason for this was simply her late start in the naval armaments race and her recent acquisition of overseas territories. She therefore had fewer of the older, more experimental armoured cruisers, but concentrated on smaller and faster vessels for employment on distant stations.

The first recognizable, sail-less cruiser types to appear in Germany were the *Greif* of 1887 and the *Kaiserin Augusta* of 1892. The former, however, was classified as an 'aviso' or station tender, while the latter was known as a cruiser corvette. The lightly-armed (two 10.5cm) *Greif* of 2,266 tonnes could be considered as the beginning of the light cruiser line, and the 6,303-tonne *Kaiserin Augusta* as the starting-point for the armoured cruiser genus which culminated in the uncompleted battlecruisers of the *Ersatz Yorck* design in 1918. Both of these early ships were, of course, coal-fired with reciprocating engines and capable of about 19 knots. *Greif* joined the fleet on 9 July 1897, but saw little active service, being used variously as an engine-room training hulk, then a mining hulk before being sold at Hamburg in 1921. *Kaiserin Augusta*, on the other hand, commissioned on 29 August 1892 and served on foreign stations in North America, Morocco and the Mediterranean until 1902. In 1914, she became a gunnery training vessel and remained on second-line duties throughout the war until sold in 1919. This ship was the first triple-shaft installation in the German fleet and she also shipped the new 10.5cm and 8.8cm quick-firing guns in addition to her main armament of two 15cm guns. The armoured or protected cruiser concept was continued with the next class whose five ships were named *Victoria Louise*, *Hertha*, *Freya*, *Vineta* and *Hansa*.

This class displaced between 5,660 and 5,885 tonnes and carried two 21cm, eight 15cm and ten 8.8cm quick-firing guns at about 19 knots with about 10,400IHP. Once again, a triple-shaft reciprocating installation was employed. These graceful ships, with their three funnels and clipper ram bows, featured a heavy tower foremast and conspicuous, goosenecked boat cranes. *Vineta*, *Hansa* and *Hertha* served abroad in the German colonies until 1905–06 and from then until 1914, all five served as training ships. Shortly before the outbreak of war, all received major refits, when they were reboilered and the number of funnels reduced to two. The heavy fore tower was also replaced by a pole mast. At the beginning of the war, they were employed for coast defence, but obsolescence limited their usefulness and they ended their days as accommodation or training hulks.

The next two ships, *Fürst Bismarck* and *Prinz Heinrich*, showed a considerable increase in size, and incorporated side armour in addition to the deck armour. They displaced

approximately 11,400 tonnes and introduced a larger, 24cm gun and twin turrets to the cruisers. *Fürst Bismarck* served in the East Asiatic Squadron during the early years of the century and then the careers of both ships followed the pattern of their earlier sisters until they were broken up in 1919–20. By 1900, there was a close similarity between the armoured cruisers of the major European powers and those of the USA, where the recent Spanish-American war of 1898 had brought global and colonial responsibilities to the small American fleet. Broadly speaking, the type had crystallized around an 11,000- to 14,000-tonne ship, carrying two or four heavy guns and a large battery of secondary armament, usually of about 15cm. This period, of course, was characterized by a state of intense rivalry between Germany and England, when Kaiser Wilhelm II was attempting to build up a fleet capable of challenging that of the Royal Navy. Hence the *Fürst Bismarck* design was probably responsible for the appearance of the British *Drake* design of 1898, but the British design carried only half the number of main guns, the twin turret being not yet in favour. Both designs carried at least half their secondary guns in low casemates where they were virtually useless in a sea-way.

The next two classes, *Prinz Adalbert* and *Roon*, were very similar in design except that the latter had four funnels. After the brief jump to 24cm guns in the previous two ships, calibre was once more reduced to 21cm with four guns in two twin turrets, one forward and one aft. Three of the four ships, *Prinz Adalbert*, *Friedrich Karl* and *Yorck* became early war losses (*Prinz Adalbert* falling victim to a torpedo from the British submarine *E8* in the central Baltic). *Roon* operated in the Baltic against Russian forces, but had been reduced to an accommodation ship by the end of the war.

The famous *Scharnhorst* class, which followed next, increased the main armament to eight 21cm guns by adding two single upper-deck mountings each side amidships. The armour belt was 150mm with 50mm teak backing, and the deck incorporated 40mm armouring. Triple-screw, triple-expansion machinery was retained for a top speed of 23½ knots. *Scharnhorst* commissioned on 24 October 1907 and *Gneisenau* on 6 March 1908. Both served from 1909 to 1910 in the East Asiatic Squadron where their subsequent fates under von Spee are well-known. This class probably represented the peak of the 'armoured cruiser' concept because the later *Blücher* more properly should be regarded as an inferior battlecruiser for reasons which are outside the scope of this book. Contemporary designs were the British *Duke of Edinburgh* and *Warrior* classes, with six 23.3cm guns; the formidable Russian *Rurik*, with four 25.4cm guns; and the US *Washington* class, also with 25.4cm guns.

In fact, the armoured cruiser concept was already obsolete by this time, for the type had been outclassed by the appearance of the battlecruiser, the first examples of which had already joined the British fleet by the end of 1908. The speed and fire-power of the battlecruiser sounded the death-knell of the armoured cruiser, replacing it in the order of battle. Subsequent German development progressed through several classes of efficient and well-designed battlecruisers, culminat-

ing in the *Derfflinger* class, with further designs remaining incomplete at the armistice. Thus the armoured cruiser was the forerunner of the battlecruiser, and the true ancestor of today's cruiser was really the smaller cruiser which had been developed in parallel with it during the last years of the nineteenth and the early years of the twentieth centuries.

Following the *Greif*, mentioned earlier, the 5,000-tonne *Irene* and *Prinzess Wilhelm* of 1888–89 were recognizable light cruiser types, armed with four single 15cm guns, disposed on the broadside. They could only make 18 knots and were actually classified as 'cruiser-corvettes'. Both served abroad between 1894 and 1901. By early 1914, they had been paid off, but remained in use for subsidiary duties throughout the war. The 4,275-tonne *Gefion*, which joined the fleet on 27 June 1894, began a long series of cruisers armed with the excellent 10.5cm gun of which she mounted ten, all in shielded single mountings. Her two-shaft triple-expansion machinery gave her a speed of nearly 20 knots, but she too saw no active service during the First World War.

A return to smaller dimensions was made in 1897–98 with the appearance of the *Gazelle* class which were classified, appropriately enough, as 'Kleiner Kreuzer' (small cruisers) and it was this type which was progressively refined during the next fifteen years into the excellent light cruiser types which were joining the Kaiserliche Marine in 1918. The development of the various ships in the *Gazelle* series varied, but was generally about or slightly less than 3,000 tonnes. On this displacement, they carried ten 10.5cm quick-firing guns, two abreast on forecastle and quarterdeck, with the remainder on the beam. The first seven ships, built between 1900 and 1901, were basically similar to one another, but the last three, *Frauenlaub*, *Arcona* and *Undine*, featured greatly increased coal bunkerage, with the result that their range was much improved. Their appearance was distinctive, with their pair of tall, very thin funnels, and extended ram bows. *Gazelle*, the first to join the fleet, was commissioned in October 1900; the last, *Undine*, was not commissioned until January 1904.

The ten ships of this group had varied careers with four (*Arcona*, *Gazelle*, *Niobe* and *Thetis*) serving on foreign stations prior to the First World War. *Ariadne* (Kpt.z.S.Seebohm) became an early war loss in the Heligoland Bight on 28 August 1914, while two more, *Undine* and *Frauenlaub*, were lost to torpedoes in the Baltic and at Jutland respectively. *Frauenlaub* was, in fact, torpedoed by the British cruiser *Southampton* during the night action and went down with 320 of her crew. *Gazelle*, *Nymphe* and *Thetis* were sold for scrap during the 1920s, but *Ariadne*, *Medusa* and *Arcona* served in the post-war Reichsmarine. *Niobe* had a most interesting career; after being sold in 1925, she eventually became the training cruiser *Dalmacia* of the Royal Yugoslav Navy. Armed now with six 8.8cm guns and fitted with tripod foremast and raked bow, she took part in the war with Italy in 1941, being captured by the Italians at Kotor. Taken over by the Royal Italian Navy, she was renamed *Cattaro* until the Italian collapse in 1943. Passing once again into German hands at Pola, she reverted to *Niobe* when she became nominally part of the German-backed Croatian Navy. Finally, she fell victim to

torpedoes from British MTBs on the Adriatic coast north of Zara on 22 December 1943.

Amazone, Arcona and *Medusa*, after service in the Reichsmarine, were hulked in 1929–30, the last two being converted to floating flak batteries at Wilhelmshaven in 1942. These ships were scuttled at the end of the war, but *Amazone* remained as an accommodation hulk until as late as 1954. She was then 54 years old!

The next design to be constructed expanded the *Gazelle* type to about 3,800 tonnes full load displacement and, with 12,000 to 14,000 horsepower raised the speed to about 23.5 knots. Armament remained at ten 10.5cm guns, but the major advance was the installation of turbines in one ship of the class, *Lübeck*, the remainder being fitted with triple-expansion machinery. The turbines in *Lübeck* were Parsons-type by Brown–Boverie & Cie and drove a two-shaft system with, initially, an eight-propeller arrangement. *Lübeck* joined the fleet on 26 April 1905. *Amethyst*, the first British cruiser with a turbine installation, had commissioned the previous year, but as yet, no other nation had adopted turbines for cruisers; the first US cruisers with turbines, *Salem* and *Chester*, were not completed until 1908. In fairness, however, it must be said, that at this time, only Britain and Germany were building cruisers in any large numbers, and it was not until 1909–10 that complete classes were fitted with turbines either by Germany or Britain. The *Bremen* class also introduced the tradition of 'town' names for light cruisers, a feature which was copied by Britain and later by the United States. This was a most valuable Public Relations exercise, affording ready-made advertising for the navy, in that each town forged close links with 'its' ship and followed her exploits closely, especially during wartime.

Like their predecessors, the seven *Bremen* class had long active careers, being involved in the fighting from the early days of the war. *Bremen, Berlin* and *Leipzig* had all served on foreign stations prior to the war, but by August 1914 only *Leipzig* was outside home waters, on the west coast of Mexico, *en route* home having been relieved by *Nürnberg*. She then joined von Spee's squadron in the Pacific. Five months later, at the Battle of the Falklands on 8 December, *Leipzig* (Kpt.z.S.Haun) was sunk in action with the British *Cornwall* and *Glasgow. Leipzig* had been at Coronel on 1 November, when von Spee's ships had annihilated Admiral Craddock's squadron, but at the Falklands the boot was on the other foot. Outgunned by the sixteen 15cm and ten 10.5cm guns of the British ships, the German cruiser went down in the darkness and icy seas with all but eighteen of her company. *Bremen* herself was the only other war loss, being mined in the central Baltic between Ventspils and the island of Gotland while in company with the destroyer *V191* on 17 December 1915. Once again the winter seas claimed many lives from both ships.

After the armistice, *Lübeck* was ceded to the UK and broken up, as were *München* and *Danzig. Hamburg* and *Berlin*, on the other hand, were retained by the post-war Reichsmarine and gave stalwart service in a training role until the early 1930s. *Berlin*, attached to the Inspector of Naval Education from 2 July 1922, was engaged upon officer training duties and made a number of foreign cruises during the 1920s in the course of which, long-range radio communications were extensively tested. At this time, the Inspector of Naval Education was none other than Konteradmiral Raeder. *Hamburg* was sunk at Hamburg during an air raid in 1944; *Berlin* was scuttled in the Skagerrak after the cessation of hostilities.

The 1903 to 1905 programmes produced further extensions of the *Bremen* design with the construction of *Königsberg* and her near sisters *Nürnberg, Stuttgart* and *Stettin*. Apart from a slight increase in dimensions as compared to the previous class, these new ships generally followed the three-funnelled, ten-gun 23/24 knots format. In visual appearance, the ram bow had now become less pronounced and the last three ships had a distinctly uneven spacing to the funnels. Technically there was little change except that, once again, one unit received direct-drive turbines in lieu of reciprocating machinery. This was *Stettin*, commissioned on 29 October 1907.

Königsberg and *Nürnberg* both joined the overseas squadron, the latter from 1910, but the former not until 1914. The outbreak of war found both still in foreign waters, with *Königsberg* (Kpt.z.S.Looff) in German East Africa and *Nürnberg* (Kpt.z.S. von Schonberg), having left Hawaii, *en route* to join von Spee's East Asiatic Squadron at Ponape (Caroline Islands). *Nürnberg* was caught and sunk by *Kent* at the Battle of the Falklands on 8 December 1914, but *Königsberg* disappeared from Dar-Es-Salaam on 31 July 1914 and operated initially in the Indian Ocean off Aden, capturing the 6,600-ton British steamer *City of Winchester* (scuttled on 11 August). British counter-measures included the stopping of all shipping in the area with the result that the German cruiser was starved of targets. More importantly, coal became a serious problem, forcing her to return south, where she took refuge in the Rufigi river down-coast from her original base at Dar-Es-Salaam. Here she remained undetected for some time, emerging in September to steam up the coast to attack Zanzibar Island where, on 20 September, she surprised the British cruiser *Pegasus* lying anchored in the harbour and quickly sank her before returning to her hide-out. She was soon located and blockaded before being sunk by British monitors in July 1915. Her crew and a number of her guns were however landed and joined von Lettow-Vorbeck's German East African Army, which remained in action until the final armistice in November 1918.

Stuttgart and *Stettin* remained in home waters. *Stettin* was involved in the action with British forces off Heligoland in August 1914; *Stuttgart* was converted to a seaplane carrier in 1918. Equipped with a large double hanger abaft the third funnel, she could carry three seaplanes. Both ships survived the war, passing to Britain and being broken up shortly afterwards.

The next two ships to be constructed, *Emden* and *Dresden*, joined the fleet from the Blohm & Voss and Danzig yards in 1908 and 1909 respectively. They differed little from previous classes except that *Dresden* had turbine machinery. At the outbreak of war, *Emden* (Kpt.z.S.von Müller) formed part of

the East Asiatic Squadron and had remained at Tsingtau as guardship and senior officer in Chinese waters when Admiral von Spee had taken *Scharnhorst* and *Gneisenau* for a three-month cruise into the south-west Pacific at the end of June 1914. The strong possibility of *Emden* being blockaded in the small Chinese outpost prompted von Spee to order her to escort the squadron's colliers to Pagan Island in the Marianas. This the cruiser successfully did, arriving on 12 August. Here, in the course of a Captain's conference, von Müller requested and obtained permission to operate detached from the squadron as a raider in the Indian Ocean.

On 13 August, accompanied by a collier, *Markomannia*, the cruiser detached and steamed south-west through the Marianas via Yap and the Palau group, and reached the Flores Sea by the 24th. Passing through the Sunda Straits, she entered the Indian Ocean, successfully avoiding the British cruiser *Hampshire* and on 8 September, captured her first ship, a Greek collier. Moving into the Bay of Bengal, von Müller quickly raised his score, sinking a further eight ships and capturing another, which was released loaded with crews from the sunken ships. His next exploit was an attack on the Port of Madras where 125 rounds were pumped into the town and the Burma Oil Company's storage tanks on 22 September. Leaving the tanks ablaze and pursued by a few futile rounds from the shore batteries, *Emden* steamed south again, rounding Ceylon and Cap Cormorin to work off the south-western tip of India. Two more ships were sunk and a third captured before *Emden* sailed further south to the Chagos Archipelago and then Diego Garcia for a short self refit.

Resuming operations, von Müller struck northwards, sinking and capturing more ships, then moved east again to attack Penang. Here, the old Russian cruiser, *Jemtchug* (1903, 3,050t, six 10cm guns), though taken by surprise, managed a few gallant salvoes before being sunk by the German's torpedoes. Fire was also returned by the ancient French gunboat *D'Iberville*, and a brave counter-attack was made by the small French torpedo-boat, *Mousquet*. This tiny 300-ton vessel, armed only with one 9pdr gun and two torpedoes, pressed home a torpedo attack in the face of heavy fire, before being overwhelmed by shellfire. Apart from capturing another ship, which he used as a transport for the wounded survivors of *Mousquet*, von Müller found no further targets in the vicinity and resolved to move south and attack the cable station in the Cocos Islands. Here, surprised in the act of destroying the installations by the Australian cruiser *Sydney*, *Emden* was finally brought to action and driven ashore a wreck. During her raiding career, the German cruiser had sunk or captured 23 ships and engaged the services of warships of Britain, France, Russia, Australia and Japan in the search for her. Kpt.z.S.von Müller became something of a folk-hero to both Germans and British.

Dresden, on the other hand, was to survive much longer, but accomplish little in comparison. Under the command of Kpt.z.S.Kohler, she had been stationed in the Caribbean prior to the war, watching German interests during the Mexican troubles. On 17 July, she sailed for Jamaica with the exiled President and his family aboard, and thence to Port-

au-Prince to rendezvous with *Karlsruhe* coming out from Germany. Here Kohler assumed command of the larger and newer *Karlsruhe* while F.Kpt. Ludecke took over *Dresden*. The latter was in fact under orders for home, but as the outbreak of war was obviously imminent, Naval Command countermanded these and instead ordered him to make ready for cruiser warfare. British and French units were converging upon the two cruisers in the Caribbean, whereupon they took steps to disappear. *Dresden* sailed from Port au Prince on 28 July, under orders to work down the east coast of South America, where there would be plenty of shipping to attack. In fact, her performance was poor and with only a small bag, she gradually moved farther south until by 31 August, she was in Gayertano Bay on the Patagonian coast. From there, Ludecke passed through the Straits of Magellan and into the Pacific by 18 September. Steaming north to the Juan Fernandez Islands, *Dresden* then struck north-westwards to Easter Island and had joined von Spee's squadron by 18 October, when he sailed eastwards towards Coronel on the coast of Chile.

On the evening of 1 November, von Spee's cruisers sighted and engaged the motley collection of British ships commanded by Rear-Admiral Sir Christopher Craddock. The British Admiral had two old armoured cruisers, *Monmouth* and *Good Hope*, together with a modern light cruiser, *Glasgow*, and the auxiliary cruiser *Otranto*. The German ships were in a tactically advantageous position, their crews well-trained and ably led. The British force on the other hand were poorly trained and effectively out-gunned. *Otranto*, having no real role in a cruiser battle, wisely sheered off and eventually escaped; on the German side, *Nürnberg*, plagued with mechanical troubles, was 25 miles astern of her squadron when action was joined and only took part in the closing stages. *Dresden*, together with the two armoured cruisers, annihilated the British armoured cruisers, allowing *Glasgow* to escape.

Dresden remained with von Spee and later took part in the Falklands battle where, when ordered by their Admiral, the light cruisers endeavoured to escape the pursuing British squadron and leave the two armoured cruisers to their fate. *Dresden*, being faster than the other two light cruisers, soon drew ahead of them and also out-paced the British ships. She inflicted damage on *Glasgow* before mist and rain obscured her and subsequently escaped under cover of the approaching darkness. Rounding Cape Horn once more, *Dresden* eventually arrived, short of coal, in Punta Arenas. Here, she managed to coal, despite being ordered out of Chilean waters as a belligerent. There followed a game of hide and seek up and down the Chilean coast for nearly three months until she was finally trapped in Cumberland Bay, Mas-a-Fuera, on 14 March 1915. Here, *Glasgow* and *Kent* engaged her, causing severe damage, whereupon she surrendered. Not long afterwards, scuttling charges exploded and she went to the bottom.

The four ships of the *Kolberg* class which followed, saw a considerable increase in dimensions, to 4,915 tonnes full load displacement. The machinery installation now became completely turbine driven, with a steam plant increased to fifteen

boilers. With 28,000–31,000 horsepower, a quadruple shaft (two in *Cöln*) arrangement drove the ships at 26½–27 knots. Probably for comparison purposes, four different turbine designs were employed: Melms & Pfenniger (*Kolberg*); AEG-Curtiss (*Mainz*); Zoelly (*Cöln*) and Parsons (*Augsburg*). Before her trials, however, *Cöln*'s turbines were replaced by Germania turbines. The increase in dimensions allowed an increase in armament, with an extra pair of 10.5cm single mountings being worked in on the broadside, making twelve in all.

Cöln and *Mainz* encountered British forces off Heligoland in the opening days of the war. *Mainz* (Kpt.z.S.Paschen), sailing from the Ems to support patrol craft under attack by British destroyers on 28 August 1914, severely damaged the British *Laurel* and *Liberty* with extremely accurate gunfire and then did the same to *Laertes* before one of the destroyers' torpedoes hit her amidships. Slowly sinking, on fire forward and aft, her port engine disabled and rudder jammed with 10° port wheel on, the stricken cruiser steamed slowly into the light cruisers of Commodore Goodenough. All four British ships opened up on the lone cripple who could only reply with an odd gun here and there. After ten minutes, on fire from end to end, the German could fight no longer. The upper decks were a shambles, and below decks a roaring inferno. *Mainz* struck her colours at 1250 and the British ceased fire, sweeping on to chase the remaining German ships. *Liverpool* stayed to rescue survivors and the destroyer *Lurcher* went alongside the German cruiser to assist in rescue operations. In the words of one British officer, 'The *Mainz* was incredibly brave.'

Cöln, flagship of Konteradmiral Maass, engaged the British *Fearless* before being overwhelmed by fire from Sir David Beatty's battlecruisers which had been called in to pull the destroyers' chestnuts out of the fire. Badly hit by *Lion* and *Princess Royal*, she had a brief respite when the battlecruisers' attentions were diverted by the unfortunate *Ariadne*. For about half an hour to an hour the ship, her engines disabled, remained unmolested until about 1325, when the battlecruisers returned and in a very short time sent her to the bottom with all her crew except one stoker.

Augsburg and *Kolberg* served throughout the war, but without particularly distinguishing themselves. Neither took part in the Jutland engagement. During the war both ships were re-armed, the forecastle and quarterdeck pairs of 10.5cm guns being replaced by single 15cm weapons. The 10.5cm guns and casements were removed from the beam, as were the midships beam 10.5cm guns. In their place were shipped two single 15cm guns on each side, making six in all. Their torpedo armament was also augmented, with a pair of trainable twin banks for 50cm torpedoes being mounted on the upper deck just abaft the after funnel. In addition, they were fitted to carry 100 mines and later, in 1918, they received two 8.8cm anti-aircraft guns. Having survived the war, both became war prizes, *Kolberg* being allocated to France and *Augsburg* to Japan. As *Colmar*, the former served in the French fleet, until stricken on 21 July 1927, but her sister, taken over in September 1920 by Japan, was not needed by that country and was broken up in Holland in 1922.

For widely different reasons ships of the next light cruiser class were to become famous or infamous depending upon

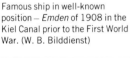
Famous ship in well-known position – *Emden* of 1908 in the Kiel Canal prior to the First World War. (W. B. Bilddienst)

one's point of view. This class, *Magdeburg*, *Breslau*, *Strassburg* and *Stralsund*, was yet another increase in the size of German light cruisers. Displacement rose by about 13½ per cent to 5,587 tonnes, but without a commensurate increase in offensive power. Instead, the extra tonnage was absorbed by improved protection and increased speed. Whereas previous light cruisers had merely a light deck armouring, this class incorporated a waterline armour belt with a maximum thickness of 60mm, albeit with some reduction in the deck armour. Turbine horsepower was increased to 25,000–35,000 and the number of boiler rooms increased to four with sixteen mixed coal/oilfired boilers in total. This necessitated a fourth funnel – a distinct departure for German light cruisers. Their speed was now 27–28.2 knots. Where armament was concerned, the only departure from previous vessels was to give the after pair of 10.5cm guns a higher command by mounting them on the after shelter deck. Surprisingly, however, the opportunity was not taken initially to make one of them superfiring. During the war, all but *Magdeburg* received seven or eight (*Breslau*) 15cm guns in lieu of the 10.5cm guns. In the case of the two seven-gun ships, the after pair were on the centre-line and superfiring.

On the outbreak of war, *Magdeburg*, having served as a torpedo trials vessel since commissioning, was based in the Baltic for service against the Russian fleet. Here, less than a month after Germany had declared war on Russia, a German cruiser force was covering a minelaying operation at the entrance to the Gulf of Finland. The weather was poor, with thick fog reducing visibility. *Magdeburg* (K.Kpt.Habenicht) ran ashore a few hundred metres off the Island of Odensholm (Osmussaar) on 26 August. All attempts to free her failed and, in anticipation of the arrival of Russian ships, her captain gave orders for the confidential books to be destroyed and the ship blown up. Before this could be completed, however, two Russian cruisers arrived and opened fire, destroying her fore-ends and bringing down the forward funnel. Much, much more serious than the loss of this cruiser was the fact that the Signals P.O. was killed and blown overboard while trying to

dispose of the code book. His body and the book were soon recovered by the Russians who, realizing the immense value of their find, magnanimously sent the book to London where it was used, unbeknown to the Germans to decipher their codes throughout the war.

Breslau commissioned on 9 October 1912 and, later that same year, formed part of Konteradmiral Wilhelm Souchon's Mediterranean Squadron together with *Goeben*. As soon as the war started, these two ships, constantly chased by British warships, began offensive operations. On 4 August, *Breslau* bombarded Bône and then proceeded eastwards to Constantinople, entering the Dardenelles on the 11th. Their successful avoidance of the Royal Navy caused the court-martialling of Admiral Troubridge and the recall of Admiral Milne, the two senior officers concerned.

Both *Breslau* and *Goeben* were 'sold' to Turkey, thus surmounting the neutrality difficulty. On 27 October, both German ships, with the Turkish *Hamadieh* and destroyers, sailed to bombard Sevastopol and Odessa, which they did on the 29th and 30th. Sinking transports and destroying harbour installations, the squadron crossed the Black Sea and practically destroyed Novorossisk town, oil tanks and all shipping in the port. Not surprisingly, an enraged Russia declared war on Turkey on 1 November! With a token Turkish crew supplementing her own crew, *Breslau* assumed a Turkish name, *Midilli*, and operated mainly against the Russian Black Sea Fleet, where she was damaged by mines in July 1915. In January 1918, however, in company with *Goeben* and now under the command of Vizeadmiral Paschwitz, she sailed into the Aegean to attack the Allied base at Mudros. On the 20th, the British monitors *Raglan* and *M28* were sunk before *Breslau* was mined off Cape Kephalo. *Goeben*, too, was mined while attempting to tow the cruiser, but then *Breslau* detonated four more mines and quickly sank with heavy loss of life.

After the war, *Strassburg* was ceded to Italy and re-named *Taranto*, while *Stralsund* went to France as *Mulhouse*. The latter was disposed of in 1935, but *Taranto* was assigned to

colonial duties in the Italian Fleet and saw service during the Second World War until scuttled at La Spezia on 9 September 1943, following the Italian capitulation. Although raised twice by the Germans she was each time sunk again by bombing.

The two cruisers of the 1910 programme, *Karlsruhe* and *Rostock*, once again slightly increased the dimensions of the 1908/1909 ships, but otherwise differed little in appearance and only slightly in performance. *Karlsruhe* was *en route* for the Caribbean at the outbreak of the First World War, whereupon, she immediately embarked on a successful career as a raider. On 4 November 1914, having just sunk the 10,500-ton liner *Vandyck*, she was on passage between Trinidad and Barbados, when a huge explosion erupted in the forecastle. This blew away all the fore-ends, killing a large percentage of her crew, who were off watch below decks or on the forecastle. For a long time her sinking was a mystery, but it is generally thought to have been caused by unstable cordite. *Karlsruhe* is credited with the sinking of eleven ships, totalling 76,000 tons.

Rostock spent most of her war as flagship of the torpedo-boat forces and, wearing the flag of Kommodore Michelsen (Flag Officer Torpedo-boats), took part in the Battle of Jutland in 1916. On the night of 31 May, *Rostock* sighted the British destroyer *Broke* and severely damaged her during the attack by the British 4th Destroyer Flotilla. In the ensuing mêlée, *Rostock* was badly damaged by a torpedo in the boiler room. At daylight the wrecked ship was scuttled by her crew, who were rescued by the torpedo-boats of the 3rd Flotilla.

The 1911 cruisers (*Graudenz* and *Regensburg*) and those of the 1912 programme (*Wiesbaden* and *Frankfurt*) followed the pattern of their predecessors, except that in appearance, they reverted to three funnels. Originally, the armament of the first pair was the usual twelve 10.5cm guns, but these were changed to 15cm during the war. Both the after guns were on the centre-line with one superfiring. The second pair of ships, on the other hand, were completed with 15cm guns.

Wiesbaden (Kpt.z.S.Reiss) was lost after fighting heroically during the Jutland battle. Hit and disabled by Hood's battle-cruisers, she became a stationary target for the 3rd Light Cruiser Squadron, then the destroyer *Onslow* followed by the armoured cruisers, *Defence* and *Warrior*, plus any other British ship that was not engaged. *Onslow* then torpedoed her with no effect, and later, Commodore Goodenough's cruisers engaged her, but failed to sink her. Miraculously, after all this shelling, *Wiesbaden* managed to launch a torpedo which hit and seriously damaged *Marlborough*. This was her last shot, however, and, drifting away, she sank some time later.

Graudenz passed to Italy after the war and *Regensburg* became the French *Strasbourg*; *Frankfurt* was employed in the well-known aircraft-versus-ships experiments by the USA in 1921.

At the outbreak of war, two Russian cruisers under construction by Schichau at Danzig as *Murawjew Amurski* and *Admiral Newelskoj*, were appropriated by the German Navy. These two 5,252-tonne ships, re-armed with eight 15cm guns and re-named *Pillau* and *Elbing* respectively, joined the High Seas Fleet in 1914 and 1915. *Elbing* was sunk at Jutland by collision with the battleship *Pommern*, but *Pillau*, ceded to Italy and re-named *Bari*, survived until 1943.

Two further 'non standard' vessels built for the navy were *Brummer* and *Bremse*. Slightly smaller than their predecessors, they carried a reduced armament of 15cm guns, having been designed as minelaying cruisers with stowage for four hundred mines. With their speed of 28 knots, from turbines originally intended for the Russian battlecruiser *Navarin*, these two ships were full of offensive potential and had some success with the gun as well as with the more obvious mine armament.

In October 1917, both ships sailed to intercept one of the regular Britain-Scandinavia convoys which consisted of twelve merchantmen (including nine neutrals). These had sailed from Lerwick on 16 October escorted by two destroyers, *Mary Rose* and *Strongbow*, with two armed trawlers in addition. *Bremse* and *Brummer* sighted the convoy, which had become rather scattered during the night, towards dawn the following morning. Both German cruisers opened fire on

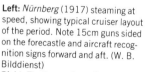

Left: *Nürnberg* (1917) steaming at speed, showing typical cruiser layout of the period. Note 15cm guns sided on the forecastle and aircraft recognition signs forward and aft. (W. B. Bilddienst)
Right: The two cruisers *Bremse* and *Brummer* were designed as mine-layers, using turbines originally intended for the Russian battle-cruiser *Navarin*. (Imperial War Museum)

Strongbow and, with customary German accuracy, hit with their first salvoes. The British destroyer received hits in the engine room and on the forecastle, knocking out her forward gun. Stopped and on fire, she was then shot up by the cruisers from as close as 200 metres. Leaving *Strongbow* in a sinking condition, the Germans closed on the convoy. *Mary Rose*, however, hearing gunfire, turned in search of it and soon located the cruisers. In a heroic dash, the destroyer closed the enemy, but with little chance of success. Out-ranged and out-gunned, she was soon at a standstill. A sitting duck, her guns being knocked out one by one, *Mary Rose* fired a torpedo and was then hit by a full salvo and quickly sank. Only ten of her crew were rescued. *Bremse* and *Brummer* then attacked the merchant ships, sinking all except two. On their return, they encountered the damaged *Strongbow* which returned their fire with what remained of her armament. The cruisers sent her to the bottom and made for home.

A little over twelve months later, both cruisers were interned in Scapa Flow where, on 21 June 1919, they were scuttled with the remainder of the former High Seas Fleet. In the early 1930s, *Bremse* was raised and broken up by Cox & Danks at Lyness.

The last classes of cruiser constructed by the Kaisermarine before the armistice were the four ships of the *Königsberg* group (*Königsberg, Karlsruhe, Emden* and *Nürnberg*) and the ten *Cöln*-class vessels. Only seven of the latter group were named (*Cöln, Wiesbaden, Dresden, Magdeburg, Leipzig, Rostock* and *Frauenlaub*), the remaining three being intended as replacements for the earlier *Cöln, Emden* and *Karlsruhe*. Thus, it will be seen that all these vessels perpetuated the names and traditions of light cruisers already lost during the war years. *Frauenlaub*, it will be noted, was not a 'town' name – the only one since 1904.

The *Königsberg* group displaced 7,124 tonnes full load and carried eight 15cm single guns at 27.7 knots. The *Cöln* type were slightly larger at 7,486 tonnes and carried the same armament. The machinery of both classes was mixed oil/coal-fired boilers and twin-screw turbines. Geared turbines had been introduced in *Karlsruhe*, and some of the *Cöln* group were likewise fitted.

The ships of the *Königsberg* group joined the Fleet in late 1916/early 1917 and saw little operational service. *Karlsruhe* was scuttled in Scapa Flow while *Emden* and *Nürnberg*, both beached on the same occasion, were used by France and Britain respectively, for experiments post-war. Only *Königsberg*, in service as the French *Metz*, was in commission for any length of time, surviving until 1936.

Of the *Cöln* group, only the name ship and *Dresden* were commissioned before the end of the war, the remainder being cancelled at the armistice and broken up. All except the last three had been launched, *Frauenlaub* as late as 16 October 1918. *Cöln* was commissioned by Erich Raeder on 10 January 1918, his first sea command after serving on Admiral Hipper's staff for some years. In May, *Cöln* joined the light cruiser group (Kommodore von Levetzow) with *Königsberg* (flag), *Frankfurt, Karlsruhe* and *Nürnberg*. *Dresden* (K.Kpt.Prince Adalbert of Prussia) commissioned in March and joined her sister during the summer. Employed on brief patrols and U-boat escort duty, the last cruisers of the Kaisermarine saw no action and were interned, and later scuttled in Scapa Flow.

By the end of the First World War, the German cruiser had advanced a considerable way from the *Gazelle* of 1899. At

Right: *Bresslau* escaped to Turkey with *Goeben* in 1914 and sailed under Turkish name (*Midilli*) & ensign. She was finally lost to mines in the Aegean in January 1918. (Imperial War Museum)
Opposite page: Caught incomplete at the Armistice in 1918 on the slip-ways of AG Weser (Bremen), these two ships are probably *Ersatz Cöln* and *Ersatz Emden*. (W. B. Bilddienst)

this time, only Great Britain and Germany were constructing cruisers in any quantity, and a limited comparison of the state of the art in the two navies is both relevant and of interest. The British equivalent of the time was probably the *Cardiff* design of approximately 5,000 tons full load displacement. They were thus smaller than their German adversaries, but possessed roughly the same speed. In terms of armament, both carried similar calibre main armament, the British vessel shipping three fewer guns. This discrepancy was not of much consequence to the British because *Cöln*'s main armament was not disposed on the centre-line (in fact, only the after pair were), while *Cardiff*'s five guns were all centre-line mounted. Thus, *Cöln* could bring only five out of eight guns to bear on the beam, while *Cardiff* could deploy all hers on either beam. Moreover, the latter's 'B' and 'X' mountings were super-firing and commanded good arcs of fire. The British design also carried double the torpedo armament. Both designs were powered by turbines (all geared in the British case) but the fuel position in Germany precluded a 100 per cent switch to oil fuel, as the British had done. In consequence, their steaming abilities still depended upon the strength of their stokers' arms to a certain extent. The British ship possessed a heavier thickness of belt armour, but was not as heavily protected on horizontal surfaces.

The remaining European powers were far behind on cruiser construction. Russia, while having laid down eight units of the *Admiral Boutakov* class at Baltic and Black Sea yards in 1913–15, was by 1917, deep in Revolution and as a result, had no modern light cruisers in service. Austria–Hungary had neglected light cruisers after the 3,500-tonne 'Improved *Admiral Spaun*' class of 1914, and apart from a brief consideration of the conversion of a 4,900-tonne hull under construction (originally for China), finally left the naval scene without any further new construction. The French Navy, too, was in a very parlous state, with all her resources having been channelled into the army. In consequence, there was little new construction for the navy. In fact, her first and only light cruiser, the *Lamotte-Picquet* had, by March 1915, already been suspended. French cruiser construction did not gain momentum until rivalry with Italy became rampant in the 1920s. Across the world, Japan had a useful if undergunned design in the 3,230-tonne *Tenryo* class, but which numbered only two. The United States, rapidly becoming a world power, had not as yet interested herself in cruiser construction.

Thus, at the close of the First World War, Germany had the second largest cruiser fleet, with about thirty afloat, although not all in first-line service. Twenty-three others had become war losses, predominantly in surface action. The Peace Treaty of 1919 led to the scuttling of eight modern vessels, and others were ceded to the victorious Allies, leaving only old and obsolete units to the post-war German Fleet. These comprised *Niobe*, *Amazone*, *Medusa*, *Nymphe*, *Thetis*, *Arkona*, *Berlin* and *Hamburg*, none of which were less than fifteen years old. In the absence of anything else, these worn-out old ships were used to re-form the new German Navy, known from 1921, as the 'Reichsmarine'.

2: THE INTERWAR LIGHT CRUISERS

Under the terms of the Treaty of Versailles, Germany had been allowed to retain only six light cruisers in commission, all of which dated from the turn of the century. Furthermore, no replacements could be put in hand until the existing vessels were twenty years old and even then replacements were restricted to 6,000 tons maximum displacement and 15cm guns. All the modern units had either been scuttled in Scapa Flow or allocated to the Allies. In point of fact, because the cruisers Germany was allowed to retain were so old, they were due for replacement almost as soon as the war was over and it was only the bankrupt state of Germany and the low standing of militarism in the Reich at that time which prevented this. Nevertheless, a start was made and in 1921 the first new unit was laid down. She was to be a light cruiser, a ubiquitous category which had served Germany well during the hostilities and would make a major contribution to the rebuilding of the fleet, particularly in terms of training value. A ship of cruiser size was especially suitable for the accommodation of numerous cadets and men under instruction, while retaining a high degree of 'military' value. As fate would have it, it was to be the training aspect in which the light cruisers were to make their major contribution to the future German war effort during the next two decades.

EMDEN

In the absence of any post-war design work, this first new light cruiser for the Reichsmarine was based upon First World War designs – a fact which has been used to denigrate the ship. But the vessel, *Emden* as she was to become, was built at a time when there was little construction of this type of cruiser in other navies. Such light cruisers as were building or recently completed were themselves First War designs or modifications thereof. Thus the British *Emerald*, American *Omaha* and Japanese *Sendai* all exhibited outdated features, particularly in their armament and its disposition – beam guns and casemates still being employed. The major exception was, surprisingly, France who, because of her circumstances during the war, had undertaken little naval construction, least of all of light cruisers. France authorized the construction of three light cruisers in 1922, the first major naval vessels she had put in hand since the end of the war. These ships, the *Duguay Trouin* class, shipped eight 15.5cm guns in twin-gun-houses, all mounted on the centre-line. Fast, but almost

unprotected, they set the standard for future light cruisers, whereas the *Emerald*s, *Omaha*s and *Emden*s represented the last wartime cruiser designs. Thus, while *Emden* was an outdated design, particularly in her original provision for coal-firing, most of her contemporaries were equally dated.

In comparison with these contemporaries, *Emden* suffered from the restriction of treaty limitations, being some 2,000 tons lighter than *Emerald* or *Duguay Trouin* and with a power plant of similar horsepower to the wartime *Königsberg* class. She was also considerably slower at 29.5 knots. The machinery installation included ten boilers in one large and three small boiler rooms. Four boilers were coal-fired, but these were removed during her major refit in 1933–34 when the steam plant was modernized by the installation of four oil-fired boilers in their place. Two sets of single-reduction geared turbines, one in each of two engine rooms, drove the two shafts, with the starboard turbine in the forward room. Between the two turbine rooms was the gearing room, thus the port turbine drove forwards into the gearbox with the gearing so arranged as to transmit the power aft once more to the shafting. This arrangement of starboard turbine forward, port aft, was adhered to in all subsequent two-shaft designs of warship. Brown-Boverie manufactured the turbines, whose revolutions at full power were 2,435rpm (HP) and 1,568rpm (LP) geared down to 295rpm at the propeller. Bunker capacity of 875 tonnes coal and 859 tonnes oil was later altered to 1,266 tonnes oil only, giving an endurance of 5,300 nautical miles at 18 knots.

The protective scheme included an armoured deck extending from the steering motor room aft as far forward as frame station 106, the bulkhead between the first and second main watertight compartments. This horizontal deck extended four metres each side of the centre-line over the boiler rooms and forward turbine room, narrowing to two metres at the extremities, being sloped downwards outside these limits to join the side plating at an angle of 40°. Thickness varied from 20mm at the ends to 40mm in the centre. A vertical waterline belt of 50mm formed the side protection. This ship, like the earlier wartime designs, also carried an armoured conning tower of 100mm maximum thickness, a feature which was retained for all subsequent German cruisers.

Originally, it had been envisaged that her main armament would comprise four twin 15cm gunhouses mounted on the

Right: *Emden* as she first completed, probably running trials. Compare tulip-shaped foretop with latter form shown below. At this time, the fore funnel was higher than the after one. (W. B. Bilddienst)

Right: *Emden*. A pre-war shot showing clearly her obsolete armament disposition. Taken probably in the early 1930s, this view shows the mainmast removed and the radio aerials carried on booms on the after funnel. The bow form is original, ie prior to her 1934 refit. (Drüppel)

Right: HMS *Emerald*. The similarity to the earlier 'C' and 'D' classes of the First World War is evident. Like *Emden* she carries a proportion of her guns on the beam, but she also has an aircraft installation. (Author's collection)

centre-line, but these did not materialize and she commissioned armed with shielded single mountings whose disposition improved on First World War designs only in that the forward pair were centre-line mounted with No. 2 in a super-firing position. Two guns were shipped on each beam, reducing her broadside fire-power to only six guns, but this was on a par with *Emerald*. The guns themselves remained the well-proven 15cm L/45 which had a maximum range of 17,600 metres. The secondary armament comprised two, later three 88mm L/45 for air defence and two twin mountings for 50cm (later 53.5cm) torpedoes. Originally four banks of torpedo tubes had been planned.

Fire-control arrangements were rudimentary and differed little from wartime cruisers, consisting of three range-finders for main armament: one atop the foremast, one on the conning tower and one aft, all 4m base. The main action centre was on the upper platform deck connected with the bridge by an armoured communications shaft. Below this command centre was the transmitting station. Three range-finders for the secondary and torpedo armament were carried on the after deckhouse and on the bridge wings to port and starboard. There was no provision for aircraft installation.

The hull design incorporated longitudinal framing with transverse bulkheads forming 23 watertight compartments of which VIII (after turbine room), X (forward turbine room) and XI (No. 1 boiler room) were the largest spaces. A double bottom extending from frames 22 to 90 enhanced watertight integrity and was used for the stowage of fuels, lubricants, water and ballast. As originally completed, *Emden* featured a tall, tulip-shaped foremast tower and a curved bow form, but immediately after trials had been run, the foretop was enlarged and the height of the tower reduced to cut down top weight. After her major refit and modernization in 1934 the height of the funnels was also reduced, but the curved bows were not altered until 1937/38 when a raked bow was fitted.

The new cruiser, known until her launch as *Ersatz Ariadne* or replacement for *Ariadne* (the oldest of the retained pre-war cruisers and therefore the first due for replacement), was laid down by the Naval Yard at Wilhelmshaven in December 1921, but work progressed slowly. Construction work took three years before she was ready for launching when the new cruiser's name was revealed as *Emden*. The selection of this name was a shrewd psychological move for her predecessor, another light cruiser, had achieved world-wide fame during the First World War when, under the command of Kpt.z.S. von Müller, she scored numerous successes while acting as a commerce raider in the Indian Ocean. Furthermore, its adoption enabled a new cycle of 'town' associations to be started which served to foster interest in the fledgling navy within Germany. To this end, both the Chief Burgomeister of Emden and the President of the Province of Hanover were invited to the launching ceremony. Once in the water, work on the new cruiser proceeded quickly, so that only ten months later, on 15 October 1925, *Emden* commissioned for service under the command of Kpt.z.S. Arnaud de la Periere. The choice of commanding officer was also a clever one, for during the earlier war this officer had been a famous submarine cap-

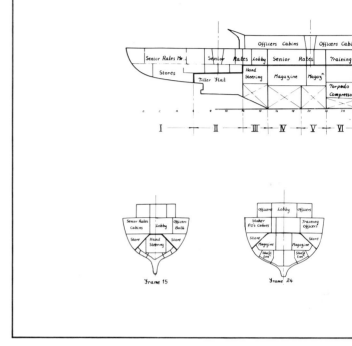

INTERNAL PROFILE AND SECTIONS OF EMDEN

tain whose daring and chivalry had gained widespread respect from friend and foe alike. It was expected that he would prove an effective ambassador in the resurrection of Germany's image abroad. Between 1925 and 1939, *Emden* made nine long foreign cruises, visiting all the major continents of the world, in the course of which many hundreds of men gained valuable sea-going experience and training. Among her several commanding officers during this period was Karl Dönitz, who later achieved fame as Flag Officer (Submarines) and who, at the close of the Second World War became the second Führer of the Third Reich, after the death of Adolf Hitler.

When the Second World War broke out in September 1939, *Emden* was eighteen years old and even older in concept, so her employment presented the Naval Staff with something of a problem. The obvious task would have been employment as an ocean raider in the manner of her famous predecessor, whose Iron Cross she carried on her bow, but several factors reduced her suitability for this role. Her low speed and distinctive warship appearance would mean that bluff could not be employed in any chance encounter with British or French cruisers in the shipping lanes, nor could she outrun them. Furthermore, the planned disguised raiders carried a similar armament, would be less easily detected and were much more economical in manpower. Their loss would be less of a propaganda coup for the enemy than that of a regular warship. *Emden*'s armament, range and seaworthiness were all adequate for a role as an ocean raider, but the advent of the Panzerschiffe and the availability of fast merchantmen

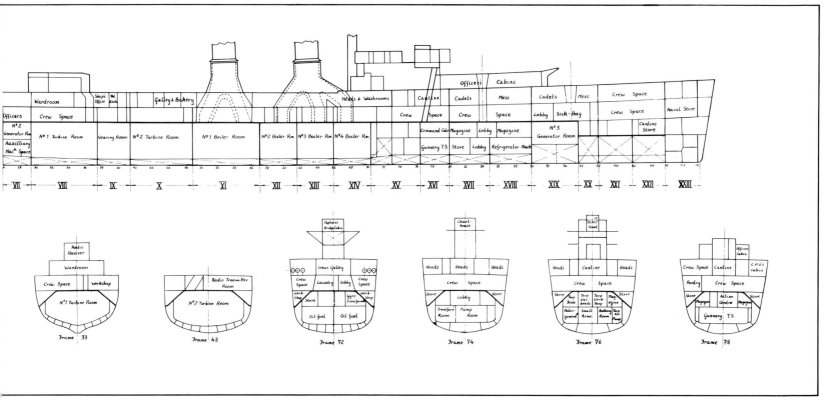

for conversion removed the need for her to be so employed. In consequence, she remained in a training role throughout the war with only occasional operational employment, for example, during 'Weserübung' and 'Barbarossa'. Thus the first post-Great War German cruiser could be summed up as a solid, reliable but obsolescent ship which had fulfilled its role in the re-building of the fleet between the wars. Her active wartime employment was restricted by her obsolete design, whereas her successors' careers were blighted by design compromises imposed by the Treaty of Versailles.

In 1928, when *Emden* was due for a refit, the question of her rearmament to the original design proposals came up. At a conference in June that year, it was confirmed that the second pair of torpedo tube banks would be installed and that although the shipping of twin gun mountings was still desirable, their installation would present some difficulties, particularly with regard to ammunition handling arrangements. So far as the twin gun idea was concerned, it was also agreed that three twin mountings would be unacceptable because of the low broadside weight; four would be the minimum acceptable. The New Construction Office was then requested to prove the weight and stability questions associated with two proposals:

(a) Four twin mountings plus two single.
(b) Four twin turrets.

The advantages of the first proposal could be summarized as follows:

(i) Little structural alteration necessary.

(ii) Could be completed within the 3-month refit period.
(iii) Relatively low cost.
(iv) No serious weight problems.
(v) One gun available each side for star shell illumination.

Against these there were the disadvantages associated with two guns in a single cradle; reduced crew protection (open shields); no splinter protection for the ammunition hoists.

The second proposal offered the advantages of good crew protection and better armouring of the ammunition supply trunks, but the turrets would require a great deal of structural alteration which was not possible to complete within the refit period and, moreover, would cost a lot of money. Finally, the additional weight could only be accommodated if the ship were converted for full oil firing. In the end it was decided that the New Construction Office should concentrate on the four-turret idea and examine the weight/stability/time and cost implications. These must have resulted in the abandonment of the re-armament ideas, for no change to twin turrets was ever made – possibly on the grounds that with such a low speed, it would have been an unwise investment. The only change made to the main armament, and this was not until during the Second World War, was the replacement of the old pattern, low muzzle velocity, 15cm L/45 guns by the newer and more powerful model 15cm TB KC/36 pattern. It is likely that this change was made because ammunition stocks for the older gun were getting low. (*Emden* fired nearly 600 rounds in shore bombardment at the opening of Operation 'Barbarossa').

THE 'K' CLASS

The first completely new cruiser design to be developed after the war crystallized during the years 1924–25 and proved to be a radical departure from the *Emden*. Chiefly responsible for the design was Constructional Adviser Ehrenberg who also had responsibility for the Type 23 torpedo-boats. Design parameters were almost exclusively bound by what could be achieved within the limits of the Versailles restrictions, for there was still an attempt to respect these limitations, in the absence of foreign contemporaries other than *Duguay Trouin*; it being accepted for the moment that the 10,000-ton 'Washington' type was not available to Germany. Thus the design requirements can be summed up briefly as the largest, fastest and heaviest gunned ship that could be built on 6,000 tonnes maximum displacement, for use as a Fleet scout and ocean raider.

The maximum calibre was fixed by treaty definitions at 15cm, and the question was, how many could be squeezed into a 6,000-tonne hull? Single guns, as in *Emden*, were out of the question. Twin turrets were the most obvious solution, but eight guns in four turrets would weigh more than nine guns in three, and the latter would give a one gun advantage over the French ships. With a three triple-turret design, the overall length and protective belt could be reduced, thereby saving weight, in comparison with a four-turret layout. In fact, weight saving was of paramount importance if a respectable armament was to be carried on such a low displacement figure. To this end, a number of features were incorporated into the design which, while helping to achieve the desired target, introduced certain weaknesses which did not become apparent until after their entry into service. In fact, these shortcomings were so marked that they ultimately prevented the ships' employment in the designed role of commerce raider. One of these features concerned the strength of the hull. Every effort was made to reduce weight by fair means or foul, in particular, incorporation of the deck-houses into the calculations for the longitudinal strength of the hull to enable the dimensions of the scantlings to be reduced. Another, but quite allowable, feature was the employment of electric arc welding on a large scale to replace riveting. However, it was early days in the art of ship welding, and design considerations in respect of welded construction could only be learned by experience. Welding was employed for some 85 per cent of the hull construction.

Like *Emden*, the new design's power plant was to be a steam turbine installation, because although the development of diesel engines for large ships was well-advanced, they would not be available for the new cruisers. Equally, the high-pressure steam concept was still in the future and as a result, the steam pressure adopted was 16kg/cm^2, the same as in *Emden*. In order to increase cruising range, diesel auxiliaries were coupled to each shaft and the main turbines could then be disengaged. In fact, the machinery installation was extremely complicated and wasteful of space, as will become evident. Six boilers (Schultz-Thornycroft pattern), two large and four small, were required for steam generation, disposed in four boiler rooms, the two forward spaces housing larger

INTERNAL PROFILE OF KÖLN

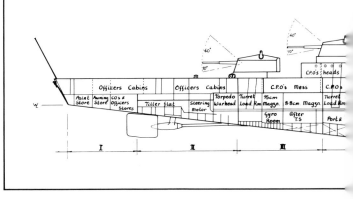

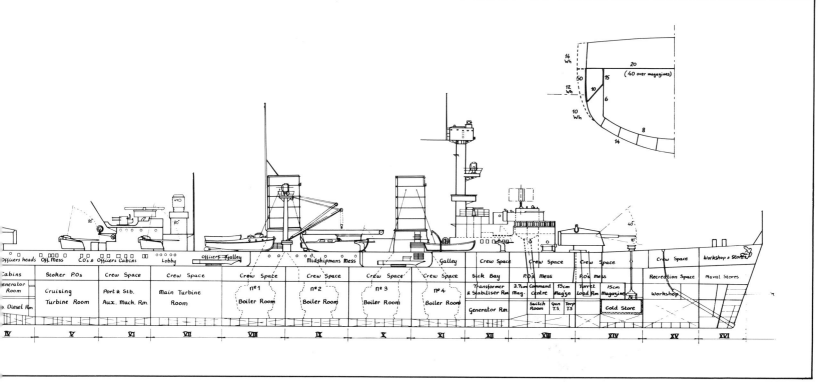

Officers heads	Off. Mess	C.O's & Officers Cabins		Lobby	Officers Galley		Midshipmans Mess		Galley	Crew Space	Crew Space	Crew Space		Crew Space	Workshop & Stores
Cabins	Stoker P.Os	Crew Space	Crew Space		Crew Space	Crew Space	Crew Space	Crew Space	Sick Bay	P.O's Mess	P.O's mess		Recreation Space	Naval Stores	
Generator Room	Cruising Turbine Room	Port & Stb. Aux. Mach. Rm.	Main Turbine Room		nº1 Boiler Room	nº2 Boiler Room	nº3 Boiler Room	nº4 Boiler Room	Transformer & Stabiliser Rm	3.7cm Mag.	Command Centre	15cm Mag'zn	Turret Load Rm	15cm Magazine	Workshop
Diesel Rm									Generator Rm.		Switch Room	Gun T.S.	Torp T.S.	Cold Store	
IV	V	VI	VII		VIII	IX	X	XI	XII		XIII		XIV	XV	XVI

boilers. Aft of the boiler spaces was the main turbine room, with a high-pressure (HP) and low-pressure (LP) rotor on each shaft. An unusual feature was that the cruising turbine was not incorporated as an extra drum on the main turbine casing, but was a completely independent installation in its own space, separated from the main turbine room by a large auxiliary machine space. Indeed, the cruising turbine room was as large as the main turbine space, as it had to be, containing as it did, two twin-drum turbines each with its own condenser. Abaft the cruising turbine room was the auxiliary diesel propulsion space, having a single 10-cylinder 900BHP MAN 4-stroke engine hydraulically coupled to each shaft. Thus the machinery installation occupied nine main compartments from frame space 42 to frame 129. Total shaft horsepower of the turbine installation was 68,000, giving a top speed of 32 knots. Each of the three ships built to this design were to receive turbines from different manufacturers, Schichau ('B'), Germania ('C') and Blohm & Voss ('D').

Electrical power was provided by three turbo-generators on the platform deck aft, two to port and one to starboard, separated by a longitudinal bulkhead. When the steam plant was dead, generating capacity was provided by two diesel sets in a space forward of No. 3 boiler room. Total power available was 540kW at 220V d.c.

Bunker capacity for fuel oil totalled 1,100 tonnes, with an additional 139 tonnes stowage for diesel fuel. During wartime operations, however, bunkerage was occasionally increased to 1,300/150 tonnes.

In comparison with the French *Duguay Trouin*, whose armour protection was scant, the new German design incorporated a reasonable protective scheme, given the displacement limits within which the designers had been forced to work. Horizontal protection comprised a main armoured deck, varying between 20mm and 40mm in thickness, which extended from side to side without any curvature to the ship's side. Vertical protection included a waterline belt, 50mm in

thickness, with 70mm transverse end bulkheads. Inboard of the main belt was a 15mm torpedo bulkhead. The main belt extended from just aft of the 'C' turret barbette to about thirty metres short of the bow. The barbettes themselves were 30mm in thickness. Further armour protection was given to the conning tower and range-finder positions.

Once the main armament calibre and number had been decided (nine 15cm guns in three triple turrets) there remained the question of their most advantageous disposition. There were only two choices: superimposed turrets, forward or aft. With four twin turrets, the French could adopt the most economical layout of superimposed turrets forward *and* aft, but three turrets presented a problem. German designs of cruiser at the close of the 1914–18 war had advanced as far as superimposed after guns. A logical extension of this would have been to increase the number of guns at each position and lead to the 'two turret aft, one forward' concept. However, it is far more likely that this disposition, the one eventually chosen, was actually decided upon in view of the intended employment of the new cruisers, i.e., as 'scouts'. In the early 1920s, naval aviation was still in its infancy and was in any case denied to the Reichsmarine. Radar too, was but a dream for the future, so that at the time that this design was being finalized, one of the cruisers' main tasks was scouting. Hence the installation of the main fire-power aft made sense because, on contact with the enemy, the cruiser was expected to report and maintain contact. Any action which did occur would then be a 'chase', with the scout as the quarry and in need of maximum fire-power aft.

This concept was equally valid in the cruiser's role as a commerce raider when her speed could always put her in an advantageous gunnery position *vis-à-vis* a merchant ship, whereas she would be expected to show a clean pair of heels to any hunting group when, once again, she would require her maximum fire-power astern. In order to counter criticism of the weak ahead fire-power (although only one gun less than

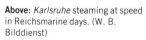

Above: *Karlsruhe* steaming at speed in Reichsmarine days. (W. B. Bilddienst)

Top right: *Königsberg* at Hamburg. Note admiral's flag at foretop. (Jansen)

Centre-right: *Karlsruhe*. Note white funnels and old-pattern single 8.8cm guns, the intended 8.8cm SKC/25 twin mountings having proved unsatisfactory. (Jansen)

Bottom right: *Köln*. Note the differences in the foretop arrangements as compared with *Karlsruhe*. (Jansen)

Right: Midships view of *Königsberg*. This view taken some time after 1936 shows the catapult and *S2* 3.7cm gun as well as the massive searchlight towers and new-pattern crane on the port side. Just aft of the funnel the new stabilized 'SL1' flak director has been fitted. (W. B. Bilddienst)

Duguay Trouin and subsequent British designs), 'B' and 'C' turrets were placed in echelon with 'B' to port and 'C' to starboard. By this means 'B' turrets arc of training was improved by a few degrees ahead of the beam to port only, while a similar situation applied to 'C' turret on starboard ahead arcs. In point of fact, the extra ahead fire achieved was relatively small and over restricted arcs, with the disadvantage of stress and blast problems on broadside firing so that this feature was not to be incorporated in later designs.

The 15cm guns, a new pattern SKC/25 in LC/25 triple turrets, fired a 45.5kg shell with a muzzle velocity of 960m/sec. Maximum range was 25,700m. 'A' turret was served by two small combined magazine and shell rooms directly below the armoured deck on the platform deck level. Between these was the handing room whence a chain and bucket hoist raised the ammunition to the guns. No. 1 magazine in particular, being so far forward, was extremely cramped. Astern, 'B' turret was served by No. 3 magazine and shell room on the starboard side of the handing room and No. 4 magazine abaft it. 'C' turret was similarly served, but in mirror fashion. Between the 15cm magazines were two further combined magazine and shell rooms for 8.8cm (fixed) ammunition. A total of 120 rounds per gun was allowed for 15cm ammunition, giving a total magazine capacity of 1,080 rounds. Both nose- and base-fuzed rounds as well as star shell were accommodated.

The secondary battery consisted of two single 8.8cm FlaK L/45 disposed on the after shelter deck just forward of 'B' turret.* Also part of the light flak outfit were four of the new SKC/30 3.7cm twin mountings sided fore and aft. A heavy torpedo outfit comprising four triple banks gave the ship a considerable extra punch and was probably prompted by a similar battery on the French light cruisers. As designed, this

---

*It had been intended to ship a new pattern 8.8cm SKC/25 but this was unsuccessful and only briefly carried.

Right: *Königsberg*. Salvage efforts during the middle war years. Note the torpedo tubes. (Drüppel)

Right: *Leipzig* at Kiel in 1939.
(Gröner)

torpedo outfit was equipped for 50cm torpedoes, but by the mid 1930s it had been re-equipped for the 53.5cm G7a type. Finally, the ship's equipment was completed by the provision for aircraft, although the Treaty of Versailles prevented the actual fitting of an installation. The conspicuous space between the funnels, visible when *Karlsruhe* first commissioned, was ample evidence that the design eventually envisaged the fitting of aircraft and catapult.

Fire-control arrangements were based upon the standard three range-finder system favoured by Germany. One was fitted above the navigating bridge, a second atop the tall foremast tower and a third on the after deck-house controlling the after arcs. The foremast equipment, some 29 metres above the waterline, had a particularly good height of command and arc of training. All were 6m base. For the secondary armament, three further 3m range-finder positions were provided, one each to port and starboard, at the base of the foremast and one on the after deck-house, this latter being the main flak fire-control position. The 3m range-finders also provided ranges for the torpedo outfit.

Cruiser 'B' was laid down at the Wilhelmshaven Naval Yard on 12 April 1926 and in just under a year she was ready for launching. After a christening address by Chief Burgomeister Lohmeyer, mayor of Königsberg, the new cruiser now named after the capital town of East Prussia, slipped into the water. Fitting out and final completion took a considerable length of time, so that it was not until April 1929 that the new *Königsberg* commissioned into the fleet. In the meantime, both her sisters, *Karlsruhe* ('C') and *Köln* ('D') had been laid down at Deutsche Werke and Wilhelmshaven respectively, to join the fleet themselves in November 1929 and January 1930. The appearance of these fine new ships was a considerable fillip to the morale of the Reichsmarine and ostensibly a good demonstration of the ingenuity of the German designers in their ability to squeeze a quart into a pint pot – a talent which

was soon to be even more strikingly demonstrated with the appearance of the 'Panzerschiffen' or Pocket Battleships.

LEIPZIG

In 1927, a further light cruiser design was developed which was a modification of the 'K' class. Although from outward appearances this design was only a minor variant of her predecessors (with a single funnel instead of two), there were in fact, considerable internal differences, particularly where the propulsion machinery was concerned. In terms of hull size, 'Kreuzer E' as she was known, displaced only marginally more than *Königsberg*, but incorporated a much needed wider beam. Apart from the single funnel, made possible by the reduction from four boiler rooms to three, the most obvious visual difference between her and *Königsberg* was the more orthodox positioning of the after turrets on the centre-line.

The boilers, still low-pressure 16kg/cm^2 types, similar to those previously installed, were shipped two abreast in the three boiler rooms, ahead of which were fuel bunkers and a diesel generator space. The boilers had a heating surface of 1,054m^2 with eighteen burners in the two aftermost boiler rooms, and 926m^2 with sixteen burners in the forward boiler room. An auxiliary boiler installation on the upper deck abaft the funnel housed two small water-tube boilers which supplied service lines and provided power when the main boilers were not flashed-up. The total installed generating capacity included two turbo-generator sets of 250kW each, and three diesel sets of 180kW each. Power supplies were at 220V d.c., with lower voltages for fire-control, damage-control and associated circuits. The main turbines consisted of a high-pressure (HP) drum and two low-pressure (LP) drums of the double-flow reaction type, with a two-stage Curtis wheel in front. An astern turbine comprising a two-stage Curtis wheel and four reaction stages was built into each LP casing. The turbines themselves were built by Krupp (Germania) and

Above: *Leipzig* at Hamburg in Reichsmarine days. Catapult not fitted. (Jansen)

were housed in separate spaces with the starboard set in the forward turbine room. Interspaced between the turbine rooms was the gearing room. Thus, the port turbine drove forwards with the propeller shaft being taken under the turbine from the 1:7.95 single-reduction gearbox, a reversion to the *Emden* arrangement. In this new design, separate cruising turbines were not fitted; instead four double-acting, 7-cylinder 2-stroke M7 30/44 MAN reversing diesel engines, each of 3,100bhp, were geared to the centre shaft through Vulcan couplings, thus making the machinery a three-shaft arrangement. Disconnecting couplings were fitted to the wing shafts for use when steaming on motors only. When using turbines only, the centre screw could be feathered, altogether a more efficient layout than that of *Königsberg*.

The hull of the new cruiser differed from the earlier type in a number of ways, but was almost as lightly constructed. Longitudinal construction was employed, with four longitudinal frames each side of the centre keel plate. Frame spacing was at 1.5 metres and the shell plating was overlapped.

The superstructure of this ship and her later half-sister was not, however, incorporated into the longitudinal hull strength calculations. Watertight sub-division was, as usual, comprehensive, with sixteen separate compartments and a double bottom extending over three-quarters of the ship's length. Welding was once again employed for a very high proportion of the hull in order to save weight. Externally, the most obvious difference was the shape of the stern and the pronounced turtle-back of the main deck aft from the break of the forecastle. Closer examination revealed a waterline bulge and bulbous bow. The protective scheme was more sophisticated and re-introduced the idea of an armoured 'carapace', in that the armoured deck, 20mm in thickness, was taken at its edges through a quarter of a circle to join the side armour at its lower edge (see sections). The curved section of the deck armour was increased to 25mm in thickness, while the side armour, inclined from the top outwards at 18° from the verti-

cal, was 50mm at its thickest point amidships, tapering to 35mm in the vicinity of the steering gear and less than 20mm in the bows. This armoured carapace extended for approximately 70 per cent of the waterline length. Within the conspicuous side bulges, which extended above the level of the upper platform deck, were bunkers for fuel oil and reserve feed water. The offensive capabilities of the new design were no improvement upon the earlier cruisers.

'Kreuzer E' was ordered from Wilhelmshaven Naval Yard and laid down in April 1928. Following previous practice, her launching address was given by Herr Rothe, the Chief Burgomeister of her name town on the River Elster in Saxony. She was the fourth ship to carry the name and the third cruiser to do so. The first vessel of the name had been a full-rigged steam corvette which joined the fleet in 1877 and served abroad, mainly in Central America, at the end of the nineteenth century. The new cruiser's immediate predecessor,

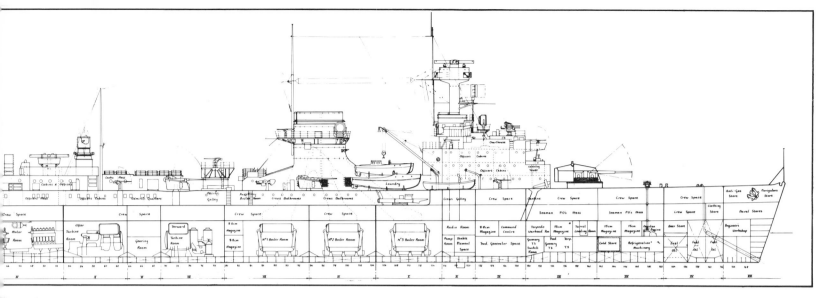

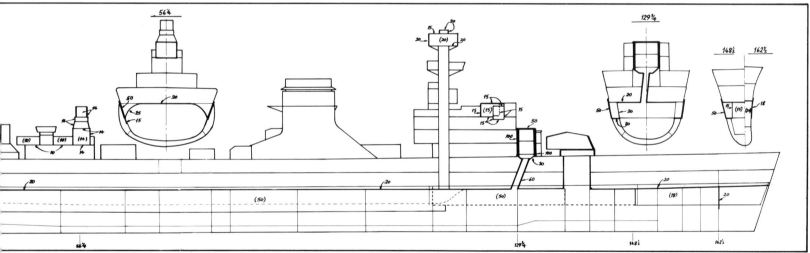

however, never actually sailed under German colours, for like many other ships, she remained incomplete in 1918 and was sold for scrap in 1921. The second *Leipzig*, a 3,800-tonne 'kleiner Kreuzer' served with von Spee's East Asiatic Squadron and was sunk in action during the Falklands battle in 1914. Almost two years were to pass between launch and commissioning of the new *Leipzig*, partly due to the final fitting out of *Köln*, then still alongside her in the basin at Wilhelmshaven. *Leipzig* finally joined the fleet in October 1931, under the command of Kpt.z.S.H-H.Strobwasser.

NÜRNBERG

There now followed a five or six years' hiatus in the development path of the light cruiser type because the naval staff could not decide upon the best type with which to continue construction. At this time there was much discussion as to whether to remain with the *Leipzig* displacement or to

increase to 8,000 tonnes. The latter figure would have given better hull strength, allowed superior protection for turrets and magazines, permitted better flak armament and an increase in speed. It was argued that it seemed necessary to match foreign designs, such as the British *Leander* and the French *La Galissonnière* types, but pressure was increasing for a switch to the Washington 'heavy cruiser' type. This complicated matters and resulted in the years 1933 to 1935 being mainly devoted to the gestation of a heavy cruiser design (to which the next chapter is devoted) and the deferment of the production of a new light cruiser design until 1936–38. The net result of this indecision was that the sixth light cruiser to be put into work, 'Kreuzer F', had to be built basically as a *Leipzig* in the complete absence of any other design. Thus the deficiencies evident in the *Königsberg* design and, to some extent, perpetuated in *Leipzig*, were carried over to the new ship as well.

Right: *Nürnberg*, seen before the war, carrying an He60 biplane. (Drüppel)

Right: *Nürnberg* passing under the Levensauer bridge in transit through the Kiel Canal. The low level of command of the conning tower (above and aft of 'A' turret) is clearly visible. (Imperial War Museum)

'Kreuzer F' was destined to be the last light cruiser to be completed and will be described in rather more detail than her forebears. This sixth light cruiser was a little longer and beamier than her half-sister, with a consequent increase in displacement of about 100 tonnes which permitted rather better hull and gunhouse protection and an enhanced flak outfit. There was, however, some loss of bunker capacity as compared to *Leipzig*. Once again, a mixed steam and diesel propulsion plant was adopted, the six boilers being sub-contracted to Germaniawerft at Kiel. The turbines, built by Deutsche Werke, consisted of an HP cylinder and two LP cylinders, with the condenser mounted abreast of the turbine and not slung below it as in later designs. Each turbine developed 33,000 horsepower and weighed 79,500kg, giving a power to weight ratio of 3.48kg/hp. Its associated single reduction gearing weighed 35,250kg. The cruising diesels, MAN 7-cylinder 2-stroke double-acting engines, were geared to the centre shaft through a Vulcan gearbox to develop

12,400bhp on this shaft. Internally, the machinery layout was basically unaltered except that the forward generator space was rearranged and an extra compartment was worked in between No. 1 boiler room and No. 2 turbine room consequent upon the re-siting of the 8.8cm guns.

Generating capacity totalled 1,300kW derived from two 350kW turbo-generators, each in its own space aft of No. 1 turbine room, and four 150kW diesel sets in the forward generator space.

The protective scheme, similar in layout to that of *Leipzig*, included a 50mm waterline belt which extended from frame 19 just aft of 'C' turret barbette to frame 149 forward. Astern of 'C' turret, the waterline belt reduced to 35mm, but the bow vertical armour was only 18mm. Like her earlier consort, the horizontal armour consisted of 20mm plate, rounded down at the sides where the thickness was increased to 25mm, to meet the vertical armour at its lower edge. Forward and aft the platform decks were 10mm thick as additional protection

below the waterline. Turret support trunks were 30mm from armoured deck to upper or forecastle decks, while the barbette rings were 60mm. In common with all German designs of the period, a heavily armoured conning tower, 100mm thick at the sides and 50mm on top, was incorporated into the bridge structure. From the base of this, an armoured shaft, 60mm thick, communicated with the action command centre below the armoured deck. Turret armour included 80mm face; 20mm sides, floor and front top; 32mm rear top and 35mm rear wall. 15mm armour protected the navigating bridge, 20mm the foretop and 14mm protected the flak control tower.

The armament of the new cruiser did not differ greatly from that of her earlier half-sister, having retained three 15cm triple turrets in a one forward two aft layout. Her heavy flak outfit was increased by one twin mounting making four in all, now sided amidships. The guns themselves remained the standard 8.8cm SKC/32 weapon. Similarly, the light flak comprised four 3.7cm twin SKC/30 mountings and four 2cm guns as in *Leipzig*. Four triple banks of torpedo tubes completed the armament. Except for the fire-power accommodated on such modest dimensions, *Nürnberg* was not particularly remarkable as a design and indeed contained some inherent defects as will become evident later.

'Kreuzer F' was ordered from Deutsche Werke Kiel on 16 March 1933 and laid down eight months later in November. Just over a year passed before the new ship was ready for launching when she received the name *Nürnberg*, once again the third cruiser of the name. The first had been lost in the Falklands in 1914. Her immediate predecessor had surrendered at Scapa Flow in 1918, been scuttled, raised and finally sunk in gunnery trials by the Royal Navy off the Isle of Wight in 1922. The new *Nürnberg* was commissioned into the fleet under the command of Kpt.z.S.Schmundt on 2 November 1935; thus she, unlike her sister light cruisers, never sailed under the Reichsmarine ensign, for with the advent of National Socialism, the fleet now became known as the Kriegsmarine and sailed under the Swastika.

Six light cruisers were now available to the fleet, a very small number considering the size of the cruiser squadrons which had been attached to the High Seas Fleet in 1918. The two most important European sea-powers, France and Great Britain, had fourteen and forty-one respectively. Of these totals, a significant proportion of each nation's cruisers were, moreover, 'Washington, 10,000-ton' types, armed with 20.3cm guns. On the other hand, a large number of the British cruisers were of 1914–1918 vintage or design and as such, were more comparable with *Emden* than with the 6,000-tonne cruisers. Nevertheless, the German force was quite clearly outnumbered and in fact, although the ships were well-armed, they were not as well-suited to ocean employment as the ships of the other two powers, as will become clear in a subsequent chapter. Thus the cruiser force, like other arms of the Kriegsmarine's surface fleet, would go to war under the twin handicaps of insufficient numbers and technical defects.

The light cruisers were extensively employed during the 1920s and 1930s in 'showing the flag' and training cruises of six to eight months' duration which took them all over the world. In 1931, *Emden* visited East Asia and Africa and in the following year, *Karlsruhe* cruised to the West Indies, Panama and the east and west coasts of America, making the first visit by a German warship to New York since before 1914. Also in 1932, *Köln* visited the Orient and Australia. In 1934, *Königsberg* and *Leipzig*, under the command of Konteradmiral Kolbe, paid an official visit to Portsmouth, the first to a British port since before the First World War. A typical itinerary was that of the cruise made by *Karlsruhe* in 1934–35. She left Kiel on 21 October 1934, visiting the following ports: Valencia (Spain), Haifa (Palestine), Bombay (India), Rangoon (Burma), Nanking and Shanghai (China), Mujajuma, Yokohama and Nagasaki (Japan), Hong Kong, Ilo Ilo (Philippines), Batavia (Dutch East Indies), Singapore, Aden, Balearic Islands and Pontevedra before reaching Germany again on 13 June 1935. *Emden*, which had left Wilhelmshaven two days after her, visited the Azores, West Indies, South America, the USA and Canada, arriving back in Wilhelms-haven on 12 June 1935. *Emden* sailed to the Mediterranean in October 1936, and the cruise included a visit to Bulgaria, where King Boris himself inspected the ship at Varna.

The possibility of war breaking out while the cruisers were in distant waters had not been neglected; each ship had orders detailing her course of action in the event of hostilities. *Karls-ruhe*'s orders in September 1933 propounded two scenarios: one in which Germany was at war and the second where Germany was not one of the combatants. In the former situation, the cruiser was to return home immediately, attacking enemy merchant traffic on the way. If it was impossible to break back home, the Commanding Officer was to conduct mercantile warfare as he saw fit. If the hostilities were with France, *Karlsruhe* was to operate to the north-west of Africa between 10° and 46° N, against troop convoys to Metropolitan France and in the Atlantic, on the merchant routes. Auxiliary mercantile raiders were to be supplied if necessary, but the cruiser's own fighting power was not to be reduced unless it were imperative. If war did not involve Germany, the cruiser's task was to protect German interests where necessary.

Hostilities did indeed break out but not directly concerning Germany when the Civil War in Spain began on 18 July 1936. The German fleet broke off manoeuvres and hurriedly fitted out for a sortie into Spanish waters. *Deutschland* (Vizeadmiral Carls), *Admiral Scheer*, *Leipzig* and *Köln* sailed from Wilhelmshaven on 23 July, charged with the protection, not only of German interests but also those of Switzerland, Austria, Sweden, Argentina, Guatemala, Chile and White Russia. During the course of this tragic conflict, all the light cruisers participated in the Spanish patrol at one time or another, operating either with the Northern Group off the Basque coast or with the Southern Group in the Mediterranean off Barcelona, Malaga, Alicante and occasionally Tangier, which was the Italian's main base. Few incidents concerned the cruisers, except a claim that a torpedo attack was made on *Nürnberg* by an unidentified submarine south of the Balearic Islands on 25 June 1937.

The continued patrolling in the Atlantic and southern Biscay waters did, however, show up serious defects in the Treaty light cruisers, caused by structural weakness. On 13 March 1937 *Leipzig* (Kpt.z.S.Schenk) was badly damaged in heavy seas which caused cracking in the upper deck and in the longitudinal girders on the port side. The discovery that all the light cruisers except *Emden* were basically unsuitable for Atlantic employment naturally necessitated close investigation. One of the contributory factors was growth due to additional equipment installed after completion, which totalled between 20,960kg (*Leipzig*) and 23,623kg (*Karlsruhe* and *Köln*). Extra equipment included loading-practice guns, stabilization of searchlights, directors for 3.7cm guns, new antennae and masting, oil-bunker heating, gun shields and power cables. *Emden*'s weight growth totalled only 2,075kg, but because of treaty restrictions, the ships after *Emden* had been constructed with a heavy armament on a lightly built hull. Weight had been saved by the use of welding, and higher longitudinal hull stresses were accepted than had been the practice prior to the Great War. Stability properties had been sufficient at completion, but the increased weights had considerably reduced margins, and unfavourably orientated hull openings had acted as stress raisers.

Cracks in the upper deck were likely to occur so the OKM ordered that the risk be minimized by reducing speed and putting into harbour in heavy weather. Cracking in the superstructure deck of *Köln* had been eliminated by extra strengthening, but was still a problem in her two sister ships, particularly around the funnel uptakes. This, however, was not considered risky unless cracks were also present in the upper deck. Cracking was also found to be initiated by sharp corner effects and welding shrinking stresses. *Leipzig* and *Nürnberg*, whose hull strength calculations had not included the superstructure, still suffered from upper-deck cracking, but were not as prone to other cracking problems as the 'K' cruisers. Nevertheless, it was necessary to avoid emptying midships bunkers first which would leave the ship's ends heavily loaded and produce hogging.

Below left: *Königsberg* entering Portsmouth in July 1934. Note old-pattern 8.8cm guns and light-coloured upperworks. Under the command of Konter-Admiral Kolbe whose flag is at the foretop, *Königsberg* was accompanied by *Leipzig*. It was the first visit to Great Britain by a German squadron, since 1914. (Wright & Logan)
Below right: *Leipzig* taken at the same time as above. Neither ship has been fitted yet with a catapult. Like *Königsberg*, this ship has also four old-style 8.8cm guns, but she has received four 2cm C/30 guns. (Wright & Logan)

Projected Programme, Light Cruisers (21 August 1939)	
Emden	Training Squadron until 1 May 1943
	Major refit May 1943–February 1944
	Training Squadron from 1 February 1944
Leipzig	Flag Officer (Reconnaissance Forces) to 1 April 1940
	Refit at Howaldt (Kiel) 1 April 1940 to 1 April 1941
	Flag Officer (Reconnaissance Forces) 1 April 1941 to 1 July 1941
	Training Squadron 1 July 1941 to 1 April 1942
	Flag Officer (Reconnaissance Forces) 1 April 1942 to 1 May 1943
	Training Squadron 1 May 1943 to 1 April 1944
	Fleet April 1944 to June 1945
	Cadet Training Ship from June 1945
Nürnberg	Flag Officer (Reconnaissance Forces) to 1 July 1939
	Refit Blohm & Voss 1 July 1939 to 1 April 1940
	Flag Officer (Reconnaissance Forces) 1 April 1940 to June 1945
	Cadet Training Ship from June 1945
Karlsruhe	Refit at KMW (Wilhelmshaven) until 1 July 1939
	Flag Officer (Reconnaissance Forces) 1 July 1939 to 1 April 1940
	Trials vessel for gunnery and torpedo Experimental Establishments 1 April 1940 to 1 February 1942
	Training Ship (Torpedo and Navigation) 1 February 1942
Köln	Flag Officer (Reconnaissance Forces) to 1 January 1940
	Refit Deutsche Werke (Kiel) 1 April 1940 to 31 December 1940
	Gunnery School Training Ship 1 January 1941 onwards
Königsberg	Gunnery Training Ship until 31 December 1940
	Refit Howaldt (Kiel) 1 January 1941 to 31 December 1941
	Gunnery Experimental Command from 1 January 1942

To rectify these problems, it was decided to increase the beam of the 'K' cruisers by 1.4m, thereby improving strength and stability. A reduction in speed to about 28 knots was the estimated penalty. The two later ships, *Leipzig* and *Nürnberg*, would be treated rather differently by receiving new side plating from the outer corners of the bulges to the edge of the upper deck. In all cases, overloading of the ends was to be avoided.

The advantage of these measures, apart from strengthen-, ing, was an increase in bunkerage, better side protection and the capability of operating two aircraft. Until completed, however, operational restrictions were placed on all except *Emden*. This meant that *Königsberg*, *Karlsruhe* and *Nürnberg* were restricted to home waters and the North Sea. *Leipzig* and *Köln* could be used in Spanish waters, but only at favourable times of the year and even then forward and aft bunkers had to be emptied. For stability reasons, the 'K' ships had to retain 680 tonnes of fuel at all times, and *Nürnberg* 150 tonnes, with a consequent effect on their endurance. After completion of these strengthening refits, it was anticipated that the service life of *Köln* would be extended to 1948 and that of her sisters to 1947. In November 1937, the re-building programme envisaged work starting in June 1938 on *Karlsruhe* at Wilhelmshaven Naval Yard, due to complete in May 1939, followed by *Nürnberg* (Blohm & Voss or Wilhelmshaven), *Köln* (Deutsche Werke, Kiel) and finally, *Königsberg* (Howaldt, Kiel) whose work would commence in September 1940. Refits in the 'K' class were estimated to need eleven months apiece, *Leipzig* nine and *Nürnberg* six. Overloading of the shipyards resulting from the Kriegsmarine's large expansion eventually caused slippage in this programme, so that by 1938, completion of *Königsberg* was being quoted as the end of December 1941. Nevertheless, *Karlsruhe* paid off on 19 May 1938 to begin her refit more or less on time, but she did not recommission until 13 November 1939, by which time Germany was at war again and the remainder of the refit programme had to be cancelled.

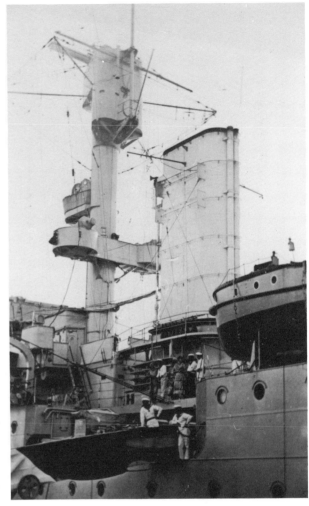

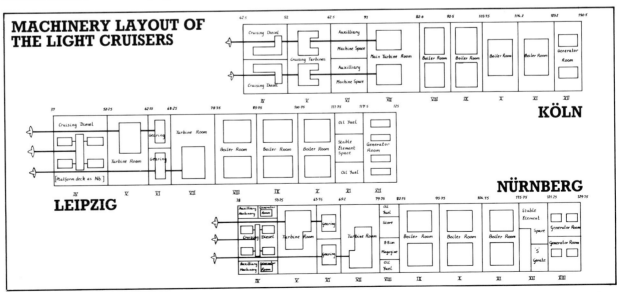

MACHINERY LAYOUT OF THE LIGHT CRUISERS

KÖLN

LEIPZIG

NÜRNBERG

3: DESIGN & CONSTRUCTION OF THE HEAVY CRUISERS

The Soviet heavy cruiser *Kirov*, used by Hitler to justify the construction of *Seydlitz* and *Lützow*. She saw action against the Finns in 1939 and the Germans in 1941/2, but never encountered her Kriegsmarine opponents. (W. B. Bilddienst)

GENESIS

The main armament of German cruisers had been standardized on the 15cm gun during the First World War after a long period of allegiance to the excellent 10.5cm weapon. Similarly, other nations, such as Great Britain and the United States, had also settled on this calibre for the majority of their cruiser types. One class of British cruisers, however, the 'improved *Birminghams*' (completed 1918–22) mounted a new and heavier gun calibre, 7.5in. During the Washington Naval Treaty discussions in 1921, the existence of these vessels under construction led to the adoption of an 8in (20.3cm) maximum gun calibre for cruisers, after pressure from the British delegation, for Britain quite naturally did not wish to be forced into cancelling these new and powerful ships. In fact, this was to act eventually to their disadvantage because, human nature being what it is, the acceptance of a 10,000 ton/8in maximum configuration soon led to this becoming the *minimum* requirement at the same time. As Britain required large numbers of cruisers for trade route protection, she was therefore forced into building fewer, but larger, cruisers when a greater number of smaller ships would have suited her better. Then, nineteen years later, on the outbreak of a new war, the vessels which had precipitated the 8in (20.3cm) gun requirement were quite obsolete and had in any case been mostly re-armed with 6in (15.2cm) guns.

The Washington Treaty thus led to the appearance in the 1920s of numerous 'heavy' cruiser designs by the major

maritime powers. These included the American *Pensacola*, British *County*, French *Duquesne*, Italian *Trento* and Japanese *Furutaka* classes. Only the Soviet Union and Germany did not initially produce such vessels, the former because her industrial and technological base was still in a state of chaos following the Revolution, while the latter was still bound by the limitations of the Treaty of Versailles. The construction of these heavy cruisers was therefore initially stimulated by artificial treaty considerations and was not the result of any evolved naval requirements. In practice, the nations concerned produced these vessels only because their hereditary or likely foes were doing so; thus, the designs produced did not necessarily meet the full stategic requirements of the naval staffs in question. There was at this time, intense rivalry in naval ambitions between France and Italy, for example, while the intentions of Japan in the Pacific were a source of concern to both Britain and the USA, particularly the latter.

So far as Germany was concerned, the existence of the Treaty of Versailles prevented the construction of heavy cruisers as such and in fact banned the construction of any cruisers larger than 6,000 tonnes. As things then stood, if a 'Washington'-type ship were built, it would have to be classified as a battleship and thus be completely outclassed by foreign equivalents. Notwithstanding the Treaty of Versailles, discussions as to the future trend of German cruiser development took place from the early 1930s, possibly in anticipation of the eventual rescinding or abrogation of the treaty.

However, the initial reactions of the Naval Staff, Head of the Design Office and Admiral Raeder, were unfavourable towards the type, predicting in June 1932 that it would soon lose favour, as already it had done in the Royal Navy, with construction switching to the smaller, 15cm-gunned *Leander* type. This situation appears to have persisted for a further eighteen months, by which time it had become obvious that while Britain was no longer building heavy cruisers, most other nations were continuing to do so, particularly, France. In a future war, therefore, Germany would inevitably encounter such cruisers and would require an effective countermeasure. After the completion of *Leipzig* ('Kreuzer E'), there was a period of vacillation on the part of the Naval Staff when they had been unable to decide upon which type to construct next. Some discussion took place upon an increase in displacement to 8,000 tonnes, allowing better strength, protection and speed over *Leipzig*, but nothing immediately came of the idea although it finally led, after a long and confused gestation period, to the 'Kreuzer M' design, as it was considered necessary to match the *Leander* and *La Galissonnière* types. Thus the *Nürnberg* ('Kreuzer F') was laid down in 1933 to the basic *Leipzig* design in the absence of anything else, and thoughts began to turn towards heavy cruisers.

Early in February 1934, the Naval Staff informed the Development Office of the basic design requirements for the new cruiser. The main requirements were:

(a) Equal to the strongest new foreign construction, specifically France's *Algérie*.

(b) Faster than the French fast battleship, *Dunkerque*.

(c) Suitable for Atlantic employment; therefore large range and good magazine capacity.

Design displacement was to be 9,000–10,000 tonnes, with a continuous top speed of 33 knots. Armament was to be either twelve 15cm guns in triple turrets or eight 20.3cm twins with a good flak outfit. Two quadruple sets of torpedo tubes, four aircraft and two catapults were demanded. A range of 12,000 nautical miles at 15 knots, with the maximum possible armour protection, completed the design demands. The main question to be resolved was obviously the gun calibre and the Development Office tabulated various pros and cons for the 20.3cm and 15cm guns. Their calculations showed that there would be a weight penalty of some 550 tonnes in the adoption of the 20.3cm option but, on the other hand, its hitting power was greater, piercing 100mm armour at 23,000 metres, which the 15cm could only achieve at 10,000 metres. Rate of fire for the 20.3cm was given as 6rpb/min, while the 15cm was naturally faster at 8rpb/min. Meanwhile, Admiral Raeder had already convinced himself that the heavier calibre was the most desirable and wished to modify the design sketch to include four 20.3cm twin turrets, four twin flak mounts, 100mm to 120mm side armour as in *Algérie*, with a good horizontal protection and four to six aircraft. By April 1934, Raeder was predicting that 20.3cm would be the calibre of the future.

This jump in calibre did involve a considerable increase in dimensions and it was probably in an attempt to compromise that a calibre of 19cm was mooted for the main armament instead of the 20.3cm. This was discussed in May 1934, at a conference chaired by the Supreme Commander of the Navy, Admiral Raeder. The merits of each calibre were argued, both of which were actually banned under the treaty. During the conference, it was pointed out by the Construction Departments that, on the nominal displacement of *Leipzig* (6,000 tonnes), only three 19cm twin turrets could be accommodated, with the disadvantage that the number of barrels in the broadside would be low and the consequent three-round salvoes would be weak – a criticism already levelled at the 'K' class light cruisers.

A better solution was held to be four 19cm twin turrets, but this was estimated to require a displacement of at least 9,000 tonnes. However, calculations showed that the difference between 19cm and 20.3cm calibre for a four-turret design, with associated ammunition, was only some 85 tonnes. It was therefore agreed to propose the 20.3cm gun and obtain agreement for this from the Chancellor.

Having resolved the calibre question, the conference turned to the problem of propulsion. The representatives from the Development Section wanted to know whether high-pressure steam or a mixed steam and diesel plant was to be adopted. Raeder and the Chief of the Construction Office favoured the high-pressure steam alternative, mainly because of the then existing problems associated with diesel plants already afloat. These had led to tactical difficulties at sea when for instance light cruisers operated in company with the 'Panzerschiffen'.

Deutschland cruised at 19 knots economical speed, but *Leipzig* could only make 13 knots on her diesels alone, and required to flash up her steam plant to reach 19 knots with a consequent reduction in action radius. Furthermore, there was a considerable weight and space penalty associated with the diesel engines of the day. Quite naturally, in view of its importance, the discussions as to which type of propulsion to install were long and detailed, the advantages and disadvantages of both modes being considered in depth. So far as the steam option was concerned, the advantages were summarized as:

  (i) Easier supply of fuel, especially during wartime, as anything could be burned. (Quite the opposite was to be experienced during the coming war.)
  (ii) Shorter shaft length required.
  (iii) Less underwater noise and quieter engine rooms.
  (iv) Steam was a valuable fire-fighting medium.
  (v) Less vibration, maintenance and fewer repairs.
  (vi) Higher overloading, i.e., 30 per cent v. 15 per cent.
  (vii) Better damage control: e.g., the turbines could be used even with water in the turbine spaces provided that the shaft seals remained intact.
  (viii) Simpler training and fewer personnel required.

On the other hand, the following disadvantages of high-pressure steam were noted:

  (a) Lower action radius.
  (b) The physical dangers of high-pressure steam.
  (c) The possibility of salting of boiler systems.
  (d) Unfavourable watertight subdivision.

Both the Construction and Engineering Offices held the view that the future trend would be towards turbo-electric propulsion, already adopted by the United States for two classes of battleships, but for the present, the Construction Office saw no clear advantage in either system, given the operational drawbacks to both. These discussions had a strong bearing on the problem as to whether to continue the diesel concept beyond *Admiral Graf Spee*, or adopt steam for Panzerschiffen 'D' and 'E'. In the event, steam was adopted for these ships, later to become *Scharnhorst* and *Gneisenau*, although their steam plant did not go to the extremes of high-pressure. As far as the new heavy cruisers were concerned, Raeder requested comparative figures for the action radii of a 10,000-tonne design, both with mixed steam/diesel and high-pressure steam options.

In June, discussions centred around a 33 knots minimum design on a displacement not exceeding 10,160 tonnes, and an alternative of only 32 knots with the weight saved being utilized for protective purposes. Finally, a displacement of 10,700 tonnes was fixed and at a further conference, held in July 1934, the Chief of the New Construction Office tabled a sketch design on this displacement of 10,700 tonnes. Maximum speed was 32 knots with a machinery weight of 18kg/hp. A total of 2,140 tonnes were allocated for protection and 1,980 tonnes for machinery. No armoured torpedo bulkhead was included, but the vertical armour was 85mm, barbettes 85mm and the armoured deck 30mm–50mm. (In the case of the deck, 50mm was only used over the steering aft.) This proposal was generally well-received but, although Raeder agreed in principle, he required certain modifications to be incorporated. These included a sloped armoured deck, an increase in the turret side thicknesses to 120mm/140mm, side armour in way of magazines to be 100mm and a compensating reduction in the belt thickness towards the extremities. He and all the other participants wished to see the deck armour increased to 50mm over the magazine spaces.

Below right: *Blücher* fitting out in 1939. Note absence of funnel cap. (Gröner)
Below: *Prinz Eugen* goes afloat at Kiel. Note the conventionally stowed anchors and straight bows. Her coat of arms is visible too. (Imperial War Museum)

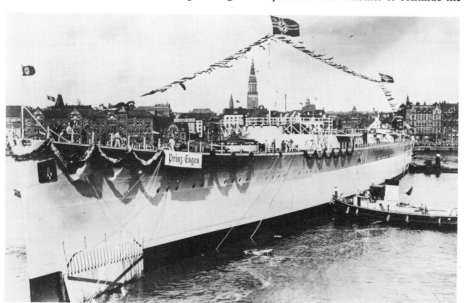

Discussions dragged on, with no real progress being made. Raeder was obviously not entirely satisfied with any of the sketch designs produced so far, and had definite ideas of his own on the subject. During the course of a conference which he chaired on 21 September 1934, he declared, 'Think what one will of the 20.3cm/10,000-tonne cruiser, the fact remains that other sea-powers have it, and our own 15cm/6,000-tonne cruisers will be outclassed.' He therefore intended to authorize the construction of two ships of this type on 1 April 1935 for completion in February 1938 and April 1939.

By October 1934, Raeder had confirmed the 10,000-tonnes, 20.3cm concept, utilizing high-pressure steam propulsion. It had proved quite impossible to incorporate the full demands from various quarters for additional protection and still remain near to the Washington limit. In fact, this was considerably exceeded despite a reduced scheme of protection, for in the final event, the main armour belt was only 80mm and that only between frames 26 and 164. Aft of this there was only a slight reduction to 70mm, but at the fore-ends, belt thickness was considerably reduced to 40mm. The main protective deck was 30mm in general with only small areas of 40mm. The upper-deck protection was at a maximum of 25mm only in the way of the main machinery spaces.

The final design configurations showed a four twin turret, high-pressure steam turbine three-shaft layout, with a very respectable high-angle armament and good torpedo outfit, but only a restricted radius of action. Detailed planning on the lead ship 'G' began in April 1935, the order for which had been placed with Deutsche Werke at Kiel on 30 October the year before. At the same time, the second ship, 'H', was ordered from the Hamburg yard of Blohm & Voss.

Adolf Hitler, the German Chancellor, had abrogated the despised Treaty of Versailles on 16 March 1935, thus freeing the Navy to begin construction of this type of vessel. In consequence, Britain quickly moved to set up a naval agreement with Germany to replace in some way the restrictions of Versailles, if only on a limited scale. The outcome was the Anglo-German Agreement of 1935, which limited German tonnage to 35 per cent of that of Britain. It was signed, amidst acclaim from both sides, on 18 June 1935.

Freed now from the shackles of Versailles and given a positive target to build to, Germany lost no time in announcing, on 9 July, a large programme of new construction, much of which had in fact already been put in hand. Raeder now had, so far as heavy cruisers were concerned, some 51,000 tonnes available. Two ships of nominally 20,000 tonnes total were on order and a third, 'J', would be ordered later in 1935. This left enough for two more heavy cruisers of the 'A' type. However, a new attempt at curtailing the naval armaments race took place in London, when France, Italy, the USA, Japan and Great Britain met in what was known as the London Naval Conference of 1936. Originally, Germany had been invited, but the French objected on the grounds that it was tantamount to acknowledging the demise of the Treaty of Versailles. The main result of the new conference was an agreement relating to submarine warfare, which is outside the scope of this book, but one other important aspect greatly concerned Germany – the 'Holiday' in the construction of heavy cruisers and battleships of more than 10,000 tonnes. If Germany were excluded from this new agreement completely, she would be free to continue the construction of the 'Panzerschiffen', which had so worried the naval powers, and similarly build heavy cruisers which other nations could not. To prevent this happening, a separate agreement was reached between Great Britain and Germany, whereby the latter would be allowed to construct the two extra ships as well as the 'Panzerschiffen' already laid down, but only under 'press of exceptional circumstances'. The net result of all this bargaining was that the two cruisers in question, 'K' and 'L', had now to be constructed as light cruisers or 'Class B' ships.

The path of heavy cruiser development now becomes rather confused by this introduction of a 'Class B' cruiser concept, and it appears as if the German Naval Staff had no real idea as to where they were going. This ban on further construction of heavy cruisers left Germany in something of a predicament, for she had only three authorized or under construction. Such a small number, coupled with the appearance of *Strasbourg* and her sister ship (which rendered the 'Panzerschiffe' obsolete) meant that any 'Class B' cruisers available would, of necessity, have to be employed on ocean cruiser warfare against French Atlantic traffic, as well as in the 'Fleet' role. The situation was exacerbated by the inherent defects in the Treaty light cruisers which had made them unsuitable for ocean employment. The initial proposals centred around a fast, high-endurance, strongly' constructed hull, with the following general requirements:

(a) Armament: 4 × 2 15cm or 4 × 3 15cm; 4 × 2 10.5cm flak. Maximum number of 3.7cm and 2cm. Minimum of 2 × 4 torpedo tubes.

(b) Armour: Effective against 20.3cm shells at 15,000–18,000m.

(c) Machinery: 35 knots continuous, i.e., sufficient over superior enemy units as well as enemy flotilla leaders. Action radius 14,000 nautical miles at 20 knots.

However, it was found that such a design would require a displacement of some 18,000 tonnes, and in its place a smaller design was proposed. This was a three triple turret, 9,000-tonnes development of *Leipzig*, which was but briefly considered before Raeder, as ever an exponent of heavier armament and armour, forced a return to the four triple turret sketch on modified requirements. These now specified the displacement as 'G', 'H' and 'J', with four 15cm triple turrets and twelve torpedo tubes. Armour was to be as 'G' and the speed and endurance at 35 knots maximum, 8,000–12,000 nautical miles. The abandoned, modified *Leipzig* concept was later resurrected and after an extremely lengthy development period, finally led to the 'Kreuzer M' design, which will be discussed later.

On 8 June 1936, Admiral Raeder, in fact, authorized the construction of the two ships to 'Class B' requirements, armed with twelve 15cm guns. Both were ordered from Deschimag at Bremen on 18 July. Orders were also placed for the guns and turrets. By November of that year, however, Hitler gave orders for both ships to complete as 'Washington' Class 'A'

Heavy cruiser building programme slippage		
Ship	Anticipated completion at:	Actual completion
	March 1937 September 1937	
G	10.10.38 1.8.39	20.9.39
H	14.7.38 3.39	29.4.39
J	15.5.39 15.12.39	1.8.40
K	12.39 1.3.40	—
L	1.7.40 1.10.40	—

heavy cruisers, after invoking the escape clause of the agreement with Great Britain. His grounds for doing so were the ships which Soviet Russia was intending to build in contravention of the treaty. These were the 18cm-gunned *Kirov* class vessels based on Italian designs, the first of which, *Kirov* herself, had been laid down on 22 October 1935. In point of fact, only two of these ships were intended for Baltic duties, so Hitler's pretext was, at best, a flimsy one. Although work on the 15cm guns and turrets continued until as late as 1941, the two ships were, by 1937, being finished as 'Class A' ships. These were the last vessels of the heavy cruiser concept to be considered by the Germans; such few further plans as were developed for new cruisers were to be light cruisers.

CONSTRUCTION

The first of the heavy cruisers laid down to the new design, was actually 'H', at the Blohm & Voss yard in Hamburg, on 6 July 1935, as Yard No. B501. The hull was longitudinally framed, using predominantly ST52-quality steel for the non-protective elements. The central keel consisted of a bottom plate (which formed part of the outer bottom plating), a 1.5m deep vertical centre-plate and a top plate which was an integral part of the inner bottom. This centre keel plate was stiffened by two horizontal longitudinals, as well as by stiffening plates on the transverse frames and at half-frame intervals. In the bows, the keel was continued as a centre-line bulkhead up to the armoured deck.

On each side of the keel, seven longitudinal frames, I to VII, at about 1.9m spacings, formed the hull shape and defined the double bottom area. Of these longitudinals, No. IV formed a longitudinal bulkhead, separating the outer bulge from the inner double bottom space, and was continued vertically as a 20cm-thick inner protective longitudinal bulkhead to meet the curve of the armoured deck, some seven metres above the keel (see page 38). In general, longitudinals I and III were not watertight, but II, IV and VI were welded oil and watertight. Longitudinal strength was further endowed by 32 longitudinal beams interspersed between the longitudinal frames and welded to the transverse frames, up to the upper deck. These transverse frames, spaced 1 to 1.7m apart, carried the load of the longitudinals. Where necessary, the transverse frames were oil and watertight, when for example, they formed part of the double bottom cellular tank construction. In other places, lightening holes were cut to save weight.

The shell plating was fully welded except where the armour plate formed part of the shell, in which case the joints between it and the armour were overlapped and riveted. Openings in the shell were kept to a minimum, but where they occurred, doubling was employed. To ensure docking strength, a box girder system was worked in between the keel and longitudinal I.

There were two main longitudinal bulkheads, the outer and the inner, the former of which partially comprised the main armour belt. Between the turrets forward and aft, a further pair of short longitudinal bulkheads, some 3.55m from the keel line and extending to the upper deck, supported the weight of the turret structures.

Twenty-nine watertight bulkheads preserved watertight integrity, dividing the ship into fourteen full watertight compartments. All bulkheads extended from the keel to the armoured deck, with most reaching the upper deck.

The double bottom (some 72 per cent of the length) was split into two separate compartment areas known as 'double bottom I' between the keel and longitudinal II, and 'double bottom II, between longitudinals II and IV. Above longitudinal IV, the double bottom was continued as a side bulge to between the armoured deck and the battery deck. This was known as the 'outer wallgang' and was divided into three oil and watertight compartments by longitudinals V and VI. Inboard of this space was another, bounded by the inner longitudinal bulkhead on longitudinal IV; the armoured deck and the 'outer wallgang'.

The main watertight compartments of the ship were identified according to the normal German practice: from aft to forward by Roman numerals I to XIV, suffixes being used to

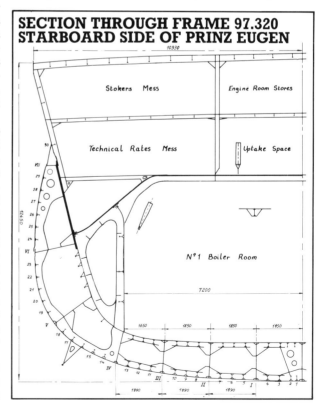

SECTION THROUGH FRAME 97.320 STARBOARD SIDE OF PRINZ EUGEN

ARMOUR OF ADMIRAL HIPPER

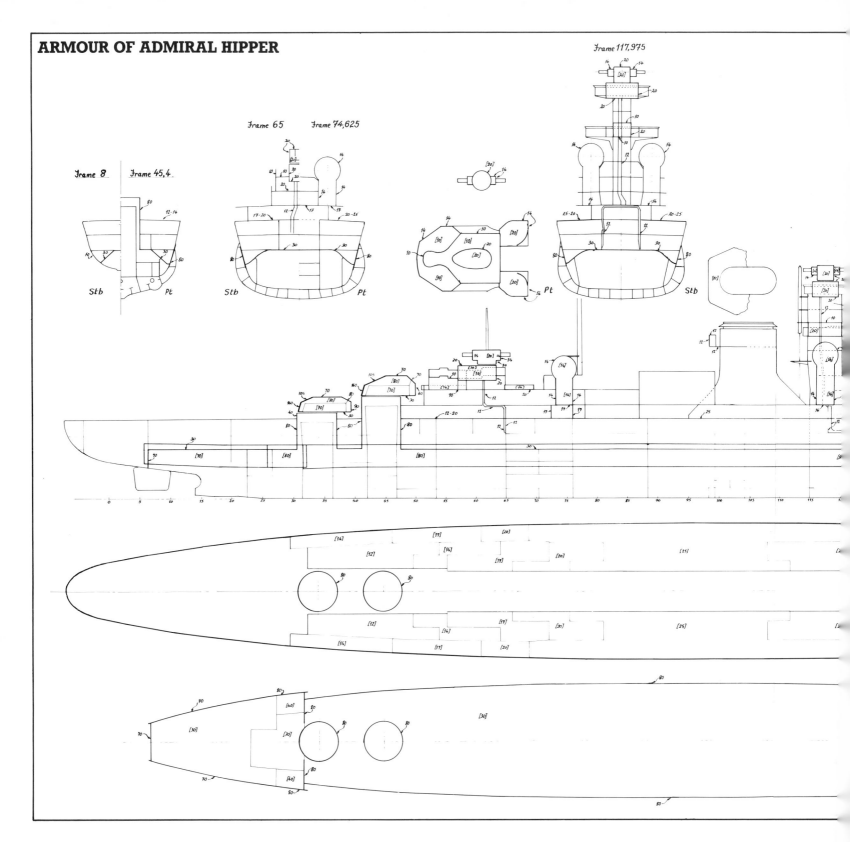

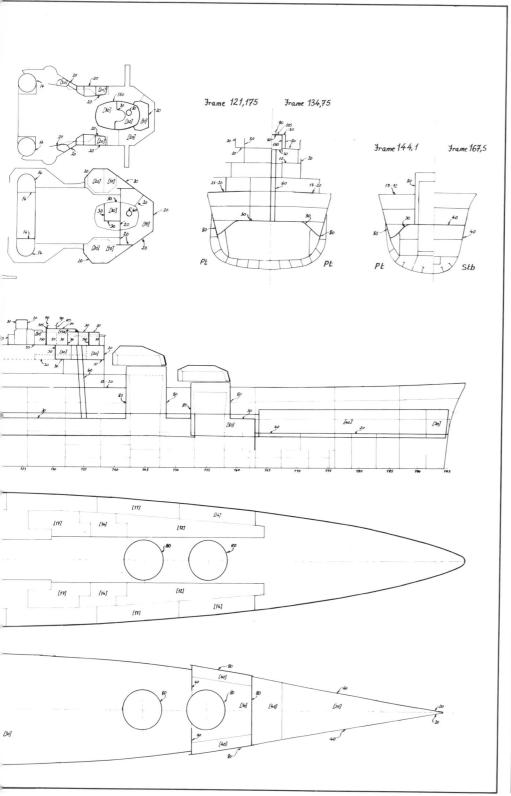

identify the deck and the individual space concerned. The ship had five main deck levels below the upper deck, known, from bottom to top as: hold, lower platform, upper platform, armoured and battery or 'tweendeck.

PROTECTION SCHEME

The main vertical protective belt extended from frame 26 to frame 164 (frames noted here refer to 'G' & 'H') in its full thickness of 80mm, being sloped outwards from bottom to top by 12½° from the vertical. Its total depth was 3.75m–3.85m and amidships at the designed light draught it extended .75m below the waterline. At the ends of the main belt a joggle, 80mm thick, was incorporated to accommodate the joint with the transverse armoured bulkheads, which closed the ends of the armoured carapace. Forward of the 80mm belt, the side protection was continued as 40mm to frame station 191.5 and thence to the bows as only 20mm. At the after end a 70mm belt, which extended to frame station 6, protected the steering gear.

Horizontal protection was split between a lightly armoured upper deck and a main protective deck below. The upper deck armouring varied in thickness from 12mm to 25mm and

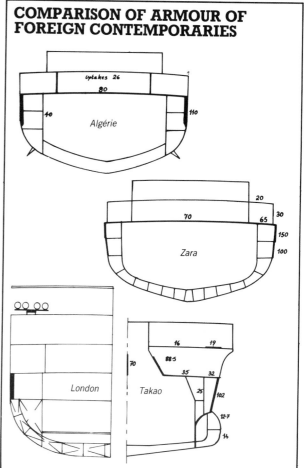

COMPARISON OF ARMOUR OF FOREIGN CONTEMPORARIES

generally extended from just outside the barbettes of 'A' and 'D' turrets and outboard of a line 3.2m from each side of the keel line. Its maximum thickness covered only a small proportion of the midships area in the way of the boiler spaces. Overlaying the steel upper deck was 55mm (85mm on the forecastle) of teak planking. The main armoured deck, 30mm in thickness, extended from frame 6 aft, to frame 163 forward. Aft and outboard of 'D' turret were small areas of 40mm armour and similarly, abreast 'A' turret. Forward of the transverse armoured bulkhead at frame 163, was another area of 40mm plate, but from there to the bows the horizontal protection was reduced to only 20mm. The 40mm areas covered part of, but not all, the magazine spaces. This armoured deck incorporated a shaped curve 2.3m high and about 4m wide, blending the horizontal protection into the vertical protection.

All armour was riveted to bulkheads, longitudinals and skin, although the hull itself was almost entirely welded. The armour type was Whn/a, a nickel steel manufactured by Krupp.

The main barbettes, 80mm thick, 6.4m internal diameter and 8.5m high, extended from the armoured deck to the base of the turrets and continued the training masses as will be described later.

Apart from the main horizontal and vertical hull protection, considerable protection was also incorporated in the various bridge and control stations. The principal component of this armouring was the conning tower on the bridge deck. Almost oval in shape, it housed the gunnery control and action conning positions within its 150mm-thick walls. The top protection, however, was only 50mm thick and was one of the rare examples of welded armour on the ship, being fabricated from about five smaller pieces. The joint between top and sides was a machined dovetail held in place by an angle with bolts, the heads of which were welded and peened when in position. From the conning position an armoured trunk led down to the command centre on the upper platform deck in compartment X. Within the upper and lower bridge areas outside the armoured conning tower, the various control positions and subsidiary director pedestals were armoured with vertical and horizontal splinter protection varying from 10mm to 30mm.

The main range-finder, atop the foremost tower, the control position immediately below it and the Admiral's bridge, all had 20mm side protection, as did the after range-finder and after control position. Each of the four flak director towers was protected by 14mm plating. Splinter protection was also provided for the boiler uptakes above the armoured deck and the searchlights on the funnel.

GENERAL INTERNAL ARRANGEMENTS

The two lower decks and spaces, the hold deck and double bottoms mainly accommodated fuel and lubricating oil tanks, as well as reserve feed, potable and washing water bunkers. Compartments IV and X, however, housed spaces associated with the fire-control systems, gyro-compass and damage control as well as a few workshops. The deck above, the lower

platform deck, accommodated further bunker spaces for fuel and water, but was mainly given over to magazine and machinery requirements. Compartments II and XI contained the 20.3cm shell rooms, these being therefore below their cordite rooms and magazine spaces for other calibres. One compartment (X) was given over entirely to the fire-control systems and contained its associated amplifier and switch rooms, but more than one-third of this deck was required for the propulsion unit.

Compartments III and V contained the three turbine units with the aftermost compartment driving the centre shaft. This space also contained a generator room. The forward space (V) shipped the two turbines driving the port and starboard shafts. Forward of these spaces, compartments VI, VII and VIII accommodated the steam-generating plant. Each contained four high-pressure boilers. Finally, the foremost space connected with the engineering department was IX, containing No. 3 generator room.

The upper platform deck, which effectively only extended between frames 10 and 47 (compartments I and II) aft, and frames 130.25 and 167.5 (compartments IX and XI) forward, was used almost entirely for the 20.3cm cordite rooms. The after section also housed the steering motors and some store spaces. The forward section accommodated, in addition to the magazines, the command centre, radio room and various gunnery switch rooms. Here too was the main boiler control stand.

The ship was fitted with a roll stabilization system based on the fluid transfer technique. This feature was built into the after end of compartment VII, almost at the mid-point of the ship's length. It comprised two tank spaces, one on each beam, cross-connected on the hold deck. The transfer of 200 tonnes of fluid could be effected by means of two turbine-blowers controlled by a pair of gyroscopes.

The 'tween deck, which was in fact the armoured deck, was given over almost completely to accommodation for junior ratings with messdecks for seamen forward and aft and stokers' messdecks amidships. Much of the space on this deck (and the one above – the battery deck) was absorbed by the boiler uptakes and barbettes. On the battery deck accommodation spaces occupied most of the available area. In the after section, compartments I to V contained cabin accommodation for senior ratings, officers and staff personnel. In general, senior ratings were allocated double cabins; the officers had singles. The remainder of this deck was divided up into various broadside messes for POs and junior ratings, 3-tier portable bunks being used for most messes. Almost the only non-accommodation space on this deck was radio room C. So far as accommodation was concerned, the internal arrangements were poor and led, in service, to congestion at action stations.

In the superstructure on the upper deck level, the aircraft hangar and funnel uptakes occupied the majority of its length, separating the officers' accommodation aft from the sick bay and other accommodation forward. The suite of cabins aft was mainly allocated to staff officers and included a separate conference room. Immediately forward of 'C' turret barbette,

the wardroom occupied the full width of the superstructure and was used only for dining purposes, being capable of seating sixty officers. At the forward end of this deck, between the end of the hangar and 'B' turret barbette, was the sick bay and accommodation for midshipmen. The medical outfit was quite extensive and comprised a seventeen-bed main ward, an isolation ward, X-ray room, dispensary and operating theatre.

The next superstructure deck level incorporated aft, the Commanding Officer's suite, consisting of day and sleeping cabins with an adjacent bathroom. At the after end and to starboard was the flag officer's accommodation, basically a repeat of the C.O.'s suite with the addition of a large athwartships conference or reception cabin. At the forward end, it housed mostly cabin accommodation, together with two flak T/Ss and ammunition handing rooms.

In the bridge structure, the lower bridge deck housed cabins for the watch-keeping officers and the First and Second Navigating Officers as well as the chart house. Abaft the chart house, in the support structure for the conning tower above, was the Action Information Centre and hydrophone office. From here, a companionway led to the upper bridge deck. This was the normal conning position for the ship and it consisted of a large open platform with a windscreen at its forward end. To port and starboard, folding wings allowed the captain good visibility when manoeuvring in confined spaces, but these were normally stowed at sea.

Under non-action conditions, the ship was generally steered from the 'Schutzhaus', a rather cramped, covered wheelhouse built onto the forward end of the conning tower. Within the 'Schutzhaus' stood, on the centre-line at its forward end, the steering position, which was a push-button system in lieu of the more normal wheel. In front of the quartermaster stood the gyro-repeater, while on his port hand stood the stand-by magnetic compass. Also on the port side, was the engine telegraph position and in the port corner, a periscope which allowed the officer of the watch a view of the chart table on the deck below. Arranged around the bulkheads of the position were the usual telephones and voice-pipes necessary for the control of the ship.

Immediately abaft the 'Schutzhaus', within the armoured walls of the conning tower, was the action conning position, entered by heavy doors from the bridge deck to port and starboard. This space duplicated the equipment of the 'Schutzhaus', but in a more comprehensive form necessary for fighting the ship. Narrow view slits were cut into the forward bulkhead, giving very limited forward vision, but this position was basically intended for use in the fully closed-down state. From this position, an armoured shaft communicated directly with the control centre on the upper platform deck.

The forward tower mast structure, abaft the conning tower, housed various cabins, the Admiral's bridge, signal and control platforms. At the extreme top sat the main rangefinder position. In respect of the accommodation, it is worth mentioning that considerable thought had been given to the needs of an on-board meteorological service for, on the bridge deck, the ship's meteorologist was allocated a good-sized

cabin and an equal-sized workroom-cum-office to port. Much use was later to be made of this facility by both *Hipper* and *Prinz Eugen*.

Kreuzer 'J', while adhering to the same fighting specification as 'G' and 'H', differed internally in a number of ways and showed differences in outward appearance. Internally, the machinery spaces were each lengthened by about .75m to 1.25m, going some way to reducing the very cramped nature of her sister's machinery layout. This increased length also allowed the provision of a double hangar, with the aircraft stowed in tandem, unlike the single hangar incorporated in 'G' and 'H'. The extension of the hangar was achieved by displacing the catapult from its former position aft of the hangar, and building the extra portion into the superstructure between the after pair of flak directors. As the catapult could not now be accommodated at the after end of the hangar because of the mainmast, and the cranes could not be brought farther aft in any case, it was instead re-positioned forward of the hangar and the cranes were moved forward to plumb it. This re-arrangement of the aircraft equipment resulted in a re-disposition of much of the accommodation on the superstructure decks.

MACHINERY
As mentioned earlier, this design adopted high-pressure steam for propulsion and dispensed with the idea of diesels for either main or cruising purposes. The steam-generating plant consisted of twelve boilers arranged in three spaces. High-pressure steam had been finally adopted on the grounds that a worthwhile saving in space, and greater fuel economy would result as compared to the steam plants of the light cruisers. The OKM assumed that the advance to higher pressures would lead to smaller boilers and pipe work, thus giving greater safety in damage-control considerations.

The boilers for the first two ships, 'G' and 'H', were built by the ships' respective builders and were of the La Mont type with a capacity of 49,895kg/hour each at 80kg/cm^2 pressure and 842°F temperature at the superheater outlet. These boilers were fitted with horizontal air pre-heaters and La Mont economizers which were located directly above the superheater with no boiler convection surfaces between. Forced circulation was employed, with two feed pumps per boiler, i.e., one on stand-by. Initially, some problems were experienced with the circulation pumps on these boilers, but these were eventually overcome. Less corrosion was experienced in the La Mont type than in the Wagner boiler except in the superheater where, despite experiments with the internal baffling in the steam drum, a carry-over of 1–3 per cent was general. There was considerable corrosion in the economizers, but little in the boiler or convection sections. To protect the economizer at low steaming rates, boiler water (manually controlled) was passed through it direct from the circulatory

Below: *Blücher* seen here as finally completed, with funnel cap, Atlantic bow, covered admiral's bridge and radar. (Bundesarchiv-Koblenz)

GEARING ARRANGEMENTS OF HEAVY CRUISERS

1. HP ahead
2. IP ahead
3. LP ahead
4. HP astern
5. LP astern
6. Cruising turbine
7. Thrust block
8. Coupling
9. Turning gear.

ADMIRAL HIPPER

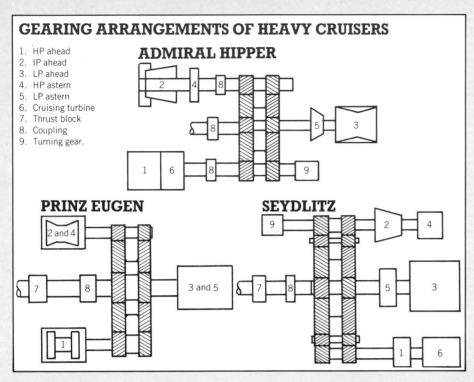

PRINZ EUGEN

SEYDLITZ

pump. The La Mont boiler, in common with the other types of high-pressure boiler, utilized Saake air turbine-driven oil burners under Askania automatic control. The small size of boiler tube employed meant that internal cleaning was only possible by chemical methods.

Kreuzer 'J' was also to ship the La Mont boiler, but 'K' and 'L' shipped the Wagner design, operating at a pressure of $59kg/cm^2$ and 400°C with a rated capacity of 68tonnes/hour. The Wagner design was, in fact, the type preferred by OKM and was used extensively in destroyers and torpedo-boats (see author's sister work, *Destroyer!*).

Plant efficiency of German boilers was generally lower than contemporary Allied designs and overall steam consumption was high due mainly to the widespread use of high-speed, high-pressure (HP) auxiliaries which were large steam users. An auxiliary boiler provided steam for secondary and harbour purposes, this being a single-ended boiler equipped with Saake burner and air pre-heater operating at $25kg/cm^2$ with a capacity of 10tonnes/hour. It supplied steam at 25, 10 and $2kg/cm^2$ to the various low-pressure auxiliaries.

The main engines, a triple-shaft installation, consisted of three sets of single-reduction geared turbines, each developing 44,000 horsepower, installed in two main engine rooms. The forward space housed the turbines on the two wing shafts, while the centre-shaft turbine occupied its own space farther aft. Both Kreuzer 'G' and 'H' adopted a turbine of

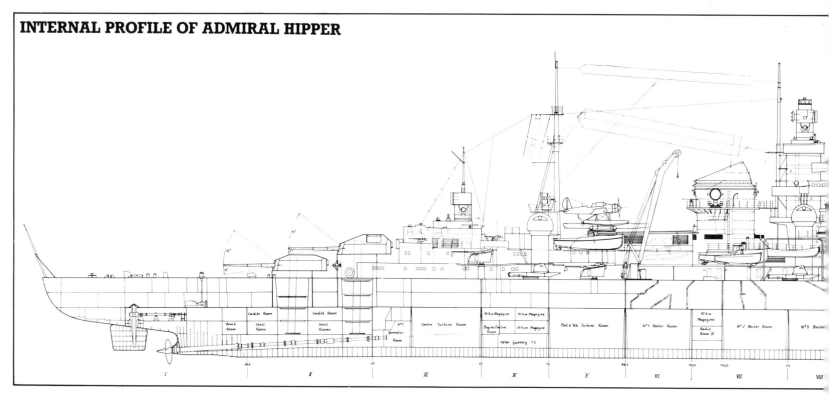

Labels on diagram: Bomb Room, Shell Room, Cordite Room, Shell Rooms, Cordite Room, Nº1 Generator Room, Centre Turbine Room, 10·5cm Magazine, 10·5cm Magazine, Engine Control Room, 10·5cm Magazine, After Gunnery TS, Port & Stb Turbine Room, Nº1 Boiler Room, 10·5cm Magazine, Radio Room B, Nº2 Boiler Room, Nº3 Boiler

Opposite page, right: *Admiral Hipper* at full speed. She is not yet fitted with radar.

Blohm & Voss design. In this, a 3-cylinder layout, the low-pressure (LP) turbine (and its coaxial LP astern unit) was situated ahead of the main wheel on to the top of which it drove through the LP pinion.

The LP turbine had a radial flow inlet stage of the impulse type. This, it was said, saved three reaction stages on each end of the unit, thus shortening it considerably. The high-pressure (HP) turbine pinion drove on to the side of the main wheel from aft, while the intermediate-pressure (IP) and HP astern set was similarly placed, driving the opposite side of the main wheel. No separate cruising turbine was fitted, but the HP turbine was provided with two groups of nozzles for cruising and four more for higher powers, the forward portion being the cruising stage. The gears themselves were of the double helical pattern, hobbed and lapped with a 40° helix, 20° pressure angle. Efficiency at full power was stated to be about 98 per cent. The three pinions on the main gear wheel allowed turbine speeds nearly as high as those in destroyers despite higher power and lower propeller rpm. On the other hand, this layout was bulky and wasteful of space, and the complex maze of steam piping around the turbines themselves led to problems of accessibility and maintenance.

In these first two ships, only the centre shaft was equipped with a disconnecting coupling, the other shafts having bolted flanges, which subsequently caused problems on active service.

Kreuzer 'J' received turbines of Brown-Boverie design. Again, this was a 3-cylinder design, but incorporated a combined cruising/HP turbine, the cruising stage of which comprised a Curtis wheel and three Rateau stages. The HP stage itself consisted of three Rateau stages. The IP turbine, a double-flow layout with one radial and nine reaction stages, also incorporated the Curtis wheel of the HP astern element. The LP turbine was once again a double-flow unit incorporating one radial and six reaction stages as well as a divided double-flow Rateau stage for the LP astern element. The astern turbine power was rated at 15,000shp per shaft.

Kreuzer 'K' and 'L' received Wagner–Deschimag turbines of rather different design, for unlike the other three ships, where the LP turbines were on the forward side of the main wheel and the HP and IP sets astern of it, all the turbine cylinders in the two later vessels were on the same (ahead) side of the main wheel. This was achieved by the use of idler pinions between the turbine pinions and main wheel, thus saving on length at some expense to breadth. In this design too, a separate cruising turbine was fitted driving through the pinion via a flexible but permanent coupling. This cruising turbine consisted of a Curtis wheel and seven Rateau stages, developing a maximum power of 12,900hp/shaft. The HP ahead turbine comprised a Curtis wheel and three Rateau stages, while the IP stage consisted of reaction stages only. The LP turbine had five single-flow and two double-flow Rateau stages. HP astern power was provided by a Curtis wheel on the end of the IP shaft, and a second on the LP ahead turbine formed the LP astern element. Maximum power was 44,000 horsepower per shaft with 320rpm; cruising power was 10,500hp/shaft maximum at 188rpm with the centre shaft uncoupled.

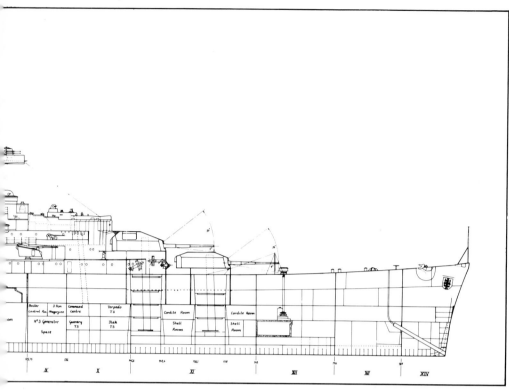

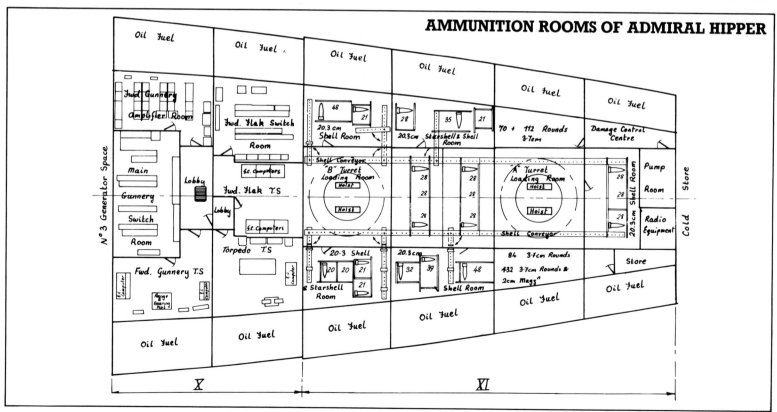

AMMUNITION ROOMS OF ADMIRAL HIPPER

SEYDLITZ AS AN AIRCRAFT CARRIER

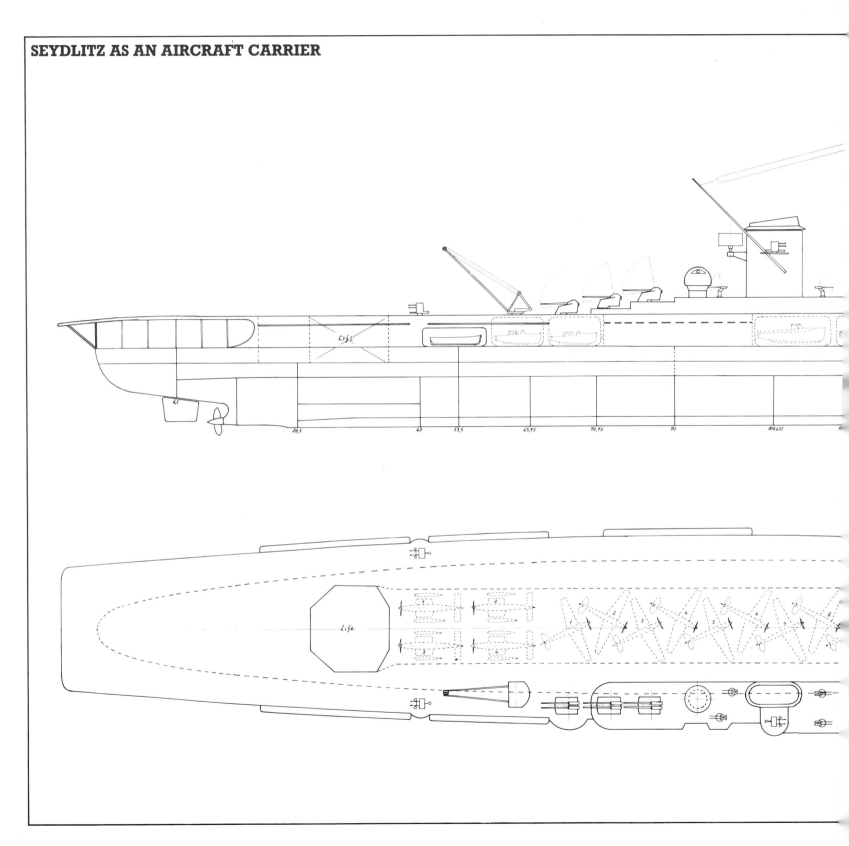

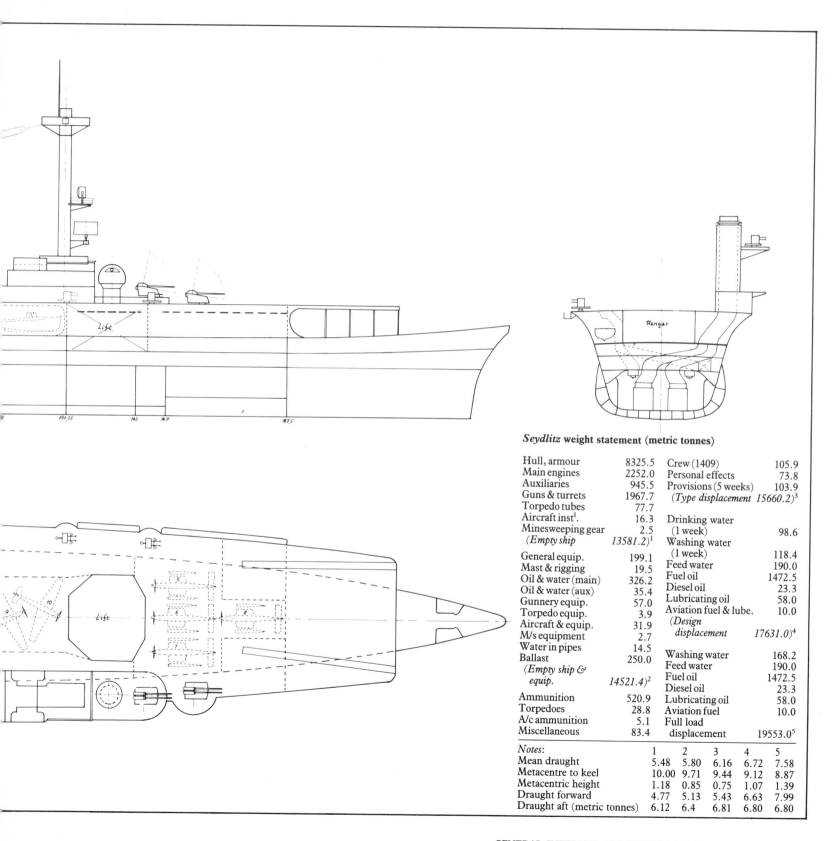

Seydlitz weight statement (metric tonnes)

Hull, armour	8325.5	Crew (1409)	105.9
Main engines	2252.0	Personal effects	73.8
Auxiliaries	945.5	Provisions (5 weeks)	103.9
Guns & turrets	1967.7	(Type displacement 15660.2)[3]	
Torpedo tubes	77.7		
Aircraft inst[l].	16.3	Drinking water	
Minesweeping gear	2.5	(1 week)	98.6
(Empty ship)	13581.2)[1]	Washing water	
General equip.	199.1	(1 week)	118.4
Mast & rigging	19.5	Feed water	190.0
Oil & water (main)	326.2	Fuel oil	1472.5
Oil & water (aux)	35.4	Diesel oil	23.3
Gunnery equip.	57.0	Lubricating oil	58.0
Torpedo equip.	3.9	Aviation fuel & lube.	10.0
Aircraft & equip.	31.9	(Design	
M/s equipment	2.7	displacement	17631.0)[4]
Water in pipes	14.5		
Ballast	250.0	Washing water	168.2
(Empty ship &		Feed water	190.0
equip.	14521.4)[2]	Fuel oil	1472.5
		Diesel oil	23.3
Ammunition	520.9	Lubricating oil	58.0
Torpedoes	28.8	Aviation fuel	10.0
A/c ammunition	5.1	Full load	
Miscellaneous	83.4	displacement	19553.0[5]

Notes:	1	2	3	4	5
Mean draught	5.48	5.80	6.16	6.72	7.58
Metacentre to keel	10.00	9.71	9.44	9.12	8.87
Metacentric height	1.18	0.85	0.75	1.07	1.39
Draught forward	4.77	5.13	5.43	6.63	7.99
Draught aft (metric tonnes)	6.12	6.4	6.81	6.80	6.80

Opposite page, top: *Seydlitz* under completion at Deschimag in 1941. In the foreground is *Z32*. (Gröner)
Centre: *Seydlitz* being dismantled for conversion to an aircraft carrier in 1943. Compare this view with the others taken earlier. (Gröner)
Bottom: *Seydlitz* under completion at Bremen. The superstructure is almost complete up to the hangar deck. Funnel base and flak director towers can be seen. (Bundesarchiv-Koblenz)

GENERATING CAPACITY

In common with all modern contemporary German designs, the generating capacity was extensive. Three separate generator spaces were provided in each of the cruisers 'G' to 'L', but the equipment therein differed slightly. All diesel sets in 'G' and 'H' were 150kW while one of the sets in the later ships was of 350kW capacity (in No. 1 generator room). The earlier ships, too, had one extra turbogenerator set installed in No. 3 generator space. All supplies were 220V d.c., of which the main power consumers were the turrets, steering motors, stern capstan and windlass. Total generating capacity of 'G' and 'H' was 2,900kW, and of the remainder 2,870kW. Converted supplies, 220V a.c., totalled 975kVA.

DAMAGE CONTROL

Particular attention was paid to damage control ability. In addition to the comprehensive watertight compartment subdivision, there was also a well-equipped fire-fighting capacity and enormous pumping ability. Three separate fire-fighting means were available: water, steam drenching and gaseous flooding. This latter technique involved the use of Ardexine gas generated in each major watertight compartment. This gas excluded oxygen and smothered fire, but it was something of a double-edged weapon for it could seep unnoticed into an adjacent compartment and asphyxiate crew members there. This in fact did occur aboard *Admiral Hipper* following her action in the Barents Sea in December 1942. The leakage seems to have taken place through cable glands in the bulkheads, a common point of weakness in German ships. There were ten independent gas generation plants, eight on the 'tween deck, one on the upper deck and one in the superstructure. *Prinz Eugen* and later ships had eleven. Ten hull and fire pumps were fitted, each of 600tonnes/hour capacity. Damage-control organization included a main Damage Control Centre, with a secondary position, and seven Damage Control groups stationed mainly on the 'tween deck.

ADMIRAL HIPPER, BLÜCHER AND PRINZ EUGEN

As the world slid once more towards war, all five ships of the class had been launched and were under completion. In keeping with German custom, their names had been kept secret until launching, so that it was not until 6 February 1937 that the first was revealed. Kreuzer 'H' was launched by Admiral Raeder's wife as *Admiral Hipper*, commemorating the Bavarian officer who had commanded the battlecruiser squadron at Jutland in 1916. (Admiral Hipper died in May 1932.) Kreuzer 'G' followed in June, being named after the Prussian Field Marshal, Gebhard von Blücher, whose appearance on the field at Waterloo had such a decisive effect on the outcome of that famous action. More than a year was to pass before 'J' reached the water; in late August 1938 she was named *Prinz Eugen* by Magda von Horthy, wife of the Hungarian Regent, Admiral Horthy, in commemoration of Eugene of Savoy (1663–1736), one of the greatest soldiers of his time. Eugene was a Frenchman whose services had been declined by King Louis, whereupon he fought for Emperor Leopold I of Austria instead. Most of his active service was concerned with driving the Turks out of eastern Europe, culminating in his famous victory in capturing Belgrade in 1717. The naming of 'J' as *Prinz Eugen* was intended to cement Austro-Hungarian relations with Germany. An army of dignitaries including Adolf Hitler, himself, attended the launching ceremony and the ship retained her Austro-Hungarian links throughout the war.

SEYDLITZ AND LÜTZOW

Kreuzer 'K' was named after the Prussian cavalry General, Friedrich Wilhelm von Seydlitz, who saw action during the Seven Years War, taking part in the victories at Rossbach (1757) and Zorndorf (1758), fighting for Frederick the Great. *Seydlitz* also commemorated an earlier ship, a battlecruiser built in 1913, which survived tremendous punishment at the Battle of Jutland. The fifth ship, 'L', did not finally go afloat until July 1939, being named *Lützow*, once again commemorating a Prussian cavalry officer, Freiherr Adolf von Lützow (1782–1834), whose Lützowsche Freikorps was destroyed by the French army in 1813. The new cruiser's predecessor had been lost at Jutland in 1916, but neither this *Lützow* nor her sister, *Seydlitz*, were destined to serve the crooked cross of Nazi Germany, the unexpected outbreak of war upsetting all plans for their completion. It is convenient, if out of chronological sequence, to describe their chequered careers at this point.

After the outbreak of war, construction of *Seydlitz* proceeded only slowly and at one time there was a possibility that both she and *Prinz Eugen* might be sold to the Russians, but Hitler vetoed the idea in November 1939. By May 1942 she was almost complete, lacking only catapult, cranes, masts and flak outfit. Construction was stopped in June and designs were prepared to convert her to an aircraft carrier. Project 'Weser 1'. Between late 1942 and 1943, the guns were removed and the superstructure was gradually dismantled until by spring of 1943, only the funnel remained standing above the otherwise flush deck.

The increase in Allied air raids on U-boat yards during the middle war years prompted the SKL to move the incomplete ship to a less vulnerable location, and the Naval Salvage Com-

Below: *Blücher* fitting out at Deutsche Werke, Kiel in 1939. Structurally complete, she has yet to receive her 10.5cm and light flak guns. No flak directors are aboard but the torpedo tubes are. Note the Atlantic bow and hull bulge. (Gröner)

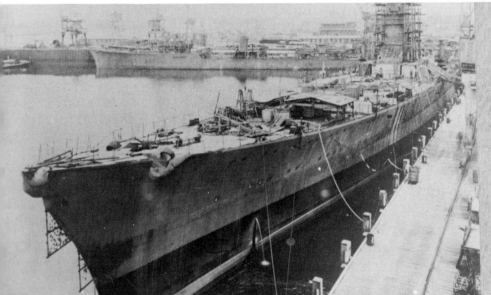

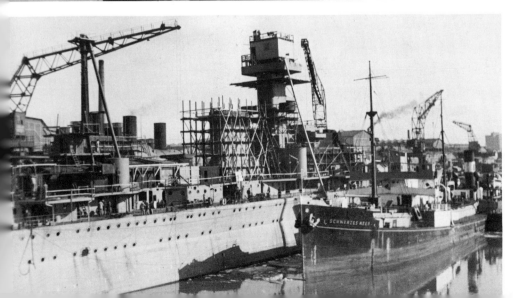

mand was ordered to take her from Bremen to Königsberg by the end of 1943. This date could not be met and by early March 1944, the ship still had not moved east. It was not until about the end of March that *Seydlitz* was taken to Kiel whence she sailed in tow of the tugs *Memmert*, *Rixhoft* and *Movensteert* on 30 March. Assisted by the ice-breaker *Pollux*, Operation 'Reiter' arrived in Königsberg on 2 April. It is not known quite how far the conversion to an aircraft carrier had progressed, but it is unlikely that much, if any, work was done at all, because by this time Germany's naval situation precluded any chance of operating a carrier. In December 1944, *Seydlitz* was re-rated a hulk.

As the Red Army approached from the east at the beginning of 1945, all useful equipment, part complete minor war vessels and ships under refit in Königsberg and Elbing were hurriedly towed to the West, but the unfortunate *Seydlitz* was not one of these; on 29 January 1945, the incomplete hulk was scuttled in the Timber harbour, her insides wrecked by explosives. A month later, Fleet Command asked if, when the Königsberg Sea Canal was reopened and communications restored with the town, *Seydlitz* could be towed out for use as valuable spare parts reserve. Pillau dockyard could only inform Fleet Command that the ship was on the bottom and there the matter ended. Her final fate is uncertain except that she fell into Soviet hands and was probably scrapped in situ or cannibalized for spares for her sister, the former *Lützow*.

Lützow too, progressed very slowly at the Deschimag yard, because of the shortage of workers, and late deliveries of such items as turbine blading. Then the signing of the Russo-German Pact on 23 August 1939, had a decisive effect upon the subsequent career of the ship, for she was to be included as part payment to the Soviet Union in return for the vast amounts of food and oil supplied to Germany under the Pact agreement. The ship was purchased by the Russians on 11 February 1940, by which time she had been completed up to the superstructure deck, with part of the lower bridge in place and 'A' and 'D' turrets aboard. Only 'A' turret had received its guns, however. On 15 April she left Germany in tow bound for Leningrad where she was to be completed at the Baltijskij Zavod imeni Ordzonikidze yard under the supervision of Konteradmiral (Ing) Feige and a team of seventy German technicians. It was originally intended to complete the vessel by 1942. Good progress was made at first, with all necessary parts and equipment being delivered. From the winter of 1940/41, however, the Russians began to notice a slowing down of deliveries which, when queried, was explained by the Germans as being caused by the war situation in the West.

In reality, deliveries had been delayed on the express instructions of Hitler, and Konteradmiral Feige himself left Leningrad on the pretext of illness in the spring of 1941. Gradually, more and more of the technicians followed, until the last left on 21 June, only a few hours before Germany invaded the Soviet Union. The ship, which in the interim had been known only as 'Projekt 53' was renamed *Petropavlovsk* in February 1941, and by 21 June was about 70 per cent complete. Her captain, Kapitan 2 Rang A. G. Vanifater, had an almost complete crew aboard, but the ship was nowhere near

operational or indeed able to steam. Vanifater endeavoured to continue completion with the assistance of his men at least to get the guns operational. By this time both 'A' and 'D' turrets were gunned and some 3.7cm flak was aboard. On 15 August 1941, the Soviet flag was hoisted for the first time and the ship became a unit of the Baltic Fleet.

When the German Army reached the environs of Leningrad in September 1941, *Petropavlosk*, now commanded by Kapitan 3 Rang A. K. Pavlovskij, opened fire on the 7th for the first time, with other units of the fleet. More than 11,000 rounds were fired by the warships including 676 by the former German cruiser during the seven days' engagement. Counter-attacks by German batteries resulted in a hit on *Petropavlosk* at midday on 17 September, which knocked out No. 3 generator room, the ship's only power source operational. Without power neither the guns could be fought nor the numerous fires extinguished following some 50 or so shell hits of various heavy calibres during the next few hours. The burning cruiser listed to port, but was prevented from capsizing by the quay wall, and the water flooding in quenched many of the fires. Ten of her crew were killed and twenty wounded. The remainder were drafted to Marine infantry units ashore.

A few specialists remained to assist salvage efforts but even with shipyard help, it was not until 10 September 1942 that the hull was finally made watertight, being raised during the night of 16/17 September and towed into the Baltic yard. Temporarily repaired, with three of the four 20.3cm guns serviceable (the left-hand gun of 'A' had been destroyed) and now renamed *Tallin*, the cruiser took part in the Red Army breakout from Leningrad in January 1944. In 31 bombardments, *Tallin* fired 1,036 rounds, before the Germans were driven out of range.

After the war, despite the availability of the wrecked *Seydlitz* for spares, little attempt was made to complete *Tallin* probably because she was an 'odd man out' in the Red Navy and possibly also because the shortcomings of the design had been exposed by the war. *Tallin* was towed into the River Neva and utilized as an accommodation hulk until the end of the 1950s, before finally being broken up.

4: LIGHT CRUISER PROJECTS

The post-*Nürnberg* line of light cruiser development had been disrupted by the appearance of the heavy cruisers of the 'Washington' type as discussed in Chapter 3, but there was still the need of a smaller ship for ocean employment. In May 1936, a broad requirement for an 8,000-tonnes ship was issued which called for a long-ranged seaworthy design intended for detached mercantile raiding in the classic *Emden* role of the First World War. This seemingly straightforward specification set in motion a train of events which was to cause a serious clash of departmental opinions and resulted in a most protracted development period. In the event, the delays experienced during design discussions prevented any ship being completed, or even reaching launching, as political ambitions rapidly outpaced Naval considerations towards the end of the 1930s.

As early as the middle of May 1936, the Construction Office had concluded that the demanded speed and endurance of a ship with four 15cm twin turrets was impossible to achieve, even on a 10,000-tonnes design, and proposed a reduction in the military demands of the project. The simplest and most efficient power plant was held to be a two-shaft installation, and for the maximum continuous speed, 100,000 horsepower was necessary. (It was not until Battleship 'H' was designed that a three-shaft layout was found to be as good as, if not better than, the twin.) The power plant would endow a top speed of 35 knots, but it was not possible to fit four twin turrets, so either three triple or three twins were proposed instead. The proposal for triple turrets was bound to be rejected because they had been the subject of criticism in the 'K' cruisers and the three twins idea could never satisfy the Kriegsmarine Gunnery lobby. This proposal from the Construction Office was, therefore, bound to lead to argument and so it proved.

By the end of August, the Construction Office had considered a three-shaft layout on 8,000 tonnes and once again reported its inability to achieve the demanded 35–36 knots. On the other hand, a two-shaft installation could reach the specified speed with an endurance of 5,800/6,200 nautical miles at 20 knots if the gun weights were similar to *Leipzig* (780t) and the armouring as in *Nürnberg*. In the following month, the Weapons Office confirmed rejection of the triple-turret layout and, in any event, it had been found that the weight of four twins was less than that of three triples, so

that by October the gun layout had reverted to the original specification.

The calculations made by the Construction Office were now called into question by the Development Office (AIV), which led to a period of inter-departmental acrimony lasting some eight months, and which had a decisive effect on eventual progress of the ship. Comparative studies of foreign designs and the recalculation of the Construction Office data led the Development Office to believe that higher-powered machinery could be installed, although endurance might prove difficult. In November, diesel propulsion was seriously considered by AIV, but despite pressure from them, a further conference on design progress did not take place until February 1937. In the course of this conference, the Construction Office stuck to its views that the installation of 100,000 horsepower on a *Nürnberg*-sized vessel was impossible, and asked for a decision between (a) a fast (35 knots) ship armed with four twin 15cm, armour as in *Nürnberg* and a large endurance on 18,000 tonnes, or (b) an enlarged destroyer, unarmoured, but capable of 40 knots, armed with six or eight 15cm guns.

Neither of these proposals was acceptable to the Development Office and quite plainly there was no reconciling the views of the two departments. In March 1937, A IV asked Reg. Rat. Dr Schmidt to investigate the problem, with particular reference to the foreign cruisers, *Montecuculi*, *Emile Bertin* and *Southampton*. This resulted in a new proposal from A IV which showed a weight distribution as follows:

Hull	2,840 tonnes		
MI	1,800	,,	Speed 34 knots
MII	450	,,	
Guns	940	,,	
Torpedo	70	,,	
Aircraft	50	,,	
Fuel	700	,,	
Equipment	550	,,	
Armour	600	,,	
	8,000 tonnes		

Simultaneously, the Construction Office issued a counter-proposal of 11,000 tonnes, 34 knots (maximum), 32.75 knots (continuous). This also, was turned down as being too large and too slow. The Construction Office then proceeded to criticise the new A IV proposal, and at the same time com-

plained that A IV had overstepped its area of design. The quarrel was now quite bitter, with eight months having elapsed and still no progress having been made towards a definitive design. Well over three years had gone by since *Nürnberg* had been laid down and there was no successor designed, let alone ordered.

The Construction Office continued to examine the design requirements and, in April 1937, reached the conclusion that the minimum tonnage required was 9,360 not 8,000 tonnes for the armament and speed specified. This was a step forward, however, for previously their contention had been, not less than 10,000 tonnes. The main difference between their view and the A IV design was in the weights of hull and machinery for which 4,250 tonnes was necessary and not 3,440 as detailed by A IV. Two months later, argument continued, the A IV design being criticized on grounds of stability, weak armour and low speed. The Construction Office insisted that at the most, 90,000 horsepower could be shipped in the parameters available, and proposed a three-shaft layout to raise endurance. A IV seized upon this proposal and wanted to install destroyer machinery on the wing shafts with a diesel on the centre one, but the Construction Office would not agree.

At the end of June, Dr Schmidt had re-worked his calculations and A IV had insisted that their design did possess adequate stability. Nevertheless, despite a personal exchange of views between the two heads of department, the two sides were as far away as ever. In a last ditch effort to reconcile views, a 90,000 horsepower, 33 knots sketch was submitted to Admiral Raeder, but was turned down as being too slow. Then, quite suddenly, on 19 July, another conference was called, attended by the Construction, Development, Engineering and Ordinance Offices, when a new proposal was laid before the participants. This envisaged a 7,900-tonnes, triple-shaft turbine layout, with 120,000 horsepower capable of 36 knots, devised by an employee of the Construction Office named Driessen. Coming more or less out of the blue, this proposal miraculously appeared to suit all parties! Four days later, the proposal was put before Admiral Raeder who asked, quite understandably, how it was possible to move from complete deadlock to mutual agreement in three weeks. The two heads of department answered this one in private after the end of the conference. What was said is not recorded!

At long last, detailed design work could now proceed. Improvements were incorporated, but without affecting displacement greatly, so that by November 1937, the specification looked as follows:

3 shafts; 100,000hp (120,000hp max.); 36 knots max.; 1,300 tonnes oil.
178m (wl), 183m (oa) × 17m × 5.05m.
Eight 15cm SKC/28 in Dreh L C/34.
Four 8.8cm SKC/32 in Dop. L C/32.
Eight 3.7cm SKC/30 in Dop. L C/30.
Four MG C/30
Eight G7a in two quadruple banks.

Power plant arrangement from forward to aft was: Generator Room/Boiler Room/Boiler Room/Engine Room/Boiler Room/Engine Room/Generator Room.

Then, in December 1937, the Engineering Office stated that it would be possible, and indeed advantageous, to replace the centre turbine by a diesel plant, and the New Construction Committee's final design showed two turbines of 40,000 horsepower each and a diesel of 36,000 horsepower giving a maximum speed of 36 knots.

In January 1938, consideration was given to arming the ship with 17cm guns, but four twin turrets entailed a weight penalty of 115 tonnes over the 15cm version and the rate of fire was slower. In view of these considerations, the change was not approved.

Admiral Raeder accepted the design on 29 April 1938, intending to construct eleven ships between 1939 and 1944 with each ship taking 2½ years to complete. The flak outfit was, in his view, a little weak, but replacement of the 8.8cm guns by twin 10.5cm was not possible on grounds of weight. Instead, removal of the catapult was considered so as to allow installation of three 8.8cm twin mountings, but this was not done. The first four, 'M', 'N', 'O' and 'P' were ordered on 24 May 1938, from Deutsche Werke (Kiel), Wilhelmshaven Naval Yard and the latter pair from Germania. Blohm & Voss, originally scheduled to build 'P', was deleted from the 'M' Kreuzer programme because of their heavy battleship work load. 'M' was scheduled to lay down on 1 November 1939 and 'V' on 1 August 1942.

MACHINERY

The machinery for six units was ordered in August 1938, their respective ships to commission between 1 May 1942 ('M') and 1 April 1944 ('R'). In the September there was a' proposal to replace 'O', 'P', 'Q', 'R', 'S', 'U' and 'W' by four 'Panzerschiffen'. Of course, whether this would in fact have been done cannot now be known. The Wagner boilers for 'M' were built by Deschimag at Bremen, those for 'N', 'O' and 'P' were to be built by their building yards under licence from Deschimag. Brown-Boverie supplied the turbines for 'M' and 'N'; Germania for 'O' and 'P', while all diesels were built by MAN. With the adoption of diesel drive on the centre shaft, the number of boilers was reduced to four, two in each boiler room, operating at 70kg/cm^2 and 465°C. Immediately aft of the boiler rooms, a single engine room accommodated the wing-shaft turbines, while the diesel plant absorbed the remaining 50 per cent of the machinery spaces. The 12-cylinder, double-acting two-stroke diesels were paired in two motor rooms with a gearing room between them. Outboard of the gearing room was a generator space to port and starboard with a third just forward of the foremost boiler room.

PROTECTION AND ARMAMENT

The main armoured deck was 20mm thick on its horizontal surfaces, but sloped at its edges, at an angle of about 45°, to join the lower side of the side belt. This sloping section was 35mm in thickness. The vertical belt itself was 50mm, with an upper strake of 30mm to upper deck level.

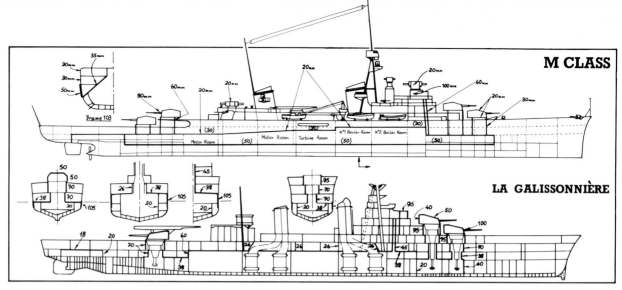

The visual appearance of this cruiser differed considerably from all previous light cruisers, mainly because of the adoption of twin superimposed turrets forward and aft. The 15cm guns, pattern SKC/28, were of the same type as those carried by *Bismarck*, having an elevation of 40° and were sited, in lightly armoured gunhouses, although the turret fronts were 80mm in thickness. A total of 120rpg plus twenty star shell were stowed in combined magazines and shell rooms on the upper platform deck. Main armament fire control was exercised by two 7-metre range-finders, one forward, one aft, together with the usual comprehensive internal fire-control spaces. The heavy flak outfit was limited to two 8.8cm SK C/32 twin mountings on the shelter deck aft, a feature which had already drawn criticism, controlled by a single high-angle director atop the bridge. This outfit was indeed light when compared to foreign contemporaries, most of which mounted eight 10.2cm or 9cm guns, but it could be argued that their employment on distant service, away from the threat of land-based strike forces, obviated the need for more. Equally, had these ships been put into service their light flak would undoubtedly have been greatly increased. As designed, this comprised four of the advanced, but unreliable, 3.7cm SK C/30 twin mountings.

Finally, the torpedo outfit consisted of only two banks of tubes instead of the four shipped by earlier cruisers, but these were quadruple instead of triple mountings so that fire-power was reduced by only 25 per cent. Four reloads were provided. Once again, a separate torpedo T/S on the hold deck and two 4-metre range-finders, one on each side of the forward funnel, provided very respectable fire-control facilities. Provision was made for the operation of aircraft, a catapult being fitted between the funnels with a hangar for a single aircraft forward of it on the upper deck. Two aircraft could be operated.

The final design proved a quite well-balanced one, and would undoubtedly have given the Kriegsmarine a useful, employable light cruiser type, unlike the 'K' ships. In comparison with its contemporaries, *La Galissonnière*, *Southampton* and *Fiji*, it carried less fire-power and was not as heavily armoured. While it could probably have outrun its British opponents, it might have had a tough time with the faster French ships, but its main task was commerce raiding for which a high speed was essential to avoid contact with enemy warships. In the event, the delays experienced during design work were such that by the start of the Second World War, only three had been laid down, on which construction was little advanced with the result that all were suspended and broken up during the war.

FURTHER DESIGNS

The Kreuzer 'M' design was the last to be put into production, but further design studies were conducted, although with little priority. In July 1937, a competition was held, for a 200,000RM prize to find the best design to succeed Kreuzer 'M'. Because of security considerations, only a restricted

Kreuzer 'M' Weight statement as at 5 May 1939			
Hull	2470	Four 8.8cm SKC/32	46.6
Armour	1000	Eight 3.7cm SKC/30	14.8
Main machinery	2375	Four 2cm C/30 (2x2)	1.8
Auxiliary machinery	520	(*Subtotal*	*457.2*)
Armament	950		
Torpedoes and aircraft	95	Low angle director	95.5
Equipment	500	Flak director	50.0
Reserve	100	Stabilization	21.0
(*Type displacement*	*8010*)	Searchlights	30.0
		Communications	40.2
50% oil fuel	500	Gyro supply system	49.5
50% water, etc	100	(*Subtotal*	*285.8*)
(*Construction*			
displacement	*8610*)	Ammunition:	
		15cm (120rpg+20	
50% fuel and water	700	Star rpg)	83.1
(*Full load displacement*	*9310*)	8.8cm (300rpg+30	
		Star rpg)	26.1
		3.7cm (1000rpg)	25.6
Emergency fuel	600	2cm (2000rpg)	5.6
Emergency full load		Saluting and signal	
displacement	*9910*)	munition	5.6
		(*Subtotal*	*146.0*)
Armament weight breakdown:		Equipment	39.4
		Margin	21.6
Eight 15cm SKC/28	394	Total (metric tonnes)	950

DESIGN OF THE WEHR DICH

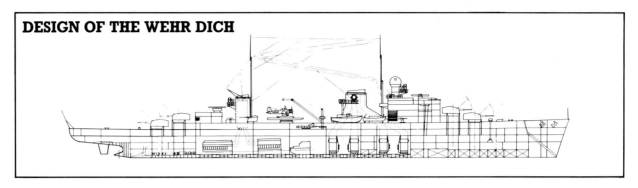

circle of entrants was invited from the major shipyards and the Naval Staff. The project parameters were:

Displacement	Less than 8,000 tonnes.
Speed	35/36 knots min. with 80 per cent fuel.
Endurance	6,000 nautical miles at 19 knots.
Guns	as Kreuzer 'M'.
Protection	50mm belt, at least 2.5m deep over magazines and boilers.
	30mm belt, outside 50mm length.
	20mm deck, 25mm slope, 30mm barbettes. (See Appendix 1.)

Four designs were submitted, known as: 'Seeadler', 'Motorkreuzer', 'Wehr Dich' and an incomplete sketch, 'Trotz Alledem'. The Seeadler entrant envisaged an 8,400-tonnes ship (and therefore over the limit!) with a maximum speed of 35.5 knots using a three-shaft combined turbine and diesel layout. Six boilers, paired in three boiler rooms, supplied the turbines. All uptakes were trunked into a single massive funnel. The most peculiar feature of this submission was in the manner of the incorporation of dual power for the centre shaft. Turbines drove the wing shafts from separate engine rooms, but while a four-diesel installation of 18,000 horsepower was geared to the after end of the centre shaft, an extremely long extension shaft was taken forward of the foremost boiler room to a third turbine space which was located *under the bridge structure*! (see page 44). This length of shafting would have led to problems in active service. Otherwise the design was a conventional four twin turret layout with three 8.8cm twin mountings disposed about the after superstructure. Internally the underwater protection was a great improvement over Kreuzer 'M'.

The Wehr Dich submission claimed 35.2 knots on a displacement of 8,128 tonnes, again with a three-shaft steam/diesel installation. The machinery layout was broadly similar in disposition to Kreuzer 'M' except that four smaller Deschimag boilers replaced the two large ones in each boiler room. The turbines on the wing shafts each developed 45,000 horsepower, and the centre diesel, 31,000 horsepower. Protection included an armoured deck two metres above the waterline, but not sloped at the edges. The waterline belt was 30mm–50mm deep. Like Seeadler, Wehr Dich envisaged a four twin turret layout, but differed externally by the need for two funnels, the after one used for the diesel exhaust.

Motorkreuzer proved to be the largest entrant, displacing 8,959 tonnes, and differed from the two designs already described by adopting pure diesel propulsion and proposing the use of three 15cm triple turrets. The latter point alone would have raised dissension at a later stage and the use of only two shafts was rejected as being overtaxing in a ship of this size. The machinery arrangement of two sets of four 12-cylinder diesels geared to each shaft necessitated four motor rooms and two gearing rooms, resulting in a very long machinery space. This in turn increased the length and consequently the weight of armour required. Deep hull tunnels for the screws, enclosing about 140° of the propellers allowed only 50mm between the tips of the blades and the tunnel surface. This would have led to vibration and vulnerability to shock damage. Externally, two funnels were needed for the diesel exhausts, and the turret arrangement was two forward, one aft.

The final design, Trotz Alledem, was not a full design as such, but an interesting machinery layout. It incorporated

TROTZ ALLEDEM MOTOR ROOM LAYOUT

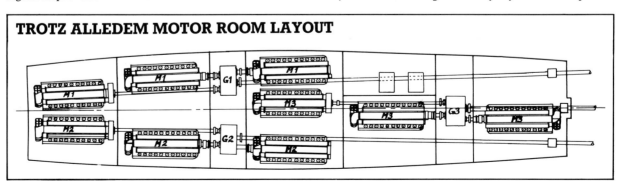

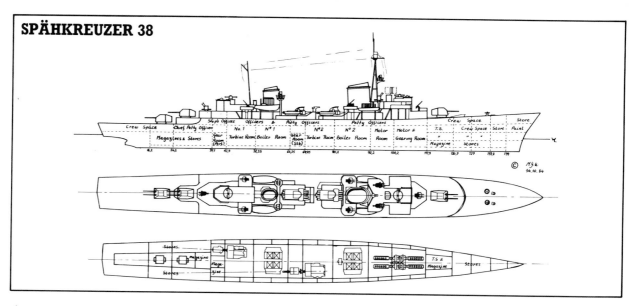

SPÄHKREUZER 38

nine 12-cylinder diesels coupled to three shafts (see page 54), each of the three engines on each shaft being in a different motor room. This could have been a great benefit to damage control, and could have permitted retention of power on all three shafts in certain kinds of action damage. In the end, none of the designs was considered superior to Kreuzer 'M', but some design points emerged which could be usefully incorporated into Kreuzer 'M'.

One final project needs to be considered, however. It will be recalled that the Construction Office had proposed and had rejected, a scheme for a super-destroyer, at the beginning of 1937. This seems to have set in train a design study of such a type which developed into a project for a Spähkreuzer or Scout Cruiser, suitable for Atlantic employment. The Staff Requirement was for a ship with superior armament to Fleet destroyers and capable of outrunning enemy cruisers. The initial definitive design was designated 'Spähkreuzer 38', a twin-funnelled ship carrying three 15cm twin mountings, one forward and two aft, as well as two quintuple banks of torpedoes on a displacement of about 6,000 tonnes full load. A mixed steam and diesel installation was planned, with boiler and engine rooms arranged on the unit principle. Unusually, the motor room, containing four diesels geared to the centre shaft, was situated in the foremost machinery space. The diesel installation developed 14,500shp and the turbines 77,500, giving a maximum speed of about 35 knots. Protection was minimal, with 15mm deck, 18mm inner longitudinal bulkhead and other areas of 12mm.

Modifications to this design led to its re-designation as 'Spähkreuzer 39', which incorporated a heavier flak outfit and better armouring on increased dimensions and displacement (now 7,550 tonnes full load). The machinery layout was reversed in that the wing shafts now were powered by the new 'V' diesels, while the centre shaft now had the turbine. The penalty for the increased protection and armament (which now also included a float plane) was a drop in speed of some

three knots, despite an increase in power to 110,000 horse-power. Protection now incorporated a 50mm waterline belt, 25mm (max.) deck and 12mm inner longitudinal bulkhead. Externally, the new design differed from the 1938 layout by having two turrets forward, one aft and a catapult between the funnels displacing the torpedoes. These twin 8.8cm were grouped around the after control position.

The 'Spähkreuzer 39' design was itself displaced by the 'Spähkreuzer 40' which showed a small increase in dimensions, but claimed an increase in maximum speed to 31.2 knots, despite the same total power installation as the 39 version. Externally, the main difference was the reversion to the one forward, two aft, turret arrangement and the reinstatement of the torpedoes at the expense of the aircraft. Internally, however, the machinery arrangements were radically revised. A unit, consisting of turbine room, generator space and boiler room, powered each wing shaft, each unit being separated from the other by a generator room and the main motor room. The overall design was a great improvement over the 'Spähkreuzer 38', giving better performance, 50 per cent greater endurance and a flak outfit equivalent to a light cruiser.

It was expected that this design would follow the Type 38 in production, but it was later cancelled as unnecessary for operations. In February 1939, the Naval Staff declared the importance of the Spähkreuzer in ocean warfare, but not at the expense of other types. On 17 February 1941 three ships were ordered from Germaniawerft as Yard Nos. 671–673 (following the original cancellation of the destroyers *Z40* to *Z42*) and designated *SP1* to *SP3*. In December 1941, the main engines were ordered for *SP4* to *SP6*, but by April the following year, construction on the Spähkreuzer programme had been suspended. Henceforth, destroyers and torpedo-boats would be the largest surface ships built by the Kriegsmarine, but the main effort was, of course, directed towards the U-boat arm.

5: ARMAMENT

15CM GUN

At the time *Emden* was designed, the standard cruiser gun was the 15cm L/45 weapon, of which large numbers had been produced during the war. As its designation implied, it was a 45-calibre gun with a muzzle velocity of 835m/sec, firing a 45.3kg projectile to a maximum range of about 17,600 metres. In its single, centre pivot LC/16 mounting aboard *Emden*, it was capable of only 27° elevation and was quite obsolete. During the later war years, *Emden* was re-armed with destroyer-pattern 15cm TBK C/36 guns which had an improved range over the First World War pattern gun, and power training. By the time that the first of the new Treaty light cruisers were designed in the middle 1920s, a new gun had been developed by the Rheinmetall–Borsig concern in Düsseldorf, which was

known as the 15cm SKC/25. Type designations were now no longer based upon the length of the barrel in calibres, but by the weapon type (i.e. 'Schnellfeurkannone' or quick-firing) and the year of design.

In comparison with the earlier gun, this new 15cm weapon featured a 60-calibre barrel with a muzzle velocity of 960m/sec. The shell weight remained the same at 45.5kg, but the maximum range was increased to 25,700 metres. Three main types of ammunition were provided: nose-fuzed HE, base-fuzed HE, and AP. The AP round was capped, with an 885-gram Fp02 bursting charge and was 3.7 calibres in length. The range of 25,700 metres quoted above was attained at 40° elevation, using a cased charge of 19.3kg of C/32 powder. An angle of 10° elevation under similar conditions achieved a

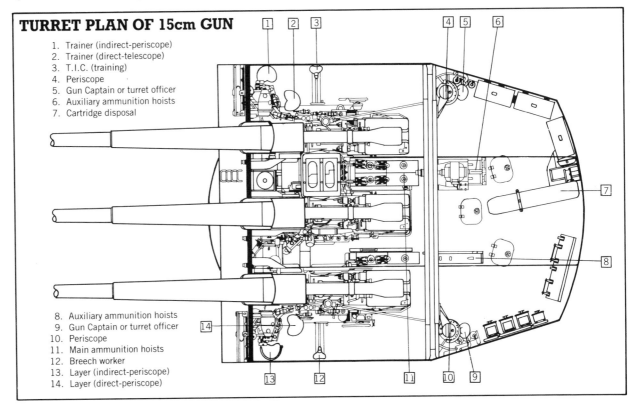

TURRET PLAN OF 15cm GUN

1. Trainer (indirect-periscope)
2. Trainer (direct-telescope)
3. T.I.C. (training)
4. Periscope
5. Gun Captain or turret officer
6. Auxiliary ammunition hoists
7. Cartridge disposal

8. Auxiliary ammunition hoists
9. Gun Captain or turret officer
10. Periscope
11. Main ammunition hoists
12. Breech worker
13. Layer (indirect-periscope)
14. Layer (direct-periscope)

range of 14,100 metres. Using reduced charges of 14.1kg, respective figures for range were 21,500 metres and 11,700 metres, with a muzzle velocity of 835m/sec. With head-fuzed HE L/45 rounds, 60mm of homogeneous armour could be penetrated at a range of 3,200 metres, but only 20mm at 11,200 metres. Rate of fire was seven rounds per minute.

To effect the necessary weight savings, the new cruiser's guns were carried in triple turrets, 'Drehturm C/25', armoured with 30mm front and 20mm sides, capable of 40° of elevation, each weighing nearly 137 tonnes. Three 'K' cruisers and *Leipzig* received this turret, but *Nürnberg* had a more heavily armoured version, with 80mm fronts and the rear increased to 35mm, pushing the weight up to 147 tonnes. The fortunes of war prevented any of the ships equipped with these guns from seeing much action, but since they had been in service for about ten years, any teething troubles had been overcome and the equipment functioned smoothly enough.

In *Nürnberg* the combined magazine and shell rooms, situated immediately below the armoured deck were ten in number, of which three served 'A' turret. Shells and charges (the latter cased), were passed via hand-throughs into the revolving structure from the handing rooms, having been manhandled from their stowage bins in the magazines. Not all magazines were adjacent to the turret handing rooms and from these, the ammunition had to be passed via another magazine which was adjacent to a handing room. The hand-throughs themselves consisted of a double scuttle arranged vertically, the upper for shell and the lower cartridge.

Rather surprisingly, in view of experiences at Jutland in 1916, in particular with *Seydlitz*, when superior anti-flash arrangements saved her and other vessels, while British ships were lost, German anti-flash arrangements had deteriorated during the post-war period. There were no anti-flash arrangements between handing rooms and magazines in the normal course of supply, and where scuttles or spring-loaded flaps were fitted between the revolving structure and the handing rooms, the fit was poor and gaps of 6mm not unusual. At the roof of the handing room, an anti-flash apron sealed the gap between fixed and revolving structures. The shells and charges were tipped into the hoist by two revolving scuttles linked together, and then lifted into the gunhouse. The main hoists were asymmetrically placed, that for the left-hand gun between the left and centre guns, while those for the centre 'and right-hand guns were between their respective guns. Loading and ramming was done by hand. Auxiliary bucket hoists were fitted to the rear of the main hoists and could supply one shell and charge by an electric winch. Training was all-electric with emergency hand-operation from the engine platform. Ammunition supply was hydraulic as was the elevation system (by 'follow the Pointer'). All guns elevated independently, but could be locked to elevate as one if required.

With the abandonment of the triple 15cm turret and the introduction of the more popular twin mounting for the Kreuzer 'M' design, a modification of the 15cm twin turret (employed as secondary armament for *Scharnhorst*) was adopted. This mounting, Drh. LC/34, utilized the newer but

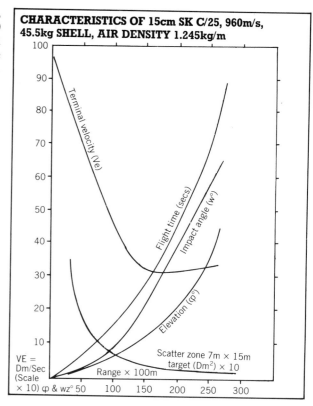

CHARACTERISTICS OF 15cm SK C/25, 960m/s, 45.5kg SHELL, AIR DENSITY 1.245kg/m

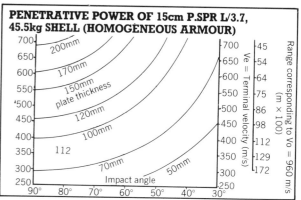

PENETRATIVE POWER OF 15cm P.SPR L/3.7, 45.5kg SHELL (HOMOGENEOUS ARMOUR)

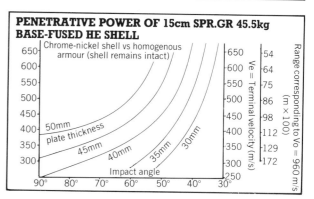

PENETRATIVE POWER OF 15cm SPR.GR 45.5kg BASE-FUSED HE SHELL

Effect of AP shell on homogeneous armour

Calibre	Impact velocity (m/s)	Range (m × 100)	15	20	25	30	40	50	60 / 200ø	70	80
P.Spr.Gr. 15cm L/4.5 head fuzed	770	32									
	700	45					400ø	300ø	crack-free		
	600	64				600ø	crack-free		crack-free		
	500	86					crack-free				
	400	112	1,200ø	900ø	crack-free	crack-free					
P.Spr.Gr. 20.3cm L/47 head fuzed	700	63							cracked		
	600	95						320ø	crack-free		
	550	115				1,200ø	1,000ø	crack-free			
	500	135			cracked	crack-free					

Note: table indicates diameter of hole punched into armour.

shorter (55cal) and less powerful 15cm SKC/28 Model gun which had a muzzle velocity of 875m/sec and a range of 23,000 metres. It fired the same projectiles, but with a reduced cordite charge of only 14kg. As fitted to *Scharnhorst*, each turret weighed 120 tonnes, but these carried 140mm armoured fronts as well as heavy side armour. For Kreuzer 'M' use, armouring was greatly reduced, lowering the weight to about 98½ tonnes.

20.3CM GUN

While the 15cm gun had had a long history of development and improvement, the 20.3cm SKC/34 gun adopted for the heavy cruisers was a completely new design and unlike the light cruiser and destroyer weapons, was a Krupp product

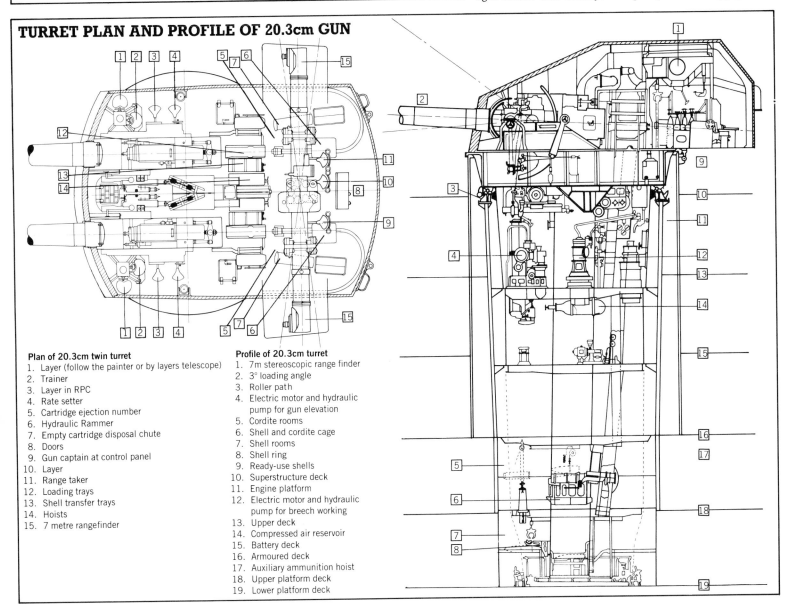

TURRET PLAN AND PROFILE OF 20.3cm GUN

Plan of 20.3cm twin turret
1. Layer (follow the painter or by layers telescope)
2. Trainer
3. Layer in RPC
4. Rate setter
5. Cartridge ejection number
6. Hydraulic Rammer
7. Empty cartridge disposal chute
8. Doors
9. Gun captain at control panel
10. Layer
11. Range taker
12. Loading trays
13. Shell transfer trays
14. Hoists
15. 7 metre rangefinder

Profile of 20.3cm turret
1. 7m stereoscopic range finder
2. 3° loading angle
3. Roller path
4. Electric motor and hydraulic pump for gun elevation
5. Cordite rooms
6. Shell and cordite cage
7. Shell rooms
8. Shell ring
9. Ready-use shells
10. Superstructure deck
11. Engine platform
12. Electric motor and hydraulic pump for breech working
13. Upper deck
14. Compressed air reservoir
15. Battery deck
16. Armoured deck
17. Auxiliary ammunition hoist
18. Upper platform deck
19. Lower platform deck

Right: Chief Petty Officer gun captain at quarters firing. Tube in his mouth is the firing mechanism although there is a second trigger on the wheel. (Bundesarchiv)

Bottom right: 20.3cm turret, *Admiral Hipper*, emergency loading of shell from ready-use rack. (Bundesarchiv)

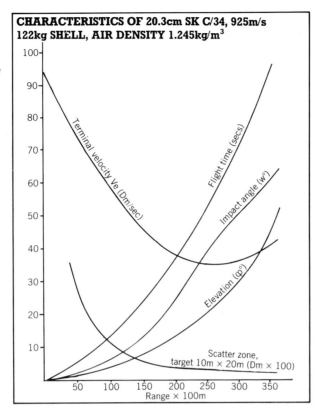

CHARACTERISTICS OF 20.3cm SK C/34, 925m/s 122kg SHELL, AIR DENSITY 1.245kg/m³

Terminal velocity Ve (Dm/sec)

Flight time (secs)

Impact angle (w°)

Elevation (φ°)

Scatter zone, target 10m × 20m (Dm × 100)

Range × 100m

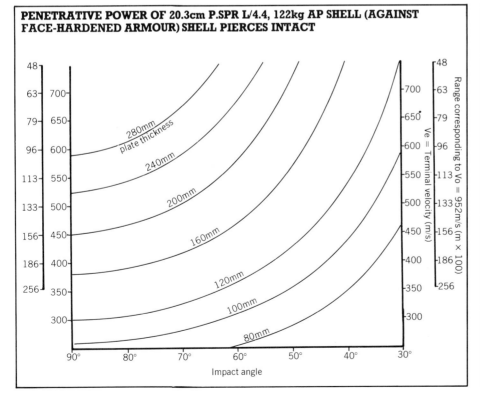

PENETRATIVE POWER OF 20.3cm P.SPR L/4.4, 122kg AP SHELL (AGAINST FACE-HARDENED ARMOUR) SHELL PIERCES INTACT

280mm plate thickness

240mm

200mm

160mm

120mm

100mm

80mm

Impact angle

Range corresponding to Vo = 952m/s (m × 100)

Ve = Terminal velocity (m/s)

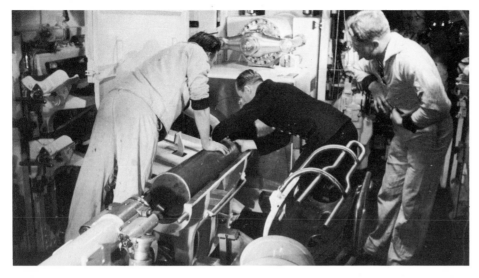

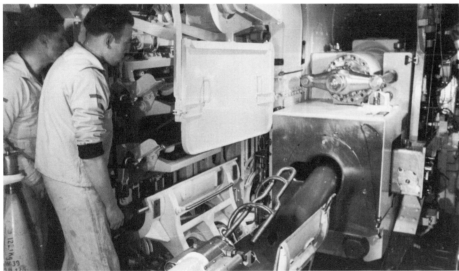

and not Rheinmetall. This 60-calibre gun, which had a muzzle velocity of 925m/sec, fired a 122kg shell, using a two-part cordite charge. The 20kg front charge (Vorkartüsche) was uncased, but the 48kg main charge (Hauptkartüsche) was brass cased. Four main types of shell were carried: Pz.Spr.Gr. L/4.4 mhb (base-fuzed AP shot with windshield); Spr.Gr. L/4.7 mhb (base-fuzed HE with windshield); Spr.Gr. L/4.7 (head-fuzed HE); Spr.Gr. L/4.7 mhb (head-fuzed HE with windshield) plus the L.Gr.L/4.5 star shell. AP and HE shells weighed 122kg except Spr.Gr.L/4.7 mhb, which weighed 124kg. The star shell round weighed 163kg. All German guns in general service used the cartridge cases for obturation and the charges, which were a close fit in the chamber, had an ignition pad at the after end with a centre flash tube made from rolled sheet propellant through the charge. Head-fuzed Spr.Gr. L/4.7 (with 8.93kg bursting charge could penetrate 50cm of homogeneous armour at 9,500 metres.

The guns were carried in twin turrets, the superfiring turrets being fitted with 7-metre range-finders. 'A' and 'D' turrets weighed 249 tonnes apiece; 'B' and 'C', 262 tonnes. All guns except those of 'A' turret had an elevation of +37°, −10° depression, 'A' turret's depression being 1° less to clear the sheer of the forecastle. Training was electric, and elevation electro-hydraulic using a water/glycerine/lubricant medium. Firing was by electro-percussion. All-elevation loading was not possible, the guns being returned to 3° of elevation for loading.

The shell rooms in the heavy cruisers were situated below the magazines which were themselves immediately below the armoured deck. Charges were manhandled into the handing room and then passed in to the cage, the front half-charge being placed on the lower shelf and the rear or main charge being carried on the upper shelf. Below in the shell rooms, shells were picked up by electric grabs and placed on roller conveyors for transfer to the handing room. In the handing room, chutes directed the shells into two troughs, which in turn tipped them into the bogies on the shell ring and thence into the cage within the revolving structure. The shell portion then picked up the cordite section *en route* to the gunhouse where shell and charges were rammed on to a swinging tray and then into the gun. Main and auxiliary ammunition hoists were provided. The ship's book ammunition stowage was 1,308 rounds of HE/AP and 40 rounds of star shell, rate of fire four rounds per barrel per minute. Towards the close of the war, ammunition supply for 20.3cm guns became something of a problem, but as early as November 1939, there were only two full outfits available for *Admiral Hipper* and *Blücher*, with one for *Prinz Eugen*. Her second could not be available before August 1940. *Seydlitz*'s supplies were in the same position, and a third outfit for all ships could not be expected until the autumn of 1941.

ANTI-AIRCRAFT ARMAMENT

All light cruiser designs initially utilized the 8.8cm FlaK L/45 gun for heavy air defence, *Emden* being fitted originally with two and the 'K' ships with three, all in single, shielded MPL C/13 mountings. *Emden* retained her single 8.8cm guns

Opposite page, top: 20.3cm turret, *Admiral Hipper*, preparing to ram home the Hauptkartusche or main charge. The rammer is in the left-hand corner. The frame between the two right-hand crew members is the spent case transfer tray. (Bundesarchiv)

Centre: 20.3cm turret, empty case being ejected from breech on to ejection transfer tray. Note ready-use shells on left. (Bundesarchiv)

Bottom: The breech end of the right-hand gun in one of *Admiral Hipper*'s 20.3cm turrets. The crewman is ejecting a spent cartridge case down the disposal chute. At the bottom left is the rammer, while above and to the left can be seen the shell loading tray adjacent to the ammunition hoist. (Bundesarchiv)

20.3cm (8in) Guns

	Germany *Prinz Eugen*	Britain *Kent*	France *Algerie*	Italy *Zara*	Japan *Takao*	USA *Wichita*
Designation	20.3cm SKC/34 in Drh T.L/C34	8in BL Mk VIII Twin Mk I Mounting	203 Mle 1924 T.Mle 1924 de 203	203 Ans/53 1929	20cm 3 Nendo Shiki 2 Gô Model E	8in Mk 9
Calibre	203mm/60 cal	8in/50 cal	203/50 cal	203/53 cal	203.5/50 cal	8in/55 cal
Muzzle velocity	925m/s	847m/s	850m/s	940m/s	840m/s	870m/s
Elevation/Depression	+37°/−10°	+70°/−3°	+45°/−5°	+45°/−5°	+70°/−5°	+41°/−5°
Range	33,500m	26,700m	30,000m	31,566m	29,566m	29,522m
Rate of fire	4rpg/min	4rpg/min	3rpg/min	3.8rpg/min	4rpg/min	
Shell weight:						
HE	122kg	116kg	120kg	111kg	126kg	152kg
AP	122kg	116kg	126kg	125kg	126kg	152kg
AP (capped)	122kg	116kg	134kg		126kg	
Cordite charge		30kg		52kg	33.8kg	50kg
Turret weight	250-260 tonnes (twin)	210 tonnes (twin)	154-159 tonnes (twin)	(twin)	171 tonnes (twin)	314 tonnes (triple)

until they were replaced by 10.5cm SKC/32gE weapons in 1944, but the other ships were re-armed with the new 8.8cm SKC/32 in twin LC/32 mountings as they became available, in the mid 1930s. This gun fired a 9kg round, with a maximum vertical range of 12,400 metres, but was considered too light for the heavy cruisers, which shipped a larger calibre, the 10.5cm SKC/33 in twin C/31 mountings. *Seydlitz* and *Lützow*, however, would have received the C/37 twin mountings had they been completed to plan. With the 10.5cm gun, shell weight increased to 15.1kg. The mounting itself was of an advanced nature, being triaxially stabilized with 80° elevation, and had a distinctive appearance. One of its main drawbacks,

8.8cm SK C/25 IN TWIN MOUNTING LC/25

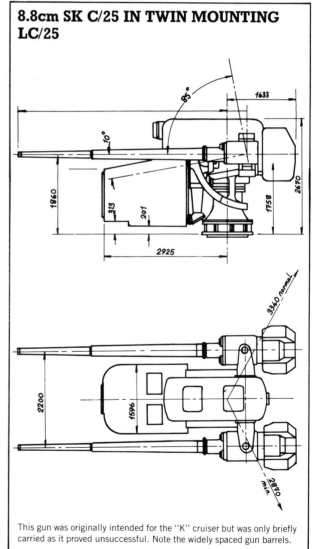

This gun was originally intended for the "K" cruiser but was only briefly carried as it proved unsuccessful. Note the widely spaced gun barrels.

10.5cm SKC/33 IN TWIN MOUNTING DOPP LC/37

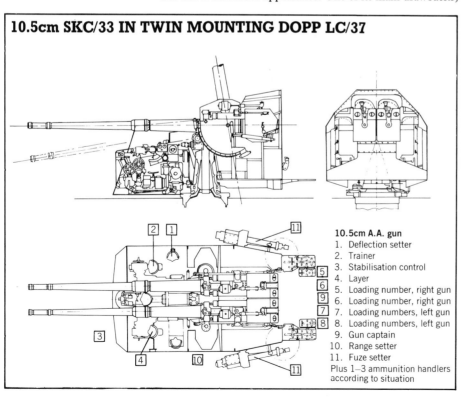

10.5cm A.A. gun
1. Deflection setter
2. Trainer
3. Stabilisation control
4. Layer
5. Loading number, right gun
6. Loading number, right gun
7. Loading numbers, left gun
8. Loading numbers, left gun
9. Gun captain
10. Range setter
11. Fuze setter
Plus 1–3 ammunition handlers according to situation

however, was its susceptibility to electrical failure as a result of insufficient attention to watertightness. (Despite its appearance, the mounting was open and not weatherproof.) Twelve men formed the gun's crew.

The C/37 mounting differed from the C/31 version by the removal of the two separate cross-roll axes and their replacement by a single one for reasons of ease of manufacture and maintenance. Cross-roll drives were strengthened in this version after sea experience with the C/31, but a proposal to use a single cradle for the guns was not carried through because of the need to use existing components. Sights were altered from flight plane predictor to vertical/horizontal co-ordinates. The secondary armament of both light (except *Emden*) and heavy cruisers remained unaltered during the war.

Light anti-aircraft defence on all classes of ship was provided by the 3.7cm SKC/30 gun in stabilized LC/30 twin mountings, and the 2cm MGC/30 gun in single pedestal mountings. The 3.7cm mounting was a triaxial, hand-worked gun, with cross-levelling by direct-acting stabilizer using two large gyros in line. Unfortunately, the potential of this gun was greatly reduced by two factors. First, the gyro system proved a hopeless failure, being unable to cope with lively movement, particularly in small ships, and secondly, it was badly affected by cold and damp which corroded the operating chains and shorted the electrics. Nearly 400 sets had been built before the defects became apparent because no foul weather sea trials had been conducted with prototypes. On the other hand, the 2cm gun merely suffered from a poor rate of fire, which was later rectified in its C/38 version.

TORPEDOES AND MINES

The cruiser's second offensive weapon was the torpedo, of which all except *Emden* shipped four triple banks. Although initially these were of 50cm calibre, by the mid 1930s, the 53.3cm G7a torpedo had become the standard weapon. The surviving light cruisers (again excepting *Emden*) landed one pair of tubes in the course of wartime refits, but while the

heavy cruisers retained theirs, only *Admiral Hipper* ever used them in earnest. Similarly, few British cruisers ever used their torpedoes.

German cruisers were generally fitted for minelaying, and the heavy cruisers were no exception, although only *Admiral Hipper* ever made use of this capability. Normally the equipment was not carried aboard, but drawn from the mining depot when required. Two sets of mine rails, each 42 metres long could be fitted to port and starboard on the quarterdeck, extending as far as the after end of 'C' turret barbette, on which up to 128 mines (dependent on type) could be accommodated. Unlike the heavy cruisers, the light cruisers performed several minelaying tasks. Finally, each cruiser carried four to six depth-charges in single cradles on the quarterdeck, fired electrically from the bridge.

FIRE CONTROL SYSTEMS

The fire-control system of the most modern light cruiser in service, *Nürnberg*, consisted of a main gunnery control position atop the foremost tower, containing two director sights forward and aft of the 6-metre stereoscopic optical range-finder. A second 6-metre range-finder was sited above the navigating bridge, and a third on the after control position. The armoured conning tower abaft 'A' turret was positioned much lower than in her half-sister, *Leipzig*, and in consequence had a lower height of command. Within this armoured position was a further gun director sight on the centre-line, and two torpedo directors sided port and starboard. Just forward of 'C' turret on the after end of the searchlight-control position was another gun director sight, while to port and starboard of it were fitted searchlight-control positions and further torpedo director sights. On the open bridge wings were fitted each side from forward to aft, a gun director column, torpedo bearing sight and two searchlight-control positions. The main gunnery transmitting station, on the hold deck below 'A' turret, was supplemented by a secondary position aft, a deck higher between 'B' and 'C' turret magazines. These incorporated a range and bearing plot together with a separate, vertical panel. Flak defence was catered for by a combined 3m range-finder/height-finder/director tower on the centre-line aft, in conjunction with a flak transmitting-station on the platform deck below it. Fuze settings and future range were predicted on a plot, and deflections were obtained by forecasting from rate of change of angle of sight and rate of change of bearing plots. Two periscopic control sights to port and starboard in each turret allowed local control of the guns. The torpedo armament had its own transmitting-station immediately forward of the main gunnery T.S.

The gunnery-control systems shipped aboard the heavy cruisers for main armament control probably represent the peak of sophistication achieved by German fire-control system designers and in consequence will be examined in rather greater detail than those of the light cruisers. The standard policy for the solution of low-angle gunnery stabilization and fire-control problems was to provide centralized gyro-stabilizer units which measured yaw, roll and pitch about the deck planes, and to feed these values to the director or gun plane resolvers. These resolvers were used to provide roll along or across the line of sight or fire, at biaxial directors or guns respectively. In addition, all important directors were provided with local line of sight stabilization. It was a Staff Requirement that directors be protected by armour, be of small size and able to control both medium and heavy guns. This led to a small, three-man director sight being developed, which had to be duplicated or triplicated in each control position because of restricted fields of view.

As installed in the first two ships, *Admiral Hipper* and *Blücher*, main and secondary systems were both advanced and overcomplicated which, while allowing flexibility, produced in practice a system difficult to maintain. The main fire-control stations were five in number:

(i) Foretop.
(ii) Forebridge.
(iii) After control.
(iv) Forward night control stand.
(v) After night control stand.

Below decks, the associated gunnery control spaces included:

(i) Forward Gunnery Control Centre.
(ii) After Gunnery Control Centre.
(iii) Gunnery Switch Room.
(iv) Reserve Gunnery Switch Room.
(v) Forward Amplifier Room.
(vi) After Amplifier Room.

The foretop or main action gunnery position contained two C/38K directors sided port and starboard, for computation of elevation and deflection. Two order transmission units C/38K (port and starboard); two SA/LA C/38K fire signal transmitters for operation of fire-bells and klaxons in the 20.3cm turrets were also fitted. In the range-finder position itself, a 7-metre optical stereoscopic unit was later supplemented by a radar ranging set, and ranges could also be obtained via the range-finders in the flak towers as well as from the night control position.

The forward and after control positions were fitted with one C/38K director unit, a fire signal transmitter and a 7-metre range-finder in each (6-metre only in *Admiral Hipper* and *Blücher*, forward position). Power training was fitted for all range-finders, but no circular cupolas were carried in the forward position by the two earlier heavy cruisers. In the forward night control position were fitted two director columns (Zielsaule C/38K), range receivers and a star shell control unit (Lg. Leitgeräte C/38K), while the after position was merely fitted with a star shell control unit (*Prinz Eugen* only). This star shell unit could receive data automatically from the Rw-Hw Geber or by hand-setting. It added deflection to the compass bearing received from the 'A Component' or main director and transmitted this with elevation data to the star shell guns.

Although the operation of this system was, in general, considered satisfactory, investigations by Dr Cordes, the Chief Technical Adviser for Gunnery and Fire control to the German Admiralty, showed that some simplification was desirable and it was decided that the order transmission units

(Befehlgeber C/38K) and fire signal transmitters could be dispensed with, as could some of the range receiver units in the director positions. In the forward and aft night control positions, the star shell control units could also be dispensed with and their functions assumed by a single control unit installed in the forward gunnery control room below the armoured deck. These changes were implemented for *Prinz Eugen* and later ships, while *Admiral Hipper* was possibly retrospectively modified.

Two master gyro rooms, one forward and one aft, provided base reference planes to the fire-control system; one, known as the 'A Component', was a continuous transmission of the ship's head which was horizontally stabilized from the second, or 'BC Component'. Values from the 'A Component' were fed via the gunnery switchboard to both main and secondary T/Ss and thence to the various parts of the system which required a ship's heading component. The 'BC Component' supplied stabilization data for pitch and roll relative to the ship's longitudinal and transverse axes. The output was fed to the transmitting stations and fire-control instruments.

Both forward and after transmitting stations contained a bearing and elevation calculator (Rw-Hw-Geber C/38K) and a main fire-control computer (Art.Schuw.Rech C/38K). The Rw-Hw-Geber supplied firing bearing and elevation data, stabilized for pitch and roll, to the guns and the stabilized optics of the director periscope. It also supplied values for target bearing, horizontally stabilized, to the fire-control computer, and contained a stabilized power output to ease the task of laying the guns in heavy weather. It was equivalent to the British Transit and Plane converter combined. The fire-control computer itself received data for range, enemy speed, inclination and course from the various range-finders and directors, and calculated the necessary firing data taking into consideration the ballistic effects of wind, air pressure and muzzle-velocity variations.

A shore-bombardment control unit, formerly fitted in the transmitting station, was later removed. Each of these two main gunnery control stations was basically equipped with the same installations except that the forward room was rather more comprehensively fitted out. *Prinz Eugen*, however, had no equipment in the after station until 1942 because her original outfit had been supplied to Russia for use with *Lützow*'s fitting out.

The fire-control system for the heavy flak outfit was also comprehensive, with four range-finder towers and two main flak director positions controlling six twin mountings disposed three on each beam. For the solution of high-angle problems, the centralized system was not followed, but each director (being of triaxial design) was provided with its own local stabilization system for yaw, roll and cross-roll, about the line of sight. It, too, was over-complicated, especially in the earlier two ships, *Admiral Hipper* and *Blücher*, leading to unreliability, inadequate accessibility and unclear layout. The later-type flak directors fitted in *Prinz Eugen* and later ships improved matters by the adoption of small gyro-stabilization with motor follow-up, but large sections of the fire-control

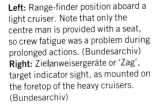

Left: Range-finder position aboard a light cruiser. Note that only the centre man is provided with a seat, so crew fatigue was a problem during prolonged actions. (Bundesarchiv)
Right: Zielanweisergeräte or 'Zag', target indicator sight, as mounted on the foretop of the heavy cruisers. (Bundesarchiv)

ADMIRAL HIPPER FIRE CONTROL SYSTEMS

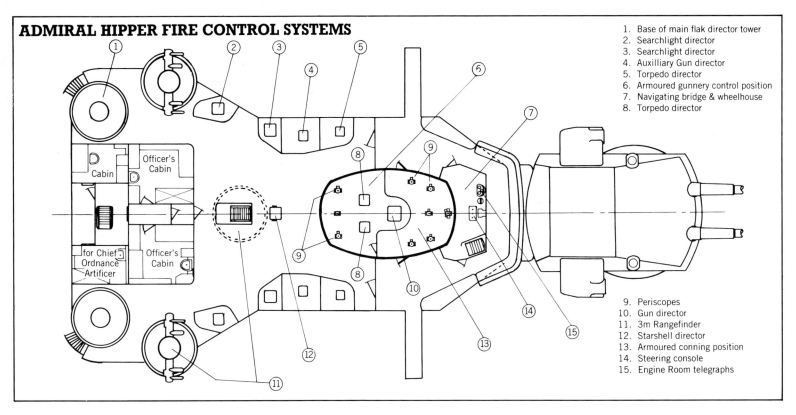

1. Base of main flak director tower
2. Searchlight director
3. Searchlight director
4. Auxilliary Gun director
5. Torpedo director
6. Armoured gunnery control position
7. Navigating bridge & wheelhouse
8. Torpedo director

9. Periscopes
10. Gun director
11. 3m Rangefinder
12. Starshell director
13. Armoured conning position
14. Steering console
15. Engine Room telegraphs

Cabin

Officer's Cabin

for Chief Ordnance Artificer

Officer's Cabin

PRINZ EUGEN FLAK CONTROL SYSTEMS

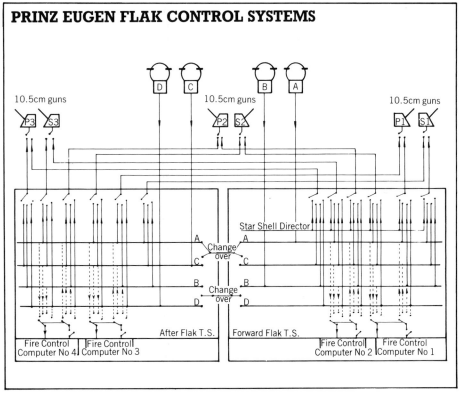

10.5cm guns

10.5cm guns

10.5cm guns

Star Shell Director

Change over

Change over

After Flak T.S.

Forward Flak T.S.

Fire Control Computer No 4

Fire Control Computer No 3

Fire Control Computer No 2

Fire Control Computer No 1

layout remained unused. As these could not be fully separated the chances of failure were obviously increased. (On the left is a schematic layout of the 10.5cm control system for *Prinz Eugen*.) The main flak control position was atop the foremast tower on which sat the main armament range-finder. On the open platform at its forward end (after end in later ships) were two flak target-indicator sights to port and starboard. Two more were fitted aft in a secondary position abreast No. 3 10.5cm mounting in *Prinz Eugen* and subsequent ships. These target-indicator sights or 'Zielanweisungsgeräte' (Zag), which had first appeared in *Gneisenau*, incorporated a 1.25-metre range-finder for computation of range and bearing. In service they were not considered fully satisfactory; the triaxial searchlight director was basically more suitable, but had the drawback of being two-man operated. Target data from the Zags could be supplied to either forward or after flak transmitting stations, wherein was fitted the AA predictor (Rechner C/VI) which computed fuze vertical and lateral deflection.

The four main flak directors, in their distinctive, triaxially-stabilized, spherical covers, contained a 4-metre range-finder and acted both as director/range-finder and plane converters from director to gun data. These directors could work with either flak T.S. and any one of three (after towers) or two (forward towers) Zags. All could supply data to the torpedo transmitting station and either forward or after searchlight directors. The forward towers 'A' (starboard) and 'B' (port) could control all the 10.5cm mountings on their respective

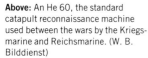
Above: An He 60, the standard catapult reconnaissance machine used between the wars by the Kriegsmarine and Reichsmarine. (W. B. Bilddienst)

sides, plus the forward mountings on the opposite beam. The after pair, 'C' (starboard) and 'D' (port), could, because of their position, control the Nos. 2 and 3 mountings on the opposite beam as well as all the guns on their own side. RPC was fitted for the entire heavy flak outfit.

The 3.7cm guns, which on earlier ships had been linked to the heavy flak control, were later provided with their own portable range-finders to simplify control arrangements.

By the time that the *Admiral Hipper* class reached service, the torpedo outfit had, like the heavy flak, become very sophisticated. Two torpedo target-indicator sights were fitted to port and starboard of the night control position forward, and two torpedo directors were fitted in the conning tower on the same level. At the extreme after end of the after main gun control position was the rate of change of bearing instrument, 'Torpedoauswandlugsmesser' (TAM), with, immediately forward of it, a target-indicator sight. Inside the armoured after gunnery station was a further torpedo director. Range was normally obtained from the 3-metre range-finders fitted to port and starboard of the bridge deck at its after end below the flak directors, but as already noted, ranges could also be provided from the other range-finders or later from radar measurements. *Admiral Hipper* and *Blücher* had an extra 3-metre range-finder on the centre-line of the bridge deck between the foremast tower and the conning tower.

Below decks the torpedo transmitting station contained all the necessary computers and instruments for spread and deflection calculation. RPC was supplied for each bank of tubes, with electrical firing from the director or, in emergency, by hand on the tube control position. The torpedoes themselves were launched by compressed air or alternatively by cordite charge. In wartime, *Admiral Hipper* and *Blücher* carried ten re-loads, six in the superstructure and four in the torpedo workshop. The later ships carried twelve, two in

lockers on the superstructure deck, six on the funnel deck and four below decks in the workshop. Loading and movement was by means of the boat cranes, overhead rails and grabs. Reloading at sea was, in practice, difficult, because of the movement of the ship and the lack of any mechanical reloading system.

SHIPBOARD AIRCRAFT

The use of aircraft aboard warships for spotting and reconnaissance purposes had become commonplace by the end of the First World War, at least in the Royal Navy. Under the terms of the Treaty of Versailles, however, Germany was barred from forming an air force and in consequence such progress as was made in the field of naval aviation was both limited and clandestine. Thus it was not until the 1930s that the 'K' cruisers began to operate aircraft after the development of a suitable catapult by Deutsche Werke. In pre-radar days, the ability to operate aircraft gave ships, especially cruisers engaged upon ocean mercantile warfare, untold advantage both in terms of avoiding superior forces and locating suitable prey. Thus it is hardly surprising that by the outbreak of the Second World War, all but the smallest cruisers of most nations were equipped to operate one or more aircraft. The first German naval aircraft to go to sea in the 1930s came from the famous Heinkel firm and was a two-seat, twin-float biplane, the He60. This aircraft had a maximum speed of 225km/hr and was armed with one machine-gun. It was issued for service with all the light cruisers except *Emden*, as well as being carried by the 'Panzerschiffen', seeing service, including the Spanish Civil War, until just prior to the outbreak of war when it was replaced by the more powerful and faster Arado 196.

The advent of the Ar.196 gave the Kriegsmarine's air arm a modern and effective aircraft for shipboard use which far out-

Above: The work-horse of the Kriegs-marine's catapult flights, the Arado 196, seen here with *Scharnhorst* in Brest. (Bundesarchiv)
Above right: *Prinz Eugen* at Krupp's Germania yard shortly before completion. (W. B. Bilddienst)

classed the catapult aircraft of the French and British Navies. Owing something to the earlier Ar.95 biplane, the Ar.196 was produced to meet a Reichsluftfahrtministerium specification, issued in the autumn of 1936, which called for a replacement for the He60 then in service with the Bordfliegerstaffeln. The Ar.196 design proved much superior to its Focke-Wulf competitor and was ordered into quantity production, both for ships' catapult flights and coastal seaplane squadrons. Its initial production version, the Ar.196A-1 (20 built), entered operational service on 1 August 1939 with Bd. Flg.St.1/196 based at Wilhelmshaven, and 5/196 at Kiel-Holtenau. But the major production version was the Ar.196 A-3, of which a small batch of 24 machines were modified as A-4s for catapult duties, to replace the by now depleted number of A-1s with the Bordfliegerstaffeln. The Ar.196 was fast (310km/hr), well-armed with cannon and machine-guns as well as being robust, acquitting itself well both at sea and in coastal duties. Aboard the light cruisers and 'Panzerschiffen', the aircraft were stowed on the catapult and on the open deck, no hangar being fitted. The more modern ships, however, including the heavy cruisers, recognized the need of efficient maintenance, and incorporated hangar facilities. As described earlier, the first two heavy cruisers had hangar accommodation for only one aircraft, while the later ships could stow two in a double hangar.

Aircraft launching was by means of a trainable compressed air-operated Type FL22 catapult, built by Deutsche Werke, with launching arcs of 75°–105° and 255°–285°. Within the hangar, the aircraft (wings folded back) sat on wheeled trollies which could be manhandled under the sliding roof for extraction by the boats' crane. Also stowed in the hangar were the larger spare parts such as floats and flying surfaces. Aircraft ammunition (sixty-two 50kg bombs, 4,000 rounds of 2cm and 31,500 rounds of 7.9mm) was stowed in a separate magazine

below decks. Aviation spirit was stored, under nitrogen protection, in four 4,250 litre tanks below the armoured deck in the outer hull spaces to port and starboard. When radar became more reliable and widely installed, it replaced the need of aircraft, and the opportunity was taken to remove the catapult and ancillary equipment from the surviving light cruisers, giving a much-needed reduction in top weight, which was partly utilized to augment the light flak outfits. Thus, *Nürnberg*, for example, initially received an extra 3.7cm SKC/30 mount on the former catapult tower.* The heavy cruisers, however, retained and operated their aircraft until the final surrender.

DEFENCE AND DETECTION SYSTEMS

Under this heading can be considered such measures as paravane equipment smoke-generators, hydrophones, 'S Geräte' and radar. All cruisers were fitted to stream paravane floats and otters, while the newer ships were also equipped with a unique bow protection boom which could be extended from the forefoot to give a lower point of attachment for the paravane wires. In addition, special sweeps were carried for use by the larger of the ship's boats. The importance of smoke protection was obviously greater before radar became fully developed, but all ships retained the ability to produce smoke, both from the boilers and by artificial chemical means. The latter method used chlorosulphonic acid, stored either in fixed tanks at the extreme stern of the vessel or in portable smoke floats which were dropped overboard to produce the necessary smoke-screen when required.

Two separate hydrophone listening systems formed the basis of the underwater detection equipment, one of which,

*It is interesting to record that trials were undertaken using a Flettner Fl282 helicopter aboard *Köln* in 1941/42. A landing platform was built over 'B' turret, but removed as soon as the trials were finished.

Right: *Prinz Eugen* in 1946,
awaiting atomic bomb trials. On the
main range-finder at the top of the
superstructure can be seen the
massive mattress aerial of the
Fu Mo26 radar. At the foretop is the
small Fu Mo81 Berlin-S aerial. On
the mainmast platform is the
Fu Mo25 aerial and on the front
portside of the flak control platform
can be seen one of the Sumatra
radar-detection dipoles

the NHG (Navigationshorchgeräte), was, as it's name implies, designed mainly for use in conning the ship. This was an accurate-bearing, narrow-beam system, employing two receivers, one on each side of the ship below the waterline. The second, more sophisticated, gear was the GHG (Gruppenhorchgeräte) which was developed primarily as a submarine detection apparatus. The origins of this system have been fully discussed in *Destroyer!*, but basically it consisted of two multiple rows of hydrophone receivers, one on each side of the hull, which could be used to obtain accurate bearings upon propeller or machinery noises from submarines, surface ships and torpedoes. The equipment aboard *Nürnberg* consisted of 32 receivers.

The 'S Geräte' equipment was also designed for underwater detection, but unlike the two hydrophone systems, was an active, not passive technique. A pulsed beam of sound was emitted by a transmitter crystal housed in a streamlined dome below the keel. On striking a solid underwater object the beam was reflected back to be detected by a receiver crystal in the same dome. The speed of sound in water being known, it was simple to calculate range from elapsed time to receipt of echo. It was similar to the British Asdic, but employed slightly different generation techniques. It, too, was susceptible to sea conditions, thermal layers and operator interpretation. Nevertheless it was an extremely valuable tool and, on occasion, even detected mines.

Serious experimentation with radar detection techniques began in Germany in the early 1930s although it has been claimed that its origins can be traced back to patents applied for by Hülsmeyer in 1904. Initially, the experiments in the 1930s were conducted under the auspices of the NVA (Nachtrichtenvesuchsabteilung) or Communications Trials Command, and later by a specially formed organization GEMA (Gesellschaft für Elektroakutische und Mechanische Apparate). The first operational sets were issued to the Fleet before the war, being fitted in *Admiral Graf Spee* and *Deutschland* and used during the Spanish Civil War.[*] These early sets were known as Type Fu Mo 22, operating on a frequency of 368MHz, 81.5cm wavelength.

None of the cruisers, however, were fitted with operational radar until January 1940, when *Admiral Hipper* and *Blücher* received a radar office on the foretop range-finder cupola, carrying the large mattress aerials for the Fu Mo 22 set. *Blücher* became an early war loss and thus had no further modifications, but nor did *Admiral Hipper* until her 1941 refit, despite the fact that *Prinz Eugen* had commissioned with a Fu Mo 27 set on both forward and after range-finder cupolas as early as August 1940. After her 1941 refit, *Admiral Hipper* carried Fu M G 40G(g0) sets on both forward and after positions which she retained until well after her return from the Arctic in 1943. Her radar equipment on rejoining the active fleet again in 1944 is not known for certain, although the Kriegsmarine Fleet hand-book of late 1944 lists her as having merely two Gema/Seetakt Fu Mo sets. During her

[*]For trials purposes, experimental sets had been fitted to *Admiral Graf Spee*, *Königsberg* and the torpedo-boat *G10* in 1937. From these were developed the operational sets.

scheduled refit, beginning in February 1945, she would undoubtedly have been fitted with new radar, including Fu Mo 25 on the mainmast. However, bomb damage prevented this refit being completed and the war ended before she could become operational again.

Prinz Eugen, after her successful return to Germany in 1942 by means of the Channel Dash, had her outfit altered; Fu Mo 26 being fitted in an enlarged radar hut atop the foretop range-finder cupola. On each side of the mattress for this set were separate antennae, thought to be for an experimental height-finding set (although her war diary at this time mentions the addition of fine-bearing equipment). This, however, was removed before the end of the war by which time her outfit consisted of Fu Mo 26 on the foretop, Fu Mo 81 at the foremast truck and, on a platform abaft the mainmast, Fu Mo 25. The after range-finder still carried a Fu Mo 23 set.

Of the light cruisers, *Königsberg* and *Karlsruhe* were lost before they could be fitted with radar, while *Leipzig* and *Emden*, being mainly employed as training ships, had a very low priority. Thus, *Köln* and *Nürnberg* were the first light cruisers to be fitted, the latter being equipped at least as early as the spring of 1941, when a Fu Mo 21 set replaced the forward range-finder atop the navigating bridge. *Köln* was similarly fitted before her deployment to Norway in 1942. By the time that *Nürnberg* went to Norway in 1942–3, her radar had been modified by the addition of a Fu Mo 22 set on a bracket secured to the foremast tower above the admiral's bridge, the vacated position on the roof of the navigating bridge being used for light flak guns.

By the end of the war, *Nürnberg* had received a Fu Mo 25 frame on the foremast tower bracket, and on a pole mainmast, stayed by two light tripod legs, an aerial for Hohentwiel K. *Emden* received a radar set in about 1942, probably Fu Mo 22 mounted at the base of the foremast tower, displacing the lower of the two searchlights. At the end of October 1944, while stationed in Oslofjord for minelaying duties in the Skagerrak, *Emden* was to be fitted with Fu Mo 26, 'Palau' passive detectors and Fu Mz 6 outfits, but these had not yet arrived in Norway. As the ship ran aground badly in December and was sent to Königsberg for repairs soon afterwards, it is doubtful if the radar set arrived in time. Certainly the 'Palau' set had not, but by the war's end, she had been fitted with a Fu Mo 25 set on the mainmast. *Leipzig* received radar on recommissioning in the autumn of 1943, being fitted with a Fu Mo 22 set on the modified, former searchlight platform on the foremast tower. This remained her only active radar set.

After a promising start in radar techniques, the Kriegsmarine soon fell woefully behind the Allies in its development. The reasons for this are complex, but it resulted in a change of emphasis from the development of enhanced capability radar, towards the evolution of equipments for the detection of radar transmissions. German surface ships and submarines had become the hunted rather than the hunters, and it became vital to be forewarned of enemy radar activity in order to take appropriate early avoiding action. This resulted in the appearance of an array of passive detectors whose

success led in turn to a further detrimental effect on the use of radar by the Kriegsmarine; if German ships could detect British transmissions, surely the converse was also possible? As a consequence, severe restrictions were placed on the use of radar in many operations to the detriment of end results. Thus the development of, for example, air warning and air gunnery sets as well as such refinements as PPI plots, suffered badly and it is of interest to compare the radar outfit of *Prinz Eugen* described above with that carried by most British light cruisers in about mid-1942. This generally consisted of Type 279 or 281 air search; Type 273 surface search; Type 284 main gunnery; three Type 285 secondary gunnery; and two Type 282 close-range AA sets.

The earliest passive receivers were the 'Biscay Cross' type (officially designated Fu M B Ant2), which were extemporized equipments first used by U-boats in the Bay of Biscay because of the increased use of radar-equipped aircraft by RAF Coastal Command. The most common receiver in surface ships was the Fu M B 4 'Samos' which used two distinct aerials. One, code-named 'Bali', was a round dipole usually fitted to the masthead to give omnidirectional warning, the other, 'Sumatra', was a loop dipole with 45° polarization, in a square frame normally fitted around the foretop screen, to give exact-bearing indication. *Prinz Eugen* carried five on her foretop: one at the front port corner, one on each beam and two covering the port and starboard quarters. *Nürnberg*, too, originally had five around her foretop, but when the later 'Palau' type became available, three were removed because the 'Palau' aerial was rotatable; only the 'Sumatra' frames covering the port and starboard quarters, where the 'Palau' set was wooded, were retained. *Leipzig* received 'Palau' on a bracket above her Fu Mo 22 and carried 'Sumatra' frames on the port, starboard and after sides of her foretop.

Instead of the 'Palau' aerial, *Prinz Eugen* and probably *Admiral Hipper* carried the 'Timor' type. This was actually a combination of 'Palau' and 'Sumatra' types, but separate aerials for the latter were still fitted. *Admiral Hipper*'s 'Timor' aerial frame was fitted at the rear of the foretop range-finder cupola, while *Prinz Eugen* had hers on the forward face below the active radar mattress. Other types of aerials, such as the Fu M B Ant3 'Bali', were also fitted, but are not generally visible in photographs because of their small dimensions.

WARTIME ARMAMENT MODIFICATIONS

Admiral Hipper In April 1940, prior to the execution of 'Weserübung', two single 2cm MG C/30 guns, in army-pattern mountings, were shipped on the top of 'B' and 'C' turrets where they remained until the ship returned to Germany for refit in 1941. During the course of this refit, the searchlight on the foremast tower was landed and replaced by a 2cm vierling. No further alterations took place until just before her transfer to Norway in 1942; on 28 February the 2cm on 'C' turret was replaced by another vierling, and a third was shipped on 'B' turret on 9 March. Flag Officer (Battleships) also proposed a mounting on the quarterdeck, as a temporary measure for harbour use only, but it is not certain if it was ever fitted. However a vierling was fitted on the fore-

castle. After her withdrawal from Arctic waters following the 'Regenbögen' fiasco, the cruiser was decommissioned and non-operational for more than twelve months. She received no new flak additions until her recommissioning in 1944 when her outfit consisted of three 2cm vierlings in triaxial mountings; two more biaxial 38/42 U mounts (probably on the funnel platform); and eight single 2cm guns as well as the original 3.7cm twin mountings.

By the spring of 1944 it was obvious that events on the Eastern Front had taken a turn for the worse, and there was a strong possibility that the ships of the Ausbildüngsverband (Training Squadron) might be called upon to provide fire support for the Army ashore. It was recognized that most of them did not possess anything like the flak defence necessary to ward off the increasingly active Russian air force, so on 10 May 1944 a conference was called to discuss the rearmament of the Training Squadron. Held at the OKM, the conference was attended by representatives from SKL, the Quartiermeisteramt, Waffenamt, Dockyards, Ausbildüngsverband Staff and from some of the major ships including *Admiral Hipper*.

So far as the heavy cruisers were concerned, it was decided to remove the forward pair of 3.7cm SK/C30 mountings and three vierlings and replace them with six single 4cm FlaK 28 Bofors, and change the single 2cm guns to LM44 twin mountings. This appears to have been carried out in *Admiral Hipper* because she was listed in the Fleet hand-book of late 1944 as having 8–3.7cm (4×2), 6–4cm (6×1), and 28–2cm (2×4, 8×2 and 4×1). By the end of the year, SKL had re-examined the possibilities for flak improvement and on 23 November 1944 proposed that *Admiral Hipper* be equipped with twenty 4cm FlaK 28, two biaxial vierlings and fourteen 2cm guns in twin LM44 mountings. Quite how these were to be disposed is not clear and it is probable that it was never fully carried out, but it is likely that the disposition would have followed the pattern of *Prinz Eugen* except that two of the 4cm guns were mounted on the forward night control stand.

Prinz Eugen This ship retained her as completed outfit until December 1941, when she was fitted with four 2cm vierlings, one each on the forecastle, 'B' and 'C' turrets and quarterdeck, while in dock at Brest. Later, in mid January 1942, a fifth vierling was mounted on the former searchlight sponson below the maintop platform. The two vierlings on forecastle and quarterdeck were, however, only temporary fittings preparatory to 'Cerberus' and were removed before the ship sailed on 'Sportplast'. When she returned to Germany for repair in May 1942 it is unlikely that any further changes had been made, but at the time of the rearmament conference, referred to above, two extra vierlings had been shipped on the funnel platform and the 2cm singles had been increased to eight.

In 1944 it was proposed that this be altered to six 4cm FlaK 28, four 3.7cm twin SKC/30 aft and twenty-eight 2cm (2 × 4, 10 × 2) guns. The 4cm guns were to have been fitted on 'B' and 'C' turrets, on the forward searchlight platform in place of the forward 3.7cm guns, and on the quarterdeck. This measure appears to have been at least partly completed, for by

the time of her collision with *Leipzig* in October 1944, she did carry both 4cm and 2cm LM44 guns. At the end of 1944, further changes were to be made, altering her outfit to eighteen single 4cm FlaK 28; six 2cm vierling and two 2cm twin LM44 mountings. All 3.7cm guns were to be removed. This final modification was never fully implemented, however, and by the time of the surrender the flak outfit consisted of eighteen 4cm; four vierlings (on funnel and abreast No. 3 10.5cm mountings), two twin 2cm on the navigating bridge and probably two more in the foretop. In addition, she retained a twin flak mounting on each side forward, below the navigating bridge. As no twin 4cm gun was, so far as is known, ever sent to sea, this mounting was probably the old C/30 twin but with gunshields. Photographic evidence of this is not positive, however, and the only shots showing this position appear to indicate gun barrel spacings much wider than those of the old C/30.

Leipzig Employed mainly on training duties, this cruiser's flak outfit had only been increased by the addition of two triaxial vierlings: one on a sponson forward of the admiral's bridge, the second at the after end of the after superstructure. Four twin 3.7cm and six 2cm completed the light armament. As part of the general augmentation of flak outfits in 1944, this was to be increased to four 4cm FlaK 28; four 3.7cm (in two twin mounts) and eight 2cm LM44 twin mountings. Quite how far progress was made in achieving this level is uncertain, but since her priority was very low in the order of refits, and she retained at least her forward vierling at the time of her collision with *Prinz Eugen* in October 1944, it is more than likely that none of this armament was ever shipped. At the end of the war she carried only single 2cm shielded guns on the quarterdeck and after deck-house, which appears to bear this out.

Köln Few changes were made to her armament until 1944, despite her deployment to Norway in 1942. By mid 1944 she was reported as having had two twin 3.7cm and two 2cm singles removed, thus halving her flak armament. Under the general flak rearmament programme of 1944, she should have received four 4cm FlaK 28 and eight 2cm LM44 twins to augment the remaining two twin 3.7cm, but once again it is uncertain if this were ever completed although the Fleet handbook implies that it was. However reports of her action against RAF bombing attacks on 13 December 1944 while in Oslofjord make it clear that no 4cm guns were yet aboard, but extra 2cm weapons had been mounted at least on the forecastle. Further augmentation of the light flak was intended in 1945 when it was planned to ship ten 3.7 FlaK 43M and twelve 2cm LM44 twins, but this was never carried out and by the end of the war *Köln*, sunk in Wilhelmshaven, had been almost stripped of light weapons.

Nürnberg During the major refit in Kiel between February and August 1942, the catapult was removed and replaced by a 3.7cm SKC/30 twin mounting. Two 2cm vierlings in army-pattern mountings were fitted, one on the roof of the navigating bridge and one on 'B' turret, while the number of 2cm single guns was increased to five: one above the conning tower, two on the bridge deck and two at the after end of the

funnel platform. In 1944, it was planned to install four 4cm FlaK 28 and at the same time remove two of the 3.7cm twins, while increasing the 2cm guns to eight LM44 twins in lieu of the former single mounts. In the event, only two 4cm were fitted, one on the navigating bridge, displacing the vierling, and a second on the former catapult tower. Two naval-pattern vierlings were shipped on 'B' turret and on the after superstructure, as well as eleven other 2cm guns, ten LM44 twins and one single. This was to be an interim outfit; her 1945 armament was to be eight FlaK 43M, two vierlings and ten 2cm twins, but the end of the war came before this could be carried out.

Emden Employed, like *Leipzig*, as a training vessel for most of the war, there was little pressure to augment this ship's armament, but in September 1942 Flottenkommando proposed a major overhaul of her flak outfit. This was to have entailed:

(a) Landing both No.4 15cm guns and replacing them with 8.8cm twin, non-stabilized mountings.

(b) Replacing the three existing 8.8cm single guns by two 3.7cm twin mountings (sided) and a 2cm twin amidships.

(c) Fitting of two 2cm singles on the foremast abreast the searchlight.

(d) Fitting of two 2cm on collapsible mountings on the quarterdeck.

The object of this was to equip her for operational duties with the Fleet, but the Barents Sea action at the end of 1942 caused all these plans to be cancelled in February 1943. Nevertheless, some alterations and additions were made, including the installation of two vierlings to port and starboard on the shelter deck abaft the beam 15cm guns. Two 2cm singles were also shipped on the after end of the navigating bridge platform. During August and September of 1944, the 8.8cm guns were replaced by 10.5cm SKC/32gE weapons, and two 4cm FlaK 28 were mounted on the bridge deck, before the ship moved to the Skagerrak for operational duty. Her remaining light armament now reportedly consisted of two 3.7cm SKC/30U, two vierlings and six 2cm twin LM44 mountings. Towards the end of the war, new plans were made for rearming the elderly cruiser when it was decided to equip her with nine 3.7cm FlaK M42 in LM42 U mountings and six 2cm LM44 twin mountings, but despite preliminary discussions with Oslo dockyard, nothing could be done about it because *Emden* ran badly aground on 9 December 1944 and had to be sent back to Germany for repair shortly afterwards.

All surviving cruisers (except *Leipzig*) were to receive two (*Nürnberg*, three) Fohn 7.3cm A.A. rocket launchers under an order dated 1945 (GK Dos 377/45).

SUMMARY AND COMPARISONS

The comparison of warships of different nations presents something of a problem, since it is extremely difficult to be certain that such comparisons are made on equal terms. It is, for instance, apparently quite easy to compare armaments for this can readily be ascertained by the naked eye, but what cannot be so easily determined is any inherent or hidden advantage or defect in any particular design. Thus, for example, the shells of one navy might not be so effective as those of another. Even more difficult to compare is armour protection, its distribution, weight and effectiveness, especially as there were different practices in determining which plating should be classified under 'Protection' and which under the 'Hull & Fittings' categories of weight statements.

More difficult still to determine, is the overall effectiveness of a ship, for quite obviously any ship is only as good as the men who man her and in consequence training levels and experience will be of the utmost importance in ship to ship engagements. Paper comparisons between warships are therefore of dubious usefulness, the acid test being, of course, war. But since many nations built ships specifically to counter the supposed technical specification of their rivals, especially where the treaty cruisers were concerned, some examination of their relative merits is appropriate here, provided that the deficiencies of such comparisons is borne in mind. So far as the German ships were concerned, the light cruisers never traded fire with any Allied ship, and only two brief actions took place between British and German heavy cruisers, both involving *Admiral Hipper*, and none at all with French cruisers. Thus the examination of relative merits must remain largely conjecture, but is of interest, nevertheless.

At the time of their completion, the 'K' class light cruisers had only one modern contemporary rival, the three ships of the French *Duguay Trouin* class; the first new British light cruisers, the *Leander* class, not completing until the years 1933 to 1935. In terms of armament, there was little to choose between German and French designs, except for a one-gun advantage to the German ships, and the gun ranges were broadly comparable. However, the protection of the French ships was much less than that of the *Königsberg*, both in terms of distribution and thickness, for *Duguay Trouin* had basically only a 19mm box citadel for the magazines, and a 20mm main deck. *Königsberg*, on the other hand, had a waterline belt 50mm to 70mm in thickness, and deck armour up to 40mm. If the German ship could have caught the Frenchman, therefore (and the *Duguay Trouin* was faster), she could probably have inflicted severe punishment upon her foe, but we must now consider one of the invisible aspects referred to earlier.

In practice, the weather would have had an important bearing on the outcome of an engagement between the two ships. The German ship had been built to very tight Treaty restrictions and suffered accordingly, as described in Chapter 2. It is not inconceivable, therefore, that *Königsberg* might have suffered more damage from stress of weather than from shell hits had the action taken place in a heavy sea. Similar reasonings could be applied to actions between *Königsberg* and *Leander* with even more disadvantage to the German cruiser. *Leander*, which was not bound by Versailles restrictions, featured much better protection than *Duguay Trouin* and was a very good seaboat, but not as fast as the French ship.

The later *Nürnberg* had rather better armour, but basically the same armament and speed as the 'K' cruisers. The design of French light cruisers had, however, progressed considerably since the completion of *Duguay Trouin*, for the new *La*

Galissonnière class, entering service in the mid to late 1930s, matched the German cruisers' fire-power and were both fast and well-protected. Her vertical waterline belt was 105mm in thickness for its full length of 107m (out of a waterline length of 170m), and 3.6m deep for all but 32m which were 1.6m deep at the forward and after ends. The main deck was 38mm thick and longitudinal bulkheads, 20mm. In any action between the two vessels, the German ordnance experts estimated that *Nürnberg*'s horizontal protection would give immunity to penetration by the French 54kg shells up to a range of 11,300 metres; above that distance, plunging fire would pierce it. On the other hand, *Nürnberg* could not pierce the French deck armour under 18,300 metres. Where vertical armour was concerned, *Nürnberg* was vulnerable at all ranges

up to 18,000 metres when struck at right-angles, but could not defeat *La Galissonnière*'s belt over 7,100 metres. In action, therefore, *Nürnberg*'s best tactics would be to keep the range above 18,300 metres and below 23,000 metres, between which ranges her side protection was safe, while having a chance of piercing the French barbettes and deck armour.

Against the British *Leander*, the 45.5kg round from the German SKC/25 could penetrate the vertical protection of the British cruiser up to 11,800 metres, whereas *Nürnberg* would be safe up to 15,300 metres. There was little to choose between immunity ranges for deck protection, but *Leander*'s 51mm magazine crowns gave her extra immunity up 21,200 metres. *Leander* had one 15cm gun less than *Nürnberg*, carrying eight 6in Mk XXIII 50-cal., but these were carried in twin turrets Mk XXII, two forward and two aft, and thus had the benefit of a better gun disposition than the German ship.

The later *Southampton* class were much tougher animals, for their 114mm belt (40 per cent of the length), 32mm deck armour and twelve guns gave considerable advantage over *Nürnberg*. The design team for *Southampton*, on the other hand, had far greater tonnage allowance to work to and in consequence could produce a better ship. If *Southampton* held the range at between 10,500 metres and 12,500 metres, she would be virtually immune to serious damage from the German, while at the same time, her 6in (15cm) BL Mk XXIII guns firing a 51kg (112lb) shell could pierce any of her opponents' armour. Of course, this is something of an oversimplification; in all the scenarios described, fighting efficiency could be drastically reduced by numbers of hits on relatively lightly protected gunhouses, bridges and director positions, without penetration of the main armour. Additionally, *Nürnberg*, too, was a Versailles product, designed down to a 6,000-tonnes displacement and suffered from the same defects as described for *Königsberg*.

None of the 'Kreuzer M' design ever saw service, but since their protection closely followed that of *Nürnberg* except for an increase in the sloped deck armour to 35mm, they could not have produced a much greater survivability factor and, moreover, had one 15cm gun less.

In the heavy cruiser category, the *Admiral Hipper* design had been produced to counter *Algérie*, the seventh 'Class A' cruiser to be built by the French, which in turn had been built to counter *Zara*. This ship was a vast improvement on the previous French heavy cruisers and was arguably the best of its type, being more of a 'protected cruiser'. Her main armament of eight 20.3cm Mk 1924 guns in twin turrets was identical with that of the German heavy cruiser, and she was good for a maximum speed of 33 knots on 12,000 tonnes displacement. In contrast to the earlier *Dupleix*, *Algérie*'s armouring totalled 2,657 tonnes (compared to 1,553 tonnes), with a main belt 110mm thick, 105m long (i.e., 58 per cent of her length). Except for about 21m of its length at the after end, this belt was between 3.8m and 4.5m deep, accounting for more than 700 tonnes of the protection weight. Internally, a 40mm-thick longitudinal bulkhead, extending the length of the machinery spaces, conferred splinter protection and acted as a torpedo bulkhead. Horizontal protection included an

80mm deck, reducing to 30mm at the ends. Magazine crowns were also 80mm.

In action against *Algérie*, *Admiral Hipper*'s deck could be pierced at ranges above 14,200 metres and her side protection at all ranges below 19,500 metres, dependent upon angle of impact. On the other hand, the French cruiser's deck could not be defeated below 27,400 metres, which was only about 6,000 metres below the maximum range of the German 20.3cm SKC/34 gun. Her side protection, however, gave immunity at ranges above 17,700 metres. Thus, if *Algérie* were to maintain the action range at between 18,000 metres and 26,000 metres, she would be fairly safe from *Admiral Hipper*'s gunfire, while at the same time retaining the ability to pierce both deck and barbette armour of the German ship (the French barbettes, too, were vulnerable at this range). Against this opponent, therefore, the German cruiser would have had a tough action and unless she closed the range right down (greatly endangering herself) would have little chance of seriously damaging her. In favour of *Admiral Hipper*, however, was the generally high standard of German gunnery and the availability of radar for ranging purposes. However, the fact that most German control instruments were manned in the standing position led to operator fatigue in long actions, with a consequent falling off in accuracy. Additionally, German fuzes were not as good as they should have been, which reduced her effectiveness considerably. In two actions, *Prinz Eugen* against *Prince of Wales* and *Admiral Hipper* against *Berwick*, a number of German shells hit but failed to explode.

The British *County*-class cruisers were in a different league from *Algérie*, at least so far as armouring was concerned, for Britain had in fact discontinued building heavy cruisers and the *County*s dated from as early as 1923. The technology of the day just did not allow the maximum 10,000 tons to be met, if eight 8in BL Mk VIII guns, high speed and good armour were to be shipped, and as a result the British ships, designed strictly according to the Treaty limits, carried little armour and became known as 'Tin Clads'. The Americans, too, were scrupulous in observing the limitations, so much so, in fact, that their first heavy cruisers came out light. Actually, *Salt Lake City* (CA25) came out 900 tons underweight when she was inclined! *Northampton* (CA26) was even lighter, more

than 1,000 tons below the limit. Other nations were less particular about observing the rules; Italy's *Zara*, being 11,870 tonnes standard displacement and *Algérie*, too, being over the limit. The Japanese *Nachi* came out almost 1,000 tonnes over the limit, while the later *Takao* was 1,500 tonnes over the odds.

All this extra weight could be, and mainly was, used to increase armour protection. The German heavy cruisers were almost 4,000 tonnes outside the Treaty limits! Thus, in comparison with the later heavy cruisers, the *County*s were lightly armoured, the *Kent*s originally having only 992 tonnes allocated for protective purposes (cf. French *Dupleix* 1,553 tonnes) with only box protection to the magazines, 25mm side plating in way of machinery spaces and 35mm deck. In the mid 1930s, the armour scheme was substantially improved by the addition of a 4½in (114mm) waterline belt.

The *County*s' deck armour would endow immunity from 20.3cm gunfire up to about 16,000 metres, and her belt above that distance for square-striking shells. With their high freeboard, however, they were large targets, and might well have suffered considerable non-vital damage internally. Moreover, the main armament's gunhouses carried only 25mm armour as against the 160mm (front) and 70mm (top and side) on the German cruisers' turrets and were vulnerable to all but the lightest splinter damage. The British 8in BL Mk VIII, carried in Mk I twin (Mk 2 in the later *Dorsetshire*s' mountings, were capable of 70° elevation and were intended as dual-purpose weapons. But this led to design complexity, and since all-angle loading was not possible, the need to return the gun to a loading angle of 10° made the ability effectively to engage aircraft merely theoretical. This complexity meant that the designed rate of fire (12rpt) was never achieved.

The range of the British 8in gun was considerably less than that of contemporary foreign guns, but RN policy considered that it was best to fight at short ranges if possible, and that the chances of hitting at the maximum ranges of foreign weapons were slim. Thus the RN accepted a lower-performance gun with a lower muzzle-velocity which, in turn, gave longer gun life. On the credit side, the more sophisticated radar fitted to Royal Navy ships as the war progressed undoubtedly gave them the advantage, particularly at night in poor weather or Arctic conditions, as the Barents Sea action showed in 1942 and the action with *Scharnhorst* at the end of 1943, when radar played a decisive part.

The other eventual member of the Allied nations, the USA, was never seriously considered as a possible opponent by the Germans, almost until the end of 1941, and little appears to have been done to compare Kriegsmarine ships with USN opponents, as was done with French and British vessels. The US early heavy cruisers, already referred to, *Salt Lake City* and *Pensacola* carried ten 8in guns to *Admiral Hipper*'s eight, but their protection would give immunity only from guns up to 5in, and a degree of protection against 6in (15cm) shells for limited ranges and angles of impact. They had no protection against 8in shells. Armour protection was gradually improved as construction progressed from the *Pensacola* to the *Northampton* and *Portland* classes, a total of ten ships, to give a

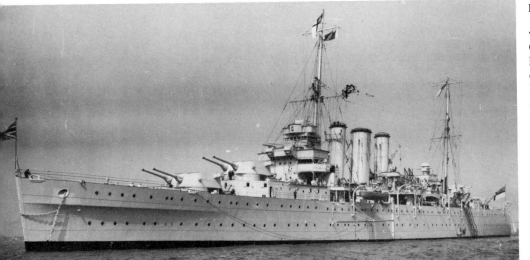

Below: Seen here in July 1935, HMS *Shropshire* was typical of the British 'County' class. Despite all the criticism of their design, these cruisers proved their worth during the war years. *Shropshire* was later transferred to the Royal Australian Navy and was not scrapped until 1955. (R. Perkins)

degree of protection against the heavier-calibre shells, but the protection of the gunhouses was very light and these ships would probably fare little better than the British *Countys* against the German heavy cruisers.

By the time of the appearance of *Wichita* (CA45) in 1939, however, the protection scheme of American cruisers had been vastly improved, based on the endowment of specified 'immunity zones' against 8in shellfire. Her belt armour, 6.4in (163mm) thick, was designed to give immunity against AP shells (90° impact angle) down to 9,200 metres (10,000 yds) compared to that of *Vincennes* (CA44), 15,140m (16,400 yds). Turret protection too had been greatly increased and was no longer just light plating, but 200mm on the fronts, 95mm on sides. Allied to the heavy protection was the availability of new AP projectiles which had been designed on the basis of being able to penetrate any thickness of armour at all angles of obliquity, but at the expense of explosive effect after penetration. These projectiles carried only 1½ per cent by weight of bursting charge compared to contemporary foreign figures of 2–2½ per cent (1.9 per cent for the German 20.3cm Pz.Spr.Gr. L/4.4). *Wichita* and her later compatriots would therefore have posed a considerable problem to the German ships and with the added advantage of superior radar and a higher percentage of sea-time (theoretically leading to better training) might have proved more than a match.

In terms of other design points, the German heavy cruisers possessed considerably better flak protection than did their contemporaries, both in numbers of guns and fire-control systems. The six gun, four-director layout of the 10.5cm outfit compared very favourably with the four-gun 4in outfit of the British *Countys* especially as the latter lacked both triaxial stabilization and a comprehensive control system. The French cruiser *Algérie* carried a similar number of guns, but of a lighter calibre (100mm/50cal), while the US ships generally carried fewer, but of a heavier calibre (5in 25 or 38 cal), neither nation's weapons being stabilized. Similarly, the 3.7cm and 2cm light flak outfits of the German ships was superior to the 2pdr and machine-gun calibre weapons of the British ships, and the obsolete 37mm French guns, at least on paper. However, as we have seen in Chapter 5, serious design defects in the 3.7cm SKC/30 reduced its effectiveness, underlining the drawbacks to paper comparisons. US cruisers were particularly poorly provided for in respect of air defence, the 1.1in quadruple AA gun proving a failure, which left the ships with only rifle-calibre guns until 20mm Oerlikons were purchased abroad.

If a ship is to be successful in action it must be able to reach the scene of the action, and to do this it must have reliable machinery of adequate power and endurance. It was in this respect that the German heavy cruisers were most deficient. Decisions made to install technically advanced machinery that was insufficiently proved led to unreliable operation and poor endurance. Compared with the conservative British and French machinery practice, and the rather more advanced US practice, the German high-pressure machinery was a weak point in an otherwise acceptable design. This might well have proved a fatal Achilles' heel in any prolonged ocean engagement or chase, as the Allied machinery was generally robust and reliable.

Finally, one other point worth mentioning is the fact that German cruisers were great consumers of manpower, as were all their ships, for reasons which are not entirely clear. Complements were often up to 500 men greater than their contemporaries, which absorbed trained men badly needed in the light escort and other surface forces. This may have been partly due to equipment duplication; for example, the three main gun-control positions and four flak director towers aboard *Admiral Hipper*-class ships all required extra manpower as did such items as the 2cm MG C/30 gun, which necessitated a crew of six men compared to the Allied Oerlikon which needed only two.

In conclusion, therefore, the German cruisers, both light and heavy, featured many technical advances in the ordnance, engineering and constructional fields, but at the same time these were in many instances outweighed by serious defects in these same fields, especially engineering and construction. Combined with a lack of numbers and a crippling shortage of oil fuel, these factors prevented German cruisers playing a full part in the war at sea, and in consequence they spent much of their careers idle after 1942, and the brunt of the Kriegsmarine's war effort was borne by the U-boat arm. Nevertheless, they could not be ignored by the British Admiralty while they remained afloat and in Norwegian or western German bases.

Below: *Pensacola*, the first US 'Washington' heavy cruiser. Built almost a decade before *Admiral Hipper*, she carried a heavier armament but was much less well-protected. Nevertheless she had a distinguished war record in the Pacific.

6: LIGHT CRUISERS IN TROUBLE, 1939

When the Second World War broke out on 3 September, the Kriegsmarine possessed only seven cruisers, of which six were light cruiser types. The sole heavy cruiser, *Admiral Hipper*, had only just completed a major refit and was not fully operational, while one light cruiser, *Karlsruhe*, had also been under refit and would not re-commission until November. Four more heavy and three light cruisers were under construction, but until these and the ships under refit were completed, the Kriegsmarine could dispose a mere five cruisers. Twenty-five years earlier, the Kaiser had gone to war with nearly ten times that number.

Initially the available cruisers were employed upon mine-laying tasks, laying and extending the 'Westwall' defensive barrage off the North Sea coast of Germany and it was appropriate that the oldest ship, *Emden*, should be the first to see action. *Emden* (Kpt.z.S.Werner Lange) had completed a minelaying sortie on 3 September and had returned to Wilhelmshaven to embark further mines for another task. During the early evening of the 4th, whilst the cruiser was manoeuvring alongside the quay, assisted by the tugs *Bussard* and *Emden*, an air raid warning sounded in the port area.

The Royal Air Force had lost no time in mounting an attack on one of the few targets then available to them, the bombing of land targets being not yet allowed. From HQ No 2 Group, Bomber Command, orders were issued to 107 and 110 Squadrons, based at RAF Wattisham, to mount a strike of five machines each on German warships in Wilhelmshaven and the Schillig Roads. Blenheim IVs from 107 Squadron, under the command of Flight Lieutenant W. J. Barton attacked *Admiral Scheer* lying at anchor in the roads, with disastrous results. All four (N6184, N6188, N6240, N6189) attacking aircraft were shot down by the warship (Pilot Officer Stephens in N6195 did not locate the target and returned with bomb load intact). Rain and cloud, had disrupted the attackers' plans, particularly those of the high-level Wellingtons of 9 and 149 Squadrons.

Flight Lieutenant K. C. Donovan, leading 110 Squadron, was fortunate in having as navigator, Pilot Officer Henderson on loan from 206 (General Reconnaissance) Squadron, who brought his aircraft right in on target. 110 Squadron intended to attack in two sub-flights of two and one lone aircraft (but again one machine failed to locate the target), using two 500lb GP bombs with 11-second delays. Bombs from the four

attacking aircraft fell close to, but did not hit, the helpless cruiser. However some good shooting by Bootsmaat von Diezelsky on one of the ship's 2cm guns, ironically led to her being damaged. He hit a Blenheim in the starboard engine, when it was only about 200 metres from the cruiser and very low. Mortally hit, the aircraft spun out of the sky and crashed into the ship's starboard side, about 1 metre above the waterline. Fires broke out in the dentist's consulting-room and the PO's mess, distorting bulkheads. Most of the damage appeared to have been caused by the aircraft's port propeller. Bombs caused further shock and splinter damage with the cruiser's complement suffering twenty-nine dead and thirty wounded. The starboard side, funnel, bridge and signal decks were peppered with splinter holes and all searchlights were put out of action. Fortunately, despite eight hits on the starboard torpedo tubes, the warheads did not explode. By a strange coincidence, the aircraft which caused the damage, (N6199) was captained by a Flying Officer Emden. His crew, Sergeants Grossie and Otty, as well as the air gunner, died with him.

The damage to *Emden* was not particularly serious, and she was back in service after only one week. Unfortunately, the same could not be said of the next victim of British attentions.

Leipzig, under the command of Kpt.z.S.Nordmann, was serving in the Baltic at the outbreak of war, being based at Kiel. At the beginning of October, she was taken into dockyard hands at her base port to commence a two-week machinery refit, during which both main and auxiliary machinery, condensers and diesels were overhauled and her boilers cleaned. After brief trials and torpedo firing practice, the ship sailed westbound through the Kiel Canal and spent the last week of the month anchored and inactive off Brunsbüttel. Moving east once more, the cruiser arrived in Swinemünde on 1 November and took part in manoeuvres with *Köln*, *Nürnberg* and *Königsberg*. Then, on the 7th, while off the Holtenau lock at Kiel on a dark, wet and cloudy night, *Leipzig* was in collision with *Bremse* and sustained damage to her starboard quarter, necessitating a week of repairs at Deutsche Werke in Kiel. On completion of these repairs, she again returned to the west for operations with Flag Officer (Reconnaissance Forces) K.Ad.Lütjens, whose force at this time consisted of *Nürnberg* (flag), *Köln* and now, *Leipzig*.

OPERATION 'NANNI-SOPHIE'

During the last quarter of 1939, the surface forces of the Kriegsmarine had been extremely active. In particular, the destroyer force had achieved considerable, if covert, success in minelaying operations around the east coast of Britain. These sorties, which have been more fully dealt with in *Destroyer!*, involved quite long passages to the lay area and, if surprise had not been achieved, could have resulted in a long chase home. In consequence, it was decided that the cruiser force should be held at sea, available for instant intervention, should the destroyers be involved in action with British destroyers or cruisers.

The first supporting sortie by the cruisers took place on 12/13 November, when the destroyers had mined the Thames estuary. By the second week in December, three sorties had been undertaken, all without incident. On 8 December, orders were issued for a new destroyer operation to mine the War Channel off Newcastle-upon-Tyne. All three cruisers were to take part in the support operation, code-named 'Nanni-Sophie'. In the appreciation of enemy forces' dispositions included in these (and all) operational orders, it was believed that strong British cruiser forces were only to be found north of the Shetland-Bergen line (i.e., the 'Northern Patrol') and that only an occasional cruiser or destroyer would be encountered on the east coast convoy route. Intelligence reports, however, had established the frequent presence of units of the 2nd Cruiser Squadron in the Firth of Forth. Three British submarines had been reported, one north of Nordeney in the southern German Bight, another north of the Texel and a third in the centre of the North Sea on the latitude of Newcastle/Sylt. This latter boat was most probably on passage either to or from her patrol station.

The cruisers were ordered to sail so as to be in a position north-east of the Dogger Bank on the latitude of Limfjord by the morning of the destroyers' return (i.e., north-west of the German declared mined area). During the morning, while awaiting the destroyers' arrival, merchant shipping was to be intercepted if seen, for which purpose, each cruiser was to have ready two prize crews. The major difference between this and previous sorties was the absence, on this occasion, of any anti-submarine escort for the cruiser force. On each previous sortie, torpedo-boats of the 6th Flotilla had accompanied the cruisers, but now not one torpedo-boat was operational. There were at this time, four torpedo-boat flotillas formed, but of these, the 1st and 2nd Flotillas consisted of only one boat each, *T1* and *T8*, both of which had been in commission but a few days. All the boats of the 5th Flotilla were in dockyard hands to refit, and the 6th Flotilla was undergoing machinery overhauls. Only *Seeadler* and *Jaguar* were running, working-up in the Baltic.

Of the destroyers, only the five detailed for the minelaying operation were serviceable, all the remainder being refitted or repairing. There was a possibility that *Schoemann* and *Lody* could be made operational in time to accompany the cruisers, but in the event, neither could be got ready in time. The absence of any anti-submarine escort caused Lütjens to modify his plans. Originally, his intention had been to use his aircraft ahead of the squadron in the reconnaissance role, but now he was forced to employ them as close a/s patrol around the cruisers. As far as the returning destroyers were concerned, he would now hold all five with the cruisers instead of the two planned, for the squadron's homeward passage. Naval Command Gruppe (West) also arranged for daylight a/s escort by sea-planes from the maritime unit at List/Sylt. Having made all the arrangements possible, given the forces available. Lütjens prepared to mount the operation, but now the weather took a hand causing one postponement after another, so that it was not until early evening on 12 December that the three cruisers weighed from Schillig Roads. Despite the delays, there was no alteration to the composition of the forces involved. No further destroyer or torpedo-boat had become available for screen duties with the cruisers.

The night passage northwards past Heligoland took place without incident, with the weather remaining fair. During the night, Lütjens passed a signal to all ships warning of the expected passage south along the same swept channel of the liner *Bremen en route* home from New York, but in the event she was not sighted. By dawn on the 13th, the squadron had reached the rendezvous area and at first light prepared to catapult the ship's float planes for close a/s patrol. Only *Nürnberg* and *Leipzig* were carrying aircraft, *Köln* being without hers, having landed her catapult in the summer of 1938. Lütjens ordered the aircraft from the flagship to patrol on the starboard side, and that from *Leipzig* the port side, both being launched about 0830. Then for the next few hours, the cruisers patrolled the area at high speed while awaiting the arrival of the destroyers.

At 1000 the ship's aircraft, which had sighted nothing other than the occasional drifting mine, were ordered to return to List at 1030, this time being selected in order to ensure adequate fuel reserves for the return flight of 160 nautical miles. Unfortunately, the intended cover from the coastal air station to replace the ships' flights had been delayed by snow, this fact reaching Lütjens at the time he had catapulted his aircraft off. There would, therefore, be a period when the cruisers would have no a/s cover whatsoever, but at this late stage there was nothing further which could be done.

SALMON'S ATTACK

At 1040, a steamer was sighted which proved to be the Danish *Charkow*. Lütjens ordered *Leipzig* to stop the merchantman and search for contraband, so the cruiser hove to and launched her cutter. While this was being carried out, the other two cruisers were ordered to form an a/s patrol to port and starboard of the stopped cruiser. However, checks showed the Dane to be on the 'Free list' and she was released. *Leipzig* was ordered to recover her boat. By 1105, the cruiser squadron had re-formed in a triangular formation, *Nürnberg* and *Leipzig* steaming abreast some 1,200 metres apart, with *Köln* astern. Working up to 24 knots, Lütjens turned his formation on to a southerly course and resumed the patrol. Ten minutes later, an aircraft briefly appeared from the clouds flashing code 'M' on her signal-lamp. The code and silhouette of the aircraft being unknown to the German force, it was

assumed that it was British, possibly a Hudson. Low cloud and excessive range prevented any flak countermeasures.

Lütjens feared that his cruisers had been located so it was a relief when at 1120 two low-flying aircraft, which were closing the squadron, were identified as the awaited air escort He 115s ('E' and 'H' of 1/506). These made current recognition signals and then turned off to starboard slightly to await the cruiser's reply. Suddenly the flight leader began to signal the ships with 'UUU' and at almost the same moment torpedo tracks were sighted from the bridge of *Leipzig* little more than 700 metres from the port side. Desperately Nordmann ordered 'hard a-port' and the speeding cruiser began to answer the helm, but oh so slowly!

The German operational orders had been correct in their assuming the presence of British submarines in the eastern North Sea, but in view of the fact that they had operated there overtly since the outbreak of war, this assumption had not required a great deal of genius on the part of the German Naval Staff. HM submarine *Salmon* (Lieutenant-Commander E. O. Bickford), a unit of the 2nd Submarine Flotilla based at Dundee, had sailed for a sixteen-day offensive reconnaissance patrol off the entrance to the Skagerrak and the Heligoland Bight. Her patrol had already achieved a measure of success, in that her torpedoes had sunk the outward bound *U36* off the entrance to the Skagerrak on the 4th. Eight days later, Bickford was attempting to stop the liner *Bremen* breaking back to Germany when he was put down by an escorting Do18 flying-boat. The next day, while dived, the First Lieutenant called his Captain to the periscope on sighting enemy warships to the north at a range of about 10,000 metres.

Bickford either saw more than was actually present or could at the time see both the cruiser group and the expected destroyers, which was unlikely, but he identified the enemy ships as being two or three ships from the *Scharnhorst* and 'Panzer-schiffen' classes as well as four cruisers. The latter he identified as two *Hipper* class, *Leipzig* and one *Königsberg* class. *Salmon* manoeuvred to attack and some forty-five minutes after her first sighting, was presented with the view of the cruisers *Blücher*, *Leipzig* and *Hipper* (sic) turning southwards in line ahead. Bickford turned west and selected the rearmost two ships, one of which was *Leipzig*, for targets. At the moment of firing his spread of torpedoes, *Leipzig* was a perfect target, beam on at no more than 5,000 metres.

In his plan of attack, the submarine captain displayed a remarkably obsolete mode of thought, for his idea was to 'wing' two ships and not just sink one, in the hope that he might be able to provoke a Fleet action. Presumably his precedents were the actions off Heligoland in August 1914, but in December 1939 the Royal Navy had little strength in close proximity to the Heligoland Bight and, moreover, the threat of air attack so close to German bases, while not yet the force it would become in less than six months' time, was nevertheless a far greater menace than existed in 1914. After firing, *Salmon* went deep and turned away at full speed on her electric motors, before hearing first one and then two further explosions. By this time Bickford was having difficulty in maintaining trim and did not attempt to regain periscope depth to observe events.

At 1125 one of *Salmon*'s torpedoes struck *Leipzig* just aft of the bulkhead between No.1 and No.2 boiler rooms. The explosion, apart from blowing a huge hole in the ship's side, destroyed both port side boilers in each of the boiler rooms and threw the starboard pairs off their mountings. The bulkhead between the two boiler spaces was ruptured and both rapidly filled with fuel oil and seawater; no one escaped from either room. The port turbine stopped almost immediately, while the starboard set, after a momentary stop when the shock shut a valve, continued to steam for a further fifteen

Right: Extract from *Leipzig*'s war diary at the time of the hit, 13 December 1939.
Below: HM submarine *Salmon*, which torpedoed *Leipzig* in December 1939, seen here in May 1935. Completed in March of that year, she failed to return from patrol off Norway in July 1940 and was presumed mined. (Wright & Logan)

Datum und Uhrzeit	Angabe des Ortes, Wind, Wetter, Seegang, Beleuchtung, Sichtigkeit der Luft, Mondschein usw.	Vorkommnisse
1125	✠ 4965	Torpedolaufbahn an Bb., Torpedotreffer Bb. mittschiffs.
		Das sofort gegebene Kommando: Hart Bb. hat sich nicht mehr ausgewirkt, da die ganze Bahnlänge bis zum Schiff höchstens 700 m betrug und von dem Torpedo nur in Sekunden durchlaufen werden konnte.
		K I, K II ausgefallen und vollgelaufen. Turbinen ohne Dampf, Motorenanlage klar für 15 sm. Elektr.Ruderanlage unklar, steuern mit Handruder, das nur schwer gängig.
		Kurz nach dem Torpedotreffer wird ein Torpedotreffer auf "Nürnberg" beobachtet. "Nürnberg" und "Köln" kommen außer Sicht.
		Schiff bleibt schwimmfähig und nimmt Kurs auf die Einfahrt zu Weg blau ◆. Gefahr des Brechens von Schotten zwingt zur Fahrtverminderung auf 10 sm.
		Der Gesamtzustand des Schiffes schließt eine weitere Fortsetzung der Unternehmung aus, ebenso ein Heranschließen an die anderen Kreuzer. Daher Entschluß, auf dem kürzesten Wege einzulaufen. Um dem außer Sicht befindlichen B.d.A. Einblick in Zustand des Schiffes und Standort zu geben werden folgende F.T.Sprüche abgesetzt.
1146		F.T. an Gruppe: "Leipzig" Torpedotreffer Mitte, kann noch 12 sm laufen, stehe 3747."
1225		F.T. an B.d.A.: Standort 3747, nur Motoren klar, Kurs 110°, Erbitte Zerstörersicherung. "Le".
		Funkpeilanlage ausgefallen desgl. vordere Kreiselanlage. Keine Kontrollmöglichkeit für achtere Kreiselanlage. Vereinigung mit "Nürnberg" und "Köln" fraglich. Zur sicheren Ansteuerung Weg blau wird Besteck-Kontrolle notwendig. Deshalb:
1312		F.T. an Gruppe: "1430 auf Peilzeichen achten Welle j.Otto j. Standort hergeben, erbitte Flugzeugsicherung.
1315	7772	Deutsches Aufkl.Flugzeug S 4 F H in Sicht. Maschine wird optisch gegeben, bei "Leipzig" zu bleiben und fliegt bis 1500 U-Bootsicherung.

minutes until starboard No. 3 boiler failed because of water in the oil fuel. The steering gear was knocked out and both gyro compasses failed although the aftermost one was later successfully restarted. *Leipzig* lay dead in the water, listing 8° to port, her only motive power being her cruising diesels which had remained undamaged. Fourteen of her crew were killed, all on watch in the boiler rooms.

No sooner had the explosion been heard by the Flagship, than two torpedoes were sighted heading for *Nürnberg* herself, which was turning hard to starboard on to a course of approximately 270° in response to an order to turn 90° to starboard after the original torpedoes had been sighted. The torpedo tracks themselves, on a course of 270°, were approaching the Flagship from the starboard quarter and the cruiser was therefore turning into the path of them. Immediate orders were issued for 'hard a-port', but with the ship moving at high speed and already in a starboard turn, the effects of reversing the helm were minimal.

The ship was still in a starboard turn when at 1127, a torpedo struck her on the forefoot in compartments VII and VIII. The lower bows were blown off and both compartments began to make water. The machinery remained serviceable, but sixteen men were injured by the explosion. At 1128 Lütjens signalled to Gruppe West 'Torpedo hits LEIPZIG and NÜRNBERG' but as a result of errors and defects, this signal was not passed and in the meantime, *Leipzig* had sent off her own signal. Three further torpedoes were then seen on

the port quarter which the Flagship avoided by steaming full ahead with helm hard to starboard. All three torpedoes exploded at the end of their run or on hitting the bottom.

The position of the cruiser force was now critical; two had been damaged, one seriously. The destroyers were not yet in sight (they had been sighted from the foretop of *Leipzig* at the moment of her torpedoing, but injuries prevented the report reaching her Captain), and the last report of their position at 1100 had put them some 35 nautical miles distant from the cruisers. It could be assumed that the attacking submarine had reported her successes and in consequence, further action could be imminent. Not only could the submarine reload her tubes, but there was the distinct possibility of other submarines, surface ships and the RAF being vectored on to the crippled ships. In the meantime, Lütjens could only signal his position to the destroyers, order them to close the cruisers urgently and use his only remaining effective unit, *Köln*, as a makeshift screen. *Nürnberg* had briefly sighted what was believed to have been a submarine periscope astern of her, and engaged with her after turret but without effect.

The situation aboard *Leipzig* was critical but, surprisingly, the ship appeared in no danger of sinking, which is quite a tribute to her watertight subdivision arrangements. The torpedo had struck on frame 89 just aft of the bulkhead at frame 89¾, about three to four metres under the waterline, opening up the hull from frames 83 to 96 (i.e., about 13 metres in length) and vertically from the double bottom to the waterline (five to six metres). The keel plate had been deformed and the armoured deck 'domed' over the port side boilers by the force of the explosions. Armoured gratings, protecting the boiler uptakes, were ripped and hanging loose, while the bulkhead between Nos. 1 and 2 boiler rooms was ruptured. All steam, fuel and service lines on the port side had been destroyed. Both boiler rooms were flooded with oil and water while the 'tween-decks area above the armoured deck in the vicinity of the explosion was similarly flooded as a result of secondary internal structural damage.

The only undamaged boiler space, No. 3, was full of smoke and was taking water slowly via the cable glands from No. 2 boiler room. The bulkhead itself remained intact as did the after bulkhead on No. 1 boiler room and the inner longitudinal bulkheads on the starboard side. More than 1,700 tonnes of water had flooded into the ship. Shock damage and electrical power failures rendered most of the telephone, fire-control and command elements unserviceable, but otherwise her armament remained intact. Nevertheless, the ship was in a serious condition and could only move on her diesels, which she did, after uncoupling the turbines, crawling away painfully to the east and safety.

Nürnberg, on the other hand, was much less seriously damaged. Flooding and damage had been confined to only the foremost two compartments on the hold and 'tween decks, although the tangled wreckage of the bows also hung down, making manoeuvring difficult and reducing her speed to about eighteen knots. No other damage had been sustained apart from shock damage to fire-control equipment. Fortunately for both damaged vessels, the weather was good, and

low cloud helped to hide their predicament. By 1200 the damage-control centre aboard the Flagship had confirmed that the forward bulkheads were holding and a homeward course was steered. Twelve minutes or so later, an enemy bomber was sighted ahead which was taken under fire. The aircraft took swift avoiding action and made a new pass from the port quarter, dropping two bombs as it did so. *Nürnberg* turned hard to port, the bombs falling some fifteen to twenty metres to starboard, shaking the after end of the cruiser, which caused leaks in the tiller flat. A second aircraft was met with heavy flak fire, but also succeeded in dropping her bombs. These missed to starboard, causing further slight shock damage.

Nürnberg was now able to make eighteen knots and continued eastwards. *Leipzig* was still to be seen on the horizon to the south whilst *Köln* steamed ahead on the port bow. One British aircraft remained to shadow the cruisers, but was driven off by gunfire. At 1340 three destroyers at last joined the cruisers, *Künne* being ordered to escort the Flagship while *Beitzen* and *Heinemann* were detached to *Leipzig*, now closing her two consorts. The remaining two destroyers, *Ihn* and *Steinbrinck* had already been diverted home because of defects. Ashore, Gruppe West set the wheels in motion to reinforce the cruisers' escort, sailing a destroyer, the 2nd Minesweeping Flotilla and an 'F' boat. All three cruisers were now sailing east escorted by destroyers and aircraft. *Nürnberg* with revolutions for eighteen knots was actually making only fifteen–sixteen knots, while the crippled *Leipzig* could only achieve ten knots.

By early afternoon in view of the difference in speeds of the two damaged ships, Lütjens had decided to sail home in two groups. *Künne* was to remain with the Flagship while *Köln* was to be left with *Leipzig* because the latter had no fire control or searchlights operational. A possible night action would require both, and *Köln* was fully effective. The two other destroyers were also to remain with *Leipzig*. Lütjens ordered *Köln* to detach for home before dawn. Fleet Command now became involved, issuing various instructions concerning deployment and routes home, but also commenting that 'Submarine attacks less likely in the inner (German) Bight'. Rather an unfortunate statement in view of later events. *Nürnberg* and her escorting destroyer pressed on for home and arrived safely off the Elbe on the morning of the 14th.

Leipzig continued her painful passage home, joined on the morning of the 14th, by *Schoemann*, *F7*, *F9*, units of the 2nd Minesweeping Flotilla, boats of the 1st 'R' Boat Flotilla and, later, the destroyer *Ihn*. At 0951, *Köln* and two destroyers (*Schoemann* and *Ihn*) were ordered to detach home by Gruppe West, leaving *Leipzig* with two destroyers and the small craft to make their own way independently. The six R-boats were disposed in an inner circular screen, approximately 300 metres from the cruiser; the four minesweepers about 1,000 metres on each beam and quarter, with the two F-boats (fast escort vessels) stationed on the port (*F7*) and starboard (*F9*) bows. The destroyers were stationed further out on the port and starboard bows of *F7* and *F9*. By noon, the squadron stood to the west of Heligoland, and with only about thirty

miles to go before entering the narrow confines of the Elbe, it seemed that little danger remained for the German ships.

URSULA'S ATTACK

HM Submarine *Ursula* (Lieutenant-Commander Phillips) had been sailed from Blyth by Captain (S) on the afternoon of 4 December, for a sixteen-day patrol south west of the Horns Reef. *Ursula*, one of the original three boats of the 540-ton 'U' class, armed with six 21-inch torpedo tubes, had first commissioned in December 1938. She had been intended for use as an unarmed target boat for anti-submarine training, but torpedo tubes had been incorporated in the design before she was completed. On the night of 12/13 December 1939, Phillips, being in some doubt as to the boat's true position, had surfaced for a fix, but the night was extremely dark and Heligoland light was not lit. At 2045 (2145 German time) this light was burned briefly, possibly in an attempt to assist *Nürnberg*, which enabled *Ursula* to fix her position by bearings and soundings. This put her close to the Nordeney lightship. Phillips now received a signal giving warning of the German cruiser force, and in response to this, closed Heligoland, dived before dawn and obtained a good fix on the island at daybreak. Having done this, he then moved south-east to await events.

During the forenoon of the 14th, *Ursula* sighted the inward bound *Köln* and her escort steaming south at a range of about 7,000m, but because of their relative positions, no attack was possible. An hour and a quarter later, however, came Phillips' opportunity; a second cruiser appeared escorted by about six ships, which the submarine captain took to be destroyers. This new target was, of course, *Leipzig*, escorted by destroyers, 'F'-boats and minesweepers, although the 'F'-boats could easily be mistaken for destroyers. *Ursula* was positioned off the port bow of the leading ship of the port screen and altered course towards the enemy formation. This brought her dangerously close to the leading destroyer on the port side, so that Phillips took his boat down to sixteen metres and turned in under her to attack.

In these confined waters, about eight nautical miles south-west of Heligoland, submarine operations were by no means easy, being hemmed in on one hand by the rocky massif of Heligoland itself, and on the other by the shallows of the North Fresian Islands. The depth of water available to the submarine at this time was about 38 metres. It was, therefore, with a good deal of courage and skill that Phillips was able to reach a firing position when he launched four torpedoes in a spread at six-second intervals at a range of 1,200 metres. After one minute, ten seconds' running time came a tremendous explosion which broke all the lights in the boat, closely followed by a second when the hydrophone operator reported HE, 'like nothing he had heard in his life'. *Ursula* had to be forced under to avoid breaking surface, and then moved slowly towards the track of the target. No depth-charges were dropped, and after 45 minutes had elapsed, Phillips moved cautiously up to periscope depth to find two escorts at the position sinking and nothing else. Elated, he concluded that two Mk VIII torpedo hits on a light cruiser and the absence of

Above: Fast escort vessel or *Flottenbegleiter*, *F9*, which was torpedoed by HM submarine *Ursula* while escorting the damaged *Leipzig* in December 1939. It will be evident why they were often mistaken for destroyers by submarine COs during brief periscope observations. (Drüppel)

Above right: *Nürnberg*, her bows damaged after *Salmon*'s torpedo. (Author's collection)

HE must have meant that it had now sunk. *Ursula* returned safely to Blyth and Phillips was specially promoted to Commander as well as being awarded the DSO for this exploit. *Salmon*'s commander received similar honours.

In *Leipzig* the first intimation of a submarine attack that Kapitän Nordmann had was the eruption of a huge explosion off the starboard bow. At least one of Phillips' torpedoes had struck home, but on the leading ship of the starboard screen, having passed ahead of the cruiser herself. It would appear that the British captain had over-estimated the speed of *Leipzig* and missed ahead. Nordmann turned hard to port and stopped his engine as further tracks were seen off the starboard bow, only 50 metres ahead. Now ordering full ahead and again turning 90° to port he managed to avoid the torpedoes. The screen was now in some confusion and no attempt was made to counter-attack the submarine. The recipient of the torpedo hit(s) was the fast escort vessel, *F9*, which was quite literally blown apart by the explosion, sinking very quickly with few survivors. To be subject to submarine attack so close to its own base was a severe shock to the German squadron and, after detaching part of the screen to search for survivors, Nordmann hurried into the Elbe, securing off Brunsbüttel early that evening.

REPAIRS AND RECRIMINATIONS

The badly damaged *Leipzig* was sent to the Blohm & Voss yard in Hamburg for temporary repairs and then moved to Deutsche Werke at Kiel where she was paid off on 27 February 1940. During repairs, the boilers were removed from Nos. 1 and 2 boiler rooms, as were all pumps, fans and steam lines on the port side. All pipe work on the starboard side into these two spaces was closed off, and the remaining steam lines inspected, tested and made good. Finally, the hull was repaired and replated in the way of the after boiler rooms. Although repairs were continued at Danziger Werft, and the ship recommissioned on 1 December 1940, she was never again fully operational since four boilers had been landed and the spaces converted to cadets' accommodation. In conse-

quence, she could make at the most 24 knots for the remainder of her career. *Nürnberg*, on the other hand, completed her repairs by the spring of 1940 although she too saw little further action, but for rather different reasons.

The torpedoing of the two cruisers, particularly of *Leipzig* with its severe damage, was a matter of great concern to the German Naval Command. Raeder was reportedly extremely critical of the use of the cruisers in such a manner. In his opinion, destroyers should escort cruisers and not vice versa, but this was not the first operation of its kind and he cannot have been unaware of the previous sorties. So far as Admiral Lütjens was concerned, he was merely following his operational orders, having made representation about the lack of a/s screen, but to no avail. Any loss, therefore, was one of the penalties to be accepted. Nevertheless, certain aspects of his handling of the sorties bear examination.

In the first place, knowing that no surface a/s screen would be available and that he must rely on shipboard aircraft, it is surprising that opportunity was not taken to embark more than one aircraft per cruiser. Originally, these vessels could embark two aircraft and despite the serious defects inherent in the pre-war cruisers, discussed in Chapter 2, this could surely have been tolerated for such a short sortie in fine weather. *Köln* no longer carried aircraft but, even so, with only four aircraft, there would have been air a/s cover at the time the submarine attack took place. Lütjens detached his own aircraft home at the limit of their endurance because he considered it too risky to stop and recover them for refuelling, yet, he happily accepted this risk when ordering *Leipzig* to launch a boat to search the stopped steamer – a totally unnecessary procedure because *Leipzig* was aware that *Charkow* was on the free-list, but it appears the Flagship did not, or at any rate did not check first.

Overall command of the operation lay in the hands of Admiral Saawächter at Naval Command Gruppe West, but tactical control was the responsibility of the Fleet Commander, Admiral Marschall, aboard *Gneisenau, but who was not taking part in the sortie.* This was a clumsy system and

although it could not, in this instance, be blamed for what occurred, it was open to errors and confusion. Marschall considered that the sending of the cruisers to meet the destroyers was an essential and important war task, on several grounds. Primarily he was concerned about the known and chronic unreliability of the Type 34 destroyers, which might have led to the need for crippled ships to be escorted home, perhaps fighting off intercepting British surface units at the same time. In this respect too, he was alive to the morale effect aboard the destroyers of knowing that support was at hand if required. Finally, Marschall appreciated the fact that the vagaries of the weather might prevent the use of land-based strike aircraft support at the crucial moment, and he preferred to have surface back-up forces on hand. An added incentive to sail the cruisers was his fear that if the destroyers were caught by the Royal Navy while the cruiser force remained anchored and inactive in the Jade, he would be seriously reproached. It appeared to be a case of 'heads you win, tails I lose!'

The question of British submarines had not been ignored in his thinking either, for Marschall was concerned over the lack of a/s screen for the cruisers. It was clear to him that those submarines in the area posed a threat to the cruisers, but he knew that war could not be conducted without risk. This risk could and had to be accepted; until now the enemy submarines had had conspicuously little success, and a chance torpedo was better than accusations of lying idle while the destroyers were in desperate need. Morale was important. Marschall's attempts to obtain a destroyer or torpedo-boat screen failed for reasons already discussed, but it would appear that he had little faith in the destroyers' a/s capabilities, believing that 'a few destroyers . . . would not seriously reduce the risk!' He would have preferred 'S Geräte'-fitted torpedo-boats and more aircraft for an effective a/s screen, although there is some contradiction later in his appreciation of the sortie, when he cites the fact of the shore-based air escort having arrived as the torpedoes were striking, as an example of the *ineffectiveness* of aerial a/s escort. This was grossly unfair, because the aircraft did not reach the squadron until *minutes* before the torpedoes had been fired, and so had no opportunity to orbit and keep submarines under. Communications between ships and aircraft were suspect; when the flight leader attempted to warn the cruisers of the torpedoes by flashing 'UUU' it was not understood, coincidentally, the recognition code for the day was 'U'!

On the whole, Marschall was not over-critical of Flag Officer (Cruisers)' handling of the first submarine incident, but was a little more critical of Nordmann for his conduct in the return of *Leipzig*. Nordmann was censured for deploying too close a screen for the damaged ship; it was considered that the screen should have been opened out to allow better use of 'S Geräte' and, by inference, earlier detection of the submarine. The loss of *F9* was judged a serious error in view of the number of a/s vessels present and the subsequent hunt was a shambles. No clear signal had been given to attack the submarine, nor had its range and bearings been reported. Few depth-charges had been dropped and the hunt such as it was, had certainly not been pursued with vigour. Marschall

appreciated, however, that Nordmann was preoccupied by the parlous condition of his own ship and could not give the squadron the attention it required. His final comments on the operation are, on the face of it, surprising, for he did not consider the incident to be of serious consequence to the sea war. *Nürnberg*'s repairs would not take over-long, and the long absence of *Leipzig* would not leave any noticeable gap which could not be borne under the circumstances then prevailing. Judging by the various margin notes in his war diary, Marschall's views were not universally shared by his superiors, but as the subsequent war careers of *Nürnberg*, *Köln* and *Emden* were, to show, they were a shrewd appreciation of the effective value of these pre-war ships.

Admiral Saalwächter, himself, had little to say concerning the incident, except that he considered cruisers to be unsuitable for the task in question, but had not prevented their employment because Admiral Marschall obviously attached great importance to their participation! He did, however, criticize Admiral Lütjens for stopping the *Charkow* and thus possibly giving *Salmon* her opportunity to attack. This was unfair, because the detailed orders for Operation 'Nanni-Sophie' were issued by Flag Officer (Reconnaissance Forces) on 8 December, two copies of which had been supplied to Saalwächter. These orders clearly stated the intention of conducting cruiser warfare while awaiting the destroyers if the weather were suitable. Considering the waters in question, this was indeed a risky exercise, but Saalwächter appears to have done nothing to countermand the intention despite his having received the orders.

A far more serious omission on the part of Saalwächter was his apparent failure to pass on to the squadron at sea, known facts about the abortive attack by *Salmon* on *Bremen*. As early as 1500 on the 12th, Gruppe (West) had received a deciphered intercept of a signal from Rugby radio station giving details of this attack. Four hours later, at 1910, Group (West) received another signal, this time from the Air Officer Commanding Maritime Units (FdL) to the effect that *Bremen*'s air escort had forced under an unidentified submarine. No position was given, but the Naval Command quite obviously knew where the liner was and should have been able to deduce the danger to the cruisers. So far as can be ascertained, no signals were passed to the cruisers and they sailed virtually into the arms of the patrolling submarine.

To sum up the incident, it was not unreasonable to have a covering force of cruisers at sea to support the returning destroyers, despite Raeder's criticism (especially in view of the suspected presence of the 2nd British Cruiser Squadron, *Edinburgh*, *Southampton*, and *Glasgow*, in the Firth of Forth), but it was certainly foolhardy to sail them without screening vessels, and loiter in an area where an enemy submarine was definitely suspected (and indeed known positively after *Salmon*'s abortive attempt to stop *Bremen* the previous day). The price for this rash undertaking was paid in lives lost and propaganda value to the enemy. On the German side, the consequences were not immediately apparent, but no doubt contributed to the later timidity of their fleet and the 'avoid losses' policy.

7: THE NORWAY ADVENTURE

'Weser time is 0515 hrs summer time' ran the cryptic signal which reached Konteradmiral Schmundt (Flag Officer, Scouting Forces) on 4 April 1940. The signal, emanating from Naval Command (Gruppe West) referred to the coming invasion of Norway and Denmark to which the code name 'Weserübung' (Weser Exercise) had been allocated.* The choice of name was no doubt intended to account for the large number of warships gathered in the River Weser area. Later that same day, the Admiral was verbally informed of the day on which the operation would take place, 9 April, five days hence. Ten groups of warships and auxiliaries were to be employed in the seizing of the two almost defenceless countries, with Schmundt commanding Group 3, tasked with the occupation of Bergen. In command of all forces west of the Skagerrak mine barrage was Admiral Saalwächter at Gruppe (West), with overall command in the hands of the SKL.

TARGET BERGEN: KÖNIGSBERG AND KÖLN

Now that the operation was finally 'on', Schmundt devoted his energy to ensuring that the task would be completed smoothly and successfully, at the same time reflecting upon the difficulties which faced him in its execution. In his view, the three most dangerous objectives in the plan were Trondheim, Narvik and Bergen. The first two lay well to the north and, unless enemy forces were already at sea in the area, were too far from British bases for the German forces to be intercepted easily. Bergen on the other hand, lay only about two hundred and eighty miles from Scapa Flow, say eight or nine hours' steaming, while for the German squadron it entailed a passage of some four hundred and twenty nautical miles. Schmundt therefore had good reason to be concerned, for if the security of the operation were breached, he could well find himself confronted with a superior British naval force off Bergen when he arrived. Added to his fears was the knowledge that all the most modern units of the fleet had been allocated to the groups ordered to Narvik, Trondheim and Oslo, leaving the remainder of the groups with a motley collection of ships wherewith to carry out the allocated tasks.

In fact, so desperate was the gamble, that every ship which could float, steam and, at a pinch, fight, was included for the operation. For Group 3, there were available two light cruisers, *Köln* (Kpt.z.S.Kratzenberg) and *Königsberg* (Kpt.z.S.Ruhfus), which the Group Commander described as 'old', though they had actually been completed in 1929–1930 and were therefore newer than a large percentage of the British cruisers. In addition, there was the *Bremse*, a training ship and the depot ship, *Carl Peters*, together with a couple of torpedo-boats and some S-boats. The presence of the two auxiliaries was a heavy millstone around his neck, for the depot ship's maximum speed was only eighteen knots. At this speed, the outward passage would take about 24 hours, giving plenty of time for possible interception. In view of this, Schmundt pressed for their replacement by *Karlsruhe*, currently allocated to the Kristiansand Force, so as to have a homogeneous squadron with a higher passage speed. His request was denied and in consequence, he laid plans, in conjunction with the Commanding Officer of the 69th Infantry Division, Major-General Tittel, whose men would be embarked, to ensure that, initially only, non-essential men would

Below: *Köln* trapped in the Baltic ice at Kiel during the winter of 1939/40. (Bundesarchiv-Koblenz)

*General von Falkenhorst (designated Army CinC of the operation) had been called to Berlin on 20 February to be told by Hitler that he was to invade Norway with a force of six divisions and that a preparatory plan was required by 1500 hrs that day. Using hastily bought Baedeker tourist guides, this he managed to do. The idea of the invasion, however, was basically Raeder's, as it would give the Navy great strategic advantage.

be carried in the auxiliaries. They could, in an emergency, be detached in Oslo and railed forward to Bergen.

A closer look at the forces allocated to Group 3 gives some idea of the barrel-scraping to which the Kriegsmarine was forced to resort in order to deploy sufficient ships for the enterprise. Neither of the cruisers was fitted as a flagship, and *Königsberg* had spent most of her time since the end of September 1939 in dockyard hands at Kiel. Not until the middle of March 1940 had she become serviceable once more. Even then, she had conducted few trials and little working-up. Moreover, some fifty crew were down with influenza and scarlet fever. Neither her guns nor torpedoes had been fired. *Köln* had new commanding and gunnery officers, the latter yet to fire his ship's main armament. *Bremse* was in dire need of repairs to her machinery and could achieve only 23 knots, while *Carl Peters* was brand-new, having only commissioned in the January! She was still on trials.

Admiral Schmundt considered two possibilities for the passage north. Should he split his force into a fast division and a slow one, steaming via different routes and meeting off the Norwegian coast, or should all his group sail in company via the same route? In fact, he chose the latter on the grounds that a group consisting of the auxiliaries and torpedo-boats would have little flak defence, there would be no a/s escort for the cruisers and, finally, it could not be guaranteed that all units would reach the rendezvous on time. This decided, he called a conference with all his captains on the 5th and the following day received the first liaison officers from the army units.

The ships forming his group were spread over three ports with only the two cruisers and *Bremse* lying in the main base of Wilhelmshaven. *Carl Peters* and the torpedo-boats were in Cuxhaven, while the seven boats of the 1st S-Boat Flotilla were at Heligoland. Loading the troops and equipment progressed smoothly at first, with trucks arriving alongside the ships at ten-minute intervals. Later on, delays occurred, caused mainly by the need to work in complete darkness for security reasons. *Köln* embarked about 640 officers and men from Infantry, Marine Artillery and Pioneer formations, while her sister took aboard a further 735 men as well as Admiral Schrader (appointed Admiral Commanding, Norwegian West Coast) and his staff. Also embarked was Oberst Graf von Stolberg, Commanding Officer of 159th Infantry Regiment. Loading of stores and equipment continued until about half an hour before midnight, when all ships reported loading completed.

The cruisers sailed shortly before midnight on the 7th, passed down the Jade and shaped course for the entrance to the Skagerrak. Already, Gruppe (West) had signalled that the Northern operation had become known to the British and that his light forces had been deployed. Whether this would affect Group 3 or not only time would tell. It was a clear but dark night as the ships passed the last lightship and left the rocky silhouette of Heligoland astern. As dawn broke, the first units of the air cover arrived, He 111s on anti-submarine patrol. During the morning watch, despite the air cover, numerous submarine, periscope and torpedo track alarms occurred,

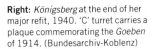

Right: *Königsberg* at the end of her major refit, 1940. 'C' turret carries a plaque commemorating the *Goeben* of 1914. (Bundesarchiv-Koblenz)

resulting in violent evasive action on the part of the ships, but by 0952, course due north had been resumed. An hour later, the weather had closed in, fog reducing visibility to less than 500 metres and a cloud base of only 50 metres. The ships' hard outlines softened then disappeared completely in the swirling fog as they pressed on, maintaining eighteen knots. *Königsberg* and *Bremse* lost contact with the Flagship during the late afternoon, but regained it a little afterwards just as *Carl Peters* and the torpedo-boats joined the squadron. At 1745 Gruppe (West) passed an enemy sighting report from an aircraft timed at 1145 (!) which reported destroyers in Q2735 on a NE course. As Schmundt quite rightly commented, such a report was useless, being six hours old. At high speed, they could already have reached Bergen.

By early evening, the fog had lifted and at 2000, when the squadron was some 20 miles west of Skudesnes, there was little cloud in the sky and good visibility. As dusk fell, the ships moved into line ahead for the night, the boats of the 1st S-Boat Flotilla joining from Heligoland at about this time. Speed was reduced to avoid arriving at the target ahead of schedule, so that by midnight, the squadron stood west of Marstein. Clouds had brought rain squalls and the wind had freshened bringing a long swell to the sea. As action stations were closed up, the manned lights ashore were doused, but unmanned navigation beacons remained lit. The thought immediately crossed everyone's mind – had the vital element of surprise been lost?

There could be no going back so, with action stations closed up, the ships continued their passage along the Norwegian coast. At 0205 the entrance to Korsfjord was reached and a challenge from a patrol vessel to starboard was answered with 'HMS CAIRO' from the signal deck of *Köln*. The patrol vessel illuminated *Königsberg* with her searchlight and fired Very signals, but took no further action. Leaving her astern, Schmundt pressed on, passing other patrol vessels, always continuing to give the impression that his ships were British. In the Vatlestrommen, an ancient, diminutive Norwegian torpedo-boat closed *Köln*, her torpedo tubes trained on the cruiser. The cruiser's signal 'English warships en route for short stay in Bergen' clearly confused the Norwegian for he made no reply, nor did he open fire. Once again, the Germans were left with the feeling that all surprise must by now have been lost, and a suspicion that the Norwegians must be saving an unpleasant surprise for them, further into the fjords.

On reaching Stangen, just before the entrance to Byfjord, the squadron stopped to allow the S-boats and cutters to go alongside *Königsberg* from whom they were to embark troops to be landed for the capture of the batteries at Kvarven and Habso. *Köln* and the remainder of the ships then resumed course for Bergen, being briefly engaged by the Kvarven battery as they passed. Several near misses were experienced, one shell passing between *Köln*'s funnels to explode on the shoreline. Increasing speed, Schmundt emerged unscathed and was soon out of the arc of training of the Norwegians' guns.

In the meantime, *Königsberg* had landed her troops following which her orders were to enter harbour and act in a fire-support capacity from Puddefjord for the troops attacking Kvarven. As she left the shelter of the cliffs off Stangen, she was immediately illuminated by searchlights and engaged by the 21cm guns on Kvarven. One shell threw up a column of water in front of her bows and a second landed abreast 'C' turret. Ruhfus ordered his signaller to send 'Stop firing – good friends' in English and, believing the shots to be only warnings, held his fire. The next round from the battery was an unpleasant surprise – it was a direct hit. This 21cm shell struck just above the waterline on the starboard bow and exploded inboard, sending a hail of splinters through the bulkheads into oil bunkers, No. 2 generator room and No. 3 boiler room. Inside these spaces, the splinters severed main and auxiliary steam lines and cables, as well as destroying electrical installations. Boiler casings were severely distorted, leading to an acute danger of steam escapes. Oil and water flooded into the ship, the oil igniting and creating a large fire which was only extinguished by flooding the boiler room and generator space. The water now stood about one metre above the floor plates. In the ship's side, the large hole was patched with collision mats. Temporary loss of electrical power rendered steering and guns useless, although the latter could not easily distinguish a target on the dark land mass in any case.

A second shell hit the starboard forecastle, abreast the 3.7cm gun and, damaging it, was deflected through cabins in the superstructure. Continuing through the forward funnel, the shell destroyed the after port 3.7cm mounting, killing or wounding all its crew. The third round struck in almost the same place as the second, causing fires on the forward mess decks. The ship was now in a sorry condition, with a hole 3.5 metres by 0.6 metres in the starboard side, serious fires below and extensive flooding. Fuel, water and fire-fighting mains had been severed, the forward funnel badly holed and the diesel exhaust punctured. Smoke billowing from the fires obscured fire control from the foretop whence control was passed to the forward director. Ruhfus quickly broke off the engagement and took his ship on into the harbour.

Inside Puddefjord, *Königsberg* attempted to anchor, but failed in the crowded waters and poor holding ground, so got under way again just as the gun battery at Eidsvaag opened fire on the cruisers. Shell splashes erupted only five to ten metres from *Köln* before both ships replied. The battery at Kvangen also joined in. *Königsberg* replied, firing full broadsides, but *Köln* could only use 'A' turret against Eidsvaag, and her 8.8cm guns against Kvangen, because S-boats and fishing vessels alongside fouled the range for 'B' and 'C' turrets. After the fifth salvo, the batteries appeared to cease fire when two Heinkels joined in with a bombing attack. However, they opened up again briefly before finally being silenced, and by mid morning all the batteries were in German hands.

Königsberg oiled *Wolf* and *Bernhard v. Tschirschky*, disembarked the remainder of the troops and set about repairing her damage, details of which had been notified to the Flagship. The squadron engineer officer came aboard to inspect the damaged spaces while Ruhfus was ordered to report aboard the Flagship. On his return to *Köln*, the squadron engineer officer gave his opinion that *Königsberg* could be

made ready for sea in a short time, but that the crew's training level might not be sufficient to guarantee this. Ruhfus and his own engineer officer disagreed strongly, insisting that the ship would need at least one to two days to regain full operational condition. If the ship were to sail that evening, she would be capable of only 22 knots or possibly 24 knots maximum. Moreover, with the holes in her side only covered with makeshift patches, her seaworthiness was suspect. In order to give his crew time to effect the necessary repairs, Ruhfus proposed that he sail on the 10th.

The damage to *Königsberg* presented a problem to Admiral Schmundt for his orders were to withdraw once the town had been secured. That morning he had received reconnaissance reports of heavy British warships at sea from the pilot of an He115 which landed at Bergen for fuel. If he waited for the damaged cruiser to effect repairs, he might well be faced with a superior enemy force outside the fjords, or be bottled up in Bergen. If, on the other hand, he sailed now, with the damaged ship capable of only 22 knots, he would be seriously handicapped if it came to a cruiser action. Admiral von Schrader proposed to Gruppe (West) that *all* the warships be retained at Bergen; he feared a British attack, and, as yet, the situation ashore was uncertain, nor were the shore batteries in working order again.

Schmundt countered this by pointing out that his orders specifically required him to leave as soon as unloading was completed, and emphasized that the longer departure was delayed, the more difficult it would be to effect a break-back to Germany. He remained adamant that the Flagship and the two torpedo-boats would leave that day (the 9th). It was unlikely that *Königsberg* would be able to leave with them, but if at all possible, she would do so. He dispatched a signal of his intentions to Gruppe (West): 'KÖNIGSBERG damaged. Length of repair not yet known. Intend break out 2200/2300 hrs with KÖLN, LEOPARD and LUCHS. Exit route depends on enemy situation.' Having made up his mind, Schmundt ordered *Königsberg* to use her aircraft for reconnaissance cover to the west throughout the afternoon and evening. In view of reports he had received throughout the day, the Admiral believed that British forces were closing in on him and that the break-back of the operational ships was rather a gamble, especially since the forecast was for good weather and clear visibility that night.

The British Admiralty had, in fact, now become aware of the German presence in Bergen and just before noon on the 9th, Admiral Layton had been detached with the cruisers *Manchester, Southampton, Glasgow* and *Sheffield*, accompanied by seven destroyers, to attack the German force. The threat, therefore, was a very real one to Admiral Schmundt. However, the course of operations of the British Fleet during that day had taken it south of Bergen, and Admiral Layton found his passage very slow-going in the face of rising seas. although only 80 miles from Bergen. Fortunately, for the Germans, the British Admiralty got cold feet and now, believing that the coastal batteries were in German hands, called off the operation. Had the sortie been pursued, they would have caught both cruisers in port, with the batteries not yet serviceable.

Königsberg was ordered to complete her repairs and regain full operational status as quickly as possible and to leave independently as soon as she could. It was briefly considered sending her into one of the more remote adjacent fjords to avoid further air attacks, but it was finally decided that it was better to keep her in Bergen where her guns could augment the shore batteries should a British attack take place.

Königsberg's Arado landed back after her first reconnaissance mission early that evening with the welcome report that no enemy forces were in the vicinity. Later on, however, a force of twelve RAF Wellingtons and twelve Hampden bombers attacked the cruisers, but failed to secure any hits despite several near misses, although some casualties aboard *Köln* were caused by strafing. At 2000, under almost cloudless skies, *Köln* and her consorts sailed for home, but in view of another bombing raid on Bergen an hour later, when it was assumed that her sailing would have been reported, Schmundt delayed his break-back by a day and lay low throughout the 9th in Mauranger Fjord, a remote side fjord off Hardangerfjord to the south of Bergen.

THE BOMBING OF KÖNIGSBERG

In the meantime, *Königsberg* had, in accordance with her orders, moved berth to the Skoltergrundskai, where her after turrets and 8.8cm guns could command the western entrance to Byfjord, and all three turrets, the northern entrance. She also lay close to civilian houses and neutral merchant vessels which it was hoped would inhibit the RAF bombers. S-boats were to be ordered alongside as floating torpedo batteries, and about one hundred of her crew were sent ashore to reinforce the land forces. After the air raids of the day, the night passed calmly. All the flak crews slept at their posts while the engine-room staffs worked throughout the night to repair the damage below.

Despite all the German ship movements the invasion had not only taken the Norwegians by surprise, but had completely wrong-footed the British. In consequence their reaction to the invasion was badly coordinated and totally ineffective in preventing the landing of the German Army. RAF bombers had mounted attacks on the various groups of warships, but with singular lack of success, and RN submarines had scored a few successes against the transports. As Admiral Schmundt had feared, the RAF reconnaissance sorties over Bergen had located and identified the two cruisers and Wellingtons were sent to attack them. When this proved ineffectual, the task of destroying the cruisers was passed to the Fleet Air Arm, who grasped the opportunity eagerly.

At this time, the main striking power of the Fleet Air Arm consisted of the torpedo-carrying, Fairey Swordfish biplane and the newer, Blackburn Skua monoplane, fighter/dive-bomber. In the closely confined waters of Bergen harbour, the torpedo could not be employed so the task naturally fell to the Skuas. Two squadrons of these were available: 800 (Captain R. T. Partridge, RM) and 803 (Lieutenant W. P. Lacy RN), both currently shore-based at RNAS, Hatston, in the Orkney Islands. Under command of the CO of 803 Squadron they were ordered to attack the two cruisers (*Köln*'s sailing having

Below: Skua IIs of 803 Squadron from *Ark Royal*, 1939/40. The Fleet Air Arm's newest aircraft and its first monoplane, the Skua had to double as a fighter as well as a dive-bomber — one of many examples of inter-war parsimony. The sinking of *Königsberg* was the Skua's crowning glory. (Fleet Air Arm)

Below right: *Königsberg* on fire and just starting to list following bombing by Fleet Air Arm aircraft in Bergen harbour on 10 April 1940. (Gröner)

gone unnoticed) in the harbour. The major problem was the distance; a return flight of approximately 660 miles – the range of the Skua was only 700. Any aircraft with less than 227lt (50gals) of fuel remaining was directed to land in Norway, well clear of Bergen. The decision was left to the pilots and would be made in the light of prevailing wind and weather. If the aircraft was serviceable on landing, pilots were instructed to consult the Norwegian authorities with a view to obtaining fuel and returning the following day. If the aircraft was unserviceable, it was to be destroyed.

On 10 April, eleven aircraft from 803 and five from 800 Squadrons, each armed with a single 500lb (227kg) S.A.P. bomb, took off from Hatston in the pre-dawn light to start their long haul across the North Sea. The strike force was divided into two groups of nine and seven aircraft, but one from the second group lost contact with her squadron and arrived about ten minutes late over the target.

The squadrons crossed the Norwegian coast and turned so as to approach Bergen from the south-east, attacking out of the rising sun. Only one cruiser was present, so the unfortunate *Königsberg* received the attentions of the entire strike force. The attack achieved complete surprise, with very little flak being encountered as the aircraft formed up in line astern and dive-bombed in turn. All the Skuas attacked in a longitudinal direction, in a 60° dive, before releasing their bombs at about 650m (2,000ft), and then flew westwards out to sea. By the time the straggler had bombed, some ten minutes late, there was no reply from the cruiser which was now smoking heavily. The aircraft received minor bullet holes, and one other aircraft, Red Leader from 803 Squadron, (Lieutenant Smeeton/Midshipman Watkinson) failed to return. This aircraft rejoined its section after the attack, but then disappeared in the clouds. Another aircraft later reported a splash in the sea. On de-briefing, the pilots claimed three hits and at least one near miss. The success of the attack was attributed to exceptionally favourable conditions, lack of serious opposition and complete surprise.

Königsberg had indeed been badly hit. The first bomb exploded on the pier, abreast the starboard side of No. 1 boiler room. Splinters cut through the thin side plating, rupturing fuel bunkers and severing steam feed pipes inside the boiler room. Live steam filled the space and burning oil gushed from the damaged bunkers. A second bomb passed through the signal deck to explode in the water alongside. The shock waves ripped open the ship's side, the outer bottom of compartment XII and adjacent spaces, and deformed the inner bottom. No. 4 boiler room, No. 4 generator room and the bilge pump space quickly filled with water which soon reached the platform deck, spilling over into the radio room, command centre and gunnery control room. The ship now began to list to port. The third bomb exploded in the auxiliary boiler room on the 'tween deck, causing many casualties and starting fires. Smoke billowed through the devastated compartments, hindering the damage-control and medical teams. Two more bombs exploded in the 'tween deck, causing more casualties, and another, in the water on the port quarter, ripped open the hull astern.

No. 3 boiler room was taking water badly, possibly because the makeshift patch had been loosened by the near misses. Water was also pouring in to No. 2 boiler room through damaged bulkheads. Since the ship had at the time only one boiler flashed up – in No. 1 boiler room – its loss naturally resulted in the interruption of power to the pumps and turbo-generators. As another hit in XII had destroyed both diesel generators there, the consequences for damage-control prospects were dire. Moreover, the fire mains on the quayside had been cut by bomb hits, which compounded the problem. It quickly became clear to Ruhfus that there was no prospect of saving the ship and in view of the danger of a magazine explosion, he ordered her to be abandoned. Men and equipment were taken off as the list to port increased, smoke poured from the amidships section and then the torpedo warheads, aircraft fuel bunker and ready-use ammunition exploded, sealing her fate. Slowly, the burning wreck rolled

over to port, leaving only her screws and part of the bottom above water. The remnants of the ship's company formed up on the quayside and, singing the 'England Song' marched off to new postings.

The wreck of the sunken cruiser was finally refloated with the assistance of nine camels on 17 July 1942 and towed keel upwards to the floating-dock area of Laksevaag, Bergen. Despite further salvage work the wreck still had not been righted by March 1943, but later efforts succeeded, possibly at the end of 1943, after which the hulk was used as a convenient berthing point for U-boats. In September 1944, *Königsberg* reportedly capsized once more and further attempts were made to salvage her. On 29 June 1944, SKL informed MOK(Ost) that the wreck would shortly be raised again and docked prior to towing her back to Germany for conversion to a flakship or, if her condition were too bad, scrapping. The Commands in southern Norway and the Baltic were ordered to find the necessary escorts for this task, orders which were received with less than enthusiasm for far more pressing tasks were in hand! In the event *Königsberg* never returned to the Fatherland and was broken up *in situ* after the war.

To the south, in Mauranger Fjord, Admiral Schmundt took the news of *Königsberg*'s loss calmly. He had also been advised by now of the loss of *Blücher* off Oslo. That evening, he sailed for home with his torpedo-boats and, joined later by two destroyers, entered the Jade without incident, late in the afternoon of 11 April. In his final comments on the operation, Schmundt notes that while he and his staff had done all they could to ensure success, luck had played a major part in the adventure. It was lucky that fog had obscured the ships' outward passage and prevented evening air reconnaissance detecting them, lucky that *Köln* was not hit in the close-quarters engagement with the shore batteries, and lucky that those bombs dropped nearby during the Wellington attacks did not explode. Finally, it was lucky that low clouds over Mauranger Fjord effectively hid *Köln* while she awaited the time to commence her return to Germany.

The Norwegian armed forces, weak and ill-equipped, were able to offer little resistance to the German invasion. At sea, the Royal Norwegian Navy could muster only four new small destroyers of the *Sleipner* class and a handful of overaged submarines, but even so, their ineffectiveness is a little surprising. None of the German invasion groups records any attacks by either surface or submarine units of the Norwegian Navy with the exception of *Olav Tryggvason* at Horten. In the close confines of the deep fjords, the German ships were at a serious disadvantage and it is probable that had the Norwegian submarines in particular been used more offensively, the surface fleet of the Kriegsmarine might well have ceased to exist after 8 April.

TARGET KRISTIANSAND: KARLSRUHE

To undertake the occupation of the southern ports of Kristiansand and Arendal, Admiral Raeder had allocated the light cruiser *Karlsruhe* (Kpt.z.S.Rieve), the torpedo-boats *Greif*, *Luchs* and *Seeadler*, together with the depot ship,

Tsingtau, and seven S-boats. *Karlsruhe* was the only unit of the 'K'-class cruisers to have undergone the major refit which had been so necessary for the improvement of their sea-keeping properties. In consequence, she had only recommissioned at Wilhelmshaven on 13 November 1939, then after a brief work-up had been employed on mercantile warfare in the central Baltic in the new year. There followed a further period in dockyard hands until the end of February, when she returned to service once more. In March, she moved to Wesermünde in preparation for the coming operation.

Karlsruhe, loaded with troops and equipment, sailed from Wesermünde at 0510 on 8 April and, clearing the estuary, set course northwards, leaving Heligoland to starboard. During the morning, the weather was anything but favourable, with calm seas, clear, sunny skies and good visibility. At midday, the visibility decreased, becoming dull, as she rounded the Horns Reef and passed the northern tip of Sylt, standing west of the Danish coast by mid-afternoon. Throughout the afternoon, visibility had steadily decreased, leaving haze with a low cloud ceiling. Weather forecasts predicted fog and Rieve resolved to increase speed so as to gain as much time as possible while he could, in anticipation of a slow, fogbound passage later. By 1620, the fog had thickened with visibility down to only ½-mile at times. At 1738, course was altered to north-east in order to rendezvous with the remainder of the group, off Hanstholm on the northernmost coast of Denmark. The fog was still thick, which delayed the assembly, but by about 0044 on the 9th, all ships except *Greif* had made contact. As this ship was assigned to secure Arendal, Rieve assumed that under the circumstances she had probably proceeded independently to her objective, and he wasted no more time waiting for her. Slowly the ships groped their way across the Skagerrak towards the Norwegian coast with the fog persisting until dawn. Half an hour later the fog began to break up a little revealing a light-buoy off the entrance to the fjord. By 0557, land was in sight and the S-boats were ordered to close the cruiser. A Norwegian seaplane appeared off the starboard bow, but turned away into the fog before any action could be taken against it. Rieve assumed that this aircraft would have reported his presence, and that he had lost the element of surprise. Delayed by the fog, it was already one hour after the planned time for the assault, and the transfer of troops to the S-boats had not yet been carried out. In view of this, Rieve decided to use the troops carried by *Luchs* and *Seeadler* for the assault against the battery on Odderoe, and to leave the eastern battery until after the town had been captured.

Karlsruhe nosed her way cautiously into the fjord. Off the starboard bow, the lighthouse on Gronningen was visible, while to port lay the small island of Oksoy and beyond that, the larger mass of Flekkeroy. At first, all was calm, but then a merchant vessel crossed the path of the inward-bound German squadron, whereupon, Rieve at once decided to use her to shelter his ships from enemy fire, only to abandon the idea when she was seen to be a German vessel! This vessel now took up a position on the port bow of the attacking force and entered with it. At 0632, the Norwegian battery on

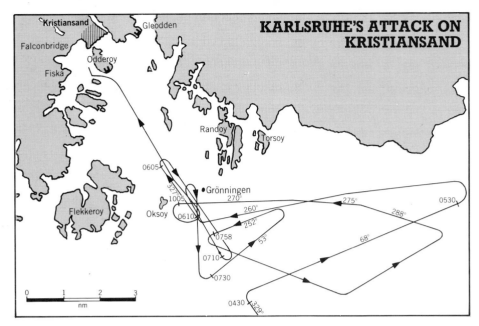

Above: *Karlsruhe*, an early wartime view, in November 1939 at Wilhelmshaven following her major refit. Noticeable modifications are the new funnel caps and tripod masts. The lower searchlight platforms have been removed. (Drüppel)

Odderoy, an island almost directly ahead, off the town of Kristiansand, opened fire. Shell splashes rose close to the bows of the German cruiser. Three minutes later, *Karlsruhe* opened fire, but was immediately at a disadvantage for only 'A' turret would bear.

As the battery presented a major threat to the success of the whole operation, Rieve decided that he had no option but to neutralize it before proceeding. To increase his fire-power, the cruiser was turned to starboard, thus opening the arcs of the after turrets. The range was about 6,500–7,500 metres. However, the narrow confines of the fjord prevented a sustained broadside engagement, forcing *Karlsruhe* to turn away and engage with her after turret group, while retiring down the fjord. In the meantime, the German merchantman had been hit and put ashore on fire, while German bombers had attacked the battery. Smoke and explosions obscured the target as Rieve turned about for a second run in. The ship's Arado was catapulted off to spot for the guns and bomb the battery, but the former task proved impossible because of radio failure. 'A' turret opened fire again, but an effective engagement of the battery, which stood 50–60 metres above sea level, with only the forward turret at close range was not possible.

Rieve turned about once more, engaged with the after turrets, but ceased fire after seventeen minutes. It was plainly impossible to subdue the battery in this manner, so a change of tactics was ordered. Rieve decided to withdraw to the south where, at the entrance to the fjord, he would gain valuable sea-room and then engage at longer range with all three turrets whose plunging fire should be more effective. While the cruiser engaged the troublesome battery, the light forces would be released to force the narrows under cover of her fire. As an extra insurance, a signal was dispatched to Group Command (Ost) requesting further bombing attacks on the coastal battery.

Between 0750 and 0829, *Karlsruhe* engaged the battery twice at a range of about 13,800 metres before fog suddenly descended again. It was not until an hour later that visibility improved sufficiently for the force to attempt to enter the fjord again, and even then conditions were deceptive and the cruiser narrowly escaped going aground on the way in. By 1025, a wind which had sprung up cleared the fog, whereupon troops were transhipped from *Tsingtau* to the torpedo-boats and S-boats for the final approaches. The resistance of the Norwegian battery had by this time been broken so that the German squadron entered Kristiansand unopposed. At midday the Norwegian flag over the battery was lowered and in the course of the afternoon naval and military forces surrendered to the Germans.

At the time of the invasion, the most effective naval units available to the Royal Norwegian Navy in the Kristiansand area were the new torpedo-boats *Odin* and *Gyller* (three 10.2cm guns; four 53.3cm TT; 30/32 knots) and the elderly submarines, *B2* and *B5*, each with four 45.7cm torpedo tubes. Given forewarning, in a position of defending confined waters studded with islands to lurk behind and led by resolute officers backed up by powerful shore defences the few Norwegian warships should have been able to stop the German forces completely or at least inflict heavy losses. That they did not do so was due to confusion and treachery in high places, allied with an insidious infiltration of German sympathisers and pacifists which undermined the Norwegians' will to defend themselves. The RNN was, with few exceptions, a navy of museum pieces but it could have achieved more than it did.

After the war King Haakon VII ordered an inquiry into the circumstances of the military authorities before and during the April invasion. The report was completed in 1950 and submitted to the King, but the Government decided that it could not be published. Thus the official side of events remains unknown, but some details of the movements of the two submarines are available. Both received orders to sail from Kristiansand on the evening of 8 April, but these orders were countermanded and neither boat sailed until 0500 the following morning, by which time the invasion was well under way. It would be interesting to know just who altered the orders and for what reason; the obvious inference is that their sailing was delayed to prevent them challenging the invasion force. As the boats sailed, the guns of Odderoya fortress could be heard in action, and as *B5* trimmed for diving she was

attacked by an aircraft. Her captain decided to sit on the bottom for some time as he deemed it inadvisable to proceed down the fjord at periscope depth with aircraft about. In fact, *B5* remained on the bottom at 40 metres for several hours as the sounds of explosions were heard from the action in the fjord. Finally, after it had been quiet for a couple of hours, *B5* surfaced and fell in with the torpedo-boat *Gyller* from whom she requested orders.

Gyller, too, had no clear orders and both put into Falconbridge on the western side of Kristiansand where the captains telephoned the local Naval Command for orders. In view of their subsequent inactivity it is likely that, in the most charitable case, the Command was confused and had no clear idea of events, or as happened elsewhere, their remaining in port was deliberately engineered. The activities of *B2* were equally ineffectual because, on diving, her gyro compass went unserviceable whereupon she surfaced and put into Fiska Verk for repairs. Thus she, too, was in port when the blow fell, but under the circumstances, the loss of the gyro compass was no reason to abandon her patrol; she must have had a magnetic compass which would have sufficed for short-range operations in the fjord.

It would appear that after the first two German attacks on Kristiansand, the Norwegian forces received orders that French and British ships should be allowed to pass, but in the poor visibility prevailing, the nationality of the ships coming up the fjord could not easily be determined. In the third attack, the Norwegians thought they saw the French ensign on the warships and so did not open fire. It was later claimed that the German naval flag 'H' (International 'T') was mistaken for the French flag which it resembled. The Norwegian Naval Commander maintained that he was unaware that the ships were German until, on boarding *Luchs*, he saw the Kriegsmarine ensign. If this was true, it demonstrates a lamentable standard of ship recognition on the part of a senior officer.

TRUANT'S ATTACK

Karlsruhe remained in Kristiansand for the rest of the afternoon, disembarking troops, supplies and equipment. Rieve's orders gave him a reasonably free hand as to when he should sail for home, but it was not intended that he delay long. In fact, he sailed at 1900, passing the entrance to the fjord at 1915. Outside in open waters, where submarines could be assumed to be operating, the cruiser, steamed a zigzag course at 21 knots. (Her passage speed was restricted to this by the torpedo-boats.) Barely three-quarters of an hour later lookouts reported excitedly that four torpedoes were approaching from starboard.

British submarines were indeed operating in the Skagerrak and Kattegat, because at this stage of the war Germany was unable to stop them getting in. Minefields had not yet been completed, and with the southern coast of Norway in neutral hands, submarines could use the deep water entrance to the Skagerrak in relative safety. This situation would change, but for the moment there were several operating off the southern coast of Norway. One of these was HMS *Truant*, under the command of Lieutenant-Commander C. H. Hutchinson. One of the new 'T' class which had begun to enter service just before the war, she had the heaviest bow torpedo salvo of any previous or subsequent British submarine type. Hutchinson proceeded to use his fire-power to good effect.

Having broken off an earlier attack on three torpedo-boats which turned out to be Norwegian, he now sighted the German cruiser to the north-west, hull down at a range of about ten miles. Twenty minutes after his first sighting, Hutchinson identified the cruisr as a *Köln*-class ship, escorted by three *Maass*-class destroyers. (The Type 23 and 24 torpedo-boats were frequently identified as destroyers by British look-outs due to their similarity at a distance.) Although initially in a good attack position, Hutchinson saw the cruiser zigzag away, putting him abaft the beam of the cruiser. Nevertheless, four minutes later he fired his full bow salvo of ten torpedoes at a range of about 3,000 metres. Two were set at 3 metres, six at 3½ metres and two more at 2½ metres running depth. Shutting off for depth-charging, Hutchinson waited anxiously for the welcome sound of hits. Two minutes later came a loud explosion, followed by another and then a third, accompanied by the sound of rending metal, the explosions being heard in HMS *Trident* which was in an adjacent patrol position. Hutchinson came to periscope depth but, sighting a destroyer approaching at high speed, dived at once to 20 metres and turned away.

For the next four and a half hours, *Truant* was hunted by two destroyers which dropped 31 depth-charges 'nearly all unpleasantly close'. After each attack, the German ships stopped to listen, using echo-sounding, but did not appear to be using an 'Asdic'-type apparatus. The a/s conditions were very good and in Hutchinson's words, the German escorts were, 'uncomfortably efficient and persistent'. Hutchinson could only hope that they would retire soon on more pressing business! During the first counter-attack, *Truant* had been taken down to 97 metres (bottom was 118 metres) in the course of which the explosions had caused the forward hatch to open and shut despite being fully clipped down. Water poured into the boat, affecting the trim and rendering both magnetic compasses useless, and most of the lighting was smashed. All machinery and the gyro compass were switched off to reduce noise.

Adding to the problems, the explosions jammed both forward hydrophones although these were later freed. 'Z' tank burst, numerous earths plagued the electrical circuits and then further explosions jarred open the main engine cooling-water inlet valves resulting in flooding at the after end. The boat was now trimmed bows up 15°, level trim being impossible to regain without pumping which would have been noisy, and the risk of oil reaching the surface. The depth of water was too great for her to lie on the bottom.

Two and three-quarter hours later, it having been quiet for about fifteen minutes, Hutchinson decided to go up for a look. More explosions were heard, although not close, so *Truant* was taken down again to 100 metres. In fact, these explosions were probably *Greif*'s torpedoes sinking the crippled cruiser. *Truant* finally surfaced after midnight, with

low batteries and foul air, having been submerged for nineteen hours. The hunters had gone and under an overcast sky, with no compasses, *Truant* set course for home and another day. Lieutenant-Commander Hutchinson received the DSO for this exploit. *Truant* survived the war, only to be wrecked off Cherbourg while in tow bound for the breakers' yard in 1946.

We must now return to *Karlsruhe*, where Kpt.z.S.Rieve had immediately ordered full speed ahead on receiving the torpedo warning, but to no avail. One torpedo struck the starboard side adjacent to or on the bulkhead between the auxiliary machine room (compartment VI) and the cruising turbine room, (compartment V). Despite three explosions being heard by *Truant*, German contemporary reports note only the one hit, although this cannot be definite in view of the conditions aboard the cruiser at the time. The explosion killed all the men on watch in the starboard auxiliary machine room as well as the two watchkeepers at the forward end of the cruising turbine room. In this latter space, the hit struck in the way of the starboard condenser which was blown apart as a dart of flame flashed athwartships. Fuel oil and water quickly entered both spaces, forcing the survivors in the turbine space to evacuate. Aft of the cruising turbine space was the main rudder motor room and No. 1 generator space. Here, water and oil was soon up to the floor plates, entering from ruptures in the bulkheads to the cruising turbine room. Attempts to get the water out failed through lack of power to the pumps. Water was also entering the port auxiliary machine space, main turbine room and No. 1 boiler room, although much more slowly. The ship's situation was serious and was reported as such by the First Lieutenant, K.Kpt.Duwel, to the Captain.

Karlsruhe lay stopped, listing 12°. A torpedo-boat was ordered up to take off the crew, while rafts were thrown overboard. No boats could be lowered through the lack of electric power. All pumps were out of action and the ship appeared to be sinking slowly. At 2045, the crew were taken off by *Seeadler* and *Luchs* and at 2110 the Captain boarded *Greif*. After the two torpedo-boats, with the crew aboard, had been detached to Kiel, *Karlsruhe* was torpedoed at 2250 by *Greif*; two torpedoes being needed to send her down. The first struck in the bows and the second abreast the mast. Slowly the cruiser sank, bows first over the starboard side until out of sight.

The loss of this ship to what appeared to be a single torpedo hit, only a few miles outside sheltered waters, was disconcerting and the action was thoroughly investigated by the Kriegsmarine, which resulted in serious criticisms of various aspects, both technical and personal. Admiral Schmundt, Flag Officer (Scouting Forces) studied the incident in depth. He recognized that the effective condition of the ship after torpedoing could now only be based on incomplete and possibly inexact verbal reports from survivors. Nevertheless, his investigation revealed disturbing errors and omissions by officers and men alike, while they were attempting to save the ship. In the first place, despite being in waters known to harbour enemy submarines, the ship was not fully closed up

and several important groups of personnel, including damage-control parties, were off watch. When the torpedo hit, there was a good deal of confusion and error in the damage-control procedures. Both the First Lieutenant (K.Kpt.Duwell) and the Chief Pump Master were in their respective messes at the time of the explosion. After the hit, the cruiser had no turbine power, although the boiler plant was initially intact. All electric power aft was lost, but power was available forward through Nos. 2 and 3 generator rooms. Calculations showed that about 2,300 tonnes of water were in the ship, 3,000 if No. 1 boiler room filled. The suction capacity of pumps in the latter was 30m/min while the leakage in this space was estimated at 50m/min and could therefore be expected to slowly fill. Nevertheless, under the calm conditions then prevailing and in view of the proximity of sheltered water, Schmundt considered that the condition of the ship would have been serious but not hopeless.

This was not the impression received by the First Lieutenant (who admittedly was on the spot) and his report to the Captain that the ship was slowly sinking led Rieve to believe that his ship was lost. Schmundt also considered that apart from the low standard of damage-control training of the crew, there were several technical aspects which contributed to the loss of the ship, in particular the shock resistance of steam valves on the turbo-generators (which closed on the explosion, thus losing electrical power) and the watertightness of electrical equipment and its ability to operate semi-submerged.

The Fleet Commander, Admiral Lütjens, considered that Rieve had discharged his task at Kristiansand energetically and successfully. After the torpedoing, the damage-control activities revealed a series of errors and inadequacies traceable to the low state of training of the ship's company. In particular, the activities of the First Lieutenant were especially criticized for failing to obtain an overall and accurate picture of the ship's condition and chances of salvage. As far as the training standard was concerned, Lütjens acknowledged the fact that operational requirements necessitated the use of ships not yet fully worked up. He also accepted the fact that Rieve's decision to scuttle the ship was based upon his First Lieutenant's report, as was his decision not to call up tugs, although he was also concerned over possible further submarine attacks on a slow-moving convoy.

Lütjens's investigations concluded that the ship could have been saved, but the energetic will to do this was absent. In his opinion, the reports of sinking by Duwell were not supported by the facts and he believed that had this officer taken charge of damage-control activities from a central command post instead of touring various compartments, a different result might have emerged.

The net conclusion as to the cause of the ship's loss was held to be a combination of inadequate training and poor damage control. Nevertheless, the Kriegsmarine appears to have made little provision for the salvage of damaged vessels during Operation 'Weserübung', despite possessing several large salvage tugs that could easily have been stationed in the Skagerrak at the time.

8: UNLUCKY BLÜCHER

The second of the 10,000-tonnes 'Washington' cruisers to enter service was *Blücher*, commissioned under Kpt.z.-S.Heinrich Woldag on 20 September 1939. The cruiser bore the name of a Prussian General, Gebhart von Blücher (1742–1819). Woldag, 47 years old, and a gunnery specialist, was a former officer of the Kaisermarine and had served in the battleships *Kaiser Friedrich III* and *Ostfriesland* during the First World War. During the early years of the Reichsmarine he held various posts ashore and aboard the old pre-dreadnought *Schleswig-Holstein* until promoted to Kapitän zur See in October 1937 and appointed to the new cruiser then under construction at Kiel. The completion of *Blücher* had been seriously delayed by numerous modifications during her construction, particularly in the later stages when the bows were altered and the funnel reconstructed. It was not until mid-November, therefore, that serious trials and working-up could begin. In fact, there was still work to be done to the machinery, and she spent all of November in the Kiel area, much of it in dockyard hands. Finally, on the 27th, the ship put to sea bound for Gotenhafen, where she remained until mid-December, carrying out various trials in connection with the main machinery, speed and endurance.

Returning once more to Kiel, *Blücher* spent a further period in yard hands for more modifications until 7 January 1940. On her release from the dockyard, she went back to the eastern Baltic where the continuance of her work-up programme was greatly hindered by the extremely harsh winter of that year. Fog, ice and a shortage of suitable ice breakers all combined to prevent her crew from completing their training. Back in Kiel by 17 January, she remained on a buoy, trapped by the ice in Kiel Bay, unable to continue her work-up until, on the 27th, she returned to the Deutsche Werke yard for further work. Here she remained until the end of March. After five months in commission, she had spent only about nineteen days at sea. The state of training of her crew was, therefore, low. This had not gone unrecognized by the Naval Staff, but the Navy's pressing need of ships to undertake the occupation of Norway over-ruled such considerations, given the small size of the surface fleet and the importance of the task.

Although it had not been planned to have the cruiser fully worked-up until 3 May, she was included in the plans for 'Weserübung' after OKM had been advised that the ship was operational for simple tasks. She had carried out no main

battery shoots, nor had action stations, damage-control and engine-room action drills been practised. All these were actually to have taken place during April. Nevertheless, the Flag Officer of her battle group, Konteradmiral Kummetz, embarked, with his Staff on 5 April, whereupon *Blücher* sailed in company with *Emden* for Swinemünde. The following day, fuel and stores were embarked, conferences were held between the Naval and Army Staffs and final preparations were made to receive 800 men of the 163rd Infantry Division whom she was detailed to take to Norway. After darkness fell, these men, together with their packs and equipment, stores and munitions came aboard and were distributed throughout the vessel.

At this time *Blücher* was still not fully operational and her magazines contained a high proportion of exercise ammunition. For security reasons this could not be landed, but was merely stowed below the live ammunition. The consequence

of this was that the Army's ammunition could not be stowed safely below the armoured deck, but had to be left on the upper deck, mostly in the torpedo workshop (compartment VII, port) and abaft the forward starboard torpedo tubes. Some were also stowed in the hangar where there were four 50kg aircraft bombs and the second Arado 196. This aircraft was empty of fuel, but the other, on the catapult, was operational although with a reduced fuel load. There was no room for the third aircraft.

TARGET OSLOFJORD

At 0600 on the 7th, the two cruisers sailed westwards once more, escorted by the torpedo-boats *Möwe* and *Albatros*, and joined the remainder of their group in Kiel, where they anchored. The night passed uneventfully until at 0300 the group weighed and sailed. Operation 'Weserübung' had begun. Steaming in line ahead the heavy cruiser preceded *Lützow* and *Emden*, with three torpedo-boats tailing behind, out of Kiel Bay and through the Great Belt, between the Danish islands of Langeland and Fyn to port, with Lolland and Sjaelland off to starboard. Steaming past the islands of Anholt and Laeso, the German squadron zigzagged its way through the Kattegat and out into the more exposed waters of the Skagerrak.

Just as the ships were entering the Skagerrak, *Albatros* received a submarine contact and flashed a warning to the Flag Ship at 1905. After several false alarms, this contact was definite. HMS *Triton* (Lieutenant-Commander E. F. Pizey) had penetrated the approaches to the Baltic and was now positioned at the northern end of the Kattegat, about midway between the Skaggen and the Swedish coast. Presented with

such a valuable target, Pizey fired a salvo from a difficult position at the German squadron, but was unable to obtain a hit; the torpedo tracks were sighted, combed and avoided. Then, while *Albatros* depth-charged the submarine and held her down, the remainder of the squadron made good their escape. The nearby *Sunfish* also sighted the German force, but was not in range for an attack. She was however, able to report their presence.

Darkness had by now fallen as the ships altered course northwards for the entrance of Oslofjord. The night was dark, but clear. As the squadron passed the outlying island of Torbjornskar just before midnight, the crews closed-up for action stations in preparation for the final approach. Suddenly a Norwegian patrol vessel loomed out of the darkness, probing with her searchlight. She opened fire on the torpedo-boat *Albatros* which had been ordered by the Flagship to capture her. The Norwegian was the *Pol III*, a converted whaler of 214 tonnes.

Aboard *Blücher*, the First Lieutenant, F.Kpt.Heymann, reported to the Captain that the ship was ready for action and was himself ordered to remain on the bridge. Shortly afterwards, the cruiser was illuminated by searchlights from the batteries on the islands of Bolarne (to port) and Ranoy (to starboard), which guarded the entrance of the fjord. The crack of a warning shot broke the quiet of the night, but the fall of shot could not be observed. A few moments later, all lights at the southern entrance to the fjord were doused. The Navigating Officer, K.Kpt.Forster, was of the opinion that the searchlights and warning shot were a protest rather than a serious intention of resistance. It is probable, however, that the battery commanders, being unsure, were reluctant to

Below: *Blücher* in her final form with Atlantic bow and funnel cap. She can be distinguished from *Admiral Hipper* by the shape of the bow and the absence of a roof to the admiral's bridge. (Drüppel)

open fire without positive identification. Batteries higher up the fjord were to have no such doubts. As for the German ships, Kummetz had issued precise orders to his group indicating the conditions under which they themselves could open fire. In essence these were: (a) open fire only on orders from the Flagship and then only if heavily engaged. Warning shots were to be ignored. (b) Searchlight illumination was to be countered with the ship's own searchlights, but permission to burn searchlights was not to be regarded as permission to open fire. The batteries at Ranoy and Bolarne fired about seven rounds in all, landing 75–300 metres astern of the ships.

Once clear of the batteries, at about 0046, *Blücher* ordered the squadron to stop in order to disembark the troops into the accompanying 'R'-boats. Six 'R'-boats took on infantrymen from the heavy cruiser and *Emden*, as the torpedo-boat *Kondor* was detached for patrol and a/s duties while the troops were being transhipped. At 0330, *Kondor*, *Albatros*, *R17* and *R21* were detached to occupy the naval port of Horten. By now most of the navigation lights ashore had been extinguished, causing Admiral Kummetz to reduce speed to seven knots to avoid forcing the Drobak narrows in darkness.

At about 0440, close to the narrows, *Blücher* was illuminated by the searchlights of a patrol vessel and from the shore. Bathed in ghostly light, the tension rose on the cruiser's crowded bridge, for not only had the First Lieutenant been ordered to remain there but the Admiral and his Staff, as well as the army officers, Major-Generals Englebrecht and Stussmann, with their aides, were present. It was impossible to locate the positions of gun batteries and fortifications along the shores of the fjord, which added to the difficulties of the fire-control officers. Suddenly, at 0521, the heavy gun battery on Oskarsborg, which lay close on the port bow, opened fire with its 28cm guns. There were, in fact, three guns in the fort: two 28cm 1891 Model Krupp weapons, known as 'Moses' and 'Aaron', and one 30.5cm gun. The latter was not in working order.* At this short range (about 1,700 metres, according to the Norwegians), it was impossible to miss and the first round struck the flak-control platform, causing heavy casualties, including the Second Gunnery Officer, Kpt.Lt.Pochammer. Inside the tower, however, there were no losses, although it rapidly filled with dense smoke.

Woldag had ordered the Gunnery Officer, K.Kpt.Engelmann, to open fire as soon as the Norwegians had fired, but no target could be distinguished and conditions in the foretop caused it to be evacuated immediately after the hit. Gun control was passed to the Third Gunnery Officer in the forward director, but he could not observe a target either and had a considerably lower vantage point. The medium and light flak, however, opened fire on anything ashore, houses, sheds, bushes – in fact, anything within range. On the bridge, shock, concussion and shell splinters caused havoc among the crowded personnel. Woldag, after ordering 'Open fire', rang for full speed ahead, hoping to force the narrows before incurring further damage.

His attempt was doomed to failure. As a diminutive Norwegian patrol vessel joined in the fight with her machine-guns, a second 28cm shell struck the aircraft hangar. Both aircraft, as well as port III 10.5cm mounting were destroyed and serious fires broke out at once. At the same moment, the 15cm battery at Drobak, only 400–600 metres to starboard, came into action with devastating effect. Twenty hits from twenty-five rounds knocked out 'B' flak control tower and the adjacent 10.5cm mounting, reducing the centre section between compartments V and IX to a twisted mass of wreckage. One of the first three hits damaged the rudder and engine-room telegraphs, leaving the rudder to port. The ship turned towards the shore, forcing Woldag to stop the starboard engine and go full astern on the port to keep her clear of the island of North Kaholmen which lay a few yards north of the main island.

Emergency steering from the tiller flat and the transmission of engine-room orders via the Action Centre and voice-pipes restored some degree of control, but at that moment, two severe shocks were felt to the hull. F.Kpt.Heymann believed initially that they had struck mines (which had been shown on Intelligence charts); others, including the Navigator, thought that they had grounded. Reports from the damage-control parties soon confirmed them as torpedo hits, however. The time was now about 0530. After three or four minutes, the batteries ceased fire as the cruiser, still making only about 15 knots, passed out of the arcs of the shore guns. Shortly afterwards, Woldag ordered his guns to cease fire.

BLÜCHER'S DEATH THROES

Astern of *Blücher*, as she had approached the narrows, was *Lützow*, followed by *Emden*. *Lützow* also received the attentions of the 28cm Kaholm guns which scored three hits, one of which knocked out the forward turret, leaving the ship devoid of ahead fire-power. *Blücher* was obviously seriously hit, on fire and, moreover, cut off from the remainder of the German squadron. Thiele, *Lützow*'s Captain, could not risk receiving the same treatment and, until the batteries had been neutralized, could not make any further progress towards his objective, Oslo. Accordingly, he assumed command of the squadron on orders from the Flagship and reversed course, intending to land his troops lower down the fjord. Only *Möwe*

*However, German inspection reports speak of three 28cm guns, all loaded and in working order.

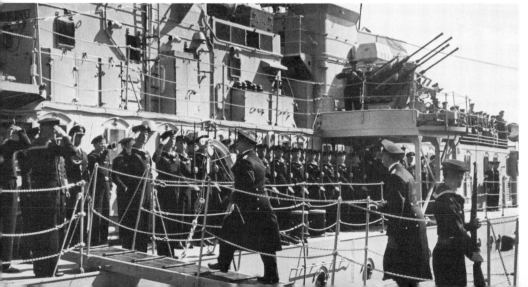

Below: Admiral Raeder visits *Emden*. Note the early installation of the vierling, in this 1940 picture. (Bundesarchiv-Koblenz)

and *Emden* heard further from the Flagship when, at 0626, she ordered the torpedo-boat up to help fight the fires. Thiele, however, countermanded this and instead ordered the landing of troops to continue leaving the cruiser to her fate beyond the narrows. This order probably saved the *Möwe* from the same fate as *Blücher*.

In the meantime, *Blücher*, despite all the hits was still under way, steering on her engines with a list of only 8°–12°. At this time no one had any reason to believe that she could not be saved. Actually, the situation was more serious than any of the ship's officers yet realized, with the possible exception of the Chief Engineer, K.Kpt.(Ing) Thannemann. Both torpedoes appeared to have struck in the vicinity of No. 2 generator room, between the two main turbine compartments. The lighting had failed as had both gyro compasses, and the 'tween decks between compartments V and VII were full of smoke. All power circuits, both a.c. and d.c., gradually failed rendering the communications circuits progressively useless. In a very short space of time, the Chief Engineer reported that the centre turbine had had to be stopped, leaving the ship moving only slowly ahead. Then both port and starboard turbines stopped, rendering the ship unmanoeuvrable. Having received the reports from the engine room, Woldag resolved to anchor, because Thannemann thought that the port and starboard turbines could possibly be restarted again in about an hour. In view of this fact, the cruiser's Captain decided not to beach her and sent K.Kpt.Czygan and Lt.z.S.Bertelsmann to the forecastle to organize an anchor party. With some difficulty, because of the list, the starboard anchor was finally let go, stopping the stricken ship.

By now, *Blücher* was in a very sorry condition. The fires in the hangar had ignited all the army stores and ammunition, producing an enormous sea of flame which linked up with the other upper-deck fires amidships. This resulted in one huge fire extending over the entire midship section, cutting off those forward from those aft. Again, the level of damage-control training was low, but the number and rapidity of the hits, together with the breakdown in communications, would have sorely tried the best-trained crew. In the Action Centre, the damage-control party had no real idea of the number or whereabouts of the various hits, so Woldag ordered Heymann

SINKING OF BLÜCHER IN OSLOFJORD

Askholmen.

Blücher is sinking 06.22

Hallangstangen.

Håøya

N. Kaholmen

9 7
10

Hit by torpedo
04.40

6

4
8

S. Kaholmen

3 1
2

Jeteén

Drøbak.

5

6° 04.21

Hit by artillery fire

Småskjær
950 m

3°

1. Seiersten AA battery 2 × 40 mm
2. Kopåsbattery 3 × 15 cm
3. Husvik battery 2 × 57 mm
4. The Main battery 3 × 28 cm
5. Nesset battery 2 × 57 mm
6. Kalkmølla battery 1 × 57 mm
7. Fugleredet battery 2 × 57 mm
8. Søndre battery 2 × 57 mm
9. Ekornredet battery 2 × 57 mm
10. Torpedo battery
■ Search-light

Storskjær
1600 m

2°

N

0   500 m   1000 m   2000 m   Oslofjord.

Frank Abelson

Below: *Blücher* seen here from the forward shelter deck of *Emden*. She does not yet seem to have the covered Flag bridge. (Bundesarchiv-Koblenz)

to find out. The scene on the upper deck was horrific. The port side, below No. 1 port 10.5cm gun mounting, was rent open and smoke and flames were pouring out, while all that remained of the torpedo workshop (where part of the army's ammunition had been stored) was a large hole in the deck. Ammunition was exploding in the fires around the hangar as well as in the vicinity of the starboard torpedo tubes where more of the stores had been secured. Steam and smoke issued from the funnel, and fire-fighting parties fought to control the many fires, but as most of the hoses had been riddled with holes from shell splinters, their efforts were in vain. Ammunition, both for the army's landing-parties and the ship's guns ready-use stock, was threatened by fire in many places throughout the ship. Some was hastily jettisoned overboard, some was returned to the magazines below the armoured

deck. Small arms munitions and hand-grenades exploded frequently adding to the general shambles on the upper deck. As the fires took greater hold and more hoses and pumps failed, the crew desperately turned to the small, hand-held extinguishers, which not surprisingly could not cope with the conflagration.

The First Lieutenant reported that the fires were getting out of hand despite the calm yet strenuous efforts of every available man. On receiving this report, Woldag stood down all guns crews, since no targets could be seen, and detailed them into fire-parties. In addition, he proposed to Kummetz that a torpedo-boat be called up to help the *Blücher*. Kummetz concurred but, as described earlier, *Möwe* received different orders from the new group commander, *Lützow*'s Captain, and so the cruiser remained isolated and alone.

Efforts to remove the wounded to less endangered areas continued in parallel with the fighting of the fires. From the fore top, scene of the original hit, the only way down was by means of ropes and hammocks because the companionway had been destroyed. Fresh winds fuelled the fires, with the resultant smoke greatly hindering the desperately embattled crew. Smoke canisters ignited by stray bullets added to the chaos and then the bombs in the aircraft hangar exploded, wrecking the entire area. On the upper deck, the torpedo crews fired off the starboard tubes, but could only remove the firing pistols from those to port because of the list and the danger to the troops in the water. This list which was only about 18° at the time, did not yet cause the Captain and Number One to give up hope of saving the ship, but they were very soon forced to change their minds.

Heymann had been assisting in the throwing of ammunition overboard near the forward starboard tubes and was on his way back up to the bridge when a huge explosion amidships rocked the ship, throwing up a mast-high column of smoke and flame. The 10.5cm magazine in compartment VII on the upper platform deck had blown up, probably because it had not been fully flooded because of lack of pressure on the fire mains.

On the engine control stand below, K.Kpt.(Ing) Grasser estimated the first torpedo to have struck No. 1 boiler room, the second, the forward turbine room. When the magazine exploded, the bulkheads between Nos. 1 and 2 boiler rooms, and probably also No. 3 boiler room, were ruptured as were the adjacent fuel bunkers. The grey smoke now became thick and black as the oil ignited. By about 0600, No. 1 boiler room, the forward turbine room, No. 2 generator room and compartment IV were flooded, while the after turbine was inoperable. With this state of affairs, it was useless to remain below and Grasser evacuated all the spaces.

The shock of this explosion had an immediate effect on the list which increased markedly. Woldag now realized that his ship was mortally hit and ordered the disembarking of soldiers and crew. K.Kpt.Zoppfel was ordered to lower the starboard cutter, which was successfully done, and the First Lieutenant detailed Kpt.Lt.Mikatsch to take over the disembarkation of the seriously wounded. The port cutter had been destroyed, and K.Kpt.Czygan had been unable to lower the

dinghies and motor boats because the cranes were unusable. All available rafts and mattresses were launched as the Captain ordered all hands on deck with life-jackets. Many of the kapok jackets secured to the rails had been destroyed by fire.

The ship was anchored about 300 metres from the small island of Askenholm, sternmost to the shore. The distance from her bows to the mainland was greater. Attempts to slip the cable and get closer to the shore to avoid losses in the icy waters failed. Amidships, the huge fire had now effectively split the ship in two with no communication between. In the bows were the Admiral, Captain and First Lieutenant, while in charge aft were the Chief Engineer and K.Kpt.Czygan. When the list had reached 45°, Czygan gave the order to abandon ship aft, and similar orders were given in the bows after three cheers had been raised for the Captain, Admiral and *Blücher*. By now the port rail was under water, and fuel oil, fortunately not on fire, was issuing from ruptured bunkers to the surface. At 0700, Woldag ordered 'Abandon ship' and the crew began to leave in a calm and disciplined manner. Many of the crew gave their life-jackets to the soldiers, some of whom had to be ordered to abandon their rifles and equipment. The cutter was badly damaged during its second trip to the rocky island and was unable to return to the ship for more wounded. Many men in the water were overcome by the fuel oil and severe cold as they struggled to reach the shore.

Blücher capsized at about 0730, flags flying, and sank slowly by the bows until out of sight. After she had disappeared several explosions were heard underwater and for a couple of hours oil continued to burn on the surface. The cold, wet and bedraggled ship's company and soldiers struggled ashore, many of the poor swimmers being more than half-drowned by the time they reached it. Others, overcome by exhaustion and the bitter cold, did not reach land alive.

To the south, the fate of the Flagship remained a mystery, with no radio communications and the gun and torpedo batteries barring the narrows still. During late morning and early afternoon, Stukas and other aircraft attacked the Oskarsborg fortress and *Lützow* joined in with her main armament. Under cover of this bombardment, the small motor vessel *Norden* broke through the narrows and reported back that the Flagship had in fact sunk. Even so, it was not until that evening that the fortress was finally secured – almost

undamaged despite the heavy sea and air bombardments – and the last survivors picked up from the islands by a torpedo-boat. With the way now open to Oslo, the occupation of the capital proceeded apace. Two months later, the whole country was in German hands.

Later investigation of the Kaholmen torpedo battery revealed it to be a bombproof redoubt in the rock at the waters' edge with three launching canals for torpedoes. In the torpedo preparation room above, there were two fully armed and fuelled torpedoes for each firing port. The torpedoes were lowered into the launching canals by steel cradles, a process which took about two minutes, and fired underwater. The sets of launch rails were parallel to one another and could not therefore fire an angled spread, although this was not a great drawback in the confined waters of the fjord.

POSTMORTEM

Unexpectedly, the *Blücher* affair raised its head again, some sixteen months after the loss of the ship, when an officer on the staff of General-Admiral Boehm, Admiral Commanding (Norway), a certain F.Kpt.Nieden, submitted a report to his senior officer in July 1941. It would appear that this officer had close contact with officers on the staff of XXI Army Corps and had been hearing their views about the conduct of Operation 'Weserübung' and the loss of *Blücher* in particular. His report indicated that in army circles, a false and damaging impression of the activities of the Navy and the actions of *Blücher*'s captain was current. Nieden detailed some of these criticisms to his superiors.

The army apparently believed that a smaller and less valuable ship should have been used to test the defences in the narrows and thereby avoid the loss of so many lives and much equipment – not to mention the ship itself. The captain of the cruiser was himself reproached on several grounds for:

(i) Not seeking to beach his ship after it had been heavily hit, in order to facilitate the landing of the troops, despite there being a suitable spot nearby.

(ii) Anchoring the ship in the middle of the fairway equidistant from either shore, so that troops who were needed on the Drobak side were in fact landed on Askenholm.

(iii) Rescue and landing of the troops – vital for the capture of Oslo – was not carried out quickly enough nor were boats put out. Floats were not inflated and launched.

Finally, the Army believed that it was only after an argument between Woldag and General Engelbrecht that the latter himself organized the rescue of the embarked troops. As a result of these experiences the Army concluded that in any future combined operation, the Army must assume overall command, with the Navy being used only for transport purposes. It was not acceptable to them that, until the disembarkation of troops, the Navy should be in command. They considered that in this instance, command should have passed, at the latest, to the Army when the ship was disabled. Similar, and to some extent more critical, conclusions were being drawn from the experiences of the 69th Infantry Division in Bergen, reinforcing the view that the Navy should play only the transport role, subordinated to the Army.

In forwarding this report, Nieden pointed out that General Gudovius, who was responsible for the Army's historical records, had visited Drobak in July 1941 and that unless steps were taken, he would receive only the Army's version of events, to the detriment of the Navy. He also noted that from his observations he did not believe there to have been a suitable place to beach the ship, and that it was undoubtedly the current which had swung the ship away from the shore while anchored.

On 30 July, Admiral Boehm forwarded this report to Grand Admiral Raeder with the comment that so far as the question of argument between the Naval and Army commanders was concerned, the General had reported to him shortly after the event that the conduct of the ship's crew and their efforts to rescue the soldiers had greatly impressed him. Nevertheless, he deemed it necessary to clarify matters in view of Nieden's report.

Raeder agreed and ordered further reports to be obtained from the surviving members of the ship's officers, now scattered throughout Europe and the Fleet, particularly Kummetz who was now head of the Torpedo Inspectorate and the former First Lieutenant, Heymann, currently serving as Director of the torpedo depot in Lorient. Woldag had been killed on 16 April 1940, when the aircraft in which he was a passenger crashed into Oslofjord. The Chief Engineer, Thannemann, too seems to have disappeared from the scene. However, all the surviving officers were asked to comment.

While this was going on, Nieden interviewed Dr Ing Paul Goerz, formerly a director of Blaupunkt Radio, who had been serving as a reserve officer on the staff of General Engelbrecht. This officer alleged that, unlike other ships in the group, *Blücher* had not instructed the embarked troops in emergency procedures while on passage. At the time of the action, the troops were below decks, uninformed of events and awaiting orders which never came. Goerz reported that in the absence of any orders from the Naval officers, the Army officers opened doors and hatches to let their men out. He also remarked on the general shortage of life-jackets. Finally, he said that while Woldag and Engelbrecht were on the island of Askenholm, the former wished to shoot himself, but was prevented by the General.

By the winter of 1941, reports were being received from some of the officers questioned. None could supply any evidence of an argument between Woldag and Engelbrecht and Kummetz specifically denied that such an event had taken place. Most, however, could recall the great shortage of life-jackets. Kpt.Lt.Gratthof remarked that a few hundred inflatable type were issued on passage – mostly to engine-room personnel. A great number of these were freely given to Army men and the remainder were given up later on orders. Ob.Ltn.z.S.Nollau confirmed that many of the Marks life-rafts were destroyed by shellhits or consumed in the fires. Those that remained were launched and used by the Army, but a number drifted ashore empty. K.Kpt.Czygan, now serving with Flag Officer (U-Boats) noted that the embarked troops were not issued with life-jackets at first, as the taking aboard of large numbers of these might have compromised the

secrecy of the operation. It was only after strenuous pleading that some supplies were received from the depot in Kiel. Even then, there were reportedly only 800 for 2,200 men aboard. Finally, Czygan reported that the troops *were* instructed in emergency procedures while on passage.

This officer also gave reasons as to why the ship was not beached. In his view there was no suitable spot on the shore line, the ship was unmanoeuvrable and the raging fires hindered all concerned. It was hoped that on anchoring, the bows would swing to starboard enabling the men to land more easily. The former First Lieutenant, Kpt.z.S.Heymann, confirmed these reasons, adding that the ship was not at first thought to be mortally hit, and she was anchored because the Chief Engineer had reported that he could probably restart the outer turbines in about an hour's time. When the true state of the ship was realized, there was no power to beach the ship even if there were a suitable place. The absence of any place to beach was confirmed by Ob.Lt.(Ing) Hirtz, now Chief Engineer of *T17*, who had been Battery Officer on Oskarsborg for a month after the loss of *Blücher*.

Ob.Lt.z.S.Frhr.von Freyberg, who was serving as an aide to Admiral Kummetz at the time of the attack, gave some details as to why the squadron acted as it did. Spies had reported that the mine barrage across the fjord was electrically fired from the shore, so that it would have been useless to go in behind minesweepers.* It was decided, therefore, to transit the narrows at as fast a speed as possible in the hope of breaking through unscathed. *Blücher* had been chosen to lead because of her strong medium and light quick-firing armament, which would be invaluable in a close-quarters action.

Finally, on the question of the ship's boats and their non-use, Ob.Lt.(Ing) Schuller, now Engineer Officer in *U568*, reported that he had been responsible for the maintenance of all boats. During the passage, they had been prepared, overhauled and were ready for use. However, their stoker crews were at action stations in the 'tween deck where they had sustained casualties from the shelling. Then fires in the hangar had destroyed some boats and lack of power prevented the remainder from being launched. When an emergency power supply was available, the boats on one side had been

destroyed, while on the other side, fire had burned out the crane's electrical system.

With these reports, SKL appears to have satisfied itself that the Navy had conducted itself honourably in the action, and that the Army's accusations were unfounded. The reports, however, probably do not tell the whole story. It is unlikely that there was no panic at all among the embarked troops, cooped-up below decks in a sinking ship. One officer did, in fact, note that some troops had attempted to get out of the scuttles to reach the upper decks. Their webbing equipment caused several to get stuck and only a few succeeded. He records panic below decks, but he is the only one to have done so.

The loss of *Blücher*, coming as it did at the same time as that of two light cruisers and ten destroyers, was a harsh blow to the Kriegsmarine. The other losses were arguably due to the unexpected fortunes of war, but the loss of the heavy cruiser was wholly avoidable. Leaving aside some of the detailed post-loss acrimony between Army and Navy, there is little doubt that better Intelligence and planning could have prevented the disaster. The Army was to some extent correct in its castigation of the Navy for attempting to force the narrows with the cruiser, but their suggestion of using a smaller ship instead would not have prevented the loss of the cruiser, because the battery commander would have held his fire until a large target was in his sights.

German Intelligence had reported incorrectly that a mine barrier existed, but did not know of the existence of the torpedoes. On the other hand, they were aware of the presence of the heavy guns on Kaholm. Thus the guns and mines (torpedoes) presented an effective barrier to the squadron, to which they had no counter. In essence, the Germans were relying on bluff and confusion in order to break through the narrows without a shot being fired. When this failed, the ships were at an immense disadvantage, steaming in line ahead in constricted waters while being engaged by heavy shore batteries. Oslo, as the capital of the country, naturally had its approaches well-defended and these not having been neutralized, heavy losses were certain. In this instance, it would perhaps have been better to abandon the idea of bluff and instead mount a pre-emptive paratroop or glider-borne attack on the islands as was later done at Eben-Emal. Alternatively, a merchant ship might have landed reconnaissance and sabotage parties during the hours of darkness while passing the narrows. As it was, in the Navy's haste to forestall the British in obtaining bases in Norway, and the need to camouflage its role as the aggressor, risks were taken which, in the case of the Oslo operation, did not come off.

The wreck of *Blücher* still lies unsalvaged on the bottom of Oslofjord, upside-down and wedged bow and stern between two rocks. Large quantities of fuel and ammunition remain aboard which cannot be removed safely, and although the wreck is now owned by the ship-breakers, Einar Høvding of Oslo, it seems the cruiser is destined to remain in her grave 70 metres below the surface.

*Subsequently a mine depot, with sufficient mines to form a four-row barrage, electrically fired, was in fact found on the small islet of Kaholm.

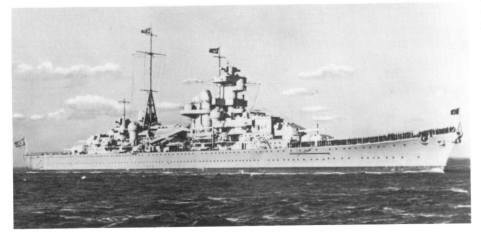

Below: *Blücher* seen at Kiel, 23 October 1939 greeting Prien's *U47* returning from Scapa Flow. Note that at this time the cruiser still has her bow shield but lacks radar. (Gröner)

9: ADMIRAL HIPPER: NORWAY & THE ARCTIC, 1940

Right: *Admiral Hipper* at Cuxhaven in April 1940. Note radar mattress at foretop, enclosed admiral's bridge and main forward searchlight. (W. B. Bilddienst)

Admiral Hipper commissioned for service on 29 April 1939, under the command of Kpt.z.S.Helmuth Heye. The selection of Heye to captain the new cruiser caused considerable comment in Kriegsmarine circles at the time, for he was junior to several more obvious candidates for the post, and indeed had only been promoted Kapitan zur See on 1 January 1939. Heye, a Saarlander, born in 1895, had joined the Kaisermarine almost twenty-five years earlier and had seen service in cruisers and U-boats during the 1914–18 war. Between the wars he had held several appointments, including command of a torpedo-boat and later, a torpedo-boat half-flotilla, as well as serving in staff appointments with the Naval Command.

Because she was the first of a new class of cruiser, with complex technological innovations, the ship was involved in long and exhaustive trials following her entry into service. As a result of these it had become obvious that a number of modifications were necessary if the full fighting efficiency of the design were to be realized. In particular, shortcomings had been exposed in the hull's seaworthiness, for it was found that the bluff bows and lack of sheer and flare forward combined to make the forecastle extremely wet in anything of a sea. Furthermore, the conning and Admiral's bridge arrangements were found to be unsatisfactory, and smoke was a problem on the tower platforms. To correct these defects of design, the cruiser was taken into dockyard hands in July 1939 for modification. During the course of this refit, a raked, 'Atlantic' bow was fitted, the bridges were modified and enclosed and a funnel cap was added. The refit considerably delayed *Admiral Hipper* in achieving 'battle ready' status, and at the outbreak of war on 1 September 1939, she was still running trials out of Kiel.

Trials and working-up continued in the Baltic for the next month or so, during which time she was visited by the Soviet Gunnery Commission, who witnessed a practice shoot against *Hessen*, when six hits were obtained. (Their interest of course stemmed from the proposed purchase of her incomplete sister, *Lützow*). Early in November, the cruiser landed her ammunition at Kiel and moved into the Blöhm & Voss yard for further modification and inspection. Here she remained until un-docked on 15 December and shifted to the fitting-out berth, but it was not until 8 January 1940 that she was able to recommence trials. The winter of 1939–40, however, was a harsh one and *Admiral Hipper*, like many other Kriegsmarine

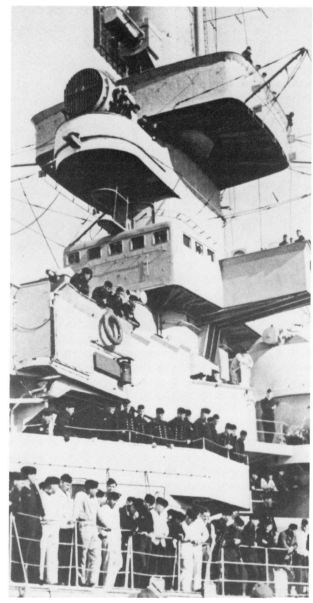

units, found her training severely disrupted by ice. In consequence, she was far from fully worked-up when ordered west to Wilhelmshaven for operational duty on 31 January. Here she was fitted with radar while lying idle until 17 February.

During the forenoon of the 18th, *Admiral Hipper* weighed from the Wangerooge Channel and sailed on her first operational sortie in company with the battlecruisers *Scharnhorst* and *Gneisenau* under the command of Admiral Marschall, the Fleet Commander (with his flag in *Gneisenau*). The object of the sortie, code-named 'Nordmark' was to attack British shipping between the Shetlands and Norway. By early afternoon on the 19th, the squadron stood to the east of the Viking Bank, on the latitude of the Shetland Islands, having swept the central North Sea without sighting anything At 1455, the operation was ordered to be broken off in the absence of targets and the squadron reversed course, reaching their base at Wilhelmshaven without further incident on the 20th. Despite its lack of material results, the sortie was a welcome opportunity for the new cruiser to work-up her crew, and much valuable experience was gained. This operation also highlighted the problems associated with her machinery, trouble being experienced with her boilers and the starboard turbine. It was to be a portent for all her future sorties. *Admiral Hipper* remained at Wilhelmshaven until 20 March, when she sailed, escorted by *Möwe* and *Wolf*, for Cuxhaven, to prepare for Operation 'Weserübung', the invasion of Norway.

TARGET TRONDHEIM

Admiral Hipper had been chosen to lead Group 2, charged with the capture and occupation of Trondheim. Accompanying the cruiser would be the destroyers *Jacobi*, *Riedel*, *Heinemann* and *Eckholdt*, under the overall command of Heye. Embarked in the ships of his command were 1,700 troops for the occupying force.

After completing embarkation of the troops on 6 April, the ships of Group 2 sailed from Cuxhaven, joining *Scharnhorst* and *Gneisenau* to the north of Nordeney during the early hours of the 7th. Throughout that day, the squadron steamed northwards in rising seas, until at 1850 they were abreast Utsire. A southerly gale was blowing, with heavy seas and hazy visibility, making conditions difficult for ships and seamen; for the troops it was a nightmare. Conditions remained poor, with the additional unpleasantness of rain, during the remainder of the 7th and into the 8th.

The poor weather and heavy seas had scattered the ships of the combined Groups 1 (bound for Narvik) and 2, particularly affecting the destroyers. Never renowned for their seakeeping, they suffered considerably in the heavy weather and with a following sea were difficult to keep on course. One of these destroyers, *Bernd von Arnim* (K.Kpt.Rechel), encountered a British destroyer, *Glowworm* (Lieutenant-Commander Roope), which had been detached from a force consisting of the battlecruiser *Renown* and four destroyers under the command of Admiral Whitworth, engaged upon Operation 'Wilfred', the British operation to mine the Norwegian Leads.

Glowworm had lost a man overboard and had requested to be allowed to search for him. The two destroyers engaged in a brief but ineffectual gun duel as the mountainous seas made the destroyers, especially the German, lively platforms.

Bernd von Arnim signalled the Flag reporting the engagement and requesting support. In response to this signal, Admiral Marschall detached *Admiral Hipper* to the assistance of the destroyer at 0922, when the cruiser was some 100 nautical miles to the north-west of the entrance to Trondheim Fjord. Heye turned about and punched through the heavy seas towards the last reported position of the action. Hampered by the seas, it was some fifteen minutes before the lookouts on the foretop flak control position reported several smoke trails ahead off the starboard bow.

Under the prevailing conditions, and with the destroyers wreathed in funnel and gun smoke, it was extremely difficult for the cruiser's lookouts to distinguish friend from foe, although it was initially believed that the destroyer to starboard was the enemy. However, this destroyer immediately morsed the cruiser and identified herself as the German ship, whereupon Heye gave the Gunnery Officer permission to open fire at 0957. Two minutes later, *Admiral Hipper* opened fire in anger for the first time with 'A' and 'B' turrets at a range of 8,400 metres. Heye's tactics were to hold the enemy destroyer ahead in order to avoid danger from her torpedoes, while accepting the consequent disadvantage of being able to engage only with his forward turrets. During the first phase of the action, the cruiser fired five salvoes, three from 'A' and 'B' turrets and then with 'D' turret as the after arcs opened and 'A' turret became wooded. After the third salvo, *Glowworm* altered course hard to port and then began to use smoke very effectively. She launched half her torpedo outfit (five torpedoes*) in a first attack, and made an enemy sighting report to *Renown*, but the launching of the torpedoes had been observed by the German ship, who managed to avoid all of them with but little effort, the torpedoes passing closely down the port and starboard sides. At the same time, one of *Admiral Hipper*'s shells struck home in the forward superstructure of *Glowworm*, wrecking the wireless office. Only part of her signal got through.

Glowworm was now almost, but not quite, hidden by her smoke-screen. The cruiser could, however, see her masthead, and in a brief second phase, fired two more salvoes into the smoke before the British destroyer turned once more, emerged from the smoke and launched a second torpedo attack. These torpedoes, too, were out-manoeuvred and at the same time part of *Admiral Hipper*'s eighth salvo struck the destroyer on the starboard side in the region of the forward funnel. The 10.5cm flak armament of the cruiser had now also received permission to open fire and scored several hits on the bridge, amidships and on No. 1 gun. Most of the destroyer's fire, in contrast, fell wide, except for one near miss to starboard. Having expended all her torpedoes, *Glowworm* turned away to port and re-entered the smoke-screen, hoping

---

Glowworm was the only destroyer of the 'G' class to receive quintuple tubes. This was a trial installation for the intended fitment of quintuple banks to the subsequent 'I', 'J' and 'K' class destroyers.

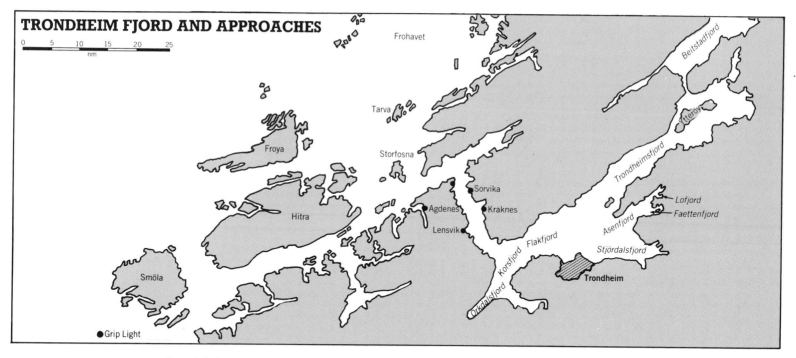

for a brief respite, but *Hipper* was fitted with radar and was able to fire a few rounds blind. Heye now resolved to chase the British ship through the smoke, and proceeded to do so. *Glowworm*, with all her torpedoes gone, and only three 4.7in guns left in action, was now hit repeatedly, the range now so short that even 2cm guns joined in. Under the circumstances, Roope decided on the only possible thing – to try and ram his adversary. Realizing what the British captain intended, Heye attempted to manoeuvre his ship so as to ram the destroyer instead, but the cruiser could not answer her helm quickly enough in the heavy seas and the destroyer hit her under the starboard anchor, ripping the hull as far aft as the forward starboard torpedo tubes.

Glowworm fell away aft, smoking and listing. At 1011, fire control aboard the cruiser was quickly shifted to the after director, under the control of the Third Gunnery Officer, and a few more rounds were fired from 'D' turret before it became clear that the destroyer had ceased fire and was obviously sinking. Heye, too, ceased fire and prepared to rescue survivors, which operation lasted about one hour before being broken off. As a result of this commendable action, some thirty-one survivors were picked up, but Roope was not among them. It was not until after the war that the full story of *Glowworm*'s lone action became known, when Lieutenant-Commander Roope was posthumously awarded the VC.

The damage to *Admiral Hipper* was extensive, but had little effect upon the fighting efficiency of the ship. The 40m-long gash extended from just below the starboard anchor to the forward starboard tubes. The torpedo tube mounting itself was destroyed. Internally, the refrigerated store and compressor rooms, as well as the meat stores had been damaged and flooded. Part of the double bottom space had been ruptured, opening up, among others, seven oil bunkers with the consequent loss of 253m³ of fuel oil. Counter-flooding reduced the list to just over 4° with about 528 tonnes of water in the ship.

Admiral Hipper had now been detached with her escorting destroyers to Trondheim for the landing. During the afternoon a British Sunderland flying-boat was briefly taken under fire but without effect, and it could now be assumed that the German intentions were known.★ In consequence of this, at 1750 Heye launched one of his aircraft, crewed by Ob.Lt.Techam and Lt.Polzen, to reconnoitre the Frohavet and western approaches to Trondheim. The air crew were given strict orders not to overfly Trondheim, and because it would be dangerous to attempt to recover the aircraft while so near to the coast, they were ordered to land in a fjord south of Trondheim and await the successful conclusion of the invasion. The aircraft completed its task, reporting the complete absence of any hostile British warships and then landed as ordered. Both aircraft and crew were captured by the Norwegians. Later, the aircraft fell into British hands and was eventually flown over to Britain for evaluation and test purposes.★★ The German force closed the coast and entered the Frohavet just after midnight on the 9th. *Hipper* led the four destroyers, as the darkened ships moved steadily on at 25 knots, leaving the Tarva islands off to port, and shaped course

★This aircraft had been dispatched at the request of Admiral Forbes (C in C, Home Fleet) to search for the German force. However, it identified the Germans as a battlecruiser, two cruisers and two destroyers, steering west, thus causing Forbes to haul off the British Fleet to the north-west, i.e., in the wrong direction.

★★The aircraft crashed on 26 April 1940 while landing at Rhu on the Gare Loch near the Marine Aircraft Experimental Establishment, Helensburgh, and the pilot, Commander C. W. Byas, RN, was injured as the machine overturned.

for the entrance to Krakvagsfjord. Sea room was now considerably reduced as the squadron penetrated deeper into the island-studded and indented Norwegian coastline. Ahead lay the Agdenes massif under which Heye turned his force to port for the approach to the entrance of Trondheimsfjord. Here the first evidence of a Norwegian presence was noticed when a solitary patrol vessel challenged the intruders, to which *Admiral Hipper* made the reply, 'Have orders from government to proceed to Trondheim. No unfriendly intent.' This clearly puzzled the Norwegian for she had been left well astern before her suspicions were aroused. In consequence, all she could do was signal 'Stop', which the Germans not surprisingly ignored, and fire some red flares, thus giving the alarm.

By 0404, the invaders had rounded Agdenes point and turned SSE to run down Trondheimsfjord itself, where the first resistance was offered by the Norwegians. Guarding the northern side of the fjord was a coastal battery at Hysnes which opened fire as the ships passed. Three rounds fell short and wide before *Admiral Hipper* illuminated the battery and silenced it with eight rounds from 'C' and 'D' turrets. No further resistance was offered by the Norwegians who, in any case, had no naval forces in the area, other than one or two small, converted trawlers. Three destroyers were detached to secure the battery with their embarked troops, while the cruiser and *Eckholdt* continued to Trondheim itself, anchoring there at 0525. Both remaining aircraft were flown off during the forenoon to reconnoitre and mop-up any unsubdued batteries, which they did quite successfully. With the troops safely ashore, *Admiral Hipper*'s main task was finished and although her fire-power would have been useful in the event of an attempt by British or French forces to re-take Trondheim, the pressing need was to get the cruiser home for repairs.

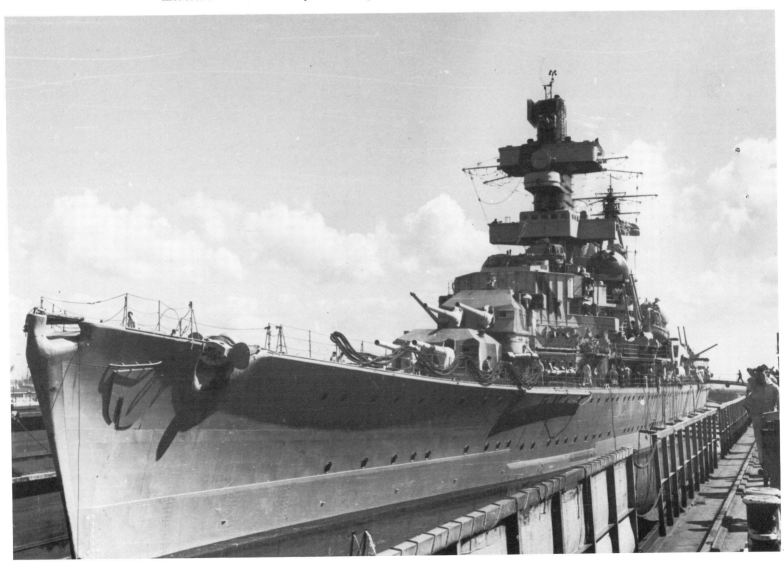

Fuel shortage and defects prevented all but one destroyer, *Eckoldt*, from sailing with *Admiral Hipper* on the 10th, and even the cruiser had precious little margin to spare. Once again, however, bad weather affected the German plans, forcing *Eckoldt* to turn back and leave the cruiser to continue alone. By good fortune, *Admiral Hipper* did not run into the British Fleet, under Admiral Forbes during the night of 10th/11th, for in the early hours of the 11th, the two forces were little more than 30 nautical miles apart. Had the opponents met, things might have been rather unpleasant for the German cruiser, for the British force consisted of the battle-ships *Rodney*, *Valiant*, *Warspite*, the aircraft carrier *Furious* and three heavy cruisers, *Berwick* (whom she would meet again), *Devonshire* and *York*. However, these were still mainly pre-radar days, and Forbes was occupied by preparations for an air strike on Tronheim planned for the 11th, in consequence, the two forces missed each other. On the 12th,

Admiral Hipper effected a rendezvous with the two returning battlecruisers, under Admiral Lütjens, south-west of Egersund and, avoiding a massed British air attack thanks to low visibility, sleet and snow, arrived in the Jade that evening.

OPERATION 'JUNO'

At Wilhelmshaven, repairs to the heavy cruiser's damage lasted until May 1940. On the 8th she began post-repair trials and then spent the remainder of May in the eastern Baltic before returning to Kiel on the 29th. Here she prepared for her next sortie which, once again, was to be in company with the two battlecruisers. This operation, code-named 'Juno' was intended to relieve pressure on German forces in the Narvik region and to attack the British base at Harstaad. The heavy units, under the command of Admiral Marschall sailed from Kiel in the forenoon of 4 June, escorted by the destroyers *Galster*, *Lody*, *Steinbrinck* and *Schoemann*. Passing through

Left: *Admiral Hipper* docking to repair *Glowworm* action damage. Bow emblem has been removed, but the support plate remains. (Bundesarchiv-Koblenz)
Right: Damage to the forward tubes caused by *Glowworm*. (Bundesarchiv-Koblenz)

Right: Hull damage to *Admiral Hipper* caused by *Glowworm* in April 1940. (Bundesarchiv-Koblenz)

the Belts and clearing the entrance to the Skagerrak mine-fields at about 1300 on the 5th, Marschall set course to the north-west at 24 knots. Throughout the day, signals had been received from Gruppe (West), giving deciphered intercepts with positions of various British warships, including submarines; *Severn*, in particular, being known to be in the Trondheim-Stadtlandet area. These signals continued the following day with a warning of heavy units leaving the Shet-lands on a northerly course, which might have been sailed to intercept the German squadron or its supply oiler, *Dith-marschen*, which had sailed ahead of the fleet.

By the evening of the 6th, the oiler had met her customers and begun to oil the battlecruisers, while *Admiral Hipper* took care of the destroyers' requirements, and then topped up from the oiler. By this time, Marschall's forces were on the latitude of the Lofoten Islands to the south-east of Jan Mayen Island. The heavy cruiser and the destroyers were ordered to take on maximum fuel in order to allow the force to press on norther-easterly as far as possible before the attack on Harstaad, planned for the night of 8th/9th. Oiling took an inordinate length of time because of inexperience and technical pro-blems, and it was not until 1745 on the 7th that all ships were fully bunkered.

Two hours after oiling had been completed, Admiral Marschall called a Captains' conference to outline the squadron orders and to air views on a plan of action. Such an event had probably not taken place since the Napoleonic and Nelsonian era! To stop the ships, put out boats and sit down to a conference on the high seas in the middle of the twentieth century was a strange action indeed. By now, Marschall had serious doubts as to the wisdom of his orders, for there had been a conspicuous lack of Intelligence regarding his target and its possible defences.

The plan of attack assumed adequate information as to the mine, boom and net defences of the Harstaad base, as well as good aerial reconnaissance information concerning the enemy ships likely to be present. Both were vital for without them the Fleet could well be hazarded on a strike into thin air. *Blücher*'s unhappy end was uppermost in the minds of many, and if the enemy fleet was not there, could the port installa-tions be effectively destroyed *even if they could be distinguished from seaward*? Was it worth risking the Fleet for a few depots and stores? Towards the end of the conference, further U-boat reports were received from Gruppe (West) which indicated three groups of ships between Tromsö and Har-staad, all steaming *west*. Earlier reports during the day had all given westerly courses, now here were more. Was the enemy evacuating? In view of the seriousness of the German position in Narvik, this seemed incredible. Finally, just before the conference broke up, a signal was handed to Marschall with a reconnaissance report from an aircraft which had managed to overfly Harstaad. Within the text of this signal were the words '. . . over Harstaad fired on by gunboat . . .' *Only* a gunboat, was there nothing else there?

For Marschall this was the final proof that he was on a wild-goose chase. He concluded that evacuation was taking place and that for him to attack west-bound ships would produce more fruitful results. Prior to this he had assumed that they were returning empty. Actually, the aircraft's sighting report had been timed at 1110 hrs and had been delayed in decoding. It was thus ten hours out of date, but it arrived at a crucial moment and made up Marschall's mind for him. He had made the correct decision, for the British were evacuating. Nevertheless, he was to suffer the consequences later for opposing the orders of Gruppe (West).

At 0033 on the 8th, Marschall signalled his squadron detail-ing his intentions, which were basically to attack the cruiser, two destroyers and two steamers, reported at 1325 the pre-vious day, to the north-west of the Lofoten Islands. *Admiral Hipper* and *Scharnhorst* would fly off their aircraft on recon-naissance patrols at 0800. At 0500, Marschall signalled his intention to attack the convoy to Admiral Saalwachter at Gruppe (West), getting, an hour later, a tart reminder that his main target orders were Harstaad. By this time he had disposed his ships in line abreast, sixteen kilometres apart, to sweep for the convoy, and *Admiral Hipper* had just sighted a ship. Another signal from Gruppe (West) now ordered the cruiser and destroyers to deal with the convoy then detach to Trondheim. The battlecruisers were still to attack Harstaad. Shore Command's interference was becoming intolerable.

Marschall ordered *Admiral Hipper* and her destroyers to investigate the sighted vessel which had by now disappeared in a rain squall. After relocating her, and her previously un-sighted consort, then identifying them finally as a trawler and an oil tanker, *Hipper* was ordered to sink the trawler while *Scharnhorst* was allocated the tanker. The two vessels were the 530-ton naval trawler, *Juniper*, armed with one 4in gun, and the 5,666-ton naval oiler, *Oil Pioneer*.

At 0700, the heavy cruiser's main armament was loaded and trained on the target, but in the absence of any reaction on the part of the trawler, as well as its low fighting power, Heye checked the main battery and instead opened fire with the starboard 10.5cm guns at a range of 2,000 metres. After the second salvo, hits were observed and the target began to list and smoke badly. There was still no reply from the trawler, which was obviously seriously damaged. Heye ceased fire and came about to inspect the enemy vessel which had still not abandoned ship and indeed appeared to break away to star-board. On seeing this, the cruiser opened fire once more, this time with the port battery scoring further hits. One minute later, fire was checked again as the trawler's list increased until finally, she capsized and sank. One man was rescued by the cruiser which had expended 97 rounds in sinking the little trawler. In the meantime, the tanker had been set on fire and, eventually, torpedoed by the destroyer *Schoemann*.

Later that morning, the aircraft were catapulted off for reconnaissance and the ships resumed their patrol line. At 0850, *Galster* reported smoke, bearing 080° which she pro-ceeded to investigate. An hour and a half later she was able to distinguish its originator, a merchantman steaming north. *Admiral Hipper* altered course to intercept and worked up speed to 32 knots. After twenty minutes, she too could see the smoke of a vessel which Marschall ordered the cruiser to sink. The target appeared to be a twin-funnelled, armed merchant-

man, and at a range of 13,000 metres, *Admiral Hipper* fired two rounds across her bows. The steamer, however, continued to hold her course and speed because, it later transpired, she believed herself under air attack and did not realize that the cruiser in the distance was German! Since her warning shots had had no effect, the cruiser fired two salvoes from her forward turrets and then altered course to open the after arcs. With all turrets bearing, seven salvoes were fired, with hits being observed after the second. The target was now stopped, listing and on fire. Her crew took to the boats, whereupon Heye ceased fire. Shortly afterwards, the burning ship sank. A total of 54 rounds of 20.3cm were required to send her to the bottom – the cruiser's fire-control crew had been confused at the start of the action by the destroyer *Lody* which had unexpectedly opened fire herself. The cruiser's first fall of shot, therefore, appeared to have an extremely wide spread. This resulted in unnecessary corrections until it was realized that *two* ships were engaging. *Lody* also fired torpedoes at the sinking ship although ordered not to do so. Both missed!

The victim, from whom 119 survivors were picked up, was the 19,840-ton *Orama*, returning empty from Norway. A second vessel in the vicinity, *Atlantis*, was a hospital ship, and under the rules of the Geneva Convention, was not attacked.

At 1305 on the same day (8th), Admiral Marschall detached the cruiser and destroyers to Trondheim for operations against convoy traffic, while he would press on and sweep the Tromso–Vestfjord region for enemy activity. For security reasons, Flag Officer (Cruisers), Admiral Lütjens, was ordered to pass Marschall's intention on to Gruppe (West) after arrival at Trondheim. While on passage to Trondheim, several signals were picked up concerning the action between the battlecruisers and the aircraft carrier *Glorious* with her two attendant destroyers. By now, however, *Admiral Hipper* was too far away to be of assistance and in fact anchored in Trondheim the following morning. Later that afternoon, the two battlecruisers entered Trondheim and anchored too.

On the 10th, Admiral Marschall decided that, in view of the now confirmed British evacuation, there was no time to lose in making a second strike at the convoy routes. Accordingly, he sailed that morning with *Gneisenau, Admiral Hipper* and three destroyers, *Galster, Schoemann* and *Steinbrinck*. (*Scharnhorst* had received torpedo damage during the action with *Glorious*). Off the Frohavet, *Hipper* sighted a diving submarine which Marschall concluded had probably reported the German squadron, and this fact, coupled with later reports of heavy concentrations of British warship groups to the north, made it appear that the German squadron had scant chance of success. Gruppe (West) was of the same opinion, and during the evening of the 11th, ordered the ships to return to Trondheim. *Admiral Hipper* remained there until the 20th, when an operation was mounted with the twofold objective of (i) creating a diversion for the homeward-bound and damaged *Scharnhorst* and (ii) attacking the British auxiliary cruiser patrol line south-west of Iceland.

Gneisenau, Hipper and *Galster* weighed from Trondheim late in the afternoon of the 20th and steamed north-eastwards up the Frohavet, entering the inner leads off Torvik and hugging the coast as far as Vaeroya before altering course and into the open sea by the Kaura lighthouse. Having left the sheltered waters under the coast, the ships met heavy weather as they struck northwards across the approaches to Foldafjord, with a large swell preventing speeds higher than nineteen knots, and making it impossible to zizag. Just after 2300, *Hipper*'s lookouts reported mastheads to the north-east, but on further investigation, these proved to be cliffs, probably in the Vikna area. While the bridge watch was concentrating on this, a torpedo explosion was observed on *Gneisenau* which was now some twenty miles east of Vikna. To the watch aboard *Admiral Hipper*, it was not clear where the torpedo had come from, and then a second was seen between *Admiral Hipper* and *Gneisenau*, causing the cruiser to take violent avoiding action.

The torpedoes had been fired by HMS *Clyde* (Lieutenant-Commander Ingram), on patrol in the area. She had sighted the German squadron at 2309 (German time) about eight nautical miles to the south-east, and had commenced an attack in the rough seas and poor visibility. At 2332, Ingram fired his six bow tubes with a track angle of 70° (i.e., almost beam on) aiming one length ahead of *Gneisenau*, estimating her speed at twenty knots. At 2336, one of these struck the battlecruiser on the starboard bow just aft of the anchor. Little shock was experienced aboard the ship, and apart from the bows, little damage was evident. Still in a port turn to avoid the torpedoes, the ship slewed around almost 90° and continued with little loss of speed. The torpedo hit in either compartment XX or XXI, flooding the foremost messdecks and fuel bunkers, but did not affect the magazine spaces of 'A' turret. *Galster* searched for the submarine without success as the damaged battlecruiser altered course a further 30° to port to prevent the heavy swell breaking over the bows. Course was reversed at 0005 and by 1005, the squadron was anchored once more in Trondheim. Both battlecruisers were now damaged and in need of dockyard repair.

Clyde, trimmed heavy because of the high seas, dived to avoid counter-attack and went far deeper than intended. To 90 metres, in fact, and because the stern was trimmed down, the depth at the after ends was about eighteen metres lower still. The pressure at this depth on the flat stern casing of this type of boat, bent support pillars in the engine room but otherwise, she escaped unscathed. Ingram, however, was later censured by Max Horten (Vice-Admiral Submarines) for not adhering to instructions for salvo firing, which stated that the point of aim of a spread should be the centre of the target. Since he over-estimated the target speed (actually eighteen knots), all but one of his spread missed ahead, and the one hit only just struck the battlecruiser's bows.

ARCTIC SORTIE

Admiral Hipper remained anchored in Trondheim Fjord until 27 June, the only incident involving one of her catapult aircraft, T3+DH. This aircraft, flown-off for an anti-submarine patrol on the 26th, crewed by Lt.z.S.Frendenthal and Unteroffizier Koch, had sighted a submarine at 0225, east of

Nordoyan light, on the northern side of Folda Fjord. An attack was made from 300 metres and two 50kg bombs dropped, straddling the boat. A second attacking pass using 2cm cannon fire appeared to score hits and further attacks on the still surfaced boat left it listing and leaking oil. When the submarine finally disappeared, air bubbles and oil were observed. After circling the vicinity for about twenty minutes, the aircraft returned to her parent cruiser claiming a submarine destroyed. The success was welcome at a time when the damage to the battlecruisers had dampened German spirits, and in recognition of the achievement, Admiral Marschall awarded the crew the Iron Cross, First Class.

In fact, the submarine was not sunk. HMS *Triton* (Lieutenant-Commander Watkins), on patrol at the northern entrance to the Frohavet, reported being attacked by an He 115 (sic) aircraft at about the right time and place, but dived to 70 metres and escaped unharmed.

The next task for the heavy cruiser was to be an anti-mercantile sweep into the Arctic Ocean. The fleet oiler, *Nordmark*, had reported some traffic from the Finnish port of Petsamo, carrying nickel to the UK, when she passed through the region the previous April, and Gruppe (West) considered it to be a worthwhile quarry for *Admiral Hipper*. Accordingly, Flag Officer (Cruisers), Admiral Lütjens, was ordered to prepare for a two to three-week sortie between Spitzbergen and North Cape. The oiler *Dithmarschen* would support the cruiser, and the auxiliary cruiser *Schiff 45* (*Komet*) was already in the area. Nine waiting positions were assigned to the oiler to cater for the cruisers' heavy fuel consumption. *Admiral Hipper*'s operational orders included a ban on attacking Soviet merchantmen or indeed stopping them. All captured ships were to be sent to Tromsö under a prize crew. Initially, Admiral Lütjens intended to operate directly off North Cape, then oil and operate between North Cape and Bear Island. Heye, the cruiser's Captain, expressed reservations about the sortie, for he believed it vital that adequate air reconnaissance be available to avoid counter-attacks by the Royal Navy from Iceland and the Faroes. He was also concerned about the poor condition of the cruiser's engines. On the 24th, a conference had been held aboard to discuss the matter. Taking part, besides the ship's Engineer Officer, F.Kpt.(Ing) Moritz, were the Staff Engineer of Flag Officer (Cruisers), Kpt.z.-S.(Ing) Dip Ing Kober, as well as a representative from OKM (F.Kpt.(Ing) Thannemann, lately of *Blücher*), and from Wilhelmshaven Dockyard (Dip.Ing. Dieke). The major question was, would the present condition of the machinery allow a two to three-week sortie, given the fact that the meeting had already decided that a four-week refit would be required in the very near future? Moritz believed that it would, given certain conditions and reservations. These were:

(a) Full battleworthiness and high continuous steaming must not be guaranteed.

(b) If adequate air reconnaissance available, then can steam on two shafts and four boilers so as to be able to undertake any necessary repairs.

(c) Breaking-back to Germany might involve long periods of high-power steaming.

Admiral Hipper sailed at 1800 on the 27th, but only on six boilers at reduced pressures to limit the stress on the machinery. High feed-water loss further complicated matters, reducing her speed to about 25 knots. At 1900 the cruiser rendezvoused with *Gneisenau*, *Nürnberg* and four destroyers off Agdenes, and remained in company until detached at 2323. While in company a signal was received from Gruppe (West) giving details of British submarine dispositions, including those of *Trident*, *Triton*, *Snapper*, *H52* and *Porpoise* of which the latter was suspected of having been ordered to lay mines off Gripholm. No sign of the submarines was evident, and as *Gneisenau* and her squadron set course for Germany, the heavy cruiser struck northwards and by midnight stood west of Ramsoyfjord, between Smola and Hitre.

From 27 July until 6 August, the cruiser patrolled the freezing Arctic waters with little success. She even went as far north as to sight the southern tip of Spitzbergen, but the expected merchant traffic proved virtually non-existent. Frequent refuelling from *Dithmarschen* and an odd rendezvous with *Alstertor* and the auxiliary *Schiff* 47 did little to alleviate the general sense of frustration. Only two ships were stopped, one of which, the 1,540grt *Wappu*, bound for Petsamo from Buenos Aires (with hides, sugar and linseed oil) was released after being searched by the crew of aircraft T3+HK. A second, the 1,940grt *Ester Thorden* out of Brando with cellulose, coal and machinery for New York, was taken in prize. Despite the cold, the two ship's aircraft were used extensively until, on the 31st, 'MH' capsized on landing and had to be sunk by gunfire. On 3 August, 'HK' disappeared leaving the ship without scout planes. Later, however, it turned up in Norway and was re-united with its parent ship. Towards the end of the first week in August, Heye intended to stay farther south because the weather was becoming unfavourable – westerly winds, high swell, fog and the possibility of icebergs all hampering the fruitless search for targets. In the meantime, Gruppe (West) recognizing the uselessness of the sortie and needing to get the heavy cruiser into dockyard hands to sort out her machinery, signalled *Admiral Hipper* on the afternoon of the 6th, ordering the sortie to be broken off. Five days later, *Admiral Hipper* was back in Wilhelmshaven.

Despite the lack of concrete success in the form of ships sunk, *Hipper*'s crew had gained much valuable experience from the sortie, in navigation, seamanship and oiling at sea. The engineering branch, too, had succeeded in coaxing the ailing machinery to keep running. The weapons branches had had little to do, but some inherent defects had manifested themselves, particularly with regard to the flak directors and 10.5cm guns. Frequent use of the ship's aircraft had refined operating techniques and would be valuable for later Atlantic sorties. On the tactical side, the absence of a 'B' Dienst (monitoring service) team aboard, the short notice at which the operation was planned, poor communications and the inability to directly contact maritime reconnaissance aircraft all became evident. Steps were taken to rectify matters, but liaison between ships and aircraft was to remain a problem for the remainder of the war.

10: HIPPER THE OCEAN RAIDER, 1940–41

After a period in dockyard hands following her return from Norway in August, *Admiral Hipper* was detailed for Atlantic raiding operations where the Naval command saw great potential in her speed and fire-power, as well as being a significant extra strain upon the hunting groups of the already over-stretched Royal Navy. She sailed from Kiel during the forenoon of 24 September and, escorted by 'Sperrbrecher' as well as four torpedo-boats, negotiated the swept channels and mine barrages in the Baltic approaches as she headed out towards the North Sea.

Her orders were twofold. The main task was to intrude on the convoy routes and sink as many merchantmen as possible. Secondly, she was to attack and sink any patrol units chanced upon in the Denmark Strait. This latter task was very much a secondary consideration. The strategic objective of the sortie was to occupy as many Royal Navy warships as possible in the hunt for her and at the same time to force the British Admiralty to draw off light forces from the English Channel to protect the convoys. If the Kriegsmarine could succeed in doing this, the forces available for the defence of the south coast of England from a German landing ('Seelöwe') would be seriously weakened.

A feint landing operation, code-named 'Herbstreise', was actually intended in the Aberdeen–Newcastle area, two days before 'Seelöwe'. The forces allocated to this task, under the overall command of Flag Officer (Cruisers) consisted of the three surviving operational light cruisers and the 7th Torpedo-boat Flotilla based on Kiel, with *Bremse* and boats from the Torpedo School. Ten merchant ships from the Norwegian routes and the large liners, *Europa*, *Bremen*, *Gneisenau* and *Potsdam*, were to form the troop transports, organized into four convoys sailing from Bergen, Stavanger, Arendal and the Rivers Elbe and Weser. Scheduled sailing date was set for 15 September 1940, but of course, 'Seelöwe' was never launched.

Trouble soon struck the heavy cruiser for she had not even cleared the Skagerrak when, on the 25th, the starboard main cooling-water pump broke down, leaving the ship on only two engines. Miesel catapulted off one of his aircraft with a signal addressed to Gruppe (Nord), B.S.O. and Gruppe (West), detailing his predicament and his intention to make for Kristiansand where repairs were estimated to need about 48 hours, and opportunity was to be taken to top-up bunkers.

The aircraft landed at Aarlborg and the signal was passed to the addressees by landline for security reasons. At 1635, Gruppe (Nord) accepted Miesel's proposal and ordered him to Kristiansand where the cruiser arrived that evening. Repairs continued throughout the 26th, with the assistance of a technician who had been specially flown in from the pump manufacturers in Germany.

Repairs and fuelling took up most of the following day, so that it was not until the dog-watches that *Hipper* was finally fit to continue her break-out attempt. Weighing anchor, the cruiser, now escorted by only three torpedo-boats (*T9* having remained behind with engine trouble) and two fighters overhead, put out into the open sea. As evening wore on, *Hipper* worked-up to 25 knots in rising seas, maintaining a zigzag course with the torpedo-boats desperately attempting to keep station. With the winds WNW, gusting Force 6–8, the slim torpedo-boats were soon unable to keep up, and as *Hipper* could not afford to lose any more time, she detached her escort and continued alone. She worked-up to 30 knots and pressed on northwards, but the increasingly heavy seas had forced a reduction to 27 knots by 2048. The seas crashed aboard, flooding the forecastle and making the navigating bridge untenable. Visibility was good and the horizon to the north and west was light, giving good possibilities for the detection of any intercepting forces. Leaving the helmsman battened down in the wheelhouse with the armoured shutters down, the watch on deck retreated to the Admiral's bridge, which, being higher, was less affected by the seas coming aboard. Unfortunately, up here there were no command facilities, only a telephone to the wheelhouse, which complicated the conning of the vessel considerably.

By midnight, the cruiser stood south-west of Boknfjord, being pounded by the heavy seas. The winds had increased to Force 8–9 gusting 11, causing her to pitch and roll badly as she endeavoured to make some headway. Trouble struck once more when the new day was barely half an hour old. In the starboard engine room, the main lubricating-oil supply pipe for the starboard HP turbine bearings fractured, spraying hot oil on to the hot turbine casing, which promptly ignited the oil. The danger was twofold: the fire was obviously serious, but more important was the fact that the lubricating-oil tank was emptying rapidly. If all lubrication failed while the turbine was still turning, the damage would be grave. There

was, therefore, no option for the Chief Engineer but to request that the ship be stopped while the starboard shaft was uncoupled.

This was necessary because even without steam on the turbine, when the ship moved the trailing shaft would spin and wreck the bearings. To Meisel, it was a bitter blow, which effectively ended his attempt to break out into the Atlantic. He decided that in such heavy weather, there was little danger in stopping to uncouple the shaft, and therefore hove to while the engine-room staffs laboured below in the wildly tossing ship. In the course of the next hour, Meisel signalled his position and damage to Gruppe (Nord) as he resigned himself to await completion of the uncoupling. In fact, the job took a little over two hours for it was not until 0235 that the engineering department reported the starboard shaft uncoupled. A relieved Meisel then rang down revolutions for 25 knots on his two remaining shafts and shaped course for Bergen. Korsfjord was reached later that morning, where attempts were made to repair the lubrication system of the

starboard turbine. By evening, a jury repair had been made, but this lasted only until the following morning when, on the return journey to Kiel, it failed once more. The remainder of the journey was made on two shafts, the safety of Kiel being attained by early evening on the 30th. Repairs were ordered to be carried out at Blohm & Voss in Hamburg.

This first sortie of one of the new heavy cruisers had now come to an inauspicious if temporary end. Disappointment and frustration were the feelings of ship's company and the higher echelons of command. Admiral Carls, commanding Naval Gruppe (Nord) expressed serious concern over the recurring technical and design faults which had jeopardized the sortie and put the cruiser herself at risk. One problem was the necessity of lying stopped in hostile waters while the shaft coupling was unbolted. Clutch couplings could have alleviated this danger by greatly reducing the time required for disconnecting the shaft. In his view, the whole course of the *Hipper* operation had been unsatisfactory. Three times the sortie had been affected by material failures and he wondered

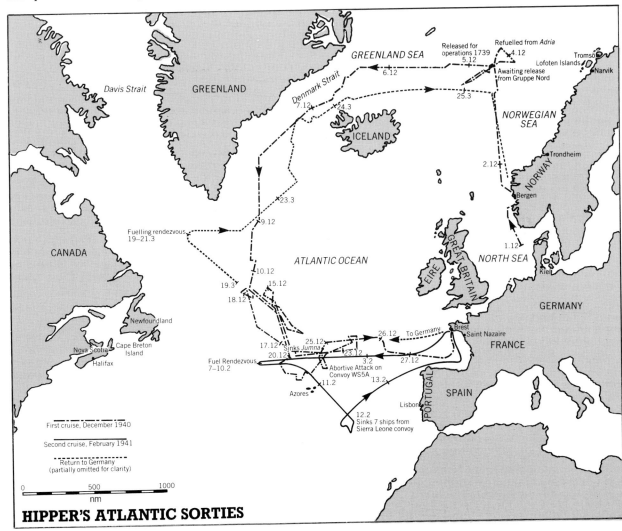

HIPPER'S ATLANTIC SORTIES

whether a few more days' preparation might have given a better chance of success. In fact, he concluded that this would have been unlikely.

The over-complication of modern machinery was such that even with detailed preparation, unforeseen defects could still occur and upset the best-laid plans. He believed that these experiences had shown that this particular class could not be used for short-notice operations without serious risk of defects. Moreover, it was not only the heavy cruisers which exhibited shortcomings. These were also all too apparent in the destroyer and torpedo-boat forces. For example, during the *Hipper* operation four out of five escorting torpedo-boats had to break off their tasks and return to port for technical and design reasons. Nevertheless, because of the weak position of the Kriegsmarine, if mercantile raiding was to be continued by the surface fleet, the heavy cruiser would have to be so used, at least until *Scharnhorst*, *Gneisenau* and the 'Panzerschiffen' were available once again. At this stage, the far greater usefulness of the armed and disguised merchant raiders does not appear to have been fully appreciated.

Admiral Hipper remained under repair at Blohm & Voss in Hamburg during October 1940 while the problems in her starboard turbine were investigated and rectified. By the 28th, however, repairs were complete and in the forenoon she sailed from Hamburg bound, via the Kiel Canal, for the Baltic and a period of trials and training. Here she remained until 17 November, when she returned westwards again, entering Kiel the following day, escorted by the 'Sperrbrecher' *Meersburg*. In Kiel she was docked for further repairs, overhaul and general fitting-out for her next operation. Fuel, provisions, torpedoes and ammunition were taken on, the ship not being undocked until three days later, on the 25th.

HIPPER'S FIRST ATLANTIC SORTIE

In the meantime, the High Command had been actively working on the cruiser's next deployment. Early in November, Flag Officer (Cruisers), Admiral Schmundt, had submitted an appreciation of the British North Atlantic convoy system to the Seekriegsleitung (SKL). This report concluded that the convoys from Halifax, Nova Scotia were code-named 'HX' and sailed every four days. In addition, every fourteen days it was believed that another convoy sailed the same route from Sydney, Cape Breton Island, these being code-named 'SC'. The convoys themselves were thought to comprise 30–40 ships, averaging 5,000 tonnes with a speed of 7–8½ knots. Passage time was twelve days, thus it was calculated that a minimum of three convoys would always be at sea, spaced some 670–820 nautical miles apart. Intelligence reports suggested that the Halifax convoys sailed at about midday with a local escort, picking up the ocean escort the following day in approximately 43° N, 57° W. This was usually an auxiliary cruiser. The convoy's route was thought to be eastwards as far as the south-eastern corner of the Newfoundland Grand Banks, where it was joined by a component from Bermuda. According to the same sources, the eastern escort joined twelve days later in approximately 54°–61° N, 17°–20° W. In the intervening period, the convoys' sole protection was an armed merchant cruiser of doubtful effectiveness. Intelligence had also deduced the presence of another route on which one convoy, 'TG6', was known to have been escorted by the battleship *Revenge* and the cruiser *Emerald*. From the strength of the escort, it was concluded that this was an important troop convoy. This information was essentially correct, the convoy was bringing Canadian troops to the UK. (They were in fact 'TC' not 'TG' convoys). As far as the 'HX' convoys were concerned, the German's initial appreciation also indicated the presence of submarine and destroyer escorts, at least on the western side. This was presumably obtained via agents' reports, but Flag Officer (Cruisers) believed these to be lease-lend or 'destroyers for bases' units on passage to the UK.

The other main traffic route of interest to the Germans was the Cape–UK route, in particular the 'SL' convoys northwards from Sierra Leone. This system was believed to operate from Freetown on a seven-day passage and to consist of 30–40 steamers, averaging about 5,000 tonnes. The escort was known to include armed trawlers, destroyers, patrol vessels and auxiliary cruisers. Intelligence reports also suggested that further subsidiary convoys joined from Gibraltar on about the latitude of Lisbon. These were thought to consist of smaller and slower ships, while off the Portuguese coast, valuable fast (over 15 knots) ships were known to be routed independently – a tempting target for a marauding cruiser.

Ober Kommando Marine broadly agreed with Admiral Schmundt's appreciation and augmented his information with further details. High Command's information suggested that the 'HX' convoys had a speed of 8–8½ knots and operated on 4-day cycles, while the 'SC' convoys were seven knots at 6-day intervals. The north-south convoys included a fast passage, 8–8½ knots and a slow one, 6–8 knots on an 8-day interval, with a 14-day passage to the west coast of Ireland.

On the question of escorts, it was confirmed that there was no mid Atlantic anti/submarine escort and the presence of destroyers merely indicated their being on delivery passage to the UK. The submarine reported by Admiral Schmundt was thought to be a Dutch boat *en route* to England for refit.

On 18 November, OKM sent a teleprinter signal to *Hipper*, asking for her state of training and battle-readiness to which the cruiser replied that, bearing in mind the continuous crew changes, the general training state was, under the circumstances, satisfactory, although the standard of action training of the crew was still insufficient. She expected to be ready for action by 25 November, assuming Kiel dockyard completed the repairs in time.

On 27 November, Gruppe (West) signalled *Hipper*'s operational orders together with further Intelligence concerning the various convoy routes, details of German and Italian U-boat operations, weathership positions and air reconnaissance patrols. *Hipper*, although sailing under the command of Gruppe (Nord), would pass into the Western Command area on crossing 60°N. One of the most notable features of her orders was that *Hipper* could attack weakly escorted convoys and that her Captain would have a more or less free hand in the conduct of the sortie. Gruppe (West) would finally order

the breaking-off of the operation, but the cruiser's Captain would do so himself if the circumstances demanded it. Logistic support for the cruiser would consist of the oiler *Dithmarschen*, assisted by the tankers *Friedrich Breme* and *Thorn*. The former was to sail from a home port, but the latter two were already in western France whence they would be sailed later. *Dithmarschen*, in fact, sailed on the evening of 22 November, bound for the first rendezvous position off Greenland.

Hipper undocked on the 25th and signalled her intention to be battleworthy by the following morning. On the 27th, Grand Admiral Raeder signalled his good wishes: 'Enemy situation permits favourable outcome of operation. Wishing you every success,' as the cruiser prepared to sail. The operation was to be known by the code-name 'Nordseetour'. At 0930 hrs, *Hipper* slipped her buoy and locked into the Kiel Canal, where she took on board a contingent of 'B' Dienst personnel under the command of K.Kpt.Schacht, as well as a representative of the SKL, K.Kpt.Hoffmann. After fuelling at Brunsbüttel, the cruiser awaited clearance to sail. When she left Kiel, it had been a hazy day with a fresh to strong southwesterly breeze, but the forecast was for winds increasing to north-easterly, Force 8–9 with very good visibility. The following day, the 28th, Gruppe (Nord) delayed her sailing in view of the weather forecast, now northerly gales with extremely good visibility, and so she lay at the quay with no communication with the shore and no leave allowed.

By the forenoon on the 30th, the gale had blown itself out. Under a clear sky, with few clouds and a light NNE breeze, *Hipper* slipped and sailed on her first Atlantic sortie. Forming up astern of *Sperrbrecher 10*, she shaped course northwards, being joined by early evening by four units of the 1st Torpedo-boat Flotilla. At sunset it was very calm and clear, but already the first mishap had befallen the operation.

At 1630 on the 30th, Gruppe (Nord) passed a signal to SKL, 'DITHMARSCHEN Quadrat EM39. Serious engine damage. Ordered return Trondheim 10kts. Propose immediate sailing of both tankers from France.' The loss of this oiler was a potentially serious blow to the whole operation, for the vessel was a purpose-designed naval auxiliary with an experienced crew and capable of about 22 knots. In contrast, the two tankers sailed from France were no more than requisitioned mercantile vessels, less well-equipped and slower than the naval oiler.

By dawn on the 31st, Marstein lighthouse was in sight as the cruiser and torpedo-boats zigzagged northwards at 29 knots. Less than an hour later, the escort was further reinforced by the arrival of boats from the 2nd Torpedo-boat Flotilla. Later that morning, *Hipper* oiled from the tanker *Wollin* in Hjeltfjord and painted camouflage patterns of dark rectangles, based upon Intelligence reports of the patterns carried by HMS *Liverpool*. The 'Hakenkreuz' on the forecastle and the red turret tops were painted out. Sailing once more, the seas became too heavy for the torpedo-boats to keep up, whereupon they were detached and the cruiser worked-up to 27 knots, crossing the Arctic Circle during the late morning of 2 December. In the afternoon, with fuel needed once more,

the tanker *Adria* was located and fuelling began. *Adria*, too, was an ex-commercial vessel and oiling was slow as both oiler and cruiser rolled in the heavy swell. *Hipper* was now in a remote part of the Arctic Ocean, midway between Bear Island and the coast of northern Norway, and here she was held by Gruppe (Nord) for the next few days to allow the two reserve tankers to reach their stations, in preparation for the cruiser's breakout.

Thorn's station was Point 'Spatz' in 47° 30′ N, 29° W which was in the central Atlantic, while *Breme* was ordered to 'Steil', an unfrequented spot in the Davis Strait between Newfoundland and Cape Farewell, the southernmost tip of Greenland. The passage to this station was of the order of 2,500 miles and would take a considerable time, some twelve days at about nine knots. Meisel was however concerned at the delay involved and having once more oiled from *Adria*, requested permission from Gruppe (Nord) to break out before the tanker reached 'Steil', in view of the favourable weather and enemy situations. Gruppe (Nord) concurred and informed Meisel that break-out orders would be issued as so soon as either tanker had reached the southern point, 'Spatz'.

In the meantime, Meisel was exercising much thought as to whether to break-out, north or south of Iceland. Finally, in view of the weather, he decided on the northern passage. It was not until 1739 on the 5th that Gruppe (Nord) finally released the cruiser for operations, and with a low approaching Iceland from the Atlantic, bringing high winds and heavy seas, the cruiser was in for a rough passage.

Hipper left her waiting area that day and steamed westwards between Bear Island and Iceland. By the end of the middle watch on the 6th, it was getting noticeably colder as they approached the Greenland ice edge, with the wind and sea gradually moving round to northerly. The seas coming aboard rapidly iced-up the superstructure, guns and wires, giving the cruiser a ghostly appearance. Four hours later, the wind had risen to northerly, Force 6–8 with high seas and a heavy swell. It was cloudy, very cold (-10°) with occasional snow showers making watchkeeping in exposed positions very uncomfortable.

Throughout the forenoon the air temperature dropped, but the early patchy fog gave way to good visibility. Numerous icefloes were sighted. Dusk soon fell after the short Arctic day, and a half moon appeared. Before midnight, the 'B' Dienst service aboard reported radio traffic in the vicinity, but, if it emanated from British patrols, nothing was seen. To the west, out of sight, lay the snow and ice-covered peaks of King Christian IX Land and King Frederick VI coast on Greenland, while eastwards lay the fjorded coast of Iceland. As the cruiser crossed the Arctic Circle once more, sea and air temperatures climbed. Running due south during the early afternoon, weather reports became ominous. A westerly storm was expected, with a low developing off Greenland. Bad weather struck some six hours later, with a strong southwesterly gale building up heavy seas. Snow and hail showers reduced visibility on an already very dark night. The heavy weather continued into the following day, with winds reaching hurricane strength by midday. The sea was white

with spray and spume, waves 15 metres high were breaking over the foretop and rolls of 30° were experienced.

Hipper groped her way south, both wing engines giving revolutions for only five knots and the centre one for seven. Steering was impossible, and some superficial damage was done to her boats and upperworks. By 2000, standing now to the south-east of Cape Farewell, the bad weather persisted. Visibility was nil and the seas remained unabated; three knots was all that could be maintained. Towards midnight, wind and sea began to reduce and continued to do so throughout the following morning, much to the relief of the exhausted crew. Fuelling was becoming necessary once more because Meisel intended making an attack on convoy 'HX93' on the 10th, but his oil position was such as to allow him to remain only one day on the convoy route before running for his tanker. To conserve fuel, the centre engine was stopped and the ship proceeded on only two shafts. Towards midnight, Gruppe (Nord) signalled *Hipper* with details of the position of *Thorn en route* for the Greenland rendezvous, and giving the time at which operational command would pass to Gruppe (West) – 1200, 12 December. (The tanker's stations had been reversed earlier).

On the morning of the 10th, *Hipper* was at last on the route which the Germans expected 'HX93' to traverse, and desperately low on fuel. To compound Meisel's problems, the starboard low-pressure turbine had sustained damage, which necessitated uncoupling the starboard shaft. On the remaining two shafts, the ship was capable of 25 knots. Her speed was therefore seriously impaired. In the opinion of the Engineering Department, the damage could not be repaired at sea; it meant either a return to Germany or running to Brest. Meisel considered the former, but fuel was a pressing problem and if he were to turn north-westwards for the Greenland rendezvous, low fuel together with top icing might cause stability problems and, furthermore, he did not know the precise position of *Thorn*, which might in turn lead to wasting valuable fuel in a search for her. Finally, the prospect of running the gauntlet through the Denmark Strait on only two shafts was not very attractive. If, on the other hand, he chose to go for the *Breme*, knowing that she was at or near her rendezvous, he might be able to make an attack on the convoy if he were lucky. Alternatively, he had just enough fuel for a direct run to Brest. In fact, Meisel took the fighting option and decided to go for rendezvous 'Spatz', attacking 'HX93' on the way. After fuelling from *Breme*, he intended breaking off to Brest. In his words, 'Better a cruiser in Brest than in Hamburg or Kiel.'

Throughout the 12th, *Hipper* searched in vain for the convoy, using much valuable fuel. In view of the fuel position, Meisel broke-off for the rendezvous the next day. The tanker was not there and it was not until after a false alarm and a signal to Gruppe (West) that she was finally located by radar at 2210 that night. An hour later, fuelling was begun. This operation took a long twelve hours before the ill-equipped tanker could be released to a new rendezvous. After engine trials, for the starboard engine had been temporarily repaired by dint of great efforts by the engineers, Meisel now intended to attack convoy 'HX94' (which had been reported to the south-east) on the 13th.

The weather now turned against *Hipper*, for by late on the 12th, wind and seas were rising and the forecast was bad. Throughout the 13th and 14th, the cruiser once more weathered hurricane-force winds and mountainous seas which peaked in strength at about midday on the 14th. Seawater cascaded down boiler and engine room fan trunkings, soaked and damaged both main-deck 10.5cm mountings, and damaged much other equipment. With rolls of 33° and a speed of only seven knots, course was maintained only by superhuman efforts of the helmsman. The weather remained poor throughout the 15th, with a deep low over the whole North Atlantic, but by early evening, winds had moderated to Force 6 and Meisel resumed his search for fuel. By the 16th, the winds had further moderated, but a heavy swell remained on the sea. *Breme* hove in sight and fuelling began as the crew relaxed and cleaned up the ship after her stormy passage. In addition to the damage already described, the torpedo tubes were found to be inoperative, due to ingress of seawater into the electrics, and a cutter had been damaged.

After oiling, Meisel's plans now were to attack 'HX95' and then move to attack 'SC15'. On the 18th, the bad weather resumed, preventing *Hipper* from using her aircraft, so that her probes for the convoys remained fruitless. *Hipper* oiled once more from her tanker on the 20th, while Meisel once again considered his position and how best he might locate the

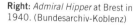

elusive convoys and so score a success. He first considered moving north-westwards with a view to attacking traffic off the Newfoundland Banks.

Here, the advantages he saw were (i) Possibility of surprise – no surface attacks had been made in the area. (ii) Bunching of shipping east of the Newfoundland Banks and (iii) Possibility of better weather. Against those, were several disadvantages, namely *Hipper*'s restricted radius of action, uncertain tanker situation, possibility of strong escorts and, not least, the vast distance from any friendly base. Finally, greatly needing a prestigious, successful attack on a weakly guarded convoy, as *Scheer* had done ('HX84'), Meisel turned to operate against the 'SL' convoy route and north-south independents. *Breme*, disguised as the Panamanian *Leda*, was dispatched to a new rendezvous in preparation. On 21 December, *Hipper* searched unsuccessfully for 'SL58' and 'SLS58', and the following day was struck once more by machinery problems, this time with the centre engine whose shaft bearings were running hot.

That morning was the first day since leaving Germany that it was possible to operate the aircraft, and it was with a feeling of great relief that her aircrews received the order to launch. Lt.z.S.Nowrat and Feldwebel Schurmann were catapulted off in one of the Arados on the first search. Nothing further was seen or heard of the aircraft, and after she became overdue, the cruiser commenced a search for the crew and any tell-tale floating wreckage. The second aircraft had been damaged on being cleared from the hangar roof and No. 3 was stuck in the hangar. By 1730, the search had been abandoned in view of the fuel situation, and reports that 'Force H' had sailed from Gibraltar. The next day, *Hipper* fuelled once more from *Breme*, by which time the third aircraft had been extricated

and mounted on the catapult. Still her searches remained without result and it was not until late afternoon on the 24th that her radar first picked up contacts which might be a convoy.

The convoy appeared to be on a southerly course, which fact Meisel took to mean that it was only weakly escorted. It was a dark night, with high seas and poor visibility, and in view of the possibility of the presence of destroyers, the cruiser's Captain decided not to attempt a night attack, but wait instead for first light. Accordingly, *Hipper* shadowed throughout the night, undetected by the convoy. Christmas festivities were cancelled in preparation for the forthcoming attack. Shortly after midnight, *Hipper* closed the starboard quarter of the convoy to attack with torpedoes, hoping that a U-boat would be deemed responsible. At 0153, three torpedoes were launched at a range of 4,600 metres, and the cruiser turned and ran out of visual range of the convoy. No hits were scored and the range, obtained by radar, was believed to be in error. After this, *Hipper* stood off to await the dawn.

At 0608, the ship was cleared for action and the convoy was closed. Rain squalls obscured visibility and a strong SSE wind blew. When the ships of the convoy became distinguishable, Meisel was dismayed to see the unmistakable outline of a three-funnelled cruiser – obviously a British *County*-class' heavy cruiser, and as such equal to her adversary.

The British cruiser, actually *Berwick*, appeared not to have detected the German ship as yet, so Meisel decided to make a torpedo attack on her, and did not initially give his Gunnery Officer, K.Kpt.Wegener, permission to open fire. The torpedo officer ordered all six starboard tubes ready to fire, but then Meisel saw another shadow beyond the British cruiser and ordered only three torpedoes to be launched. This caused delays on the tubes and in the meantime, *Hipper*, having run parallel with the convoy, had turned, at about 0630, to close it and was now getting uncomfortably near to *Berwick*. At 0639, *Hipper* opened fire on the British cruiser with her main armament, but smoke from the guns, spray on the gun-control optics and generally poor visibility prevented observation of the fall of shot for the first two salvoes. The blast effects of the 20.3cm gunfire also put the torpedo-tube training gear out of action so no torpedoes were fired. This mishap robbed *Hipper* of a good chance of success against the enemy ship. The 10.5cm guns opened fire, first upon *Berwick* and then shifted to the merchantmen. After a couple of minutes, *Hipper* shifted her main armament on to what was believed to be a destroyer, attacking under cover of a smoke-screen. This was probably either *Bonaventure* or *Dunedin*, which were also part of the escort, for by ill-fortune, *Hipper* had not found a lightly escorted merchant convoy, but the troop convoy, 'WS5A', bound for the Middle East. Also present was the aircraft carrier *Furious* carrying crated aircraft in a transport role.

Berwick, whose company had already closed-up for dawn action stations before the enemy was sighted, increased speed and altered course towards the German, opening fire two minutes after *Hipper*. As Meisel took avoiding action to port

Below: Detail view of *Admiral Hipper* at Brest in 1941. (Bundesarchiv-Koblenz)

to avoid the torpedoes of the 'destroyers', the British shells fell close by to port. By now *Hipper* was withdrawing, engaging *Berwick* with her after turret group, and the other cruisers with her 10.5cm guns. The directors had to switch target frequently, and smoke was a problem to the after control position. Meisel himself was hindered by the poor view aft from the bridge platform. *Berwick* fired only intermittently with 'A' and 'B' turrets as and when the enemy could be observed, but Wegener's shooting was good despite the fact that it was not until 0658 that smoke and spray had diminished sufficiently to allow proper gunnery control.

At 0705 *Hipper* scored a hit on the *County*'s 'X' turret which disabled it and killed four of its Marine crew, although it did not explode. Then, changing to AP shells, three minutes later, abreast 'B' turret below the waterline, causing flooding. *Berwick*'s fire was generally close grouped, but short, although some 'overs' forced Meisel into avoiding action. A third hit amidships struck S1 4in mounting which deflected the shell through several bulkheads before it exploded, about 18 metres away, in a funnel uptake. A final hit on the side belt was deflected into the bulge where it exploded, flooding about 13 metres of the bulge space. After this hit, rain squalls obscured the antagonists, and by 0714, *Admiral Hipper* had managed to break contact. The hit forward on *Berwick* flooded the lower steering position, forcing the coxswain to evacuate to the upper position as Captain Warren took his ship back to rejoin his convoy. The German cruiser had fired 174 rounds of main armament during the brief engagement in which, apart from *Berwick*'s damage, two ships of the convoy, including the *Empire Trooper* (13,994 tons) were damaged.

The indecisive action was a narrow escape for *Hipper* and it is difficult to understand why, even when acting as a ferry carrier,

Furious did not have one or two aircraft on stand-by for a/s patrol work or torpedo strike. This would have given a much greater degree of protection to the convoy and might have ended *Hipper*'s career there and then. The omission of a defence flight is all the more surprising given the loss of *Glorious* as an example.

Meisel's next pressing need was for fuel if he were to remain active. In his opinion, however, he had reached the limit of his crews's endurance and his ship was in need of repairs. He therefore resolved to move north and then head east for the Bay of Biscay and a safe dockyard. Later that morning, the lookouts reported a shadow in the rain which turned out to be a fast-approaching merchantmen. A quick exchange of signals revealed it to be the 6,078-ton James & Nourse steamer, *Jumna*. *Hipper*'s guns opened up as the radio office jammed an attempted 'Raider' signal by the unfortunate merchantman. To speed her sinking it was necessary to put two torpedoes into her before the cruiser withdrew northwards at high speed. *Hipper* had now at least scored a success, however small and, low on fuel and stores, made for Brest, arriving on the 27th.

This first ocean raiding sortie by one of the new heavy cruisers, which lasted 28 days, produced a wealth of experience although little material result, apart from forcing the Royal Navy to mount numerous patrols and sorties in the attempt to intercept the raider. However, as *Hipper* remained undetected until 25 December, her diversionary effect was more limited than it might have been. So far as actual experience was concerned, the two major features which emerged were the low action radius of the type, and the temperamental nature of the machinery. The low endurance meant that her captain was continually preoccupied with the question of fuel and Meisel recommended that a minimum of two fast oilers was necessary

Below: *Admiral Hipper* at Brest on 28 January 1941, just a few days prior to her second Atlantic raiding sortie. Single 2cm guns in land mountings can just be discerned on 'B' and 'C' turret roofs. (Gröner)

in the operational area, as well as reserve tankers in the Greenland area. Apart from its fuel consumption, the high-pressure steam installation was, particularly in *Hipper*, chronically unrealiable. In consequence, her deployment far from a base was problematic and risky. Much credit is due to her engineering staff that she managed to remain at sea at all.

The severe weather encountered throughout most of the sortie tested the design of the hull and equipment sorely. The hull itself proved extremely seaworthy, but the heavy seas found weak spots in the equipment. Particularly prone to problems were the torpedo tubes, flak and flak directors, mostly of an electrical nature. Operational experience also showed that the bridge was badly laid-out and cramped, while the siting of the chart-house a deck below was particularly criticized. Sea conditions also proved the very limited capabilities of catapult aircraft, for on only three days was launching and recovery possible. Furthermore, it was found that the design of the hangar roof door left much to be desired. Other detrimental features were the lack of effective clear-view screens in the covered bridge, poor layout below decks, leading to confusion when action stations was sounded, and lack of any means of quickly disengaging a propeller shaft.

Positive features were the extremely valuable nature of the radar installation and the presence of the 'B' Dienst team aboard. No problems were experienced with the main armament.

On balance, therefore, the Naval Staff cannot have been too impressed with the heavy cruiser's suitability for this mode of warfare, but they were to send her out again, this time with greater success. In the meantime, however, she needed at least four weeks in dockyard hands to repair her machinery and the sea damage sustained.

Flag Officer (Cruisers), Admiral Schmundt, broadly agreed with Kpt.z.S.Meisel's report and commended his toughness and perseverance. In particular, he applauded his decision not to return to Germany. The admiral himself concluded that so long as heavy escorts were used on convoys, a single cruiser was insufficient, and heavy escorts would be employed as long as the ship remained a threat in Brest. He recommended that two cruisers, or various combinations of battleships and cruisers, as the ideal solution. The battleships, having the radius of action while the cruisers had torpedoes. One suspects however, that in any such combination, the cruiser would be a millstone round the battleship's neck. Unless of course, it were a light cruiser, which was ruled out anyway for reasons already discussed. He went on to say that if later experience were to show that the employment of the cruisers, with their known weaknesses, from Brest continued to be unsuccessful, they should be employed with the Italian Navy (whose ships also had low-action radii). How he proposed to get a heavy cruiser through the Straits of Gibraltar is not recorded, except that he considered it not impossible on a dark night.

SKL, in their appreciation of the sortie, agreed that Meisel was correct in not attacking independents (he had taken great care to avoid being seen, as ordered) but that in future, these opportunities must not be missed. Admiral Schmundt's proposal about the Mediterranean was not concurred with

because in the view of SKL, the main target was the Atlantic convoys.

HIPPER'S SECOND ATLANTIC SORTIE

Hipper remained under repair until 27 January, when she was undocked and prepared for trials, which were carried out on the 29th. She was now ready for another strike at the convoy traffic. In the late evening of 1 February, the cruiser, escorted by *Sperrbrecher 9*, *Beitzen*, *Seeadler*, *Greif* and *Kondor*, nosed out into the Atlantic swell and set course westwards, but only 24 hours later, Meisel was already concerned about fuel. On the 4th, the tanker *Spichern*, was located and prepared for oiling. This tanker, another exmercantile vessel had been fitted-out as a replenishment vessel in great haste and, moreover, her crew were woefully inexperienced. Not only did *Hipper* have to send a boat with an oiling party to the tanker to assist operations, but Meisel also thought it necessary to pass a note to her skipper outlining the great importance of her task and the need for speed and dexterity. *Hipper* fuelled again on the 5th, 6th and 7th, while awaiting the orders that would release her to attack convoys.

Loitering in mid-Atlantic, *Hipper* listened to the signal traffic from Gruppe (West) and U-boats at sea. Meisel expected to receive permission to attack on the morning of the 9th, as by then, *Scharnhorst* and *Gneisenau* would have reached the 'HX'

Right: *Admiral Hipper* in dry dock at Brest in January 1941. Note depth-charges on the stern, and the angle of the port after flak director. (Gröner)

convoy routes. *Hipper* would then act as a diversionary force for the two battlecruisers. On the evening of the 8th, she was able to monitor signals between BdU (Flag Officer U-Boats) and *U37*, which was shadowing convoy 'HG53'. This appeared to be a suitable target. Meisel anticipated attacking the scattered merchantmen after the convoy had been broken up by air and U-boat attacks.

His orders were to attack the north-south convoy routes with permission to operate as far south as 30° N. He, in fact, saw his best opportunity in the southern half of his area of operations, i.e., south and south-east of the Azores. Here, his diversionary activities would be farther from the 'HX' convoy routes and would stretch the British forces that much more. He would have a vast area of unfrequented ocean in which to disappear; the weather would be kinder, and *Hipper* would be able to use her speed to advantage, and probably employ her aircraft to good effect. Finally, a major point was the presence of the tanker, *Breme*, to supply the fuel-hungry cruiser. On the other hand, if at any time after the successful appearance of either *Hipper* or the two battlecruisers, Fleet Command or Gruppe (West) wished or needed to combine the two forces at a fixed time and position, *Hipper* would be far to the south and, unless refuelled, might arrive at the rendezvous with insufficient fuel for any tasks she might be ordered to undertake by Admiral Lütjens, aboard *Gneisenau*.

Below: Portside midships view, *Admiral Hipper*. (Bundesarchiv)

Still the cruiser loitered undetected and inactive, avoiding independent merchantmen and topping-up her tanks at every opportunity. Her 'B' Dienst squad picked up signals from the convoy escort, reporting attacks by aircraft and giving its position some 400 nautical miles west of Gibraltar. On the 9th, Gruppe (West) intimated to Meisel that they suspected that Admiral Lütjens, once he had attacked the 'HX' convoys, might move south to join the heavy cruiser, but as yet this was only supposition. It fitted in well, however, with Meisel's appreciation of the probable train of events. At 2125 that day, *Hipper* began to move eastwards in anticipation of her release which actually came at 2320, after Admiral Lütjens signalled that he had been detected by enemy forces. This was probably the battlecruiser's abortive attack on convoy 'HX106' which was guarded by the veteran battleship, *Ramilles*, which, in fact, only sighted one enemy and reported her as possibly a *Hipper*-class cruiser.

Throughout the 10th, *Hipper* moved east at speed, to close the convoy which *U37* had been ordered to shadow. At 1644, however, Meisel was dismayed to intercept a signal from Flag Officer U-boats to *U37* informing her that there would be no further air attacks on the convoy and that she should sink the remaining nine vessels. There was now a distinct possibility that the cruiser, having burned a vast quantity of valuable and scarce fuel oil, would now strike at thin air. U-Boat Command must have been aware of *Hipper*'s orders from Gruppe (West), but it was not until 1920 that the cruiser's orders were confirmed and *U37* so informed. *U37* then lost contact with 'HG53'!

On the 11th, in poor weather, with rising seas and swell, the cruiser, steaming at 25 knots, continued the search, but it was not until early afternoon that any success was enjoyed, when lookouts reported a lone merchantman steering a northerly course. *Hipper* stopped her with a shot across the bows and stood off in case she was a Q ship. The merchant ship was the 1,236-ton *Iceland*, out of Seville and bound for Glasgow via Gibraltar with a cargo of oranges and general goods. She was a straggler from 'HG53'. After her crew had taken to the boats, the cruiser sank the abandoned ship with gunfire and a torpedo. *Iceland* was, interestingly, an ex-German prize, being formerly named *Delia*. From her crew, a great deal of detailed information was obtained regarding the composition and intentions of her late convoy. *Hipper* still had not located her main quarry, however, and to assist her *U37* was ordered to re-locate and maintain contact with 'HG53'. In the event she was not required, for a little before midnight, *Hipper*'s radar detected two contacts at a range of 15,500 metres, but it was not the particular convoy for which she had been searching.

From midnight until the early hours of the 12th, *Hipper* circled the unsuspecting convoy, while assessing its size and escort strength. From her observations, she deduced it to be only weakly escorted and making about seven knots on a northerly course. In the darkness and even with her radar, the cruiser underestimated the size of the convoy which, in fact, consisted of nineteen ships which had left Freetown on 30 January and was known as convoy 'SLS64'. Twelve were British, four Greek and three Norwegian. Most importantly,

however, as far as *Hipper* was concerned, was the fact that they had no escort at all. *Hipper*'s luck had turned at last.

In the darkness, of course, Meisel did not know that the ships were unescorted and resolved to attack at first light in order to avoid brushes with torpedo-armed destroyers at night. As the night wore on, the weather deteriorated with a high north-westerly swell, low cloud, poor visibility and occasional rain, factors which would not aid the attack of a scattering bunch of ships in the dawn light. During the morning watch, Meisel took the cruiser round to the western side of the convoy whence he intended to launch his attack. At 0515, a sudden improvement in visibility found the cruiser some 20,000 metres west of the convoy aiming to attack its head and thus force it to turn in confusion. Meisel intended to attack the nearest steamer with all his armament, and then engage the enemy escort. To the north and west, the horizon was lighter than in the south and east, where dark clouds and rain persisted. The cruiser rolled heavily, but remained dry and fully battleworthy. As the sky lightened, the watch on the bridge were amazed to see ship after ship come into view with no sign of an escort. The count rose, seven now ten, now eighteen defenceless ships under *Hipper*'s guns! Meisel could not believe that so many ships could be sailed unescorted. At 0618, he gave permission for the main armament to open fire, followed two minutes later by similar orders for the torpedo armament. The lighter weapons were used against bridges and superstructures, while the main guns fired at the hulls. Using four-gun salvoes, *Hipper* began her work of destruction as the convoy commodore aboard SS *Warlaby* ordered his consorts to scatter.

Some of the steamers were armed and made a brave, but ineffectual, reply to the German fire. After ten minutes, having fired all her starboard torpedoes, *Hipper* turned on to a westerly course and continued to engage with her port armament. Confusion reigned as the steamers scattered, some making smoke as they did so. One had already sunk, while several more were on fire and listing badly. At long last, Meisel was able to send off the cherished signal: 'To Gruppe West. In action enemy convoy, 6 to 10 steamers Q CF80 – HIPPER.' Between 0642 and 0646, six steamers had been sunk, but already the Gunnery Officer, K.Kpt.Wegener, had reported to the captain that two-thirds of the 20.3cm head-fuzed ammunition had been shot away. Another merchantman was reported sunk and three others were burning fiercely when the Torpedo Officer, Kpt.Lt.Bülter, reported to the Command Centre that all twelve loaded tubes had been used, with eleven observed hits. Only two of the reserve torpedoes had so far been loaded because the re-load system was badly designed and the reserve torpedoes were not easily accessible. The levels in the shell rooms fell rapidly as four more ships were engaged and sunk by the main turrets, leaving few nose-fuzed HE shells remaining.

The remnants of the convoy were now well and truly scattered, rain, smoke and fog obscured the area and the cruiser was almost out of ammunition. At 0740 Meisel broke off the action declining to chase the few steamers left in sight. As the officers and men in the various control and director positions compared notes, Meisel reckoned his score as being

thirteen ships totalling 75,000 tons, but only four names could be confirmed: *Perseus* (estimated 10,000t), *Borgestadt* (3,924t), *Shrewsbury* (4,542t) and *Oswestry Grange* (4,684t). In fact, in the confusion, Meisel had over-estimated his score and actually, his tally was seven ships at 32,806 tons.* In view of his fuel and ammunition position, Meisel now decided to break off the operation and return to Brest, signalling this intention to Gruppe (West). About an hour later, Gruppe (West) acknowledged, but were not wholly in favour of his return as evidenced by their reply: 'Assume pressing reasons for return. Otherwise fuel and re-ammunition from BREME and remain at sea as a diversionary force and in the interest of the overall operation.' Meisel, however, stuck to his original intentions and set course for Brest, where the ship arrived safely on the 14th, having approached the French port from the south to avoid detection. She had by this time, only 370m³ of fuel remaining.

A number of conclusions could be, and were, drawn from the successful completion of this second cruise by the heavy cruiser. The major finding confirmed what had already been experienced during the first cruise – these ships were basically sprinters and did not have the endurance necessary for really successful commerce raiding. Both Kpt.z.S.Meisel and Fleet Command laid great stress on this point in their respective post-mortems. To illustrate this, the cruiser had steamed 1,300 nautical miles at speeds of between 15 and 27 knots, to reach her first tanker rendezvous. This took 57½ hours and consumed 1,135m³ of oil, i.e., 40.5 per cent of her bunkerage. Then, during the period 5–10 February, she oiled seven times in all. The tankers were therefore a vital factor in raiding operations, which necessitated their being highly trained and efficient. Unfortunately, this was not always the case. Furthermore, it was thought necessary to have better control of the tankers from land, in order that they were punctual at rendezvous.

As far as actual locating and attacking of the convoys were concerned, experience showed that U-boats and aircraft were the best means of determining the composition of the convoy and the strength of its escort. Radar could not do this. The ship's own aircraft could obviously carry out these tasks, but once again, it was found that the weather in mid Atlantic severely restricted the operation of catapult-launched aircraft. In the timing of the actual attack, four options presented themselves: attacking at night, day, dawn or dusk. As a night attack involved the possibility of encounters with escorting destroyers, it was found better to confine such attacks to the use of torpedoes and not reveal the presence of a surface unit. On the other hand, a daylight attack could hardly be expected to achieve surprise and the escort would have to be defeated first. Attacking at dusk might achieve surprise if the position of the target was known beforehand, but if the escort resisted strongly, there was a serious probability that the merchantmen would scatter and be lost in the approaching darkness. Location and destruction would then be very time-consuming and inefficient. All things, considered, therefore, the best possibilities appeared to be offered by a dawn attack. This

*The other three sunk were *Warlaby*, *Westbury* and *Dorrynane*, all British. *Volturno*, *Lornaston* and the Greek *Kalliopi* were damaged to varying degrees.

could achieve surprise and if the escort could be overwhelmed quickly, long hours of daylight remained for the sinking of the convoy.

The other major factor to emerge was the great usage of ammunition and the danger of being left with insufficient HE shells to engage destroyers successfully. Re-ammunitioning at sea was not possible simultaneously with oiling, and had to be a separate operation because the Kriegsmarine used the astern hose technique. In any case, both oiling and ammunitioning were very much dependent on the prevailing weather. This, to some extent, explains Meisel's reluctance to replenish at sea after his attack, when in all probability he had stirred up a hornets' nest. However, by not remaining on the high seas, his diversionary effect was restricted in the extreme. *Hipper* had also expended, besides the 247 rounds of 20.3cm, twelve torpedoes, and it was in the torpedo department that the most serious design drawbacks manifested themselves. The six starboard tubes had been used first and when empty, preparations were begun for re-loading. Before any were loaded, however, the forward port tubes were fired and since the reserve torpedoes were stored on the port side, the first two torpedoes were loaded into the port forward bank. This took about twenty minutes. The other two for the starboard side were put on to trollies, which ran from the port side round to the starboard tubes, but as the ship was rolling so badly that there was a serious danger to men and torpedoes, the attempt had to be abandoned. It was not until the ship altered course that the operation was satisfactorily completed. The remaining six reserve torpedoes were stowed on the superstructure deck with their warheads in the warhead store below decks. These could not be manoeuvred quickly into a loading position.

So ended *Hipper*'s second (and in fact last) Atlantic raiding cruise. Such operations had been proved more suitable for the large radius, diesel-engined 'Panzerschiffen'. *Hipper*'s machinery, besides being uneconomical, was also unreliable, rendering her a constant source of anxiety whenever at large on the oceans. Three months later, however, the Kriegsmarine was to have one more attempt using these heavy cruisers on the high seas.

Hipper now needed to return to Germany, in order to refit and have her machinery investigated, but this posed something of a problem for the High Command. Not only were the battlecruisers still operating in the Atlantic, but *Scheer* was also scheduled to return to Germany very shortly. With so many ships at sea, the British were bound to try and intercept some of them, with the consequent danger that operations against one German ship might ensnare another. The cruiser could not stay in Brest, because that dockyard could not refit her, and it was too dangerous. Constant air raids had not yet hit the ship, but on 24 February, fifteen bombs fell within 200 metres of her. It was only a matter of time before she was hit. The cruiser was sailed on 15 March, and after refuelling at a rendezvous south-west of Greenland, some time between the 19th and 21st, broke through the narrow ice-bound passage between Greenland and Iceland on the 23rd during bad weather. Rounding Iceland she set course south and after fuelling at Bergen, reached Kiel safely on 28 March.

11: PRINZ EUGEN GOES TO WAR

The first, and as it turned out, the only unit of the modified 'Hipper'-type heavy cruiser to see service, *Prinz Eugen*, commissioned at Kiel on 1 August 1940. Her captain was the popular Lübecker, Helmuth Brinkmann, who had joined the old Kaisermarine in April 1913 and seen service in battleships, cruisers and torpedo-boats during the First World War. One of his post-war appointments had been the Aviso, *Grille*, whence he was posted to the Naval Defence Department (Marinewehramt), becoming its Chief before receiving his appointment to the new cruiser in 1940.

The war came early to *Prinz Eugen* for on 2 July 1940, while still in the final stages of fitting-out, the ship had been hit by a bomb during an RAF raid on Kiel. This struck the ship on the port side, destroying a motor boat, severing power cables to the guns and causing some structural damage to the galley bulkheads. Commissioning was not over-delayed and after her entry into service, *Prinz Eugen* spent the next four months engaged mainly on trials or post-completion modifications in and around Kiel dockyard. Then, in the new year, she commenced working-up in the Baltic, interspersed with further times in dockyard hands. By April, when it had been decided that the new ship would accompany *Bismarck* on her Atlantic sortie, she still had to carry out gunnery shoots, exercises with the 24th U-Boat Flotilla and in-company exercises with *Bismarck* herself, the intention being to have her operational by the 23rd. While in Kiel dockyard at this time, an additional steering position was installed on the Admiral's bridge as a result of experience aboard *Admiral Hipper*. The 'PRINZ' as she was affectionately called, sailed from the Deutsche Werke yard on 8 April and moved eastwards to Gotenhafen to begin preparations for her intended sortie. Here, in addition to the exercise programme, speed trials were carried out on the Neukrug measured mile in heavy rain and poor visibility. On 75 per cent full load displacement, a speed of 32.84 knots was obtained.

On the 22nd, *Prinz Eugen* sailed from Gotenhafen once more, and after exercises with *Bismarck*, set course for Kiel, escorted by the 'Sperrbrecher' *Rothenburg*. Late the following afternoon, the Sperrbrecher led her charge into Kiel Bay, being some 700 metres ahead of the cruiser, when an underwater explosion erupted in the wake of the escort, only 20–30 metres off the cruiser's starboard bow. The whole ship shook to the force of the detonation, losing power and steam. Hand-steering was quickly engaged and the starboard engine was soon operational again. The forward gyro-compass and degaussing equipment, however, were knocked out temporarily. After 28 minutes, the Engineer Officer, K.Kpt.Graser, was able to report the centre engine serviceable, but it was a further 20 minutes before all engines were working. Slowly, the damaged ship limped into Kiel and made fast at the Deutsche Werke yard for inspection and rectification of the damage.

The explosion, probably caused by a ground mine laid by the RAF, had ruptured fuel bunkers, torn one turbo-generator from its foundations and damaged the propeller shafts, as well

Right: *Prinz Eugen* in 1941, prior to 'Rheinübung'. The spherical shields have not yet been fitted to the forward flak director towers. (Drüppel)

Opposite page: *Prinz Eugen* at Gotenhafen in April 1941, prior to 'Rheinübung'. Note separate elevation to the 20.3cm guns, the left gun of 'Anton' turret is at maximum elevation, the right at maximum depression. In the background is *Cap Arkona* and astern of her either *Deutschland* or *Hansa*, employed as accommodation ships. (Gröner)

as inflicting a great deal of shock damage to electrical and fire-control systems. It was not until 2 May that the ship could be undocked, and a further nine days passed before passage back to Gotenhafen could be undertaken, where the final preparations for the Atlantic sortie, codename 'Rheinübung' were to be made.

OPERATION 'RHEINÜBUNG'

Admiral Lütjens, the Fleet Commander and senior officer of the squadron, came aboard on the 18th to confer with Brinckmann and outline his orders and intentions. These included the following points:

(a) If the weather situation were favourable, the squadron would oil at sea from the oiler *Weissenburg* and not enter Korsfjord as intended. Luftwaffe reconnaissance of Scapa Flow would safeguard this operation.

(b) The break-out would be achieved using the Denmark Strait, taking advantage of ice, fog, high speed and radar.

(c) Torpedo attack by *Prinz Eugen* only on orders from Fleet.

(d) Ship's company not to be informed of the objectives until on passage north.

(e) Camouflage paint to be retained for the moment. In case a long stay in Trondheim was necessary, suitable coloured camouflage materials to be prepared.

(f) Aircraft to be operated through Fleet Commander with clear written orders. On reconnaissance flights, attacks prohibited, the object being to remain undetected. Optical recall to be used.

(g) Tankers to be priority prizes.

(h) Ammunition to be conserved.

Details were also given concerning attacks on neutrals, submarine dangers and oiling on passage.

At 1112 that same morning, tugs pulled the heavy cruiser off, allowing her to raise steam in the Bay and prevent the possibility of choking the condensers in the shallow, muddy harbour. That evening, *Prinz Eugen* weighed and sailed, joining *Bismarck* the following day. The great adventure had begun! Passing westwards, the squadron cleared the Great Belts and steamed into the Kattegat where, on the 20th, the Swedish cruiser *Gotland* was sighted, an unfortunate occurrence for the Germans since it was likely that news of their passage would soon reach British ears.

Their fears were actually quite justified for the C in C of the Home Fleet, Admiral Tovey, received Intelligence of the German squadron's movement that same day. Reconnaissance air patrols were launched immediately and already the hunt was on. Meanwhile, the ships pressed on northwards, and by 0900 on the 21st, stood off Kors Fjord, anchoring in Kalvenes Bay shortly after midday. Here steamers came alongside as makeshift torpedo protection and the oiler *Wollin* moved up to refuel the heavy cruiser, pumping a little over 700 tonnes into her tanks. While oiling continued, the camouflage scheme was overpainted grey on the orders of the Fleet Commander. The stay in the Norwegian fjord was brief and both ships weighed at 1930. Passing through Hjelte Fjord, they reached the open sea, accompanied by their escorting destroyers. Steering north-

Opposite page, top: *Bismarck* photographed just prior to 'Rheinübung'. Note she still has her camouflage pattern, which was not painted out until after her arrival in Norway. The carmine turret tops stand out clearly in the sunlight. The guns in the foreground are the after turrets of *Prinz Eugen*. (W. B. Bilddienst)
Centre: *Norfolk*, typical of the standard British 'Washington'-type heavy cruiser. Three funnels, slab sides and a general clutter of boats and equipment give the design an out-dated appearance as compared to the *Hipper* class. Note too the paucity of both fire-control equipment and AA guns.
Bottom: *Hood* in the 1920s. By the time she met *Bismarck* and *Prinz Eugen* in 1941 her 5.5in guns and aircraft had been landed, but other equipment had been added and her displacement increased somewhat. (National Maritime Museum)

wards under cloudy skies, the squadron continued its sortie, the destroyers being detached in the morning hours of the 22nd. At midday, the ships were about 220 nautical miles north-west of Trondheim, steering 320° under cloudy skies, with a SSE wind. Shortly afterwards, Lütjens signalled his intentions for the following day to his consort, orders which basically consisted of readiness and steaming instructions. Outside friendly aircraft range now, the coloured turret tops and the 'Hakenkreuz' on forecastle and quarterdecks were painted out, so as not to make it too easy for enemy reconnaissance planes to determine their nationality.

North-east of Iceland, the weather began to close in, with rain falling and the likelihood of further deterioration (which would favour the undetected break-through). This probably persuaded Admiral Lütjens to cancel the oiling rendezvous with *Weisenburg* and take advantage of the prevailing weather. By the evening of the 22nd, visibility was down to only 300–400 metres and the ships, steaming at 24 knots, could not see each other. Aboard the *Prinz* Brinckmann was relieved, the weather seemed to be on their side! His meteorologist predicted that it would extend as far as the southern tip of Greenland, and if so their undetected passage would be much easier, because they believed that the patrolling British cruisers were not yet fitted with radar.

As the ships forged ahead on a generally westerly course, the weather continued to deteriorate. Fog, cloud and rain made watchkeeping and lookout duty a cold, miserable task despite the foul-weather gear. At 1200 on the 23rd, the two ships were about 75 miles off the north coast of Iceland, shaping course around the declared British minefield and making for the north-eastern entrance to the Denmark Strait. In the early evening, *Bismarck* closed-up action stations, reporting a vessel to starboard, which turned out to be an iceberg! They had reached the ice edge and came round to port to run down the Denmark Strait and head for the open Atlantic. After the previous poor visibility and rain, the air was now very clear, with good visibility to starboard towards the ice, while to port, the Icelandic coast was shrouded in mist. Conditions had turned a little against them.

Zigzagging now through the broken ice floes, *Bismarck* and *Prinz Eugen* threaded their way south-west, hoping that the patrolling cruisers could be avoided. This hope was shortlived; less than half an hour after entering the straits, *Bismarck* detected a shadow, off to port, which quickly disappeared into the mist that had descended once more. Aboard *Prinz Eugen*, too, the hydrophones and radar had detected the stranger, who in those latitudes could only be one of the anticipated British cruiser patrols. Both ships closed-up to action stations, while the lookouts strained to identify the foe. *Bismarck* led the cruiser through the ice-littered sea, a pregnant silence pervading the frosty air. In the brief moment when the enemy had been visible, its three funnels had been recognized – a County-class heavy cruiser. Then at 1922, *Bismarck* fired her first shells in anger, loosing five salvoes from her 13.8cm guns at the British ship, which *Prinz Eugen* could not initially see. The target was, in fact, *Norfolk* (Captain A. A. L. Phillips), Flagship of Rear-Admiral Wake Walker, commanding the 1st

Cruiser Squadron. She managed to avoid the shells and slip back into the mists, to transmit an 'enemy sighted' report. Unbeknown to the Germans, a second cruiser had also made contact a little earlier and, being equipped with radar of modern pattern, was able to keep contact while remaining unseen. This ship was the *Suffolk* (Captain R. M. Ellis). At one point, *Norfolk* closed and actually opened fire on Lütjens' squadron, but the range was too great and her shells fell far short. Both cruisers remained in contact throughout the evening and night of the 23rd/24th, their propeller noises clearly audible to those aboard the German ships, who realized with some foreboding that this tenacious contact holding in poor weather could only mean that the British *did* have radar. It augured ill for the future.

In fact, the first misfortune had already befallen the Germans, for the shock of *Bismarck*'s gunfire had disabled her radar; she was blind forward. In consequence, *Prinz Eugen* was ordered to lead the squadron and act as its eyes – a change which was to have important consequences in a few hours' time.

The 24th brought snow, carried on a gentle breeze under leaden clouds, as the ships forged on at thirty knots, avoiding the occasional icebergs dotted about the straits. Throughout the middle watch, the sky remained overcast, but the wind freshened as time wore on, and the rising seas began to break over the forecastles of the ships. It remained cold. Ominously, the 'B' Dienst monitoring service aboard the German cruiser informed the bridge that the shadowing cruiser was reporting to her Command the speeds and course alterations of the German squadron, quickly and efficiently. Interception by the Royal Navy could now be only a matter of time.

CONTACT

British measures to intercept the powerful German squadron depended initially upon the battlecruiser squadron (Vice-Admiral L. E. Holland), consisting of the *Hood* (Captain R. Kerr) and *Prince of Wales* (Captain J. C. Leach), which had been sailed from Scapa Flow just after midnight on 21 May. Accompanying the two capital ships were the destroyers, *Achates*, *Antelope*, *Anthony*, *Echo*, *Electra* and *Icarus*. Their orders were to proceed to Iceland, refuel in Hvalfjord and await the expected break-out of the German ships. Following the discovery that *Bismarck* and her consort were no longer in the Norwegian fjords, a report to this effect reached Admiral Tovey (C in C Home Fleet) on the evening of the 28th.

The Home Fleet consisted of *King George V*, *Victorious*, *Repulse*, four cruisers and seven destroyers, and sailed for Icelandic waters on the 22nd. By the time that *Norfolk*'s sighting report was received, it stood about 200 nautical miles south-east of Iceland, Tovey having already concluded that the most likely break-out route would be via the Denmark Strait. Far to the north-west, *Hood* and *Prince of Wales* patrolled off the Rekyjanes peninsula at the south-west corner of Iceland, ideally placed to intercept the German ships. The seas were increasing, making conditions aboard the escorting destroyers difficult, but for the moment they held on. Just after midnight on the 23rd, *Suffolk* lost contact with *Bismarck* as a result of the

treacherous visibility conditions then prevailing in the northern part of the Strait.

A visual error on the cruiser's bridge brought about by mirage conditions, led to the belief that the German battleship had reversed course and was closing *Suffolk*. After reversing course herself, it was not until radar contact had faded that *Suffolk* realized the error, but despite returning to her original course and increasing speed, contact was not regained. The direct result of this was that Holland decided to alter course northwards to increase his chances of interception, based unfortunately on a wrong guess as to what the Germans would do now that they knew they had been discovered. Actually, Lütjens continued south-westwards rather than turn back, so Holland missed him. Then at 0210 on the 24th, *Hood* and *Prince of Wales* turned south once more, with the destroyers being ordered to continue searching to the north. This left the British force in a poor position, without destroyer support and in a tactically unfavourable deployment.

Aboard *Prinz Eugen* and the Flagship, there was as yet no inkling of the nearness of British heavy units, as they held course for the open Atlantic. The brief Arctic twilight had given way to an overcast dawn with a moderate north-westerly wind blowing off the frozen icecaps of Greenland; visibility was about ten nautical miles. Just after the change of watch, at 0400, the hydrophone office aboard the heavy cruiser reported HE bearing 286° (ship's bearing, i.e., broad on port beam). The presence of capital ships was still not suspected, and the hydrophone report assumed it to be one of the shadowing cruisers. Then at 0537, 'B' Dienst reported a new unit signalling off to port and four minutes later, a similar report of a second unit on the same bearing. Two ships in company could mean an intercepting squadron and Brinckmann immediately closed-up his ship to action stations. The Gunnery Officer, K.Kpt.Jasper, raced up to his action station in the foretop where he joined the officer of the watch, Kpt.Lt.-Schmalenbach (who was also Second Gunnery Officer) and scanned the horizon. Four objects were visible, three to port and one on the starboard quarter. Of the former, two in company were on the beam and approaching at high speed. The two single ships were obviously the shadowing cruisers, but the other pair were difficult to identify, other than as enemy, their angle of approach being so acute. Initially neither Jasper nor his colleagues believed that they were battleships, but rather that they were 10,000-ton cruisers, possibly the *Exeter*, *Birmingham* or *Fiji* (sic), and were rather surprised that the British would actually attack such a powerful German squadron with only two heavy cruisers.

As engagement drew closer, the well-oiled gun drill swung into action aboard the German ships. Shells and charges were loaded into ammunition hoists, directors tracked the targets and the range-takers continued to call out the rapidly closing range. The heavy guns elevated and sought out the target, fed by data compiled deep inside the ships where, aboard the *Prinz*, the Commander, F.Kpt.Stoos, kept watch in the Command Centre below the armoured deck. In the foretop, Jasper was still unable accurately to identify his opponents and, still believing them to be cruisers, selected HE base-fuzed

rounds for action. He had in any case to fire the first salvo with nose-fuzed HE because these were already at the guns as ready-use ammunition in case of contact with auxiliary patrol cruisers in the Strait.

The British ships were the first to open fire at 0553 when the range was about 24,500 metres. On their angle of approach, the 'A' arcs were closed, reducing their fire-power to only four 15in and six 14in, but the flash of the guns left Jasper in no doubt that these were no cruisers. Admiral Holland had ordered that fire be concentrated on the leading, or left-hand ship, in the belief that this was *Bismarck*, but the officers in *Prince of Wales* realized that this was not so, and disregarded the order. As the flash of *Hood*'s guns died away, the officers in *Prinz Eugen*'s foretop could clearly see her guns trained not on *Bismarck*, but on themselves. They were under enemy fire for the first time! Brinckmann gave permission to open fire at 0555 and Jasper fired almost immediately, taking *Hood* as the target. The heavy cruiser fired a full eight-gun broadside at a range of 20,200 metres as the shells from *Hood* arrived, bracketing the German ship and throwing up huge columns of dirty water. The fall of shot from *Prinz Eugen*'s first salvo could not be properly observed and a second full salvo was fired. This bracketed *Hood* and was followed by a third, one shell from which struck the British battlecruiser on the boat deck in the vicinity of the main mast, starting a fire which glowed brightly and appeared to pulsate, throwing the after structure into sharp silhouette. Brinckmann now ordered his Gunnery Officer to shift target left and engage the second enemy which hitherto had been left unmolested. In consequence, the directors swung off *Hood* and missed the dramatic finale to the action.

At 0559, *Prinz Eugen* opened fire with a full salvo on *Prince of Wales* at a range of 16,000–17,000 metres and continued firing with forward and after turret groups alternately. *Bismarck*'s secondary armament was also engaging this target, which quickly suffered hits, the first of which, on the compass platform, killed or wounded every man there except Captain Leach. *Prinz Eugen* claimed two hits on the port side aft from her first salvo.

In the meantime, *Bismarck*'s guns, which had fired with chilling accuracy from the outset, landed a salvo around *Hood*, one or more shells of which struck the British ship, causing an enormous explosion in the vicinity of the after turrets. A huge column of smoke and flame shot skywards with turrets, guns, superstructure and wreckage being thrown high into the air, reminiscent of the fate of other British battlecruisers at Jutland, 25 years earlier. The explosion, of what can only have been her after magazines, broke *Hood* in two, just as she was being turned to allow 'X' and 'Y' turrets to engage. The 42,500-ton ship sank within three or four minutes. There were but three survivors from her ship's company of 1,419 men.

After their eighth salvo, high up in the foretop of *Prinz Eugen*, the fire-control crew tracking *Prince of Wales* saw her alter course violently and then through their sights came the awesome view of the remains of *Hood* projecting bows up from the water at an angle of about 45°. Avoiding the remains of her consort, the unfortunate *Prince of Wales* now received the attention of both main and secondary armaments of the two German ships. With part of her armament defective, her reply was weak and she was soon suffering badly, being hit by at least three shells from *Prinz Eugen* and four from the Flagship. As the range had dropped, even the 10.5cm heavy flak aboard *Prinz Eugen* had joined in, firing 78 rounds before being forced to engage a shadowing Sunderland aircraft. During the engagement the German cruiser made a violent alteration of course when the hydrophone office reported torpedoes approaching, one or two of which Brinckmann believed that he saw. Actually, it is doubtful if these were more than a figment of the imagination, for although *Hood* was fitted with two torpedo tubes above water on the beam, she was never on a firing bearing, and certainly not at the time when they would have had to have been launched to arrive at *Prinz Eugen* at 0505 or thereabouts.

The range gradually opened again and after 28 salvoes, the ships' turns caused the funnel gases to obscure the range and then the forward turrets became wooded. Control was shifted aft, where Lt.z.S.Albrecht took over in the after director, engaging with 'C' and 'D' turrets until ceasefire at 0609 when the enemy, covered by smoke, was obviously disengaging. During the brief engagement, it lasted a mere 24 minutes, the heavy cruiser had fired a total of 157 rounds main armament and 78 10.5cm rounds on surface targets. *Bismarck* had expended 93 rounds of 38.1cm ammunition. Unbeknown to the German gunners was the unreliable nature of their fuzes, for of the three 38cm shells which struck *Prince of Wales*, only one exploded, and of four 20.3cm rounds from *Prinz Eugen* which found their target, but one exploded. *Prinz Eugen* had received no damage at all, but *Bismarck* had received three hits from *Prince of Wales* which, although not serious in themselves, forced Admiral Lütjens to revise his plans for the Atlantic sortie.

The three hits on the Flagship struck the port side; one exploded in No. 4 generator room, having penetrated the armoured deck, and caused further flooding in No. 2 port boiler room. The flooding could, however, be contained for the time being. A second hit in the bows on compartments XX and XXI destroyed or contaminated several oil bunkers, while the third caused insignificant structural damage. Five men were slightly injured. It was the hit in the bows which was to have the most significant influence on 'Rheinübung' for the shell passed straight through the lightly armoured bows just above the waterline, allowing about 2,000 tonnes of seawater to flood the forward compartments. This cut off or damaged the fuel feed pumps serving the foremost bunkers and, as a result, some 1,000 tonnes of precious oil fuel could not be tapped. The consequences of this on the ship's endurance is obvious, but in addition, her speed was reduced by two knots and a tell-tale trail of oil was being left in the wake. *Bismarck* was now down 3° by the bow and listing 9° to port, but counter-flooding reduced this to a certain extent.

The action was a tactical success for Admiral Lütjens, but he would have preferred an unobserved entry into the North Atlantic – his target was the mercantile sea lanes, not the capital ships of the Royal Navy. Aboard *Prinz Eugen* there was general satisfaction with the ship's performance, the only sour note

being the question of the non-use of her torpedo outfit. Brinkmann had given permission for the torpedo armament (under the command of Kpt.Lt.Reimann) to open fire when in range almost as soon as he had given the same orders to the guns. No torpedoes were launched and at about 0501 Brinkmann had repeated the order, but still the torpedoes remained in their tubes. This led to later criticism of Reimann for missing a vital opportunity.

In fact, the angle of approach of the British ships had been so acute, that at first there was no likelihood of torpedoes being effective. Then, after *Hood* had been hit and *Prince of Wales* altered on to a more favourable inclination, there was some disagreement as to the correct range figure. While this was being confirmed, the surviving British ship had begun to take such punishment that she turned away, and while the torpedo control position was deciding if she had turned towards or away, the only opportunity for torpedo use had passed. Thereafter, the range opened. In fact, the range was never less than about 13,000 metres and then for only a matter of minutes (possibly only two or three). Since the maximum range for a G7a torpedo was only 15,000 metres at 30 knots, the running time would have been some fifteen minutes. The chance of the enemy being in the same position as the torpedo after this length of time was very remote and it was not unreasonable for the TO to withhold his fire and await a better opportunity. Later, Flag Officer (Cruisers) and the new Fleet Commander, Admiral Schniewind, both considered that every opportunity should have been taken for torpedo attack and Reimann suffered some censure. It was recognized, nevertheless, that training was inadequate and a mere two days' torpedo practice in the Baltic was no real grounding for action conditions.

PRINZ EUGEN ALONE

The German ships had now succeeded in breaking out into the Atlantic, but in doing so had stirred up a hornets' nest. They continued south-westwards after making the unpleasant discovery that *Bismarck* was leaving a trail of oil – a result of a hit in the bows. This would make it doubly difficult to shake off the tenacious shadowers, which now included the damaged *Prince of Wales* as well as the two heavy cruisers. In the course of the morning, the weather deteriorated, with an easterly wind and a slight swell. Rain squalls and mist reduced visibility and only infrequently did the cloud cover break to reveal a watery sun. By midday on the 24th, Lütjens had already decided to break off the sortie because of fuel loss and reduced speed (28 knots), but intended to release the cruiser for mercantile warfare if the shadowers could be eluded. *Bismarck* herself would make for Saint-Nazaire for repairs – a decision which surprised the SKL who had expected Lütjens to return to Germany the way he came out. The reasons behind Lütjens' decision are not known, but it is likely that he considered a second attempt at forcing the Straits after repairs in Germany would have much less chance of success and that, operational once more in Saint-Nazaire, the Atlantic would be much more accessible.

During the afternoon, *Prinz Eugen* received Lütjens' intentions for the shaking off of the shadowers. At a suitable time, during a rain squall, on receipt of the code-word 'HOOD', the Flagship would break away west, leaving the cruiser to continue on the original course and, on breaking contact with the enemy, make for one of the supporting oilers and commence mercantile warfare. At 1540, the first attempt at eluding the shadowers was made. *Bismarck* steered away to starboard and was quickly lost in the mist. Fifteen minutes later, a reconnaissance aircraft found the cruiser, only to be met with a barrage of flak before disappearing in the haze and then, barely 20 minutes after she had left, the Flagship reappeared. She had run into a cruiser off to starboard. A second attempt was made at 1814, when *Bismarck*, after ordering the cruiser to drop back a little, altered to starboard and detached.

Brinckmann did not know the exact intentions of the Fleet Commander, but saw two possibilities: a break-back to Germany or Norway or, to make for the French Atlantic coast. In his opinion, the former would have involved the greatest risk, bearing in mind the shadowers. For the heavy cruiser, the pressing need would soon be fuel; she had only 1,350m^3 remaining (45 per cent of capacity). Two oilers, *Lothringen* and *Belchen*, were scheduled to be stationed south of Greenland, the former in the entrance of the Davis Strait and the latter closer to the south of Greenland's Cape Farewell. However, no confirmatory signal that they were on station had been received, and a detour to the north-west, besides being possibly fruitless, would also bring his ship within air reconnaissance range or into contact with US vessels, which would surely report him. Two other oilers, *Esso Hamburg* and *Spichern*, were definitely known not to be in position, but they were on passage and their approximate position was known. Brinckmann decided to go for the southern group on the grounds that: (i) better weather would give him a better chance to see patrols on the horizon and avoid them, thus sparing fuel; (ii) wider sea room to avoid pursuit; (iii) less chance of US air patrols; (iv) the further south, the longer the nights.

The decision was a difficult one to make, for it involved a passage of some 1,000 nautical miles and it might be necessary to use every drop of available fuel. A signal was sent to Gruppe (West) informing them of the critical fuel situation and the intention to go for *Esso Hamburg*. Two hours later, Gruppe (West) replied with the position of *Spichern* (BD78), in mid Atlantic, roughly on the latitude of Cape Sable, Nova Scotia, and some 1,200 miles off. *Esso Hamburg* was even further away.

Prinz Eugen continued southwards throughout the remainder of 24 May, the seas rising as the day wore on. The wind had increased to north-westerly Force 6, and the seas swept the forecastle, throwing spray over the forward turrets and bridge. The sky was overcast and the visibility poor with foggy patches. Of their consort they heard little and now, alone, the heavy cruiser rolled on through the night. The weather remained heavy into the next morning, during which time, avoiding action was taken on detection of individual ships – refuelling was the top priority. By evening, the weather had moderated, with the wind backing WSW, and the cloud cover had broken up. The high ground swell had subsided and visibility increased to reveal a clear horizon. The day passed

uneventfully, but the need to locate an oiler was becoming pressing. On the morning of the 26th, Brinckmann believed that his auxiliary could not be far away and ordered her to transmit homing signals. It was a bright, clear and fortunately calm day, ideal for oiling at sea. Suddenly both the foretop lookouts and hydrophone office reported a ship. Slowly the sunlit upper works of an oiler appeared over the horizon – it was *Spichern*. The fuel crisis was over!

Preparations for oiling were begun immediately and oil soon began to flow into the cruiser's tanks, which were down to only 480 tonnes of which 300 tonnes could not be pumped out. Oiling was a time-consuming exercise even with trained crews, so that it was not until 2230 before oiling was completed with 2,815m^3 being taken on board. *Prinz Eugen* could now begin her planned attack on the merchant shipping routes. Her orders were to operate on the 'HX' convoy routes, west of 35°W, and for this purpose, two auxiliaries, *Kota Pinang* and *Gonzenheim*, were detailed to act as reconnaissance ships stationed in the western Atlantic. Since these two would not be on station until late on the 27th, Brinckmann decided to make a brief northwards sortie after completion of oiling, towards the southern sector of the 'HX' route, hoping to encounter independents and, if the hunt for *Bismarck* had drawn off as much of the Royal Navy's strength as expected, possibly weakly escorted convoys as well. If *Bismarck* were sunk, however, he expected that this sortie would be untenable, in which case he would top-up his tanks and replenish 10.5cm ammunition from *Esso Hamburg*, then operate to the south.

On the 27th, *Prinz Eugen* moved west to search for the two auxiliaries and give them their orders. During the morning, however, news of the torpedo hit on *Bismarck*'s steering came through and cast gloom over those who were informed of it. It seemed certain that the Flagship was doomed. Then a signal from Gruppe (West) reached the cruiser to the effect that an Italian submarine had reported 'five battleships' steering south-west at high speed. The position of these ships, to the northeast of the Azores, led Brinckmann to believe that they might be chasing *Prinz Eugen*. In view of this, he decided to abandon his passage towards the 'HX' convoy route. To avoid the suspected pursuing squadron, Brinckmann briefly considered escaping to the north, but he discarded the idea because it would bring him within range of air patrols. A run to the west was also inadvisable because of the reported presence of the US coast-guard cutter, *Spencer*, which would, in all probability, make a report which could be overheard by British forces.

He decided to run south and operate, based on the oiler *Breme*, as *Ermland* was not yet available. His target was now to be the New York–Lisbon route, and the auxiliaries to the north would have to wait until the dust had settled. A further problem which manifested itself was the ship's machinery. Having operated at mainly high speeds since the 19th, it was in dire need of attention. During the afternoon, news of the end of *Bismarck* was received, casting a gloom over the cruiser. A sense of frustration was evident at their not being present to aid the Flagship, but merely cruising about the empty ocean. Actually, had the cruiser been present, she too would have been overwhelmed.

Prinz Eugen refuelled from *Esso Hamburg* the next day and, having received reports that the British Fleet was withdrawing to base after sinking *Bismarck*, intended to move further south to intrude on the USA–Portugal routes. This move, however, was frustrated by continuing and increasing machinery problems. A high-pressure steam leak on the main line between No. 1 and No. 2 boiler rooms on the port side prevented the port turbine from developing full power, and the starboard turbine was restricted by a damaged propeller blade, possibly caused by ice in the Denmark Strait. The main cooling pump for the centre engine was overloaded because of the high water temperature, and the port one was in a similar condition. At one point the port engine stopped and it was found that a bearing in the LP turbine was damaged. Added to these

problems was a high feed-water loss. Maximum speed was reduced to 28 knots and it was not impossible that further, more catastrophic damage might occur. The ship's main advantage over the armed Merchant Raiders, its high speed, was now gone and in view of the unreliable state of the machinery, it was decided to break off the Atlantic sortie.

On the 31st, Brinckmann signalled his intentions to Gruppe (West) and, having been met by the 5th Destroyer Flotilla, arrived safely in Brest on 1 June. *Prinz Eugen* had been at sea for fourteen days, steamed 7,000 nautical miles and consumed 6,410m³ of fuel for no visible return. Not only had the *Bismarck* been lost, but British crypto analysts had broken the German codes and as a result, the efficient and widespread support ship system was decimated. Of the ships assigned to 'Rheinübung'

for *Prinz Eugen*'s support, *Gonzenheim* was intercepted by *Nelson* and *Neptune* on 4 June, scuttled herself to avoid capture and was torpedoed by the cruiser. *Esso Hamburg* also scuttled herself on interception by *London* the same day. A similar fate befell *Friedrich Breme* (*Sheffield*) on 12 June and *Lothringen* was captured by *Dunedin* three days later. *Kota Penang* lasted longer and escaped the searches in June, but ran into *Kenya* in October *en route* to the Indian Ocean to supply U-boats. Overall it was an expensive exercise for the Kriegsmarine and, in fact, the last of its kind although further sorties were planned up to as late as early 1943, but none ever reached the Atlantic. *Prinz Eugen* now found herself trapped in Brest together with *Scharnhorst* and *Gneisenau* and was to spend the next eight months in that port.

Below: *Prinz Eugen* arrives in Brest after 'Rheinübung'. Note the paint eroded by the action of the bow wave. (Bundesarchiv-Koblenz)

12: THE BALTIC, 1940–1943

Consequent upon the German–Soviet Non-aggression Pact and the subsequent division of Poland by those nations, the Baltic became a peacetime theatre of operations for the Kriegsmarine since, of the other nations bordering the sea, Sweden was neutral and Finland strongly pro-German. No British or French forces ever penetrated farther than the Kattegat, nor was there any attempt to operate in Germany's 'back-yard' as happened in the First World War when British submarines operated from Russian bases. This latter strategy was, in any case, no longer tenable because there was no sympathetic base available in 1939/40. The absence of opposition and the limited range of the RAF during the early war years allowed the Kriegsmarine a first-class training area which was utilized to the full. In fact, with the build-up of the U-boat arm and the need of large numbers of seamen and technicians for the minesweepers, a/s and patrol craft from the Arctic to the Mediterranean, it assumed vital importance. To supply the necessary sea-going training facilities, the surviving light cruisers were withdrawn from active front-line service and once again assumed their former peacetime role. Their usefulness was, in any event, greatly reduced by the severe operational restraints placed upon them as described in Chapter 2. After the success of 'Weserübung', there remained only four light cruisers, *Nürnberg*, *Leipzig*, *Köln* and *Emden*, of which *Leipzig* was of little use for anything but training, following her torpedo damage in 1939. In the training role, their main advantage lay in their ability to accommodate large numbers of trainees and space for training them. OKM ordered them all to be used for training on 15 February 1941.

Emden had returned to Swinemünde from Oslo (where she had been employed as a radio link) on 8 June 1940 after which she remained under minor refit, or otherwise non-operational, until mid August. During this time, many of her company were drafted to man ships captured in French ports. At the beginning of November 1940, she landed her ammunition, disembarked her crew to the accommodation ship *Monte Olivia* and was docked at Deutsche Werke (Kiel) for overhaul. This extended to February 1941 when she joined the training squadron. On her return from Norway, *Köln* spent two weeks idle at Kiel before moving east to Swinemünde where she remained until 11 May 1940, when she was ordered to Wilhelmshaven for operational duty with Gruppe (West). By the 14th, she was anchored in Wilhelmshaven, loaded with mines, but because of the prevailing weather, did not sail until the 16th, when, in company with *Grille* (also mine-laden) and escorted by *Beitzen*, *Schoemann*, *Heinemann*, *Kondor* and *Greif*, she put to sea on a sortie to the Fisher Bank. The lay proceeded without incident and after returning on the 18th, further mines were loaded for a second operation with the same ships. As the squadron returned to base, *Köln* and *Grille* were ordered to the Baltic. After a brief interlude with the Schiffes Artillerie Schüle (SAS) (Naval Gunnery School) at Sassnitz, *Köln* spent from mid June to mid August in the Kiel area, much of it in dockyard hands at Germania or Deutsche Werke.

Save for a minor collision with *U70* on 16 August, the next three and a half months were uneventful, taken up mainly on exercises and training in the southern Baltic. Back in Kiel once more at the beginning of December, *Köln* embarked mines from *Lauting* and sailed with *Nürnberg* on 4 December for an operation off the entrance to the Skagerrak. Elements of the 1st and 2nd Torpedo-boat Flotillas escorted the two cruisers, but heavy seas and gale-force winds caused Gruppe (Nord) to abandon the operation. *Köln* returned to Swinemünde where she disembarked her deck load, remaining in the area until allocated for training duties. The crippled *Leipzig* recommissioned at Danzig on 1 December 1940, under the command of Kpt.z.S.Stichling, almost a year after her torpedoing and was immediately used for training purposes. Finally, the newest light cruiser, *Nürnberg*, having completed her torpedo damage repairs by the end of April 1940, spent a brief period in Norwegian waters from June to July, before returning to the Baltic for training duties.

The duties of the training cruisers were fourfold:

(a) Basic new-entry training of seamen and technical recruits, including weapons training.

(b) Senior rates training.

(c) Junior officer training.

(d) Target ship, trials and experimental duties.

All courses were of three months' duration, the trainees forming the bulk of the ship's companies with only a small nucleus of trained men. In consequence, the ships were no longer capable of operational deployment; only a proportion of their flak outfits and the essential damage-control installations were maintained at readiness. Dockyard time was to be reduced to the barest minimum, commensurate with their ability to fulfil the training role.

Right: The unfortunate *Luchs*, lost while escorting *Nürnberg* home from Norway in 1940. (W. B. Bilddienst)
Below: *Nürnberg* in June 1940 lying in Trondheim. Evident is the camouflage pattern and the Arado Ar 196 aircraft. (Bundesarchiv-Koblenz)

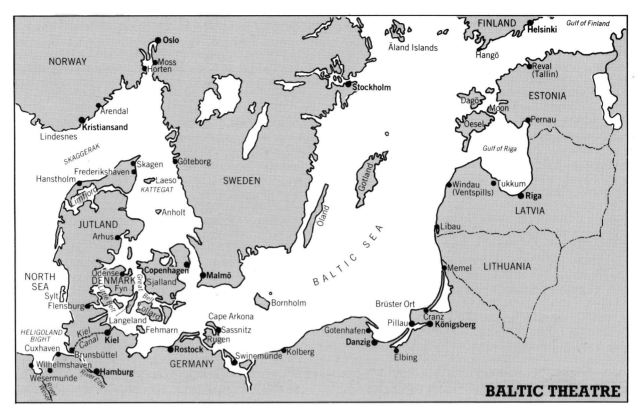

BALTIC THEATRE

WAR IN THE EAST

Only four months were to pass before this routine was disrupted by the launching of the invasion of Russia – Operation 'Barbarossa'. Hitler unleashed his armies against the Soviet Union at 0315 on 22 June 1941, to begin a carnage which was to lead to the eventual defeat, not of the USSR, but of Germany herself. In the beginning, however, all went in Germany's favour and her armies were soon thrusting deep into the occupied Baltic states, where they were initially greeted as liberators. It was not until the SS and Gestapo formations moved in behind the front-line troops that the local population began to revise their opinion.

During the early stages of the conflict, the involvement of naval forces was limited to light forces and submarines, with much emphasis on mine warfare. Then, in September, the possibility of the Soviet Fleet's making a sortie from Lening-rad, led to the formation of the 'Baltenflotte'. This force was stationed at the western entrance to the Gulf of Finland and was built around the new battleship, *Tirpitz*. Of the cruisers, *Köln* and *Nürnberg* were allocated to the northern group, while *Leipzig* and *Emden* belonged to the southern group. The latter ships were the first to go into action, using their guns in support of the Army ashore, which was being delayed by strong Soviet resistance on the Baltic island of Oesel. This large island lies across the entrance to the Gulf of Riga and its southern peninsula, known as the Sworbe, controlled the northern side of the Irben Strait, the only route into the Gulf from the west. The Army had captured much of the low and thickly wooded,

limestone island, but the Sworbe peninsula itself remained in Soviet hands.

On 23 September, *Leipzig* and *Emden* accompanied by *T7*, sailed from Swinemünde, oiled at Pillau and then sailed to the captured Latvian port of Libau, where they arrived the following evening, having been delayed by fog. While on passage, orders were received from Flag Officer (Cruisers) for an early bombardment of the Sworbe by the two cruisers. In Libau naval harbour, Kpt.z.S.Stichling, who had been appointed Commander of the Southern Group, issued tactical orders to the ships under his command (the two cruisers, *T11*, *T7*, *T8* and later, *S104*). In the meantime, *Leipzig* embarked her aircraft for spotting and a/s purposes. The operation was timed to commence at dawn on the 26th, and was code-named 'Weststurm'. Little air opposition was anticipated, and only a few motor torpedo-boats were thought to be available to the Soviets, although the presence of submarines could not be discounted. Ashore, there was believed to be a heavy gun battery on the southern tip of the peninsula, and another at Kaunisbaa was suspected, though details were lacking. On the previous day the front line had been at Salmo. The object of the bombardment was to disrupt Soviet rear echelons and lines of retreat, not to direct supportive fire so close to the front-line. The initial target zone was the Kaunispe–Kargi–Loupollu area, particularly the airfield. Further targets would be engaged at the direction of the Army ashore.

On the evening of the 25th, the squadron cleared Libau and proceeded northwards for the entrance to the Gulf of Riga,

under an overcast sky and in calm seas. Off to starboard, the overgrown sandy dunes of the Latvian coast slid by in the darkness, as further radio orders came in detailing the requirements of the 61st Infantry Division whose formations were engaged on Oesel. At about dawn, *Leipzig* flew off her aircraft in preparation for the task ahead, but daylight still had not fully broken so Stichling reversed course for a time, while awaiting better light. At 0600, the cruisers opened fire on the northern target zone. For the next five hours, six bombardments were fired, five on the northern zone and one on the southern. The torpedo-boats also engaged, using their single 10.5cm guns. Altogether, *Leipzig* fired 327 rounds of main armament, *Emden* 245 and the torpedo-boats 51 rounds. After recovering her aircraft which, because of poor observation conditions, had been employed on a/s duties since the start of the action, the squadron withdrew from the coast to await further orders.

These were received in the course of the afternoon, being basically a repeat of 'Weststurm' the following day. In the meantime, minesweepers would continue the gun action inshore. After an uneventful night, the German squadron closed the coast again to begin its second bombardment, *Leipzig* launching her aircraft again as dawn broke. Five minutes after the Arado took the air, the ship's guns opened fire. This time the shore battery replied, shell splashes from heavy guns rising short of the bombarding ships. Stichling withdrew the escort out of the danger area, but otherwise, the Germans were unhindered by the Soviet guns. More signi-ficantly, the Arado reported the presence of four MTBs in Labaru harbour. Less than an hour later, the Captain of the 18th Minesweeping Flotilla reported enemy MTBs at sea. By now, the enemy shore batteries were engaging the ships, with calibres estimated to be at least 28cm for the southern battery and probably 15cm or 18cm for the second. Although no hits had been suffered by the ships, it began to appear that this second operation would not be as uncontested as the first. On the other hand, the Arado reported effective gunfire and Stukas had also been in action, clearly visible from the ships.

Opposition from the Soviet Navy finally materialized at 0917 when four MTBs attacked from the south-west. These four boats, *TKA72, 82, 92* and *102*, under the command of Kapitan Lieutenant Gumanenko, were probably the units located by air reconnaissance that morning, and had sailed to attack the bombarding squadron. They were first sighted by the foretop lookout in *Emden*, whereupon, the shore bombardment was broken off. Both cruisers increased to full speed as Stichling ordered his escort to deal with the attackers. Two minutes after first being sighted, the MTBs were taken under fire by *Emden* with her forward guns at a range of 10,000 metres, before she altered course to engage with all her armament. *Leipzig* opened fire a few minutes later, engaging the right-wing MTB at a range of about 6,000 metres. The target turned to starboard and laid smoke which obscured the area and caused a confused mêlée to develop. *Leipzig*, having scored no visible hits, ceased fire and waited for another target to appear. Barely half a minute later, the silhouette of a second MTB came into view.

After several more misses, this boat too turned off to starboard then received heavy hits and blew up.

Both cruisers now engaged the MTBs in a confused action for the next twenty minutes or so, before the range was fouled by the torpedo-boats moving in as ordered, to drive off the Soviet boats. This they succeeded in doing and by 1000, the brief action was over. The German ships observed only one torpedo track and had not sustained any damage. They had fired 153 (*Leipzig*) and 178 (*Emden*) rounds to claim two MTBs sunk. The actual losses sustained by the Soviets are difficult to determine precisely, but it is known that *TKA82* was lost. In the confusion of the noise and smoke, it is possible that both cruisers claimed the same boat. *T7*, *T8* and *M151*, which had chased the retreating MTBs to the south, soon came under heavy and accurate fire from the shore batteries before being recalled to rejoin the cruisers. Five bombardment runs had been made before the appearance of the MTBs, during which time *Leipzig* had fired 320 rounds, and her consort, 217.

The squadron withdrew from the coast once more and shaped course south to return to Libau for fuel and ammunition. During the afternoon, *Emden* detected radio transmissions whose origin was unknown, but nothing untoward occurred until half an hour later when the ships were some twenty miles west of Windau. At 1427, lookouts reported torpedo tracks to starboard; simultaneously, *T7* also signalled a submarine alarm. Both cruisers turned hard to port as a torpedo passed ahead of *Leipzig*, whereupon *T7* dropped depth-charges. While *Leipzig* was dodging these torpedoes, further torpedo tracks were sighted to starboard and the listening plots in both cruisers recorded a second submarine contact. *T11* joined *T7* in a hunt for the submarines, leaving *T8* to protect the cruisers. After three-quarters of an hour, *T11* and *T7* were ordered to rejoin the cruisers, having lost contact with the submarines, and course was resumed southwards. Once again, the reconstruction of events from the Soviet point of view is hampered by their uncooperative nature, but there is no doubt that *Shch317* did carry out an attack on the cruisers at this time. However, there is no evidence (other than from German records) for the presence of a second boat.

That evening, the cruisers anchored in the outer harbour at Libau while the torpedo-boats went into the naval harbour to refuel. This operation was to be *Leipzig*'s only active contribution to the war at sea, and having successfully carried it out, she was ordered to Kiel for repairs. *Leipzig* and *Emden*, accompanied by *T11* and *T8*, sailed from Libau on the 28th, bound for Kiel where *T11* and *Leipzig* arrived the following day, having detached *Emden* and *T8* to Gotenhafen *en route*. *Leipzig* entered the Deutsche Werft yard for repairs and overhaul, remaining there until 20 October.

To the north of Oesel, lies the smaller island of Dago which, together with the small island of Moon, commands the northern entrance to the Gulf of Riga. Soviet possession of these islands had enabled warships and auxiliaries, trapped in the Riga area, to be withdrawn through the narrow and shallow Moon Sound to the relative safety of the Gulf of Finland. Even the damaged cruiser *Kirov* had been brought safely through after the sound had been specially dredged. Then, when German land forces reached Pernau and thus secured the whole mainland coastline of the Gulf of Riga, the Soviets were still able to pass MTBs and light craft into the Gulf to interdict German supply traffic, although with scant success. It was intended by the German Army Command that the Baltic islands would be taken by thrusts from Estonia to which end, a small bridgehead was secured on Dago on 16 September, after the 61st Infantry Division had landed on Moon Island two days earlier. In order to mislead the Russians, however, feints from seaward were arranged to give the appearance of a landing by troops on the western side of Dago. For this purpose, the cruiser *Köln* (Kpt.z.S. Huffmeier), together with the torpedo-boats *T2*, *T5*, *T7* and *T8*, as well as minesweepers of the 1st and 4th Flotillas, were to bombard the batteries on Cape Ristna (Operation 'Ostpreussen'). While this was proceeding, a minor landing would be made on the south coast of the island.

Köln sailed from Gotenhafen in the forenoon of 11 October, being joined an hour or two later by *T2* and *T5*. *T7*, having fouled her propellers, would follow later. It would appear that *Köln* did not have a clear idea of the exact position of the gun battery to be attacked, for her Gunnery Officer had to ask

Below: *Leipzig* in Baltic waters, 1941. Note catapult and after tubes removed, and camouflage scheme. (W. B. Bilddienst)

K.Kpt.Erdmann (in command of the torpedo-boats) for details of its location. These he supplied to the best of his ability. By about 0800 on the 12th, the cruiser had reached her position to commence the first bombardment run, having loitered to the west, out of sight of land, as ordered, until the landing had begun. The target lay at Ristna, on the western end of the densely wooded Kopu peninsula. A range of hills ran the length of the peninsula, but at the Ristna end, it was low and sandy with the trees beginning a little way inland. The lighthouse on the northern tip of the peninsula provided a good landmark for the location of the battery which was believed to consist of three guns of about 18cm calibre, with a range of 25,000–30,000 metres. The weather was fine, and visibility was very good as the cruiser began her task. On her first run, *Köln* fired 124 rounds and the shore battery replied with three salvoes. During her second run, only 35 rounds were fired, because ranging and observation were difficult. The Ristna battery was considerably more active on this run, firing some fifteen salvoes and getting uncomfortably close on several occasions. Apart from a splinter hit near 'C' turret, however, *Köln* sustained no damage. Nevertheless, the accuracy of the fire forced constant changes of course, and smoke laid by the torpedo-boats hampered fire control to a certain extent. The minesweepers and torpedo-boats also joined in the engagement, and after a further 126 rounds from *Köln*, the battery was silent and wreathed in smoke. Whether this was due to damage or shortage of ammunition was not certain. The following day, two more runs were made, *Köln* firing a total of 256 rounds and, once again, the smaller ships joined in. This time there was no reply from the shore. By late morning, after the torpedo-boats had completed their shoot, the cruiser set course to return to Gotenhafen, where she arrived the following morning. Reportedly, she had been unsuccessfully attacked on the 13th, by the Soviet submarine *Shch323*, but the cruiser remained unaware of the attempt.

Thus ended the light cruisers' involvement in 'Barbarossa' and they returned once more to their training duties. However, it would appear that their temporary operational use in the eastern Baltic led to consideration of their being generally more actively employed. In the autumn of 1941, it was proposed that *Köln* and *Nürnberg* be allocated for duties with the Fleet. This led to a mild conflict of opinion between Flottenkommando and MOK (Nord) as to the usefulness of the ships in question. Both *Nürnberg* and *Köln* had spent almost the whole of 1941 in the training role, and although the OKM had scheduled each for a six-weeks' refit (*Nürnberg* 15 January–28 February 1942; *Köln* 1 March–15 April 1942), this was not, in the opinion of the Fleet Commander, sufficient for operational employment. The minimum refit period for anything other than a training role would be three months. More seriously, there were just not the trained men available within the fleet to fully man the ships. At the same time, their use in an operational theatre would reduce the output of trainees by nearly 2,000 seamen and more than 1,000 technical ratings per year. Finally, neither ship would be ready before April 1942, nor was either suitable for use in the Atlantic or northern Norway. The views from MOK (Nord) were rather different, it being suggested that as the end

of the war was still not in sight, it would be prudent that, of the four light cruisers, one be kept fully manned and a second mechanically reliable so as to have one ship available at any time should it be needed. Because of her poor seakeeping properties, *Nürnberg* was not considered suitable, and *Leipzig* was out on grounds of low speed. This left *Köln* and *Emden*. Both would need augmentation of their flak outfits, but otherwise were suitable for the envisaged employment; *Emden*'s weak torpedo armament being offset by her good seakeeping and adequate gun armament.

By February 1942, it had been decided to use *Nürnberg* and *Köln* with the Fleet, to which end both were to be put into refit, the former at Deutsche Werke (Kiel). *Nürnberg* required a turbine change, while *Köln* needed work on her turbines, boiler re-tubing, burner modifications, the addition of radar and the removal of the after banks of torpedo tubes. It was estimated that neither could be operational before July 1942. In the event, *Nürnberg* did not sail for Norway until 11 November 1942, and it was *Köln* which sailed first for northern waters, on 9 July (see Chapter 14).

Leipzig and *Emden* remained in the Baltic, employed in training duties, but *Emden* was available for limited operational deployment as required. She was scheduled to remain in the Baltic as a training cruiser until the end of March 1943 when, after a refit, she would be sent to Norway as from August 1943. However, the débâcle in the Barents Sea on 29 December 1942 led to the cancellation of this schedule on 16 February 1943, and she remained in the Baltic. *Leipzig* operated in the eastern Baltic until paid off at Libau on 4 March 1943. *Köln* finally returned to Kiel from Norway on 8 February 1943, paying off on 1 March. *Nürnberg*, too, returned from northern waters in 1943, reaching Kiel on 3 May before going to Wilhelmshaven for refit. All the light cruisers were now in Baltic waters once more, and a pseudo peace atmosphere reigned until 1944 when the Soviet forces began their westward offensive. In January 1943, *Prinz Eugen*, having aborted a second attempt to reach the 'zone of destiny' – Norway – remained in the Baltic operating in a training role from April 1943, while the damaged *Admiral Hipper* had previously returned to Kiel on 7 February, where she received orders to pay off at Wilhelmshaven on 1 March. On the 11th, the cruiser moved under her own power for the last time in more than a year and passed through the Kiel Canal to arrive in Wilhelmshaven on the morning of the 12th. The following day, a Marine flak detachment arrived on board with its own 2cm guns, to take over the ship's air defence, and preparations were made to land both heavy and light flak mountings. Kpt.z.S.Hartmann relinquished command of the ship on the 16th. He ended the war as Port Commander, Oslofjord. Aboard his former command, meanwhile, preparations continued for her de-commissioning, including the application of a suitable camouflage. Finally, on 28 February, *Admiral Hipper* was paid off and the following day, turned over to dockyard control. A month later, Wilhelmshaven Naval Yard was ordered to send the ship to Libau, where *Leipzig* already languished. Under tow, the sorry cruiser arrived in Pillau to which port she had later been redirected, on 17 April 1943.

13: 'CERBERUS' AND 'SPORTPLAST', 1942

In the dockyards of Brest, the German squadron, consisting of *Scharnhorst, Gneisenau* and *Prinz Eugen*, had been subject to heavy air attacks ever since their arrival after operations in the Atlantic during 1941. First one ship then another had received bomb damage, frustrating all the efforts of the SKL to resume Atlantic raiding. It was only a question of time before one or more of the ships was sunk or put out of action completely. *Gneisenau* had been torpedoed in a daring attack by Flying Officer Campbell of 22 Squadron RAF on 6 April 1941. Then *Scharnhorst* received five bomb hits at La Pallice on 24 July.

Nor did *Prinz Eugen* remain unscathed; on 2 July, while lying under camouflage nets in dry dock, she was hit during an air raid. Brinckmann believed himself in the most secure corner of the dockyard, but a stick of six bombs straddled the ship diagonally from port quarter to starboard bow.

The second bomb struck the cruiser on the port side, just aft of 'B' turret, penetrated the armoured deck and finally exploded in the gunnery amplifier room which was completely destroyed. The force of the detonation also distorted the deckhead of the amplifier room (which formed the deck plates

of the Command Centre above), bowing it upwards by about ½-metre and ripping the plates open. Inside the Command Centre, the Commander, F.Kpt.Stoos was closed-up with his action crew. Blast, fire and gas effects wreaked dreadful havoc: Stoos and some sixty others being killed or later dying of wounds, including Bauoberfähnrich Burkhardt, the son of the ship's designer. The structural effects also included damage to the bulkhead between the amplifier space and No. 3 generator room, gyro room and the forward gunnery transmitting-station. The ship's bottom plates also received damage. A lengthy repair period was required, and it extended until the end of the year, the ship being finally undocked on 15 December. Four vierlings were now installed: on the forecastle, quarter deck, 'B' and 'C' turrets and, a few days later, a fifth was fitted on the forward searchlight platform. Early in January 1942, the forward flak directors were finally fitted with their distinctive spherical housings which had not been available on commissioning. After brief machinery trials at the beginning of February, *Prinz Eugen* finally declared herself battleworthy on 7 February.

OPERATION 'CERBERUS'

In Berlin, Grand Admiral Raeder had hoped that the Brest squadron would be able to recommence Atlantic raiding in February, but Hitler had other ideas. He was deeply involved in 'Barbarossa', the invasion of Russia, and wanted nothing to distract him in the Atlantic. Raeder was surprised to receive orders to bring the ships home and by the Channel route at that. He and his staff were violently opposed to such a risky move, wanting to use the safer, north-about route.* Hitler was obdurate, the ships must return to Germany using surprise to force the Channel – they were urgently required in his 'zone of destiny', Norway. Only one alternative was offered to the admirals – pay off the ships and send their guns to Norway instead! Faced with such an alternative, the Naval Staff had little choice and accepted the Führer's demands. In fact, this

---

*Actually, as early as May 1941, SKL had planned the passage of heavy cruisers and 'Panzerschiffen' from Germany to the Atlantic via the Channel route, following the loss of *Bismarck*.

was one occasion when Hitler was unquestionably correct in his assessment of the situation. Planning went ahead rapidly and by late on 11 February, the squadron was preparing for sea. Destroyers and torpedo-boats had been collected from the Baltic and Norway to form an escort, while the minesweeping flotillas had worked unceasingly to lay out a mine-free route from Brest to Heligoland.

Under cover of darkness and in the course of an air raid, the squadron sailed unobserved and undetected by the submarine patrols (currently *Sealion* and *H34*), rounded Ushant at high speed, shaping course for the Channel Islands. Luck was certainly on the Germans' side, for Coastal Command's air patrols experienced radar failures and missed the ships completely. Rounding Alderney and skirting the Cherbourg Peninsula, the air escort arrived at dawn on the 12th, as Admiral Ciliax altered course to cross the Seine Bay. Not until the Germans were off Le Touquet did the RAF sight the ships, and then the pilot of a Spitfire reported them as a convoy and its escort. Later, it was realized that these were in fact the Brest squadron and slowly, the British put together the pieces of the puzzle and launched a series of sporadic and uncoordinated attacks on the ships as they forged on up-Channel. The whole course of events pertaining to Operation 'Cerberus' is a complex story of bad luck, short-sightedness and sheer heroism on the British side, which resulted in a Board of Inquiry at the time, and has been studied in depth by naval historians ever since. The subject demands, and has received, book treatment in its own right. Here we shall follow only the fortunes of *Prinz Eugen* as she sailed home to Germany.

Throughout most of the passage the weather favoured the German ships; grey skies with low cloud and fresh winds, bringing choppy seas. *Prinz Eugen*'s passage remained uneventful until 1320 on the 12th, when she and the port side of the escort came under fire from the Dover batteries. For about a quarter of an hour, shell splashes erupted from the sea, short on the port side, before the cruiser passed out of range. Hardly had the shelling subsided when an abortive attack by MTBs developed which the destroyers dealt with, followed by the heroic attack by Lieutenant-Commander Esmonde's six

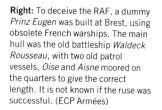

Swordfish of 825 Squadron, FAA. *Prinz Eugen*'s look-outs detected the first Swordfish at 1344 on the port quarter. The port side heavy flak opened fire immediately. Four aircraft could be seen, one of whose torpedoes exploded on impact with the sea on release. Three of the four planes were claimed shot down by *Prinz Eugen* for the expenditure of 47 rounds of 10.5cm. Destroyers and torpedo-boats astern engaged the remaining aircraft.

An hour later, further bombing attacks developed, but without effect, one twin-engined bomber being claimed shot down. At 1530 *Scharnhorst* hit a mine and stopped, but *Gneisenau* steamed on, followed by *Prinz Eugen*. Throughout the afternoon, intermittent air attacks took place, also an imagined submarine attack. At 1643, surface units were detected off the port bow, being provisionally identified as a cruiser and three destroyers. Brinckmann immediately rang down for full speed as shell splashes bracketed his ship, opening fire himself as soon as the smoke from the 10.5cm guns cleared enough for the directors to acquire target. The opening range was 53,000 metres when the first full salvo was fired at the leading destroyer, which was on an almost parallel course. Gun-smoke and the following wind obscured the foretop, with the result that control was passed to the forward director atop the bridge, as torpedo discharges were observed on the enemy ships. Turning violently, the German ships successfully avoided them and continued the action.

It was a confusing fight; the German gun-control crews were never really certain at any time whether their target was a new one or the same one. One enemy ship, probably *Worcester*, was seen to be heavily hit and on fire and although it was believed that she was sinking, such was not the case. The damaged destroyer was escorted home by *Campbell*, *Vivacious*, *Mackay* and *Whitshed*. This action lasted only eleven minutes. Aircraft bombing and torpedo attacks continued throughout the afternoon and evening, but failed to inflict any damage to *Prinz Eugen*, except some personnel losses to machine-gun fire.

In the early evening, as she endeavoured to close *Gneisenau*, the WSW wind had risen to near gale-force and the cruiser's bows began to dig deep into the shallow seas, forcing the forecastle vierling's crew to be withdrawn. 31 knots were all which could be obtained and as the Flagship did not wish to reduce speed, the cruiser was detached with the 3rd Torpedo-boat Flotilla for escort. By this time, the ship's position was not accurately known and at times speed was progressively reduced to only five knots as the water shoaled. DF fixes later gave a better idea of the ship's position, but the conditions prevailing at midnight on 12/13 February were unhelpful to say the least. The winds were now gusting gale force with driving rain and sleet. There was no moon. At 0143, the cruiser was ordered to Brunsbüttel together with *Gneisenau*, but there were no pilots or tugs available, and the cruiser had to steam back and forth outside until 0800 when both ships passed into the Elbe under escort.

TO NORWAY

In Brunsbüttel lock, Brinckmann received orders to replenish fuel and ammunition, take on torpedoes and warheads and

embark his aircraft in preparation for *Prinz Eugen*'s move to Norway. By the 19th, this had been completed and the ship prepared to sail. After taking aboard more than 250 men returning from leave and bound for Norway, *Prinz Eugen* put to sea once more, navigating the ice-choked Elbe and, joined by her escort (*Beitzen, Jacobi, Ihn, Z25* and *Seeadler*), proceeded northwards through the German Bight in company with *Admiral Scheer*. The British Admiralty had gathered Intelligence of the impending moves through 'Ultra' decrypts, the movement of Luftwaffe units to Norway, and from naval orders setting special W/T watches.

The beginning of the operation itself, was only given away by the sudden increase in W/T traffic with surface units, on Kootwijk radio from the 20th. Accordingly, they alerted the air patrols and torpedo-bomber squadrons. One of these patrols from No. 16 Group Coastal Command, in fact sighted the squadron off the Dutch coast on the morning of the 20th, whereupon, a torpedo strike was launched. The 'B' dienst troop aboard the cruiser deciphered its sighting report an hour later, '2 battleships, 3 cruisers probably 4 destroyers off Limfjord, course 360°.' Immediately on receipt of this, Vizeadmiral Ciliax, whose flag *Prinz Eugen* wore, ordered the squadron to reverse course, a ruse which successfully avoided the British torpedo attack. At 1432, Ciliax was ordered by Gruppe (Nord) to break off the attempt and return to the Elbe, but a couple of hours later, this order was rescinded and at 1746, Ciliax received instructions to proceed to Skudesnes and thence to Bergen via the Inner Leads. Course northwards was

resumed late that evening and by midnight on the 21st/22nd, the squadron once more stood west of Limfjord. During the morning of the 22nd, *Prinz Eugen* took aboard pilots off Karmsund for the difficult negotiation of the Inner Leads. Shortly after this, two RAF aircraft found the ships by chance and although one was shot down, the Admiralty again knew where their quarry lay.

By early afternoon, *Prinz Eugen* had anchored in Grimstadfjord whence, almost a year ago, the 'Rheinübung' adventure had begun with such high hopes. Passage northwards was resumed that night, reaching the open sea about an hour before midnight. The sky was completely overcast with a moderate WSW breeze carrying rain and reducing visibility to about 3–4 nautical miles. The moon shone intermittently through the occasional gap in the clouds, but as the middle watch wore on, the rain turned to snow, visibility perceptibly decreased and a northerly swell developed. During the morning watch, the wind increased to Force 5, gusting, and visibility was further reduced. Seas began to break over the forecastle bringing the danger of icing, for it was bitterly cold. The watch on deck miserably scanned their allotted sectors and longed for the change of watch at 0800 when they could retire to the stuffy fug below decks. At 0630, Grip Light came over the horizon, but was frequently lost in the squalls as the squadron shaped course for the Ytrefjord and the southern approaches to Trondheim.

The approaches to Trondheim, a major German base in Norway, were patrolled by British submarines at all times, the current boat being HMSM *Trident* (Lieutenant-Commander

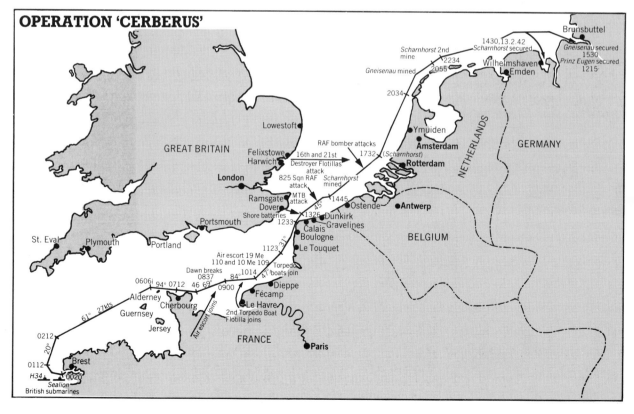

OPERATION 'CERBERUS'

Sladen) which had not sailed until the 19th. On the morning of the 23rd, *Trident* lay stopped, about 19 nautical miles due east of Grip Light, when the enemy ships were sighted dimly aft of the beam to port. Sladen manoeuvred to close the target which was quickly identified as 'a "Pocket Battleship" leading a cruiser with three escorting destroyers – one ahead and one on each beam'. *Trident* fired a dispersed salvo of seven torpedoes or would have done so had not an order been misinterpreted and the salvo checked after only half the torpedoes had been fired. After the third torpedo was running Sladen dived and awaited events.

Aboard the cruiser, the premature detonation of one torpedo was heard at 0702, somewhere astern to port, but its cause was a mystery. Three minutes later, *Prinz Eugen* herself reeled under the impact of a torpedo which stopped all turbines and forced open the steam safety valves. The noise of escaping steam deafened all on the bridge and it was some time before communications with the engine room could be resumed. Damage control reports came in quickly and it was soon obvious that the rudders had gone although by some miracle, the propellers remained undamaged despite some flooding of the centre-shaft tunnel.

Ciliax believed the explosion to have been caused by a mine, but Brinckmann correctly assessed it as a torpedo hit, but could not be sure if it was from an aircraft or a submarine. Whichever it was, his ship now lay stopped and disabled in an extremely dangerous area. The extreme stern hung down in the water and eleven men, mostly soldiers and Todt-organization men *en route* to Trondheim, had been killed in the explosion. They had been berthed aft, as had the ship's two Luftwaffe officers for the Arado, who were among the 25 wounded. After attempts to steer with main engines, Brinckmann finally managed to turn the ship from broadside on to the sea and shape course for the safety of the fjords. The destroyers closed-up and an air escort appeared overhead as the cruiser limped in at about ten knots. *Z25*, *T5* and *T12* as well as *Schoemann*, shepherded the casualty towards Trondheim during which time, the ship's trim was improved by the transfer of all the shells from 'C' and 'D' magazines forward – a task which took about eleven hours! Slowly but surely the distance to Trondheim reduced until *Prinz Eugen* was able to anchor in Trondheimfjord at midnight on the 23/24.

Once in the safety of the fjord, Brinckmann and his men were able to take stock of the damage. The torpedo had struck the aftermost watertight compartment, destroying it almost completely and leaving the stern hanging down at a drunken angle from frame 6½. The tiller flat and steering motors were flooded or damaged, and the rudder jammed 10° to port. The centre and starboard shaft tunnels both were making water which could be held only with difficulty. Other damage was relatively minor, but the ship would obviously be non-operational for some considerable time.

The torpedoing of *Prinz Eugen* meant that now all three units of the former Brest squadron were damaged and unserviceable. The question is could the cruiser's damage have been avoided? and here a number of factors must be considered. In the first place, while no specific Intelligence of any identified British submarine operating in the vicinity was available to Gruppe (Nord), (as had frequently been available in the past), the danger of British submarine attack was well-known to the Kriegsmarine. In view of this, it had been intended to provide a very strong escort of destroyers and torpedo-boats for the passage to Norway, but the intention had been frustrated not, as on many occasions by poor serviceability, but by weather and sea conditions, in this case, ice. The winter icing had trapped two of the 2nd Flotilla's five torpedo-boats in Cuxhaven and three of the 3rd Flotilla, all of which were sorely needed for 'Sportplast'.

Jaguar, *Iltis* and *Seeadler* of the 5th Torpedo-boat Flotilla did sail with the escort, but for some reason were sent back to Heligoland on the evening of the 25th. Thus the squadron continued with just the five destroyers which was perhaps a reasonable escort for two heavy units. However, after the squadron had sailed from Bergen, snow and poor visibility during the early hours of the 23rd, coupled with a course change an hour later, caused the destroyers to lose contact with their charges. When the visibility improved, only *Z25* and *Schoemann* regained contact. The other three, for reasons which Admiral Carls at Gruppe (Nord) found incomprehensible, turned back to Bergen instead of holding course at best speed. Ciliax, perhaps unaware of this, reduced speed in the approaches to Trondheim, possibly in the belief that the

missing three would catch up. Whatever his reasons, it was an extremely dangerous thing to do in these waters, especially as no zigzag was being steered, and he paid the penalty. No blame or accusation of negligence can be laid at the door of the Luftwaffe in this instance, for the co-operative effort set up for 'Cerberus' still held sway; fighter cover had been promised and arrived at dawn. Finally, it was puzzling why none of the ships detected *Trident* on their very sophisticated hydrophone and 'S-Geräte' outfits.

The initial estimate of the work involved in repairing the stern proved optimistic, for the damage was greater than first thought. Kiel dockyard received orders to build a jury rudder, while Marineoberbaurat Dr Strobusch was brought to Trondheim to supervise the repair work which was carried out by the staff of the repair ship *Huascaren*. By the end of March, the difficulties incurred caused the provisional trials date to be put back to mid April, and it was expected that fitting the new rudder would take two to three weeks. On 10 April, work was stopped to allow trials of the ship without rudders, which were carried out the following day. These showed that at speeds up to 21 knots, the ship could be steered on the engines with some difficulty and that sea conditions up to 4 or 5 should present no problem. By the 13th, Kiel dockyard signalled that the jury rudder would leave Kiel aboard the supply ship *Karnten* the next day and in fact, it arrived in Trondheim on the 21st.

Fitting took until 9 May, and after trials in the eastern end of the fjord, *Prinz Eugen* was finally ready to sail for home and full repairs. With the jury rudders, speeds of up to 31 knots could be employed in an emergency, but it was thought prudent not to exceed 29 knots. The major problem was, in fact, the time taken for the ship to respond to helm commands and the doubling of the normal turning circle radii, bearing in mind the narrow passages on the Inner Leads' route south.

The transfer of the damaged cruiser back to Germany, code-named 'Zauberflöte', presented a considerable problem, for it was unlikely that the progress of repairs had gone unnoticed. Some attempt was made to use *Admiral Hipper*, then present in Trondheim, as a cover for the departure of *Prinz Eugen*, including the adoption by the latter of the same camouflage pattern as *Hipper*. Assisted by tugs, *Prinz Eugen* manoeuvred out of the nets in Lofjord just before midday on 16 May, to begin the hazardous journey home. After passing across the entrance to Orkdalsfjord, where her sister ship flashed 'greetings and *bon voyage*', Brinckmann skirted the cliffs of the northern side of Trondheimsfjord in order to keep out of the bright sunlight, because the only paint available in Trondheim had been a light gloss type which was not too suitable for camouflage purposes. During the afternoon, off Agdenes, the escort joined. Two destroyers (*Z25* and *Jacobi*) and two torpedo-boats (*T11* and *T12*) were to accompany the

Left: Extract from *Prinz Eugen*'s war diary at the time of *Trident*'s torpedo hit on 23 May 1942.
Right: *Prinz Eugen* lying off Kiel in October 1942. A faint trace of a residual 'wave'-type camouflage pattern is just visible on the original print. Vierlings are fitted on 'B' and 'C' turrets. (Gröner)

Right: A 'T'-class submarine, many of which were in contact with German cruisers off the coast of Norway and the Skagerrak in 1939–42. The upper bow (external tubes) are visible as are the forward firing midships tubes. (P. A. Vicary)

Below: *Prinz Eugen* in US hands bound for the Pacific and the atomic bomb trials. Points to note are the removal of the 20.3cm guns from 'A' turret, the starboard flak director landed, as is most of the light flak. Gone too is the main range-finder on the conning tower where special test equipment has been installed. (USN)

cruiser home. Both destroyers were bound for dockyard refits, but could hold the cruiser's maximum speed, while the short legs of the torpedo-boats would necessitate their refuelling part way home and consequent temporary absence from the escort.

The first mishap occurred only one hour later after the ship had worked up to 26 knots. While manoeuvring to enter the Trondheim Leads, between the mainland and the island of Hitra, Brinckmann suddenly found his ship turning hard to starboard as the steering failed! Rapid orders for emergency full speed astern saved the situation, but the rocky cliffs were uncomfortably close. On investigation, it was found that the steering had been mistakenly switched from power- to hand-working, fortunately without serious mishap. Passage was continued at high speed, with the intention of rounding the dangerous area off Stadlandet in maximum darkness, and thence via the Inner Leads where the narrow Skatestrommen could be transitted in daylight. By midnight, the ships were crossing Haugfjord and steaming for Stadlandet at 24 knots. The weather was uncomfortably good, with some 10–15 nautical miles visibility but so far, the enemy had not yet put in an appearance, although radar transmissions were continually detected throughout the early hours of the 17th.

The Skatestrommen narrows were successfully passed, without the assistance of the tug *Atlantik*, which had been stationed there as a precaution, and then speed was again increased to 26 knots. At dawn, a new air escort joined as the ships continued through Asfjord making good progress until later in the morning, *Prinz Eugen*'s port engine developed defects which necessitated a slower speed while repairs were effected. Then came the first indication of enemy activity when a signal was received via Flag Officer (Destroyers), who was engaged in escorting the northbound 'Waltzertraum' operation,* to the effect that 18 Group Coastal Command aircraft were extremely active off the Norwegian coast during the early hours. It seemed likely therefore that 'Zauberflöte' would be, or perhaps already had been, detected.

Off the entrance to Karmsund, a signal was received from Gruppe (Nord) ordering the cruiser not to enter Karmsund as it was blocked, but to loiter between Bommelen and Bergen until it was cleared. It was not clear if the reason was due to mining or the presence of enemy ships, but in any event, Brinckmann reversed course. (Actually it had been mined by Hampdens of RAF Bomber Command). Towards midday, condensation trails were observed over the ships from which it was assumed that the British had located them, but it was hoped that their north-easterly course would cause British Intelligence to deduce them to be the *Lützow* group. After reaching Hardangerfjord, Brinckmann received a signal from Gruppe (Nord) to the effect that the fairway outside Karmsund was now clear and that he could proceed provided that the torpedo-boats streamed their sweeps ahead of the cruiser.

Passage south was resumed once more and, off Bommelen, the ship's aircraft was flown off for close escort and reconnaissance. Nothing untoward occurred until the evening of the 17th, when a Hudson aircraft approached too close and was taken under fire, then chased by the fighter escort before

*Transfer of *Lützow* to the Norwegian theatre.

disappearing into the clouds. Barely seven minutes later, the long-anticipated air attack finally materialized – a large number of low-flying aircraft were located off to starboard, at a range of some 40,000 metres.

Prinz Eugen had, in fact, been sighted by reconnaissance aircraft while still in the Trondheim Leads and a close watch was kept on her thereafter. *Lützow* too had been sighted *en route* north, with the result that the whole striking power of RAF Coastal Command had been put on stand-by. The crews of 42 Squadron, whose Beaufort torpedo-bombers were based at Leuchaurs in Scotland, were preparing to mount a strike against *Lützow*, but on receipt of reports that the enemy ship had reversed course, stood down again. Meanwhile, their sister formation, 86 Squadron, based at Wick, took off just after midnight to attack *Prinz Eugen* off Stadlandet. No contact was made with the German ships, although some of the sixteen aircraft were sighted by the *Prinz*'s look-outs at long range. *Prinz Eugen* continued her passage homeward, being next reported outside Karmoy, steaming south at about seventeen knots during mid-afternoon on the 17th.

This time, the RAF launched a two-pronged attack in a determined effort to sink the elusive cruiser. From Leuchars, 42 Squadron (Wing-Commander Williams) got airborne with twelve Beauforts, escorted by four Beaufighters and six Blenheims. The latter machines were to make dummy torpedo runs as well as provide fighter cover. At Wick, 86 Squadron put up fifteen Beauforts, with an escort of four Beaufighters. Finally a high-level diversionary bombing force of twelve Hudsons took off for the Norwegian coast. The plan of attack called for 42 Squadron to make landfall some 50 miles south of Mandal and then to sweep north-west towards Lister, while 86 Squadron were to sweep south-east from Egero Island with the intention of executing a pincer attack on the damaged cruiser. A shadowing aircraft reported the location, course and speed of the German ships, to guard against any doubling-back tricks, but the Beaufighter so engaged was attacked by the cruiser's BF109 air escort with the result that in the confusion of defending itself, a wrong position was reported. This actually had little effect on 42 Squadron's operation, for at 2015, rather earlier than expected in view of the incorrect position report, they sighted the enemy and manoeuvred to attack. The weather was good, visibility excellent and the sky clear as Williams ordered the attack to commence.

Jacobi reported torpedo tracks to starboard, and fired warning Very lights, then the cruiser herself sighted further tracks, but it was believed at first that these were submarine torpedoes because the aircraft did not appear to be in a suitable attacking position. Very quickly, the action developed into a confused mêlée as torpedo-bombers, fighters, destroyers, torpedo-boats, as well as the cruiser, joined in the fray. After a couple of rounds of barrage fire from 'B' and 'C' turrets, the range closed quickly allowing the light flak to join in. The six escort fighters and the ship's Arados were vectored to the centre of the attacking wave, while the ship's guns engaged the wings. Torpedo tracks and ships' wakes criss-crossed as frantic attempts were made to avoid the aircraft's missiles, while the aircraft themselves flew low overhead, strafing any available

target. Explosions erupted in the sea and the sky was black with smoke from exploding shells. Twisting and turning, *Prinz Eugen* managed to out-manoeuvre all the torpedoes from the first wave of six aircraft, and then did the same against the second wave. Twelve minutes after it had all begun, the enemy aircraft had disappeared, leaving the ships' crews jubilant at their escape and counting the number of aircraft claimed destroyed. *T12* claimed two, *Prinz Eugen* six, and one by the ship's aircraft. In fact, only three of the Beauforts were shot down and one of the Beaufighters ditched on the way home.

After the end of the torpedo-bomber attack, there was a brief attack by Hudson bombers without effect, losing one of their force. 86 Squadron were unfortunately affected by the shadow aircraft's incorrect position report, for they turned north (instead of south) along the coast, running into fighter attack from Stavanger airfield, which caused the loss of four machines. The remaining aircraft reached home without having sighted their target at all. From the British point of view, it was a costly and disappointing result, the first combined torpedo and bombing strike with escort cover, failing because of poor coordination and faulty reconnaissance reporting. Nevertheless, the experience gained was later put to very effective use along the Norwegian coast from 1943 to 1945.

The German squadron continued into the Skagerrak without further molestation, rounded the Skaw and reached the safe waters of the Kattegat. By the evening of the 18th, *Prinz Eugen* was secured alongside in the Scheerhafen at Kiel, preparatory to beginning full repairs, and the following day came under the tactical command of the Ausbildüngsverband (Training Squadron). After de-ammunitioning, a floating crane came alongside and lifted out all the 10.5cm mountings. The cruiser then moved into No. 5 dock at Deutsche Werke where she was suitably camouflaged. Some 3½ months were estimated for repairs. On 31 July, Kpt.z.S.Brinckmann bade farewell to his crew and a couple of days later left the ship. On 1 September he was promoted to Konteradmiral and two weeks later took up his new appointment as Chief of Staff to Naval Gruppe (Süd). In the meantime, repairs continued, the ship being undocked at the beginning of August and moved to the Germania yard until 7 October when she returned to Deutsche Werke.

Here, on the 8th, her new captain, Kpt.z.S.Voss, joined her as she approached completion of repair. Like his predecessor, Hans-Erich Voss had served in the Kaisermarine, mostly in cruisers, and between the wars had held a number of shore appointments as well as a tour as Gunnery Officer aboard *Admiral Graf Spee* when first commissioned. The stocky, energetic Stettiner was keen to make his new command operational as quickly as possible, but he was destined to be disappointed in his desire to get into action. His short tenure of command was to be dogged by misfortune, for less than two weeks later, 33 of his crew were drowned in Kiel harbour when their picket boat was rammed and sunk by a ship. Nevertheless, despite air raids and a shortage of dockyard workers, the repairs were by now nearly completed, and by 20 October ammunition was being re-embarked. On the 27th, a little over six months after repairs had begun, Voss took his ship out to sea, bound for Gotenhafen where he was to commence work-up training. It was intended that *Prinz Eugen* return as soon as possible to Norway to reinforce the strike-force in northern waters which earlier had been deprived of her services by *Trident*'s torpedo. To this end, Voss pressed ahead with his training until the beginning of January 1943, when he was ordered to take his ship back to northern waters.

The movement of *Prinz Eugen* to Norway was code-named Operation 'Fronttheatre' and covered the sailing for northern waters, not only of the heavy cruiser, but also of *Scharnhorst*. Both ships weighed from Gotenhafen Bay during the afternoon of 9 January, the battlecruiser wearing the flag of Admiral Schniewind (CinC Fleet). It was not until the 11th that the ships began passing through the Belts, a fact that was already of concern to Kpt.z.S.Voss, as was their passage in daylight. The weather, moreover, was fair, although cloudy, and overhead eight Focke-Wulfs provided the fighter escort through the coastal waters. Voss's fears were justified, for at 1306, an aircraft was briefly sighted before being lost in the mist. A minute later, the 'B' Dienst crew passed a decrypt of the aircraft's sighting report to Voss – it gave their composition and speed. Half an hour later a second report was picked up. For the time being, Schniewind continued north, although taking the precaution of opening up his formation and putting the flak crews at a high degree of readiness. Voss, himself, thought that any attack would take place at about sunset and, in fact, Admiral Tovey had instigated strong air reconnaissance sorties and sailed six submarines as well as cruisers and destroyers in an attempt to catch the German ships.

The attempt came to naught, for Schniewind had reversed course late in the afternoon of the 11th, when it was obvious that their passage could not have been made undetected. *Prinz Eugen* was ordered to return to Gotenhafen, a decision which Voss personally thought to be wrong. He favoured putting into a port in southern Norway, whence they could sneak out at a later date unobserved. From the entrance to the Skagerrak to the Leads was not a long way, and the ship had made the passage quite successfully in reverse when damaged. Gotenhafen, after all, was a long way east. Voss, however, could but obey orders, and by early afternoon on the 22nd, his ship was back in that port.

Admiral Carls knew the likelihood of attack in the Norwegian Narrows now that the enemy had been alerted, and had decided that it was not worth the risk. There was, in any case, no rush, and he intended to sail the ships again when the weather was more suitable and enemy activity had died down. The new attempt, code-named 'Domino' took place towards the end of the month, when both ships sailed from Gotenhafen on the 23rd. This attempt was no more successful than the first, for they were sighted and reported on the 25th, causing Gruppe (Nord) to order their return again. Voss still maintained that a port in the Skagerrak–Kattegat area would have been a better refuge, but once again *Prinz Eugen* was ordered to Gotenhafen. Perhaps he suspected that his ship was fated not to return north, and indeed that proved to be the case, for *Scharnhorst* finally sailed alone on 8 March, reaching northern waters in safety. *Prinz Eugen* spent the rest of the war in Baltic waters.

14: NORTHERN WATERS, 1942–1943

We now return to follow the fortunes of *Admiral Hipper* after her arrival back in Germany at the end of March 1941. She had then begun a badly needed refit at the Deutsche Werke yard in Kiel, during which her bridge was modified and her bunkerage increased by alterations in the double-bottom spaces. This refit extended until the end of October, when sea trials were begun. These soon showed up the woefully inadequate training of the ship's company, many of whom had not the first idea of shipboard life or the sea, when, on 28 November the ship sailed east to begin work-up training based at Gotenhafen. Speed trials on the measured mile at Neukrug gave a figure of 32 knots, with 50 per cent fuel in calm, deep water at a boiler pressure of 78kg/cm^2. After refit her draught was 30cm greater than before.

The training period continued into the New Year, when severe icing conditions in the Baltic during January curtailed many of the planned exercises. By the end of January, the ship was back in Kiel where Blohm & Voss required some three weeks to fit degaussing cables and apply a new camouflage scheme. A month later, *Admiral Hipper* was ordered west to Brunsbüttel where Meisel hoped to complete his work-up in the Heligoland Bight. On 1 March, she arrived in snowed-up Brunsbüttel (where the upper deck was painted white for camouflage purposes), but because of the dangers of mines and air attack, training in the Heligoland area was not approved. Passing back to Kiel, further dockyard repairs were necessary to rectify ice damage to hull and propellers as well as the installation of a Fu Mo B set from *Gneisenau*. The ship had actually been ordered to Norway for operational duty and sailed from Kiel via the Kaiser–Wilhelm Canal on 18 March.

Escorted by the destroyers *Z26*, *Z24* and *Z30*, as well as the torpedo-boats *T15* and *T16*, the heavy cruiser steamed northwards in rough weather, arriving without incident in Trondheim on the afternoon of 21 March. Here she came under the operational command of Flag Officer (Battleships), but took no part in operations until July, when a major strike was prepared against the Allied convoys to North Russia. The target was to be convoy 'PQ17' and the operation, code-named 'Rosselssprüng'. On the evening of the 2nd, *Tirpitz*, wearing the flag of Admiral Schniewind, sailed from Trondheim accompanied by *Admiral Hipper*, the destroyers *Galster* and *Riedel* with *T15* and *T17*. In the fjords, the low clouds were unbroken with gusting winds and driving rain as the ships moved through the choppy waters towards the open sea. They were actually bound for Altafjord far to the north, where Schniewind's group were to join forces with Vize-admiral Kummetz, Flag Officer (Cruisers) and his Group 2. The destroyers *Lody* and *Ihn* joined from the Lofoten Islands as the squadron forged northwards.

The next day, things began to go awry, when Kummetz signalled that the pocket battleship *Lützow* had run aground in fog, damaging her bottom, but Gruppe (Nord) ordered the sortie to continue despite the mishap. Then, in the early afternoon, both *Lody* and *Riedel* ran aground in Grimsoystraumen and had to be left behind. Group 1 finally anchored in Altafjord early in the evening of the 4th. Throughout the day, continuous reports were received from Luftwaffe aircraft and shadowing U-boats giving details of the convoy's position, composition and escort; the latter appeared to consist of at least one battleship and five heavy cruisers if the reports were to be believed.

In fact, 'PQ17' did have a considerable escort for the close component consisted of two British (*London* and *Norfolk*) and two US cruisers (*Tuscaloosa* and *Wichita*) under the command of Rear-Admiral Hamilton, RN, while the distant cover was provided by the Home Fleet with two battleships, an aircraft carrier, two cruisers and fourteen destroyers. The close escort was scheduled to proceed as far as Bear Island and the Home Fleet was to operate in the waters north-east of Jan Mayen Island. Despite the fact that only three of the merchantmen had been lost to air attacks, by the evening of the 4th, by which time the convoy stood some 240 nautical miles due north of North Cape, the British Admiralty, aware of the presence of the powerful German squadron in Altafjord, ordered the convoy to scatter. The reasons for this decision, which had resounding effects, not least on morale, are still hotly debated today, for the result was a massacre of the defenceless merchantmen. In essence, the Admiralty feared that a surface ship strike had been launched and judged the convoy safer if it scattered. In fact, 21 merchant ships were sunk by aircraft or submarines and the surface ships never got near them.

Tirpitz and her squadron, now comprising *Admiral Scheer*, *Admiral Hipper*, seven destroyers and two torpedo-boats, weighed from Altafjord at 1104 on the 5th, but it was not until an hour later that Schniewind was given clearance to start 'Rosselsprüng'. Off Rolvsoy, the Soviet submarine *K21*

(Commander Nikolai Lunin) claimed to have attacked *Tirpitz* and damaged her, but if such an incident did occur, it went completely unnoticed by the Germans! On reaching open waters, one of the patrolling submarines, *Unshaken*, sighted the squadron and reported it. Her message was picked up by the 'B' Dienst troop aboard *Admiral Hipper* and deciphered some two and a half hours later. Meisel feared that it could influence their entire operation. He was to be proved correct, but probably not quite as he had foreseen. Later that evening, Meisel's men deciphered a second sighting report broadcast by Cleethorpes radio, and originating from a shadowing Catalina of 210 Squadron RAF, giving an accurate position but not an accurate course. They had also been reported by *P54*, which had been unable to attack. With their position compromised and the convoy scattered to the four winds, the chances of success for the surface ships was poor, while the possibility of their being subjected to air or submarine attack was correspondingly high. Under the circumstances, therefore, it was not surprising that at 2130 hours, Gruppe (Nord) ordered the operation be broken off. Course was thereupon reversed and by mid-morning on the 6th, the squadron was anchored in Langfjord, later moving to Altafjord. Perhaps in order to console the squadron, Gruppe (Nord) later signalled that the sinking of 27 ships of the convoy and the scattering of the rest, meant that a worth-while target for the surface ships no longer existed. Meisel, however, saw here a possibility that his cruiser with four fast destroyers might be able to catch some of the remaining merchantmen and requested permission to do so. His hopes came to nothing for Schniewind did not allow his request (nor a similar one from Flag Officer (Destroyers)) although appreciating the spirit of the signal.

The fleet returned once more to Narvik, arriving on the 8th. Here the cruiser remained, until early September when the fleet, less *Tirpitz*, was transferred back to Altafjord.

The light cruiser, *Köln* (Kpt.z.S.Baltzer) had also now been transferred to Norwegian waters, having sailed from Swinemünde on 9 July. *En route*, she took part in a minelaying operation in the Skagerrak before continuing north to Trondheim where she arrived on the 15th. Her stay there was brief and uneventful and she moved further north at the beginning of August, reaching Bogen Bay, Narvik by the 6th. Her passage between Trondheim and Narvik, made at 25 knots, produced the extremely unwelcome finding that under war conditions, her fuel consumption was actually 21.7m³ per hour instead of the ship's book figure of 16.1m³. This would have a serious effect on the ship's endurance which, for a usable bunkerage of 1,175m³ would now only be 1,350 nautical miles at 25 knots (or 2¼ days' steaming). Furthermore, when lying at three hours' notice for steam, it was necessary to keep one main boiler flashed-up – the small auxiliary boiler being insufficient. This too had an adverse effect on fuel consumption. It was not only the fuel problem which was to affect the unfortunate *Köln*; the pre-war restraints upon her seagoing activities were held by the SKL to be equally valid under war-time conditions, despite the serious shortage of ships. In consequence, all the proposed operations of the light cruiser were cancelled for one or both of these reasons. The first such operation to be affected was 'Rasputin', a minelaying sortie to the Matoshkin Straits between the islands of Novoya Zemelya, planned for August. *Köln*, carrying 160 mines and accompanied by two destroyers with 80 mines each, were to lay a field at the western entrance to the Straits. The distance to the Straits, however, was at the limit of the ship's endurance, despite the Naval Staff's agreement that seawater could be admitted to the fuel bunkers as fuel was used up and thereby ensure adequate stability. In the end, the operation was cancelled as was 'Meisenbalz' a later combined operation with *Admiral Hipper* and the 8th Destroyer Flotilla against convoy 'QP14' in September. This latter

Right: *Admiral Hipper* in northern Norway at the end of 1942. Noteworthy are the camouflage scheme and the vierlings fitted to the superimposed turrets. Visible on the foretop range-finder are a FuMO 27 radar aerial (front) and a 'Timor' radar search receiver aerial (rear). (Gröner)

operation was aborted due to a lack of sufficient air reconnaissance reports about the convoy's progress.

Admiral Hipper, now wearing the flag of Vizeadmiral Kummetz, left Bogen Bay on 10 September, accompanied by *Admiral Scheer*, *Köln*, *Z23*, *Z27*, *Z29*, *Z30* and *Beitzen*. In open waters, the destroyers *Z23*, *Z27* and *Beitzen* led the larger ships in a broad arrow formation, with the three cruisers in line abreast. *Z30* and *Z29* covered the port and starboard flanks respectively. As the ships left Galvefjord, they were sighted by the submarine *Tigris*, then on patrol off the Lofoten Islands. *Tigris* was loitering submerged, the calm, glassy sea and good visibility necessitating sparing use of the periscope. The first indication of activity was the appearance of an He115 aircraft off the entrance to the fjord, obviously an a/s patrol. Ten minutes later, the foretop of a capital ship was sighted, bearing 190°, range about nine to ten miles. *Tigris* commenced an attack, on what quickly proved to be an enemy squadron of three large ships, escorted by a number of destroyers. The aircraft overhead, which got very close to the submarine at times, and the calm sea, presented problems in tracking the enemy, but by 1450, *Tigris* was about 10° on the port bow of the centre ship (*Admiral Scheer*) and right ahead of the port wing ship (*Köln*), range about six miles. *Köln* then altered to starboard and the He115 re-appeared, forcing *Tigris* down to 15 metres. Returning to periscope depth a few minutes later, *Tigris* found the He115 gone and a very favourable attack position developing.

The range to *Köln* had dropped to 500 metres and that to *Admiral Scheer* to 1,500 metres approximately. (*Scheer* had actually been identified by the submarine as *Tirpitz*). *Tigris* manoeuvred to give a broad beam shot, the screening destroyers passing very close as the submarine waited for the desire track angle. This distracted the CO somewhat, causing him to miss the best firing angle and making it necessary to come round to port, before firing a salvo of five individually aimed torpedoes. Aboard the warships, the submarine's presence had gone undetected and even when the torpedoes exploded (after hitting rocks on the bottom?) it was initially believed that high-level bombing was the cause. In consequence, no counter-attack was mounted by the destroyers and *Tigris* withdrew unscathed, although chastened by her failure to secure any hits. The German squadron arrived in Alta without further incident on 11 September.

'Rasputin' was superseded by 'Zarin,' which was carried out by *Admiral Hipper* and four destroyers towards the end of September, for which *Köln*'s participation was to be limited to the provision of a five-man prize crew! The minefield was to comprise two rows of mines, off the north-west coast of Novaya Zemlya. *Admiral Hipper* loaded 96 mines from the mine-tender *Irben* and, after being delayed by bad weather (which probably accounted for *Köln*'s non-participation) sailed on the evening of the 24th, escorted by *Z23*, *Z28*, *Z29* and *Z30*. Rough seas considerably hampered the destroyers which could only make fifteen knots and by the early hours of the 25th the small squadron was still punching its way to the north-east, west of North Cape. The strong northerly winds, overcast sky and rain squalls reduced visibility, made watch-keeping duties miserable and prevented an accurate fix of the ship's position. By evening, it had begun to snow, further exacerbating the situation, so that the following morning, in the absence of a precise knowledge of their position, Admiral Kummetz was already considering a 24-hour postponement of the lay. Things must have improved, however, because the operation was continued, with the destroyers being detached in the forenoon of the 26th, to form a north-south reconnaissance patrol across the middle of the Barents Sea, thus protecting the cruiser's flank, as she pressed on further east.

Some five hours later, the snow-covered mass of Novaya Zemlya could be picked out of the mist. The seas had moderated and the wind had dropped, but the leaden, low-lying clouds continued to cover the whole sky, obscuring the mountain silhouette and preventing a positive identification of landfall. Meisel and his navigators had not had a good astronomical fix for more than 24 hours, and it was vital to get one if the minelaying were to be successful. Their sole source of topographical information was the British *Admiralty Pilot* for the area, but even that was sparse in detail. Meisel crossed the entrance to the Matoshkin Strait and slowly closed the coast, hoping to locate the Admiralty Peninsula with the intention of achieving a fix on Cape Speedwell on its southern coast.

At 1720 on the 26th, the Cape was sighted and there were sighs of relief on the bridge. *Admiral Hipper*'s position was now accurately fixed at last! Altering course away from the coast, Meisel increased speed and laid his mines to the north-west of the peninsula. During the lay, signals were detected emanating from a Soviet ice-breaker to the north, and Meisel suggested that after finishing the lay, the cruiser should attack it (and the convoy presumed to with it). Kummetz vetoed the suggestion – it was not in their orders! It took nearly four hours to lay the mines in the requisite pattern; this was, in fact, the first and only time that the heavy cruisers were used in this role. *Admiral*

Below: The loneliness of service in the rugged arctic Norwegian fjords is captured in this shot of *Admiral Hipper*, taken in 1942. Her camouflage scheme is hardly effective in these surroundings. (Imperial War Museum)

Hipper retired westwards and, after rendezvous with her destroyers at about midday on the 27th, reached Kaafjord the following morning undetected by the enemy.

Results achieved by this minefield are not known, nor is evidence of merchant traffic on this route well-documented, but it was hardly as busy as the Britain to Murmansk route.

Köln remained an embarrassment to the Naval Staffs in the far north for nothing could be found for her to do. After the cancellation of 'Meisenbaltz' and 'Rasputin', her next proposed employment was Operation 'Blitz', a naval strike against suspected enemy weather stations on Bear Island. This was to be carried out by *Köln* and four destroyers, two of which were to embark a landing-party of about 50 marines. One of the criteria for the operation was the non-participation of the army! It was planned to execute this sortie at the end of October or early December, dependent on the Russian convoy cycle. In the event, the Luftwaffe got there first, parachuting a three-man team into the north-west of the island on 19 October, to lay out a glider landing strip for use by a Luftwaffe weather reporting base. High cross-winds and incomplete preparation of the landing strip led to the attempt being abandoned. What happened to the men on the ground is not known, but the operation proved that there were no Allied forces on the island. In consequence, and in view of the general shortage of fuel, 'Blitz' was cancelled as was a similar operation, 'Donner', against Jan Mayen Island by destroyers.

BATTLE OF THE BARENTS SEA

The year 1942 was now drawing to a close, but in its last dying hours, the cold and forbidding Barents Sea would witness an action which was to have far-reaching and unforeseen consequences for the Kriegsmarine. At this time, German Naval forces in the Norwegian theatre were considerable and were to be increased even further, but for the present there were *Tirpitz* in Trondheim (although not fully effective), *Nürnberg* at Narvik and *Admiral Hipper* with *Lützow* in Alta. With these last two ships were six destroyers, and three more destroyers were at Trondheim.

On the British side, there had been considerable discussion, following the sailing of 'PQ18', as to the optimum size for a Russian-bound convoy. Admiral Tovey pressed for and received permission to split the next convoy into two parts; the smaller group would be more manageable. While agreeing with Tovey, the Admiralty ordered that the cruiser covering force should press much farther east into the Barents Sea and not turn back at about 25° E as previously. This decision was to have an important bearing on subsequent events. After the prefix 'PQ' had acquired such a stigma following the 'PQ17' débacle, the convoys were redesignated 'JW' and 'RA' to denote outward- and inward-bound convoys respectively.

The next convoy to sail for Russia, fifteen ships and an oiler, was designated 'JW51A'. It sailed from Loch Ewe on 15 December and arrived undetected in Kola Inlet on Christmas Day. The second part of the convoy, 'JW51B', left a week after the first with an escort of six destroyers and five corvettes, trawlers and minesweepers under the overall command of Captain R. ST. V. Sherbrooke in *Onslow*. By the forenoon of 31 December, after a gale had broken up the convoy, four separate groups of British ships were scattered about the Barents Sea. The main group of twelve ships, with most of the escort, was moving due east, while to the north, some 45 miles off, was a straggler and one trawler escort. North-east of the convoy stood the fleet minesweeper, *Bramble* searching for stragglers. The cruisers *Sheffield* and *Jamaica*, under the command of Admiral Burnett, were about thirty miles north of the convoy. The two cruisers had accompanied 'JW51A' right through to Kola, and had then sailed again on 27 December to cover the arrival of 'JW51B'.

Unlike the first half of the convoy, 'JW51B' had been detected by the Germans, *U354* having sighted it some 50 nautical miles south of Bear Island on the 30th. That same morning the report reached General Admiral Carls, Flag Officer Gruppe (Nord), who immediately passed the information to Admiral Kummetz in Altenfjord, and ordered Admiral Klüber (Flag Officer Northern Waters) to put *Admiral Hipper* and six destroyers at three hours' notice. *Köln* was not included. Then Kpt.z.S.Gerlach at SKL agreed to *Lützow's* being included in the operation. Just after midday, Admirals Klüber and Kummetz received orders for immediate readiness and a further reconnaissance report from *U354* gave details of the convoy's composition. According to the U-boat, it consisted of six to ten steamers with a weak escort of destroyers and possibly one light cruiser. Carls was delighted – it was exactly as he had hoped. Here was a magnificent opportunity to gainfully employ his surface fleet which had been idle for so long. Nevertheless, he was aware that the situation might alter and that the U-boat might not have seen all of the escort, particularly any off lying cruisers. 'B' Dienst had, in fact, detected cruisers in the Barents Sea on the 27th.

Carls telephoned Klüber to discuss the employment of *Lützow* and *Köln* and, in view of the expected forecast of winds Force 6–7, ruled out participation by the latter. *Lützow* would be included as her low speed would be no particular disadvantage in this instance, while her heavy guns might prove decisive. Some of the operational instructions discussed are particularly interesting: (a) capture of individual merchantmen desirable; (b) no time to be wasted on rescuing enemy crews; (c) a few captured mercantile skippers valuable for interrogation; (d) rescue of enemy crews by the enemy undesirable. The first sign of the usual reluctance to hazard the surface fleet now became apparent when Konteradmiral Fricke, Chief of Naval Operations, telephoned to say that there must be no risk to *Lützow*. While his concern was probably connected with his subsequent plans for this ship, of which more later, it was a portent of things to come. Carls himself signalled Klüber to the effect that it was possible that the escort might have been reinforced from Kola, and that he should ensure that his forces report any increased escort immediately to SKL and Gruppe (Nord). Klüber repeated this information to Kummetz, specifically mentioning two cruisers and ordering him to avoid action with superior forces, later amending this to include 'equal forces'. Finally, early that evening, SKL agreed to *Lützow's* participation. She had in fact cleared Kaafjord boom two minutes earlier!

Right: This well-known view of *Nürnberg*, anchored in Bogen Bay, Norway, shows the effectiveness of her camouflage to good advantage. (Gröner)

Below: *Lützow* lying in a Norwegian fjord in 1942. (W. B. Bilddienst)

Admiral Kummetz took his ships to sea late in the afternoon of 30 December. Within the fjords, it was calm with light winds and very good visibility, but some three hours later, on reaching the open sea and steaming into the Loppahavet, heavy snow began to fall, and there was a high swell from the north-west. After such long periods of idleness in sheltered waters, seasickness was already taking its toll among the ship's crews. At midnight, having successfully avoided the British submarine patrols, currently *Graph, Unruly, Trespasser* and *Seadog*, Kummetz's force stood west of North Cape, shaping course for the Barents Sea and the last known position of the convoy. To find the convoy, Kummetz intended to string his destroyers out in a north-south line, with *Admiral Hipper* behind the northernmost wing destroyer and *Lützow* similarly placed to the south. In this formation he would sweep due east at 18 knots, hoping to come up on the convoy from astern. Coding problems delayed the executive signal for the commencement of this manoeuvre and, in the meantime, a signal from *U354* reported the position of the convoy at 2030 hours on the 30th. This put the ships farther south than Kummetz had expected and he decided to shift his reconnaissance line twenty miles farther south. Shortly afterwards Kummetz received another signal, this time from Admiral (Northern Waters) giving details of *Lützow*'s 'Aurora' operation against mercantile traffic north of 70° N, between 5° and 35° E. Stange, Captain of *Lützow*, received these orders with considerable surprise; it would appear that he did not know that he was to detach at the conclusion of 'Regenbogen'.

The new position of the convoy meant that the time for the start of the reconnaissance sweep had to be brought forward by half an hour, but in the event, a search was not necessary; the German forces ran into the enemy. At 0800, *Lützow*, at the southern end of the German formation, stood about 110 nautical miles north of Tanahorn. Here the weather was fair, with slight seas and only occasional snow squalls. Seventy miles or so to the north, *Admiral Hipper* groped her way through the dark Arctic pre-dawn, her radar sweeping for the elusive convoy. At 0720, visual contact was made with two shadows off to starboard, forward of the beam, at a range of about 12,500 metres. Initial estimates of their course and speed was 045° sixteen knots. The German cruiser altered course towards the unknown vessels in order to reduce her silhouette, and thus remain unseen until the onset of the brief Arctic twilight when her chances of success would be that much better. Reducing speed and continuing round to starboard, *Hipper*'s lookouts quickly found more and more shadows in the gloom. They had found the convoy! Kummetz's contact signal was received in *Lützow* far to the south, and she immediately altered course and increased to 24 knots to close the flag.

Eckholdt, the most northerly of the destroyers, received orders to close the convoy and shadow while *Admiral Hipper* drew off and shaped course around to the north with the intention of driving the merchantmen south into the guns of *Lützow*. It was probably this destroyer which was one of the two sighted by the corvette *Hyderabad* at about 0820, but as this ship was expecting the arrival of two Soviet destroyers, she took them for these and made no report. Ten minutes later, *Obdurate*, stationed on the starboard beam of the convoy, also sighted these two destroyers crossing astern. She was at once ordered to investigate and hauled round to do so. It was some

Below: Only four of the 'O'-class destroyers received their designed armament of four 4.7in guns, of which *Onslow* was one. All her consorts at the time of the Barents Sea action were armed with 4in guns. This photograph shows *Offa*, identical to *Onslow* except that the lattice mast was not fitted until 1943. (Ministry of Defence)

little time before *Obdurate* could identify the destroyers in question because of poor visibility, but the matter resolved itself when the German ships, after altering on to a parallel course, opened fire to starboard. It was but a brief action: *Beitzen* did not open fire at all; *Z29*'s forward gun misfired twice, and only *Eckholdt* may have got off a few ineffectual rounds before the British ship swung back into the gloom to report to her flotilla leader. Captain Sherbrooke immediately concentrated his four Fleet destroyers and took them out on the port quarter of the convoy to engage. Aboard *Eckholdt*, however, Kpt.z.S.Schemmel was more concerned with shadowing than action; as yet, his orders were to act as contact holder.

The three northernmost German destroyers now moved up towards the Flagship as the convoy received smoke protection from the sole destroyer remaining, *Achates*. *Onslow* with only *Orwell* in company at the time, sighted the German cruiser at 0939 as she began to engage *Achates* with her main armament. The appearance of the British destroyers on an attacking course forced Hartmann to disengage with *Achates* after only five salvoes and concentrate on the threat from *Onslow* and *Orwell*. *Achates* had been hit, but not seriously. For the next half-hour or so, the destroyers skilfully held off the heavy cruiser, weaving in and out of the smoke and mist, making use of every trick in the book to baulk their superior opponent. *Admiral Hipper*'s forward radar set had been put out of action by the shock of her guns when they first opened fire, and because of icing on the lenses of range-finders and director optics, the cruiser's shooting was initially poor. At 1008 Sherbrooke sent *Obedient* and *Obdurate*, his two weaker ships, armed with only 4in guns, back to the convoy, lest the German destroyers, whose position was uncertain, got among the merchantmen. With his two remaining ships, Sherbrooke continued to hold off the heavy cruiser and neither side scored any hits until about 1020, when the fortunes of war suddenly swung in favour of the Germans. *Onslow* had closed *Admiral Hipper* off her starboard bow and the range had steadily dropped to 8,500 metres as the British destroyer continued to threaten with her torpedoes. *Admiral Hipper*, whose after radar was operative, engaged her very effectively with 48 rounds, obtaining hits with two consecutive salvoes, while her 10.5cm guns fired on *Orwell*.

Four heavy shells smashed into the British flotilla leader, grievously damaging her. Both No. 1 and No. 2 guns were put out of action, serious fires started in the forward messdecks, and the side of the engine room was holed. Shell splinters from a hit on the funnel rained down over the destroyer's open bridge, one of which seriously wounded Captain Sherbrooke, forcing him to hand over command to Lieutenant-Commander Kinloch of the *Orwell*. The British destroyers turned away under smoke as a providential snow squall obscured them from the heavy cruiser, which continued south-eastwards, her three destroyers trailing after her.

Unknown to Kummetz, Admiral Burnett, with *Sheffield* and *Jamaica*, was only some fifteen miles to the north-west of him, but as yet, the British Admiral could not be sure which ship was the enemy in view of the multitude of radar contacts and the atrocious visibility. Nevertheless, he was closing fast and the German's time was running out. *Admiral Hipper* continued to the east and quickly came into contact with another British

Below: *Sheffield*, seen here escorting a troop convoy for the north African landings, sailed north a few weeks later and was flagship of Admiral Burnett at the time of her engagement with *Admiral Hipper* in the Barents Sea. (Imperial War Museum)

warship off the starboard bow. This was actually the minesweeper *Bramble* (Commander H. T. Rust), which was still searching fruitlessly for lost merchantmen. *Bramble* (armed with only two 4in guns) desperately took avoiding action and made smoke, but at such close range, now only 5,500 metres, the diminutive minesweeper stood little chance. *Admiral Hipper* opened fire with both main and secondary armament, scoring hits on the target's forecastle with her third salvo, exploding the ready-use ammunition.

As he initially believed his opponent to be a destroyer, Hartmann then swung north to avoid any torpedoes, so that the crippled minesweeper became lost in the smoke and snow. Ordering Schemmel to sink *Bramble*, the Flagship then reversed course south again, anxious to get at the convoy, for the few meagre hours of Arctic twilight were fast slipping away. After some confusion, *Eckoldt* turned to execute her orders, taking with her *Beitzen*, who fired four salvoes at the blazing wreck before being ordered to cease fire by *Eckoldt*. The flotilla leader then signalled her intention to finish off the minesweeper herself and became lost in the gloom astern of *Beitzen* as she turned east towards *Bramble*. *Admiral Hipper*, meanwhile, closed the convoy and sighted its escorting destroyers once more, catching *Achates* unprotected by the smoke-screen. Hitting with her first salvo, the German Flagship quickly reduced the destroyer to a shambles, killing or wounding many of her company, including her Captain, and leaving her on fire with a serious list.

Commander Kinloch now took *Obedient*, *Obdurate* and *Orwell*, which had moved to the south of the convoy to ward off attacks by the newly appeared *Lützow*, out towards *Admiral Hipper* to relieve pressure on the now defenceless *Achates*. Faced with the threat posed by three destroyers, *Admiral Hipper* was forced to shift fire to *Obedient* who was near-missed, sustaining some splinter damage. As a result, of her W/T being put out of action by this, Kinloch ordered *Obdurate* to take over command, but already, the German ship was turning away to the north to avoid the threat of torpedoes. As she did so, she suddenly came under accurate and heavy fire from the north-east. *Sheffield* and *Jamaica* had finally arrived!

At 1130, a forest of shell splashes erupted close to the heavy cruiser, giving Kummetz and Hartmann a rude shock. Initially, no one aboard *Admiral Hipper* could make out their new assailant for the visibility to the northern horizon was considerably worse than to the south and *Sheffield* had opened fire at a range of some 10,500 metres. *Admiral Hipper*'s guns and directors were at this time engaged on bearing red 200°, whereas her new assailants appeared to be off her starboard beam. At 1132, she altered course due north and then sighted two cruisers to the north-east, before turning to starboard again on to a parallel course to the enemy. Before she could complete this turn however, a 6in shell hit her below the waterline, about half a metre below the armour belt in the way of frame 124, No. 3 boiler room. (The ship was at this time listing well to port under the influence of the starboard turn, thus exposing her vulnerable side.) This shell passed through the side plating and exploded in the adjacent fuel bunker, which was still full, deforming the inner bulkhead to the boiler room. Splinters

Opposite page, top: *Hazard* a fleet minesweeper, very similar to her sister *Bramble*, sunk in action with *Admiral Hipper* in the Barents Sea in December 1942. (Author's collection)

Centre: The destroyer *Achates* as she appeared during the action in the Barents Sea in December 1942. She has been modified for escort duties and now carries only two 4.7in guns and one bank of torpedo tubes. (Imperial War Museum)

Bottom: The light cruiser *Jamaica* in 1942. (Imperial War Museum)

BATTLE OF THE BARENTS SEA   Phase One

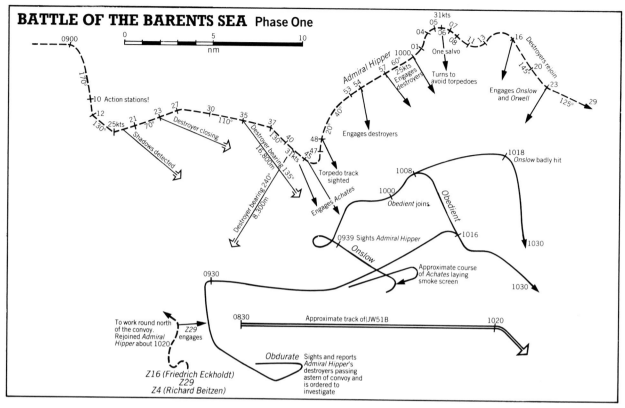

0   5   10
nm

0900
170°
10 Action stations!
12
130°   25kts   21   70°   23   27   30   110°   35   37   40   48   45   47   31kts
Shadows detected
Destroyer closing
Destroyer bearing 135°
Destroyer bearing 240°
6 800m
8 300m

Admiral Hipper 1000
53 54   57   60°   25kts   01   04   05   31kts   07   08   11   13   16   Destroyers rejoin
20   40°   20°
Engages destroyers
One salvo
Turns to avoid torpedoes
145°   20   23   125°   29
Engages *Onslow* and *Orwell*
Engages destroyers

Torpedo track sighted
Engages *Achates*
1008
1000   *Obedient* joins
Obedient
1016
1018   *Onslow* badly hit
1030
1030
0939 Sights *Admiral Hipper*
Onslow
Approximate course of *Achates* laying smoke screen

0930
To work round north of the convoy. Rejoined *Admiral Hipper* about 1020
Z29 engages
0830   Approximate track of JW51B   1020
Obdurate   Sights and reports *Admiral Hipper*'s destroyers passing astern of convoy and is ordered to investigate
Z16 (Friedrich Eckholdt)
Z29
Z4 (Richard Beitzen)

The Arctic Theatre of Operations

Franz Joseph Land
Spitzbergen
KARA SEA
Novaya Zemlya
GREENLAND SEA
BARENTS SEA
Bear Island
Battle Area
Kolguyev
North Cape
Altafjord
Lofoten Islands
Hammerfest
Tromsö
Kirkenes
Narvik
Murmansk
Kola
NORWAY
SWEDEN   FINLAND
USSR
Archangel

Phase Two

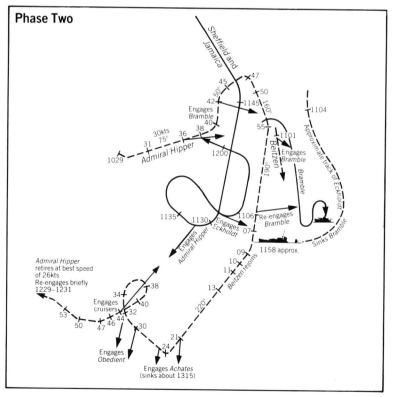

Sheffield and Jamaica
45   47   50
50°   1145   160°   1104
Engages *Bramble*
42
40
30kts   75°   36   38   55   1101
Engages *Bramble*
31   1029   *Admiral Hipper*   1200   Beitzen   061°   Bramble
Approximate track of Eckholdt
1135   1130   Engages *Eckholdt*   1106   Re-engages *Bramble*   07
Engages *Admiral Hipper*
09   1158 approx.   Sinks *Bramble*
Admiral Hipper retires at best speed of 26kts Re-engages briefly 1229–1231
10
11   Beitzen rejoins
13   220°
34   38
Engages cruisers
40
53   32
50   47   46   44   30   21   24
Engages *Obedient*
Engages *Achates* (sinks about 1315)

pierced the thin plating, causing rapid flooding in No. 3 boiler room.

It was not until 1134 that the directors re-acquired target, and fire opened on the British cruisers. The first salvo was short, but the director optics were iced-up and smoke obscured the range, making correction difficult. Her second salvo remained unobserved, because *Admiral Hipper* was now turning hard away from her antagonists as she received two more hits at 1135. The first struck the ship on the port side, at frame III, above the waterline, piercing the upper section of the side protection and passing across the 'tween deck, wrecking the welding shop and messdecks before lodging against the starboard side. Fires broke out immediately and seawater flooded through the holes in the hull as the ship turned. Almost at the same time, a third shell hit the port side of the hangar and exploded within, setting fire to the aircraft and throwing splinters through the hangar floor which pierced water and steam lines.

By this time, *Admiral Hipper* had turned away from the British ships and the smoke from the hangar fire obscured the after director while the forward director's optics were iced-up once more. It took about 2½ minutes to clean them, by which time Hartmann had ceased fire, having only fired twenty rounds. In view of the presence of an equal enemy force and the damage sustained by the Flagship, Admiral Kummetz ordered the action to be broken off. As he felt it unwise, because of his ship's condition, to go south into the convoy, and was reluctant to release his destroyers, Kummetz withdrew to the west.

As Admiral Burnett's ships gave chase, they chanced upon two destroyers crossing their port bow. The nearest of the two was the German flotilla leader, *Eckholdt*, returning from despatching *Bramble*, while some way ahead of her was *Beitzen*,

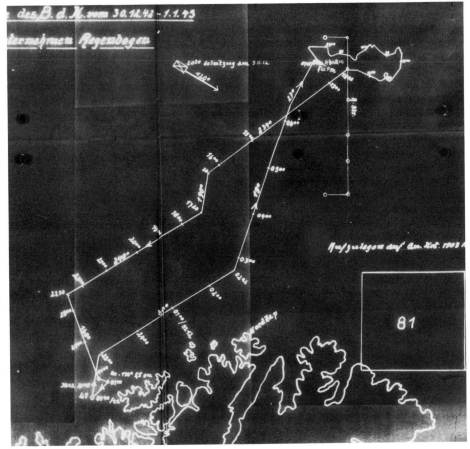

moving to rejoin the flag. The next few minutes were disaster for *Eckholdt*, for in the confusion of the fast-moving action in atrocious visibility, she had completely lost her bearings, signalling *Admiral Hipper* at 1141 'See cruiser and destroyer bearing 300°. Is it you?' followed a minute later by 'In which direction from convoy are you?' (to *Hipper*). As *Admiral Hipper* replied 'North of convoy', *Sheffield* opened a crippling fire on the German destroyer which immediately signalled accusingly to the Flagship 'You are firing on me.' *Beitzen*, which could just make out events astern, quickly made to her flotilla leader 'No, English cruiser', but it was too late, and the unfortunate *Eckoldt* was shot to pieces at point-blank range. She blew up with a dull explosion and sank quickly, taking all her crew with her.

While this vicious little action had been going on north of the convoy, Stange's *Lützow* had now closed from the south. As anticipated, the convoy had been turned into her guns by the presence of the Flagship to the north. *Lützow* had actually picked up the convoy at 1042 off to port, then altered course to starboard, thus crossing ahead of the convoy's track. Snow squalls obscured vision and the overcast sky made the light so poor that it was difficult for Stange to identify individual targets. His raider detected many contacts, but could not distinguish friend from foe, and he decided to hold off and await an improvement in visibility, while he loitered at about twelve knots.

Stange signalled his intentions to the flag and later altered course further eastwards, still keeping his destroyers with him. It was not until 1126 that he finally reversed course and steamed NNW to close the convoy again and rendezvous with *Admiral Hipper*. Just visible through the snow and smoke to port were the ships of the convoy, but it was not until 1142 that *Lützow* opened fire at a range of 16,000 metres. Five minutes later, her secondary armament opened fire too, but quickly ceased because her optical range-finders too were iced-up and the results from the radar were unsatisfactory. The British destroyers turned to threaten the 'Panzerschiff', laying smoke as they did so. *Lützow* opened fire once more, hitting one merchant ship before smoke obscured the targets again and the destroyers withdrew northwards to engage *Admiral Hipper* which had re-appeared. At 1203 *Lützow* received the 'Break off' signal from Kummetz and at 1205 she ceased fire and retired to the west.

Admiral Hipper's re-engagement with the destroyers was brief and ineffective, and the German Flagship quickly disengaged, now intent only on returning to her base. The British cruisers gave chase, bracketing and near missing *Lützow* as both German ships replied with a few salvoes before breaking contact with their pursuers at about 1400. In the meantime, the crew of the battered *Achates* had lost the unequal struggle to keep their ship afloat and she had capsized and sunk at about 1315.

BITTER RECRIMINATIONS

As the sound of gunfire died away and the Arctic night began to close in once more, both sides could take stock of the situation and consider their reactions. For the British, it was very much a success, for despite the loss of a destroyer and a minesweeper, with one more destroyer damaged, the skill and professional handling of the weak escort had prevented the loss of a single member of the convoy, despite the superiority of the attacking forces prior to the appearance of Admiral Burnett's cruisers. But what of the German reactions? Ashore in Kiel and Berlin far to the south, the High Command and the Führer, himself, waited for positive news of the victory, which was surely within Kummetz's grasp, for Herbschlieb's reports from *U354* had painted a graphic picture for the Naval Staffs to conjure with. The signal to break off the action was the first indication that success might be other than total, but it was to be many hours before the full story was known in Germany.

In the Barents Sea, Kummetz's flagship limped home with No. 3 boiler room blackened and burned out from a serious fire following the hit. Several men had been killed and a number wounded, and three of her diesel generators had failed because of water in the fuel lines. The starboard turbine lost steam and had stopped, there being no way left to switch it to one of the remaining two boiler rooms. In one of these, No. 2, the bilges were flooded and as the level rose above the floor plates, there was a danger of that room losing all power. By mid-afternoon, only one boiler, in No. 2 room, remained on line and apart from that, three of the turbo-generators and three of the diesels had by now stopped. As the steam pressure dropped, the port turbine ran down. It was later restarted, but throughout the afternoon, it was touch and go to keep the boilers flashed-up and on line. Late in the afternoon, the water was once more up to the floor plates in No. 2 boiler room and every effort had to be made to keep it in check. Efforts to flash-up the other three boilers in this space remained unsuccessful as seawater flooded through the cable glands from the derelict No. 3 boiler room. Despite strenuous efforts on the part of the damage-control parties, the water level rose ever higher until at 1733 the one remaining boiler failed and the port turbine finally stopped.

The proud *Admiral Hipper* could only crawl home now, but the enemy surface forces were far away and the patrolling submarine *Graph*, which did sight her, could not get in an attack. By 0528 the Flagship had anchored safely, in Kaafjord. Of the other ships, *Lützow* had remained undamaged, fired but a few rounds and had only damaged a merchantman. Her 'Aurora' sortie had been cancelled in view of the presence of the British cruisers. The destroyers had accomplished nothing and had lost their flotilla leader.

Far away in East Prussia, Adolph Hitler waited impatiently for news of his Fleet's victory. Admiral Krancke could tell him nothing and could only counsel patience, but the Führer's last shred of patience vanished when a Reuter's dispatch came in giving the British account of their action in which a few destroyers had driven off a heavy cruiser, a 'Panzerschiff' and six destroyers. Fury gripped the German leader as he launched into a tirade against the Navy, its big ships in particular – they were useless and should be scrapped. Even by late afternoon on 1 January, there was still no report from Altenfjord because the Flagship had remained anchored in the fjord until the forenoon of the 2nd when she moved into her usual net-encased berth and secured finally to the telephone buoy.

Above, left: Extracts from the short-wave radio log (UKW), showing the last contacts with the destroyer *Eckholdt*.
Above: *Eckholdt*, which was sunk during the action in the Barents Sea in December 1942, while vainly trying to regain contact with *Admiral Hipper*. This photograph was taken pre-war and her appearance had been considerably altered by 1942. (Drüppel)
Left: Befehlshaber der Kreuzer's rough sketch of the Barents Sea action area, 30 December 1942 to 1 January 1943.

The precise reason for the delay in a report reaching the 'Wolfsschanze' was probably political – the Navy did not quite know how to explain their failure and was playing for time. Admiral Klüber signalled Admiral Kummetz at 0245 on 1 January while the ships were still on their way home, requesting a brief report of events and successes. Two hours later, Kummetz did in fact signal a brief report, which detailed the loss of *Eckholdt* and the damage to the Flagship as well as the claim of three enemy destroyers damaged and one probably sunk. Kummetz claimed that it had been coded-up in anticipation, but had been delayed partly to avoid compromising their position and partly because of more urgent signals, notably requests for tugs.

Kummetz's first report was not received by Admiral Klüber until 0655, whose comment was that it was neither very complete nor informative. Notably absent was any mention of *Lützow*'s performance. This report was repeated to Admiral Carls at Gruppe (Nord) where it was received at 0909. Twenty minutes later, Klüber confirmed Carls' fears that *Admiral Hipper* had been unable to break through the convoy's escort. Thus a report was available in Kiel by the morning of the 1st, although a brief one. The absence of any claims of success were obviously tacit admissions of the operation's failure and it would appear that no one dared break the news to Hitler until mitigating factors had been found. Consequently, the airwaves, telephone and teleprinter lines between Berlin, Kiel, Narvik and Altenfjord were alive with activity (when they were not cut) as the SKL desperately tried to piece together the events of the action. Kummetz, with some justification, maintained that he could not give an accurate overall report until the various ship's reports had been studied by himself, but it is unlikely that such consideration would have delayed things had there been adequate successes to report.

Leaving aside the acrimony which was building up to a head between Grand Admiral Raeder and the Führer, the SKL were obviously extremely concerned about the way in which the action had been fought and the circumstances surrounding it. Konteradmiral Meisel, Chief of the SKL, himself a former captain of *Admiral Hipper*, criticized Admiral Klüber's signal to Kummetz at 1648 on 30 December, which emphasized the risk question ('equal opponents'). Meisel rightly considered it an additional and severe restraint on Kummetz and his ship's captains – but had not all German operations been conducted under similar restraints? However he seems to be referring to Klüber's altered wording of the instruction, which gave it more force than SKL intended.

Actually, the culprit here was probably Carls, for he had instructed Klüber to order Kummetz to break off if the enemy strength was *nearly* equal! Stange in *Lützow*, too came in for some heavy and probably justified criticism for his timid approach. If, under the weather conditions then prevailing, he had judged it imprudent to approach the convoy, he should have used his destroyers to scout for him. They would quickly have found the escorts drawn off to the north. Tactical commands and communications during the operation as well as post-operation reports left a lot to be desired and as for the radio commentary from *U354* ('I see only red'), well . . .!

Admiral Carls agreed about the conduct of *Lützow*, but allowed that an experienced officer would probably have acted differently, particularly in the handling of the destroyers. He too underlined the necessity of giving the officers on the spot freedom of action, but as Meisel remarked, the loss of *Bismarck* still coloured the Führer's thinking in this respect.

Admiral Schniewind (CinC Fleet) concurred with Admiral Kummetz's tactical plan – experience had already shown it to be necessary to destroy the escort to ensure success. In his view the weather had played a decisive part in the course of events, and it certainly caused confusion on both sides. He was more lenient with Stange's actions, possibly in view of this, and supported the decision of *Lützow* to stand off. In a close mêlée, her low speed and slow-firing heavy guns would have been a disadvantage.

Apart from the irresolute handling of *Lützow*, the most striking feature of the action was the contrast between the German and British destroyer handling. While the British ships turned to fight at every opportunity, the German destroyers were kept under close leash by each cruiser. It could be argued that the British had to keep snapping at the enemy in order to keep him at bay, but had the German flotilla been sent in to engage them, perhaps the two heavy ships' fire control could have had undisturbed shooting against the merchantmen while the destroyers fought it out – at least until the arrival of *Sheffield* and *Jamaica*.

Which leads to the next question, why was the British cruisers' arrival such a surprise? It was known that they had arrived at and sailed from Kola before 'Regenbogen' was launched; 'B' Dienst reports on the 27th confirmed the fact. Admiral Klüber correctly concluded that they were *en route* to join the convoy reported by *U354* and it may have been the reason behind his proposal for *Lützow*'s participation. A warning of the possible presence of these two cruisers in the vicinity was passed to Kummetz by Klüber at 1500 on the 30th, so that Flag Officer (Cruisers) was aware of their existence. Once action was joined however, and no cruisers could be seen, it seems to have been assumed that their supposed presence was a false alarm. During the action itself, the poor visibility necessitated constant use of the radar for gunnery ranging and it may be that search sweeps were not carried out as frequently as prudence required (*Admiral Hipper*'s radar log is not clear on this point). Neither the forward nor after sets detected the British cruisers until almost the moment that they opened fire on *Admiral Hipper*. In consequence, the unfortunate German Flagship was caught completely unawares. This situation might well have been prevented by the judicious stationing of a destroyer as flank protection for the heavy cruiser.

So ended 1942 and the New Year began with an inauspicious start. The repercussions of 'Regenbogen' eventually led to the resignation of Grand Admiral Raeder and the order to decommission or scrap the major units of the surface fleet. Despite the success of Admiral Dönitz in reversing this policy to a great extent, it was the end of the surface ship's active participation in the war in the west, with the exception of *Scharnhorst* and the inactive *Tirpitz*. The cruisers returned to the Baltic where they spent the remainder of their careers.

15: THE BALTIC, 1943–1945

As we have seen, by mid 1943, all German cruisers had been withdrawn to the Baltic and, moreover, only *Prinz Eugen*, *Nürnberg* and *Emden* were running. Until the spring of 1944, training duties were the order of the day, under the command of the Ausbildüngsverband or Training Squadron. Then, increasing pressure from the Soviet armies, together with a fear of invasion from the west, led to re-activation of the cruiser force. *Leipzig*, which had re-commissioned under the command of Kpt.z.S.Hulsemann on 1 August 1943, remained on training duties, now (from 26 August 1944) captained by Kpt.z.S.Sporel, but *Prinz Eugen* was operational and *Admiral Hipper* had been brought forward from reserve with the intention of having her available for operations from November 1944. In February 1944, *Köln*, in use as an accommodation

ship/training hulk since June 1943, was towed to Königsberg where she was taken in hand for refit at the Schichau yard, which extended until the end of May. *Emden* and *Nürnberg* continued their training duties.

Towards the end of June 1944, Soviet forces were seriously threatening Finnish positions on the Karelian front in the area of Viborg. Landings had been made by the Soviets to secure the off-shore islands in Koivisto Sound, supported by strong elements of the Soviet Fleet. The Finnish IV Army Corps was forced to withdraw from the Mannerheim Line and fell back to Viborg. Finnish and German light forces were committed to the battle and gained some initial respite, but the position was obviously grave. In order to give the Finns some more tangible and material help, SKL ordered *Prinz Eugen* to the Gulf of

Right: *Nürnberg,* forecastle deck in 1944. Two 2cm LM44 twin mountings have been shipped in echelon on the forecastle. (Drüppel)

Finland in the middle of June. The heavy cruiser, now commanded by Kpt.z.S.Reinicke, lay at Gotenhafen under short notice for steam until 19 June, when the Flag Officer (Training Squadron) Vizeadmiral Thiele and his staff came aboard. At 0600, she slipped and sailed, escorted by the torpedo-boats *T10* and *T11*, together with the fast sloop *F10*. Later, two destroyers of the 6th Flotilla were to join from the Gulf of Riga, where they had been operating. Under clear sky and in calm seas, the squadron pressed onwards making good speed. The expected destroyers failed to appear and the only ships encountered were *T3*, *T8* and *T12* of the 2nd Flotilla, *en route* from Türkü to Libau to refuel. In the early hours of the 20th, Üto lighthouse hove in sight and after picking up Finnish pilots and liaison officers, the squadron anchored. The torpedo-boats refuelled from the cruiser and later in the afternoon, both were put under the orders of the Naval Commander (Gulf of Finland), but remained for the moment with *Prinz Eugen*. Both sailed for Reval however, that same evening. During the day, the situation with regard to air cover, anchorages, etc., was discussed and, to the east, *T31* was lost in the fighting off Koivisto.

Soviet troops had landed in the Koivisto area and were attacking Viborg from the south. The situation for the ships in the Aaland islands was unsatisfactory, because facilities of any kind were entirely lacking to support the squadron. Flak and submarine defences were poor and the absence of shore supplies forced all ships to keep up steam with a consequent high consumption of fuel oil. And for what? There was little prospect of action against surface units worthy of a heavy cruiser, and the dangers of air attack were only too obvious. Nevertheless, on the morning of the 25th, the German squadron was further strengthened by the arrival of *Lützow* with her escort (*T3*, *T4* and *T12*) and in the afternoon, *Z28* arrived. (*Z25* and *Z35* had arrived earlier). The following day, however, *Prinz Eugen* and two torpedo-boats were ordered south once more, and on the 27th, the cruiser sailed with *T3*

and *T12*. After detaching the torpedo-boats to Libau, *Prinz Eugen* reached Gotenhafen the following day.

By July, the German Army in Estonia was being pushed westwards by spearheads of the Soviet Army. Pskov, at the southern end of Lake Peipus, had fallen to the Third Baltic Army on 23 July and, by the 27th, General Bagramyan's First Baltic Army had captured the important railway centre of Shavli in the north of Lithuania, and thrusting towards Riga, had cut the last rail link between Estonia and East Prussia on the 31st. Here he swung north-westwards again, capturing the town of Tukkums on the road from Riga along the southern shore of the Gulf, and the only escape road to the south from Riga itself, on 1 August. In order to re-establish lines of communication with the city and the parts of western Estonia still in German hands, Colonel-General Schoerner launched elements of his Baltic State Army Group in a counter-attack, which stalled in the face of fierce Soviet resistance.

To break the deadlock, naval gunfire support was called for and *Prinz Eugen*, then lying at Gotenhafen, was detailed for the task. Held at ever-decreasing notice for sea, the heavy cruiser finally received orders on the 18th to sail the following morning. At 0700 on the 19th, she sailed, accompanied by units of the 2nd Torpedo-boat Flotilla, under the overall command of Vizeadmiral Thiele. Off the Irben Straits, the destroyers *Z28*, *Z25*, *Z35* and *Z36* joined, then the squadron passed between the tip of the Sworbe peninsula and the northern coast of Lithuania, before rounding the low sandy point of Kolkasrags, whose wooded hinterland lay shrouded in darkness. Entering the Gulf of Riga proper, Thiele took his task force south-eastwards down the Gulf as the hours of darkness ticked away. Ruhnu Island dropped astern to port and later, the featureless outline of the low shoreline to the west revealed itself in the grey light of dawn.

The target was the town of Tukkums, which lies a few miles inland on the south-western corner of the Gulf. *Z28* and *Z25* were allocated several subsidiary targets on the coast where

Soviet positions were known. All three Arados (T3 + KH, MH and CH) were catapulted off for forward observation, strafing and bombing duties in support of the counter-offensive by General-Major von Strachwitz's armoured corps and units of the Waffen SS under SS Stürmbahnführer Gross. The early morning mist over the sandy coast rather hampered observations, but at 0802, *Prinz Eugen*'s main armament opened fire for the first time in her career against land targets. The first bombardment centred on the railway station, which was also bombed by the ship's aircraft. In the meantime, the destroyers' guns supported the break-out of the Riga garrison. A second bombardment took in the south-western corner of the town with the aircraft once again taking part. Several engagements with Soviet Air Force IL2 and DB3 aircraft took place, during which some minor damage was incurred by the German planes. Finally in a third phase, a Soviet gun battery north of the town was taken under fire and silenced. After completion of this task, and in the absence of further requests from the army, Thiele withdrew from the Gulf, detaching the destroyers to Oesel and the 2nd Torpedo Flotilla to Libau *en route* to Gotenhafen, where *Prinz Eugen* arrived safely on the afternoon of the 21st. It was a job well done and the ship's company took great satisfaction in having made a positive contribution to the German war effort after such a long period of inactivity. Schoerner, as a result of this action, was able to hold Riga until October, when elements under the command of Generals Yeremenko and Maslennikov captured the town on the 13th. The German forces were now bottled-up in the Kurland, whence their only escape route was by sea to East Prussia.

The cruiser's next operation, a direct result of the Finnish cease-fire on 4 September 1944, took her once more to the entrance to the Gulf of Finland. Here she was to act as distant cover for one of Germany's most futile actions of the war. Presumably so as to continue the blockade of the Soviet fleet, Hitler ordered that the island of Hogland (Suursaari or Ostrov Gogland) be taken from the Finns and held as a fortress. This small island, no more than six miles long and at most, one mile wide, lies roughly in the centre of the Gulf of Finland, between Kotka bay in the north and Narwa bay to the south. It is partially wooded and steep to in most places, affording poor anchorage and possessing no good harbours. Given the facts and its situation, less than ninety miles from Kronstadt, the German intentions were at best foolhardy, but probably suicidal, for there was a strong Finnish garrison on the island.

Initially, *Lützow* and the boats of the 2nd Torpedo-boat Flotilla had been detailed as distant cover, but representations from Reinicke to MOK(Ost) secured substitution of *Prinz Eugen* for the 'Panzerschiff', and on the evening of 12 September, Vizeadmiral Thiele, commanding the 2nd Task Force, broke out his flag aboard the heavy cruiser. The following evening, she slipped from Gotenhafen and anchored off Hela, where *T1*, *T4*, *T5*, *T9* and *T10* of the 2nd Torpedo-boat Flotilla (K.Kpt.Paul) joined her. Her orders called for the squadron to remain west of 22° E because of the threat of air attack, but this meant they were some 200 nautical miles from Hogland, and a swift intervention in the operation would be impossible. Not only this, but the possibility of

having to make a high-speed dash to the island in an emergency, meant that the fuel-hungry torpedo-boats would have to be continually topped-up with oil. To this end, it was finally agreed to station the oiler *Lissa Essberger* in Tagga Bay, between Oesel and Dago, and to detach the torpedo-boats there at frequent intervals. On the morning of the 14th, the squadron sailed, receiving during the day, the information that the landing was scheduled for 0200 on the 15th. Passing Libau in mid-afternoon, the torpedo-boats were detached as planned, while the cruiser loitered to the west of Dago. By the following morning, after the torpedo-boats had rejoined, ominous reports were already being received from the invasion island; the Finns, in accordance with their treaty with the Soviets, were resisting fiercely. By mid-morning of the 15th, MOK(Ost) had reported that the harbour and ports to the north-west of it were in German hands, but Finnish resistance was continuing. One R-boat (*R29*) and one tug had been sunk, and the retiring minesweepers and launching craft were under continual air attack.

Throughout the morning the squadron itself was subject to desultory airborne torpedo attack, but without effect. The dismal reports from Hogland, as well as a signal from Army Command reporting the start of the long-awaited Soviet offensive in Kurland, must have made the reasons for the squadron's presence superfluous by this time, for any intervention into the narrow mine-, aircraft- and MTB-infested Gulf of Finland was plainly suicidal. An intervention into the Gulf of Riga in support of the Army in Kurland seemed more likely. *Lissa Essberger* was ordered to Reval later in the day, while the cruiser oiled her torpedo-boats, then moved north towards Üto, in order to escort a homeward-bound net layer group out of the Finnish lands. Contact with the landing forces having been lost hours earlier, *Prinz Eugen* sailed for Tagga Bay, passing the 3rd Torpedo-boat Flotilla on its way north to the Aaland Sea. Later one of these boats (*T18*) fell victim to Soviet aircraft rockets while stopped and searching an Estonian refugee boat. These aircraft may well have been searching for the heavy cruiser. After lying at anchor throughout the 16th, orders were received to sail for Gotenhafen the following day. During the night the eastern horizon was aglow with gunfire as the Soviet offensive continued – a stark reminder to the ship's companies of the desperate position of the Reich. On the 17th, the task force sailed, not having fired a shot in anger, returning to Gotenhafen on the 18th.

Prinz Eugen's stay in port was brief; two days later she was at sea again, this time covering the withdrawal of merchant vessels from northern Finland, consequent upon Finland's withdrawal from the war. More than 1,000 miles almost due north of Gotenhafen, General Lothar Rendulic's mountain troops on the Murmansk front had been thrown back by the Soviet Army, commanded by General Meretskov, and forced to withdraw westwards. His options were: evacuation to the south from Kemi at the head of the Gulf of Bothnia; by sea from Kirkenes or Petsamo, or by road into northern Norway. The quickest and probably safest way would have been via the 'Arctic Highway' which ran from Petsamo via Valo on Lake Inari and thence through Rovaniemi to Kemi whence his forces

Left: *Prinz Eugen*. This photograph is of uncertain date but was probably taken in 1943 or 1944. Noteworthy is the faded camouflage paint. (Gröner)

could be shipped back to Germany. The Finns, however, denied this route to the Germans as well as the inland route to Norway, with the result that Rendulic was forced to use the slow and tortuous coastal road. His retreat is outside the scope of this narrative, but as a result of the Finns' actions, his supply base and logistic support at Kemi were rendered useless. Consequently, it was decided to evacuate the base and sail all supply ships south at once. In Kemi at this time, were six merchant vessels of various sizes, the tanker *Hanna* and three naval ferry barges, *F379*, *F517* and *F599*. At a passage speed of no more than eight knots, it would take some 48 hours for the convoy to reach the entrance of the Gulf.

Straddling the entrance to the Gulf of Bothnia, lie the Finnish Aaland Islands, upon which were sited coastal batteries. The attitude of these batteries, in view of events in the north and east, was uncertain, and it was highly likely that any German warships passing northwards would be engaged. In consequence, the covering force was ordered to remain south of the islands and only close the batteries if they opened fire on the merchant ships. It was expected that the merchantmen would be allowed to pass unopposed, but the MFP landing craft were clearly naval vessels and might provoke a reaction.

The Second Task Force (Vizeadmiral Thiele) sailed from Gotenhafen during the evening of the 21st and proceeded northwards the following morning. Accompanying *Prinz Eugen* this time were *Lützow*, the destroyers *Z35* and *Z36*, and torpedo-boats *T1* and *T8*. *Z25*, *Z28* and *T9* would join from

Libau, whence they had been operating in connection with the evacuation of Reval. After anchoring on the Homburg Bank, south of Gotland, because the steamers' sailing had been delayed, the squadron reached its waiting position on the morning of the 23rd. *Prinz Eugen*'s Arado had been catapulted off with pilot charts for the homeward bound merchant ships, returning later that morning as the ships loitered off Enskar. The first steamer hove into view at about 0730 and nearly two hours later the last MFP had entered the open Baltic without reaction from the batteries. The operation had proceeded faultlessly! After detaching the steamers, with *Z25*, *T1* and *T8*, to Danzig, and the MFPs unescorted to Libau, the task force returned to Gotenhafen late in the forenoon of the 25th.

By the beginning of October, the Soviet Army had re-occupied all mainland Estonia, having captured Reval on 22 September. Assaults on the Baltic islands were under way, Moon Island being taken on the 30th and Dago by 3 October. Most of Oesel was also in Soviet hands and Riga finally fell on the 13th, having been cut off since the 10th when General Bagramyan reached the coast between Memel and Libau. On the direct orders of the Führer, the Sworbe peninsula was tenaciously held by the Germans, and covered the Irben Straits while Riga was evacuated. To support the Army once more, the 'Prinz' and *Lützow* put out from Gotenhafen on 11 October with units of the 6th Destroyer and 3rd Torpedo-boat Flotillas. Despite a conflict of opinion between MOK (Ost) who favoured a gun support action off Memel, and Admiral (Ostliches Ostsee) who favoured the Sworbe, the task force finally went into action of Memel.

Here, between the early afternoon of the 11th, and late afternoon of the 12th, the ships bombarded the hilly, wooded coastal strip around the town itself. Shore batteries returned the fire, but without effect, while attacks by torpedo-bombers were equally unsuccessful although strafing resulted in some casualties in the exposed light flak positions. By the early hours of the 13th, *Prinz Eugen* was safely anchored in Gotenhafen Bay, having expended 633 rounds from her main armament. The effects of her gunfire are impossible to assess, but it certainly caused a lot of shock damage within the ship herself! (It did, however, result in a message of thanks from the XXVIII Army Corps, Gross Deutschland Division). Thick fog blanketed the sea as the heavy units awaited refuelling and replenishment of magazines in preparation for further bombardments of the advancing Soviets.

The need to relieve the hard-pressed Army was urgent and the dense fog caused an unwelcome delay. It was intended to sail *Prinz Eugen* after replenishment by the evening of the 14th or, at latest, on the morning of the 15th. Re-ammunitioning *Lützow* was delayed and in consequence, *Prinz Eugen* sailed without her, accompanied by *Z35*, *T21*, *T13* and *T9* at midnight on the 13th/14th; *Lützow* would follow later. In the forenoon of the 14th, action was once again joined off Memel where, despite communications problems and bad weather, some 246 rounds were fired in support of the forces ashore. The *Lützow* contingent joined in the afternoon and, after withdrawing from the coast during the night, bombardment recommenced the following morning. In all, eighteen targets were

Below: Ammunition expenditure by *Prinz Eugen* off Memel, 11–15 October 1944.

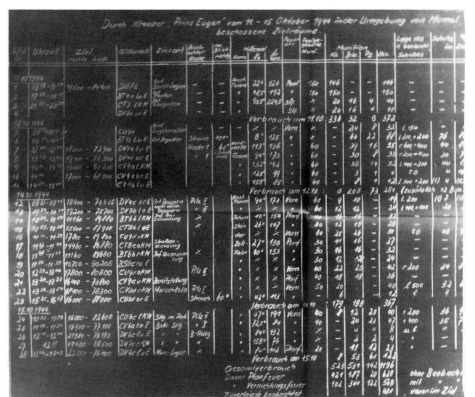

engaged, the 'Prinz' having expended 368 rounds, more than 50 per cent of her outfit. By this time, the ammunition position was giving cause for concern, and emergency arrangements had to be made to ship extra supplies into Gotenhagen from arsenals further west and from Norway, where it was now no longer required.

After completion of their task, the ships turned for home. The weather was by this time closing in, with fog thickening as the ships groped their way south. Events now became affected by operational requirements in the Skagerrak, where an Allied landing had been feared for some time. A contingency plan ('Wallenstein') had been devised to counter this threat, and the minefields at the entrance to the Skagerrak were to be reinforced, for which latter task the lame-duck light cruiser, *Leipzig*, then lying in Gotenhafen, was detailed. As recounted previously, this ship had been of little use other than for training purposes because of damage early in the war, but for the current job, she was adequate. However, she required docking to effect minor bottom repairs, and could not be ready before the 14th. She sailed from Gotenhafen on the 15th, bound for Swinemünde, where she was to load mines for onward passage to the Skagerrak. Thus, the unfortunate ship was outward bound in very foggy and dark conditions while the 'Prinz' was inward bound at the same time.

At 2005, a signal was received by Fleet Command from the 2nd Task Force, detailing its ammunition replenishment requirements and giving its eta as 2200 in Gotenhafen, but hardly had this signal been sent than the bridge watch aboard

the heavy cruiser was horrified to see lying across their bows, the shape of another ship, only metres away. Despite a last-minute order for emergency full speed astern, the sharp bows of *Prinz Eugen* cleaved into the hapless *Leipzig*, for such it was, before the whirling propellers could do anything to check the bigger ship's forward motion. The momentum of the 18,000-tonne vessel carried her deep into the flimsy light cruiser which lay almost cut in half under the ghostly illumination of lamps from *Prinz Eugen*'s bridge. Fortunately for *Leipzig*, she remained impaled on *Prinz Eugen*'s bow; if she had slipped of, she could well have either broken in two or sunk, before damage-control measures could become effective.

The heavy cruiser had struck *Leipzig* almost amidships, between the bridge superstructure and the funnel, on the port side. Both No. 2 and No. 3 forward boiler rooms were breached and flooded, while the compartments forward and aft of these spaces were taking water also. Some 1,600m³ of seawater flooded into the ship and all power and lighting was lost. Eleven men were known to have been killed, and a further six were missing. Thirty-one more suffered injury in the collision. The damage to *Prinz Eugen* was less serious. Her bows had been destroyed from 3 metres below the upper deck down to the keel, and there was flooding of the lower forward compartments up to the armoured deck. Both ships now lay locked together some 2½ nautical miles east of the Hela peninsula. It was dark and starless, with patchy fog and poor visibility, but there was considerable danger of enemy attack despite being so close to a home port. Tugs, escort vessels and salvage craft were

Below: Still locked together many hours after the collision, this view shows a number of points of technical interest. *Prinz Eugen* has received an interim flak modernization – here two twin 2cm LM44 mountings are visible on the forecastle and a 4cm flak 28 Bofors on 'B' turret. *Leipzig* has had a vierling added atop the admiral's bridge, FuMO 25 (large) aerial and above that the smaller FuMB 'Palau' frame. Two, possibly three FuMB 4 'Sumatra' frames are mounted on the foretop. (Imperial War Museum)

Below, top right: At the moment of separation, no longer supported by *Prinz Eugen, Leipzig* is now noticeably lower in the water. Lying alongside to starboard is a Type 37 torpedo-boat supplying power and pumping capacity to the casualty, while one of the tugs stands off. (Imperial War Museum)

Below, bottom right: The damaged bows of *Prinz Eugen* after ramming *Leipzig* in October 1944. (Imperial War Museum)

called up immediately, as damage-control parties worked throughout the night preparing to separate the two stricken vessels. Finally, the following morning, attempts were made at separation by the heavy cruiser going astern, but to no avail. It seemed as if they would never be separated and at one stage, *Prinz Eugen* signalled that if further attempts failed, she would attempt to push *Leipzig* towards Hela! This would almost certainly have broken the light cruiser in two, but happily after tugs had pumped vast quantities of water out of *Leipzig*, a final attempt was made by holding *Leipzig* with tugs, while *Prinz Eugen* used full astern power on her screws. This time the attempt succeeded and at 1430 the 'Prinz' was able to signal that she was at last free from the light cruiser. All the tugs and salvage vessels could now concentrate their attention on *Leipzig* and after transferring the remainder of the Task Force staff to *T4*, *Prinz Eugen* proceeded into Gotenhafen.

Aboard *Leipzig*, conditions were serious, but not desperate in terms of the ship sinking, for there seemed little chance of that despite the damage that she had received. She could not proceed under her own power because after her torpedoing in 1939, she possessed only two boilers, both in her forward boiler room (No. 3) and this had now been put out of action. No. 2 boiler room, converted to accommodation for trainees, was also flooded and, but for the change of watch just prior to the collision, would have been crowded with men who must surely have been casualties. Her diesels could not be started and as a result, the damaged ship arrived in port under tow, reaching Gotenhafen at about midnight on the 17th. Her excess draught caused by the flooding presented problems in docking, and it was some time before a suitable berth could be found.

Directly after their arrival in Gotenhafen, the two ships were visited by the CinC (Fleet) Vizeadmiral Meendsen-Bohlken, for the consequences of the loss of *Prinz Eugen*'s services for any length of time were serious. Initial estimates of repair times were four weeks for the heavy cruiser, while *Leipzig* was adjudged irreparable under the yard conditions then prevailing. On 16 November it was decided to pay the ship off, reduce her to hulk status for instructional purposes, and draft the majority of the ship's company elsewhere. It was intended that she remain in this status until May 1945, and not be required for further service until August 1945. The war's progress dictated otherwise!

An emergency repair conference was held at Gotenhafen's Deutsche Werke offices on 17 October to examine the repair position for *Prinz Eugen* at which was present an array of top brass, indicating the importance of the task in hand. Chaired by the CinC (Fleet), the meeting was also attended by Konteradmiral Rogge, Flag Officer (Ausbildüngsverband), his Staff Engineer and Flag Lieutenant as well as Professor Burkhardt, the designer of the cruiser, and the shipyard director, Herr Kausch, among others. Figures were tabled which showed that an estimated 42,500 man-hours work were necessary, of which 30,000 were represented by steel work repairs to the hull. This was plainly unacceptable, especially as Admiral Dönitz indicated that the ship was part of the 'Wallenstein' plan and as such had a priority only below that of the U-boat programme. After some discussion, Burkhardt,

who had a particular affection for his ship (his son had been one of her casualties in the bomb hit at Brest in 1940) undertook, by cutting all red tape and official channels, to complete repairs within two weeks. In fact, it took a little longer, even though some of the work was cut out, including re-installation of the bow protection equipment, so the ship was not finally out of dockyard hands until 7 November.

Prinz Eugen returned to operations on 19 November when she sailed that evening, bound for the Sworbe. Hitler had ordered that at least one heavy cruiser should be in support of the beleagured defenders of the narrow peninsula, and the heavy cruiser had once again been detailed for the task. Groping his way out of Hela Bay, escorted by four boats of the 3rd Torpedo-boat Flotilla (*T21*, *T16*, *T13* and *T19*), Reinicke took the heavy cruiser northwards into deteriorating weather. By early morning on the 20th, the seas had become heavy, there was solid cloud overhead and rain driving on the wind, as *Z35*, *Z36* and *Z43* joined from the Irben Straits. Visibility was now down to only one to two miles, with the wind having risen to Force 6–7. Conditions such as these could obviously render the whole task impossible. Off the Sworbe, Flag Officer (Task Force) sent the destroyers inshore to test conditions, for the heavy cruiser could not approach the shore in visibility of less than two–four miles, without knowing her position accurately. As a result, the heavy cruiser spent the whole morning fruitlessly steaming about off-shore until towards midday, visibility improved. Finally, at 1405, *Prinz Eugen* was able to begin her task. Her shooting was reported good by the forward observers ashore, while the enemy shore batteries (approximately 15cm guns) reply was inaccurate. Every round had to count for by this time, supplies of 20.3cm ammunition were very low, and it was not certain after the following day's expenditure, whether any more ammunition would be forthcoming.

During the night the squadron withdrew seawards, loitering off the northern tip of Gotland throughout the hours of darkness before closing the coast the following morning. Weather and visibility were no better, with the result that one of the destroyers received orders to lower a cutter carrying a marker flag to assist the heavy cruiser in positioning herself. In the meantime, the enemy shore batteries once again opened fire on the Task Force, but failed to secure any hits as the cruiser manoeuvred off-shore. Not until 1048 could permission to open fire be given, when a number of different targets were engaged on the instructions of the forward observers ashore, until ceasing fire at 1540. In the course of the two-day operation, *Prinz Eugen* had fired 255 rounds on the 20th, and 259 rounds during the 21st, as well as nearly 200 rounds of 10.5cm gunfire. She had now expended her ammunition allowance and accordingly, withdrew from the coast then, in the lee of Ostergans Holme, transhipped Admiral Rogge (Flag Officer Task Force) to *Admiral Scheer* which was to continue the task of gunfire support off the Sworbe. *Prinz Eugen* returned to Gotenhafen the following day, where appreciative signals were received from General-Oberst Schoerner (O.C. Herrsgruppe Nord) as well as Admiral (Eastern Baltic) and CinC (Fleet).

The numerous and frequent shore bombardment tasks performed by *Prinz Eugen* during the last six months of 1944, now meant that her guns were overdue for re-lining, for which purpose she went into dockyard hands at the beginning of December. At the same time, opportunity was also taken to modernize and augment the flak outfit. Conditions in the dockyards were, by this time, rather desperate, with frequent air raids disrupting working hours and only intermittent electricity supplies available. Not surprisingly, therefore, the dockyard period took up the whole of December and extended into the first week of the New Year, and it was not until the end of January that *Prinz Eugen* resumed operations against the Soviet Army.

Unlike *Prinz Eugen*, the Kriegsmarine's only other remaining heavy cruiser, *Admiral Hipper*, played no further part in any wartime operations after 1942. Having languished unrepaired since 1943, she could not be readied for active duty without a considerable amount of dockyard work. In March 1944, the SKL did actually decide to repair the ship, with the intention of having her ready for operational duty in Baltic waters from November 1944. She was taken in hand at the Gotenhafen yard where repair work continued until the end of June, but by the end of the year she was still not fully operational despite further dockyard time. During this time,

she was on several occasions considered for shore bombardment tasks, but because of her low standard of efficiency, no operations were ever conducted by *Admiral Hipper*, although she had been earmarked as a possible flagship for the Task Force.

Towards the end of 1944, it was finally decided to overhaul the ship properly and to fully repair No. 3 boiler room. She was to be at the Gotenhafen yard by 1 December at the latest, although repairs would not be started immediately because the necessary parts were not available.

The refit period was scheduled to extend from 1 January 1945 until 15 March, and both heavy cruisers were to be fully operational by the end of that month. On 3 January, de-ammunitioning began and preparations were started to land the flak guns for overhaul. As the month progressed, the situation on the eastern front deteriorated, with the result that on the 19th, *Admiral Hipper* was ordered to retain some of her 10.5cm guns and re-embark ammunition for her 3.7cm and 4cm weapons; in an emergency, 10.5cm ammunition would be obtained from her sister ship. The ship was under eighteen hours' notice for steam, but on the afternoon of the 22nd, both she and *Emden* were ordered to prepare to move, readiness being reduced to three hours. Flak ammunition was re-embarked, but the ship was far from effective since only one engine was working and only the forward pair of flak directors were serviceable. That evening, orders came to embark 20.3cm ammunition, but no movement order arrived until the 29th, when she was ordered to sail at 1600. Even then delays occurred and it was not until late afternoon on the following day that the cruiser limped out, escorted by *T36*, the two ships carrying some 1,700 refugees.

Out at sea, the refugee ship, *Wilhelm Gustloff* had been torpedoed by the Soviet submarine *S13*, at a position on *Hipper*'s route west. The danger of a further attack on the lame cruiser prevented her participation in the rescue operations and reluctantly, but correctly, Kpt.z.S. Henigst had to watch the liner sink by the bows and capsize while he manoeuvred his ship past the mass of lifeboats, floats and wreckage. More than 6,000 people had been aboard the liner and few survived. Many had been trapped below decks or killed in the explosions, but for a while, a number survived in the freezing seas and on the life-rafts. Henigst ordered *T36* to assist in rescue operations, while he took his ship on to Kiel. Only about 650 people were finally rescued. *Admiral Hipper* secured in the Deutsche Werke yard at Kiel on 2 February, to begin her refit which was not destined to be completed. In the course of an air raid on 3 May (in fact, the last operation against Germany by RAF Bomber Command) the ship was heavily hit and settled on the bottom of the dock.

By 20 January, the Soviets had thrust deep into East Prussia, cutting Gotenhafen and Danzig off from the Reich, Königsberg, capital of East Prussia, was also cut off and the town of Elbing, to the south, was threatened. Memel had fallen on the 27th and its garrison were retiring along the narrow spit of land between the open Baltic and the Kurisches Haff. The operational orders of the 2nd Task Force were simple – to keep open the lines of communication along the coast from the

Below: *Admiral Hipper* bombed and sunk in Deutsche Werke, No. V dock, Kiel May 1945. (Imperial War Museum)
Bottom: *Admiral Hipper* being broken up at Kiel in August 1947. (Gröner)

Nehrung and thence to Pillau where the retreating Army could be evacuated by sea. *Z25*, together with *T33* and *T23* of the 5th Torpedo-boat Flotilla were also to take part in the operation.

On 26 January, Reinicke, with serious misgivings, took his ship into the beleagured port of Gotenhafen to embark ammunition, a task which took until late evening. The threat of heavy air raids was ever-present and, in fact, Danzig suffered the following day, hence Reinicke's worries, especially as the start of the sortie was delayed. Snow now began to fall from the overcast sky and fog patches reduced visibility considerably. It was very cold and snow fell throughout the day. Finally, the Task Force put to sea at 0000 on the 29th, reaching their firing position about eight and a half hours later. A few minutes later, Cranz church came into view and at 0850 the cruiser, her guns trained to port, opened fire on Reich territory for the first time. For almost ten hours, the ships engaged a variety of targets during the course of which, *Prinz Eugen* fired her 2,000th round in shore bombardment. During the night the ships withdrew to Hela, re-engaging at 0755 the following day, until poor visibility forced a cease-fire during the afternoon. A total of 850 rounds had so far been fired by the cruiser during the two days of action. The action was repeated on the 31st, during which sortie, the ship's aircraft also took part, after which the ships returned once more to Hela to replenish fuel and ammunition.

This operation was, in fact, the last to be performed by *Prinz Eugen* for some time; ammunition for 20.3-calibre guns was very scarce, and since 28cm ammunition was in greater supply, the 'Panzerschiffe' took over the bombardment tasks. By March, there were two battle groups operating, one centred around *Lützow*, commanded by Vizeadmiral Thiele and the other commanded by Vizeadmiral Rogge. Throughout March, *Prinz Eugen* bombarded targets around Gotenhafen, Zoppot, Danzig, Tiegenhoff and Ladekopp in a vain bid to stop or delay the seemingly invincible Russian Army. Despite all the Kriegsmarine's efforts, the German Army was forced relentlessly back, Gotenhafen falling on 28 March and Danzig two days later.

Huge numbers of troops and refugees were evacuated to the west under cover of the warship's protection, an activity which continued even after the cease-fire in May. Soviet aircraft and light surface forces attacked on numerous occasions, but failed to inflict any serious punishment on the bombarding ships (*Z34* was the only exception, being torpedoed though not sunk off Hela on 15 April). Once again, however, casualties were numerous among the exposed flak crews. By the 30th, the last evacuations were taking place from Oxhoft where *Prinz Eugen* again provided off-shore support, being hit the following day by rockets from Soviet aircraft which killed nine men. There were now only about forty rounds of 20.3cm ammunition remaining, and the heavy cruiser took her last target under fire on the evening of 4 April, having, during the last month, expended 4,871 rounds from her main armament and more than 2,500 from her 10.5cm guns in support of operations ashore. *Prinz Eugen* was now unable to play any further part in the eastern catastrophe and, on 10 April, sailed west by stages, arriving in Copenhagen on the 20th where, together with

Nürnberg, the two ships represented the last of the Kriegsmarine's big ships.

Like *Admiral Hipper*, the remaining light cruisers played little or no part in the traumatic events in the eastern Baltic. *Köln*, after her re-activation, arrived in tow at Pillau on 17 February 1944 to begin a refit at Königsberg, and was recommissioned on 1 April. The refit extended until about June. Following this, she was employed on training duties until ordered to the Skagerrak for minelaying in October 1944, sailing for Horton from Swinemünde on the 7th. Here she remained until early in the New Year, when as a result of near misses, and poor general condition – her shafts were defective which restricted her speed to only fifteen knots, she was ordered to repair in Germany. *Köln* returned to Kiel on 12 January 1945, then transitted the Kaiser-Wilhelm Canal to Wilhelmshaven where she docked on the 14th. Like *Admiral Hipper*, *Köln*'s refit too was brought to an abrupt end, this time by the 8th USAAF on 30 March while still in dock. Settling on the bottom, her upperworks were above water, her flak guns still serviceable, but as an effective unit her career was over.

Nürnberg, the newest light cruiser, spent most of her career from 1943 onwards as a unit of the Ausbildüngsverband, operating in the Baltic until ordered for duty in the Skagerrak on 25 December 1944 to replace *Emden*. She sailed from Swinemünde on 3 January 1945, accompanied by *Linz*, and arrived in Oslofjord on the 8th. Here, she was employed on minelaying sorties, wearing the flag of Konteradmiral Kreisch (Flag Officer Destroyers). Her general efficiency level was low, due to continual changes of cadet courses, but it was intended that she work-up for duties in the eastern Baltic as soon as possible. Unfortunately, training and fuel problems were such that the ship remained inactive in Copenhagen from February until the surrender in May 1945.

The veteran cruiser *Emden*, having spent nearly all her war service in Baltic waters was also ordered to the Skagerrak in September 1944, sailing from Swinemünde on the 11th. While navigating Oslofjord on 9 December, she ran heavily aground east of Flateguri Island and was unable to get free until the following day. On the 16th, Admiral Dönitz ordered her to repair at Schichau (Königsberg) where she docked on Christmas Day. Her repairs were also frustrated by enemy action, this time by the Soviet Army which, by the evening of 21 January, was only 40 kilometres from Königsberg. *Emden* was almost ready for undocking when her repairs were abruptly broken off with the intention of towing her out to Pillau on the 24th, in order to be ready for sea on the 28th. On the afternoon of the 23rd, *Emden* was ordered out of Königsberg and, after oiling at Pillau, to proceed to Gotenhafen and re-embark her guns. Strict orders were given that any refugees must only be taken as far as Pillau, on no account were they to be taken to Gotenhafen – conditions were bad enough there already. After loading the Hindenburg Sarcophagus, the cruiser reached Pillau on tow on the 24th, but could not proceed from there until the 26th because her engines were still in pieces! On the 30th Kpt.z.S.Kahler finally got to Gotenhafen where the guns were quickly remounted. He could now defend himself, but could only steam at ten knots! At last, on the afternoon of 2

February, *Emden* sailed west accompanied by *TS6*, *TS9*, *T11* and the tug *Boreas*, arriving in Kiel for completion of her repairs at Deutsche Werke on 6 February. In April, she was damaged during an air raid and at the end of the war remained unrepaired, being scuttled in shallow water in Heikendorfer Bay, Kiel, where she was broken up in situ after the war.

Only *Leipzig* now remains to be dealt with. Never repaired fully after 1939, this ship remained a lame duck throughout the war and after the collision in October 1944, was virtually a wreck. The hole in her hull measured some ten metres by ten metres, opening up the side from upper deck to the keelson which itself was bent, and many of the tank spaces had been ruptured. Temporary repairs carried out at Gotenhafen involved a pair of 500mm × 150mm channel bars some ten metres long being welded longitudinally to the hull, above and below the waterline to stiffen it, and the opening being plated over. All her boilers were either damaged or removed and although four new boilers were available on the dockside, no renewal was made to the steam plant. *Leipzig* remained in dockyard hands until January 1945 when, toward the end of the month, SKL decided to use the ship as a floating battery and not to withdraw her to the west. Ammunition was embarked, scuttling preparations were made and her berth was shifted to the outer harbour on the Oxhoft side. Two days later, it was decided to shift berth once more because in her present position she was too close to the bunkers of the Naval Commander and Fortress Commander, and the ship was an obvious bombing target. Experience with *Tirpitz* had also shown the importance of preventing capsizing, so a suitable bed on the harbour bottom was to be prepared. On 16 February, she test fired her guns against a convenient wreck and was adjudged an operational battery. It is believed that *Leipzig* joined in the last desperate land battles around the port of Gotenhafen during March, before escaping from that port on its capture by the Russians on the 28th. Capable of only a very slow speed, *Leipzig* crawled west on her diesels, finally reaching Aabenraa, a small Danish fjord, north of Flensburg on the Little Belts, where she surrendered in May 1945.

Left: *Nürnberg*. Visible here is a 2cm gun added in front of the navigating bridge, and the aerial of the FuMO 24/25 radar on a bracket of the foremast. Three of the 'Sumatra' FuMB 6 radar detection aerials can also be seen around the foretop. (Drüppel)

Right: *Nürnberg*. A 'goofers' piknik' in 1944 during gunnery exercises. 2cm LM44 twins are visible on the forecastle and a 4cm flak 28 at the extreme left, above the army officer. The bridge wing is swung inboard. The three equipments manned on the starboard side are, from aft: searchlight director (with the long frame), torpedo director and an auxiliary gun director. (Drüppel)

16: POSTSCRIPT

Following the Allied Tripartite Agreement at Potsdam, the surrendered cruisers were allocated to the USA (*Prinz Eugen*) and the USSR (*Nürnberg*), while the derelict *Leipzig* was to be destroyed as a 'Category C' vessel. *Leipzig* was brought down from Aabenraa to Kiel and then towed to Wilhelmshaven where she languished until the summer of 1946. 'Category C' ships had, under the conditions of the Potsdam agreement, (Article 7) to be either broken up or sunk in deep water by not later than 15 August 1946; at the same time, opportunity was taken to dispose of some of the vast quantity of munitions (including gas shells) belonging to the Wehrmacht. The rust-streaked and silent cruiser, whose war-time career had been one of misfortune, left Wilhelmshaven under tow on the morning of 6 July 1946, with only a towing party aboard. The passage north through the German Bight and along the coast of Denmark was a slow one and it was not until the 11th that she was finally in place and ready for scuttling in the deep water trench south-west of Farsund in southern Norway. The tugs moved alongside to take off the towing party and at 1059, the scuttling-charges were fired. *Leipzig* exploded and went to the bottom in a cloud of dirty, black and grey smoke.

Nürnberg, the most modern of the light cruisers, passed into Soviet hands and was put into dry dock at Wilhelmshaven to forestall any attempt at scuttling by her German crew if her

Right: *Leipzig* en route for scuttling under tow. Her armament has received little augmentation during the war and she is unusual in that she has single shielded 2cm guns. Just forward can be seen the make-shift repairs to the port side. (Drüppel)

Below right: *Leipzig* at her scuttling position. The tug has taken off the towing crew prior to firing the scuttling charges. (Drüppel)

Bottom right: *Nürnberg*. De-ammunitioning ship at Copenhagen in May 1945. Note shield fitted to the 3.7cm SKC/30 mounting. (Imperial War Museum)

Below: Another view of *Nürnberg* at Copenhagen in 1945. Noteworthy items are the 'Hohentweil' radar on the main mast, vierling on 'B' turret and the numerous 2cm LM44 twin mountings. (Imperial War Museum)

Left: *Nürnberg* sailing for Libau in 1946. Several 2cm guns in LM44 shielded twin mountings can be seen. The 'Sumatra' aerials have now been removed from the foretop front, leaving only a rotating 'Palau' aerial. On the main mast truck is the FuMO 63 'Hohentweil K' set and atop the bridge is a single 4cm Flak 28 Bofors. (Imperial War Museum)
Below left: *Nürnberg* at anchor in the River Neva, Leningrad, about 1955. Her appearance is little changed with the exception of new radars and a repositioned mainmast. (Drüppel)
Below right: View of the former *Lützow* in Soviet hands post-war. (BDZ)

transfer to Russia became known. The Soviet crew came aboard on 16 December 1945 and in the New Year, hoisted the flag of Vice-Admiral Rall of the Soviet Navy before sailing for Libau on 2 January 1946, accompanied by *Hessen, Blitz, Z15, T33* and *T107*. The Soviet Navy re-named the ship *Admiral Makarov*, commemorating an officer of the Tsarist Navy who lost his life outside Port Arthur during the Russo-Japanese war of 1904. During her career in the Soviet Navy, *Admiral Makarov* served as Flagship of the 8th Fleet (Vice-Admiral F. V. Zogulya) before being withdrawn from active service and employed as a training vessel. She remained in this duty, based at Leningrad, until about 1959 when she was observed at Kronstadt in the August of that year, partially stripped. In the summer of 1960, it was reported that the last surviving Kriegsmarine cruiser was being broken up in the coaling harbour at Leningrad.

The handsome *Prinz Eugen*, immaculate and well-maintained, was taken over by the US Navy and moved initially to Bremen which was under US control. On 5 January 1946, the ship was officially placed in service (but not in commission) as *Prinz Eugen*, designation 1X–300, Commanding Officer, Captain A. H. Graubart, USN, who was himself of German extraction. In New York, eleven officers and 275 enlisted men embarked in the transport *General Anderson* for passage to Le Havre to form the cruiser's crew. *Prinz Eugen* sailed from Wilhelmshaven on 13 January 1946 bound for Portsmouth (UK) for fuel and thence to Boston Ma, where she arrived on 23 January. For the next six weeks or so the ship remained in the Boston area undergoing minor repairs, trials and examination by the USN, but her final destination was the Pacific and a possible Valkyrian fate. She, like many surrendered Imperial Japanese Naval vessels and obsolete US

warships, had been allocated to the Atomic Bomb experiments at Bikini Atoll, Operation 'Crossroads'.

Prinz Eugen (1X300) sailed from Boston on 10 March 1946, for San Diego via the Panama Canal. While on the Atlantic coast, much of her special equipment in the radar, sonar and gunnery fields had been landed for evaluation by the relevant USN departments, while at the same time additional equipment concerned with the forthcoming 'Crossroads' tests had been installed. Thus both 20.3cm SKC/34 guns from 'A' turret, P2 and P3 10.5cm SKC/33 twin mountings, and most, but not all, of the 4cm FlaK 28 were removed, as was the forward range-finder cupola and the starboard forward flak director. The catapult was removed. A box structure topped by a radar dish replaced the forward range-finder.

On the west coast of the USA, operating out of San Diego and San Pedro, *Prinz Eugen* (1X300) conducted high-speed trials, served as a target for Subron 3 and had her underwater detection equipment evaluated, as well as being briefly docked for necessary voyage repairs. Eventually some of the sonar equipment was removed and, before the ship finally sailed for Pearl Harbor, the remaining German personnel, some 134 officers and men, were to be landed at San Diego. Leaving the east coast on 11 May 1946, the ship reached Pearl Harbor on the 19th, where she was to form, with USS *Pensacola* and *Salt Lake City*, temporary Cruiser Division 23 for the duration of the tests. *Prinz Eugen* (1X300) remained in Pearl Harbor preparing for the tests until 3 June when she sailed once more, accompanied by the Fleet tug *Sioux* (ATF75) *en route* for her final destination, Bikini Atoll, 2,100 miles east across the Pacific, where she arrived on the 9th.

The first nuclear test, 'Able' took place on 1 July 1946, when a bomb was dropped from a B29, fuzed to explode above the

water. The former German cruiser anchored some 1,500 metres from the centre of the blast area suffered remarkably little damage (although the paint was completely stripped from her side facing the explosion), but the second test, 'Baker', exploded under the water's surface, resulted in damage and buckling to the hull plating. Nevertheless, she remained afloat and on an even keel. Following this second test, the ship was towed to Kwajalein, another island in the Marshalls, south-west of Bikini. It was intended to use the surviving ships as targets for the US Navy, but by now, the heavy cruiser was highly radio-active, and the commander of the joint Task Force had to report that it would be impossible to decontaminate the vessel to a point where she could be made continuously habitable within the next few months. Accordingly it was proposed to utilize her in test 'Charlie'. This was agreed on 16 August and on the 30th it was decided to decommission the ship (but note earlier re-commissioning). She was taken out of service on 6 September 1946. The invisible effects of the blasts were by now becoming apparent. Shock waves had loosened underwater fittings, pipes and glands, with the result that serious flooding developed. On 21 December the flooding suddenly increased to a point beyond the pumping capacity of the salvage vessels, and a list developed, sufficient to put the lower scuttles under water. Urgent action was required to prevent her capsizing and the ship was beached on Carlos Island, but capsized the following day, 22 December 1946. She remains on a reef at Enubuj, Kwajalein to this day, having been stricken from the USN records on 10 June 1947.

Right: *Prinz Eugen* surrendered at Copenhagen in May 1945. Shown here to good advantage is a 10.5cm SKC/33 mounting with, just above and left, a covered vierling and forward of it, a 4cm Flak 28 Bofors. At the foot of the mainmast is the main searchlight platform with 'C' and 'D' flak directors on each side of it. An Arado Ar. 196-A3 floatplane sits on the catapult. (Imperial War Museum)

Below: *Prinz Eugen* under escort to Wilhelmshaven in 1945. An interesting study of comparative heavy cruiser designs. Note that *Devonshire* has landed 'X' turret. (Imperial War Museum)

APPENDICES

I. SHIPS' TECHNICAL DATA

EMDEN
Displacement:
Full load: 6,990 tons/7,102 tonnes.
Standard: 5,600 tons/5,689 tonnes.
Length: 155.1m (oa), 150.5m (wl).
Beam: 14.3m.
Draught: 5.93m (full load), 5.15m (standard).
Machinery:
Four coal-fired marine and six oil-fired marine boilers, 16kg/cm². (The coal-fired boilers were replaced by oil-fired types in 1934).
Two shaft Brown Boverie & Co. single reduction geared turbines.
46,500shp = 29.4 knots.
875 tonnes coal plus 859m³ oil = 6,750nm at 14 knots.
Later: 1,266m³ oil = 5,300nm at 18 knots.
Three diesel generators = 420kW at 220V d.c.
Armament:
Eight 15cm L45 in MPL C/16 (120rpg).
Two (later three) 8.8cm L45 in MPL C/16 (400rpg).
Four 50cm torpedo tubes in two twin mountings (later replaced by 53.3cm pattern torpedoes).
About six 2cm C/30 single guns had been added by the outbreak of war.
120 mines.
By autumn 1944, her armament had been altered as follows:
Eight 15cm Tbts K C/36.
Three 10.5cm SKC/32gE.
Two 4cm FlaK 28 (Bofors).
Two 3.7cm SKC/30U.
Twenty 2cm C/38 (2 Vierling, 6 twin).
This was intended to be modified to:
Nine 3.7cm FlaK M42.
Twelve 2cm C/38 (twins).
Protection:
Deck: 20–40mm.
Belt: 50mm.
Conning tower: 100mm.

KÖNIGSBERG, KARLSRUHE and KÖLN
Displacement:
Full load: 8,130 tons/8,260 tonnes (8,350 tons/8,433 tonnes *Karlsruhe* after refit 1939/40).
Standard: 6,650 tons/6,756 tonnes (6,730 tons/6,837 tonnes *Karlsruhe* after refit 1939/40).
Length: 174m (oa), 169m (wl).
Beam: 15.3m (16.6m *Karlsruhe* 1940).
Draught: 6.28m (full load), 5.56m (standard). (*Karlsruhe* 6.20m after refit).
Machinery:
Six oil-fired marine boilers, 16kg/cm².
Two shaft single reduction geared turbines (Schichau – *Königsberg*, Germania – *Karlsruhe* and Blohm & Voss – *Köln*).
Two MAN ten-cylinder four-stroke diesels for cruising purposes.
68,000shp = 32.5 knots. Diesels 1,800bhp = 10 knots.
1,184m³ oil plus 261m³ diesel oil = 3,100nm at 13 knots.
Two turbo generators plus three diesel generators = 180 plus 360kW at 220V d.c.
Armament:
Nine 15cm SKC/25 in triple turrets LC/25.
Six 8.8cm SKC/32 in twin mountings LC/32.
Eight 3.7cm SKC/30 in twin mountings LC/30.
Four 2cm MG C/30 in single mountings LC/30.
Twelve 50cm torpedo tubes in four triple mountings (later, in about 1934, replaced by 53.3cm pattern).
120 mines.
Two aircraft, one catapult.
Note: These ships completed with an extemporized FlaK battery of old 1916 pattern 8.8cm single guns until the new 1932 model was available. Two or three of these were carried until replaced

initially by two twin mountings on the centre-line forward of 'B' turret. Later two mountings were sided port and starboard and a third retained on the centre line. Similarly, there were considerable delays in the fitment of the 3.7cm and 2cm guns.
By late 1944, the light FlaK was to be altered to:
Four 4cm FlaK 28 (Bofors).
Four 3.7cm SKC/30.
Sixteen 2cm Kg C/38 in twin mountings, in the only surviving vessel, *Köln*.
Protection:
Deck: 40mm (maximum).
Belt: 50–70mm.
Conning tower: 100mm.
Turrets: 20–30mm.
(*Karlsruhe*, following her rebuilding, received new side plating 10–14mm thick and a new upper deck of 16mm.)

LEIPZIG
Displacement:
Full load: 8,250 tons/8,382 tonnes.
Standard: 6,515 tons/6,619 tonnes.
Length: 177.1m (oa), 165.8 (wl).
Beam: 16.2m.
Draught: 5.69m (maximum), 4.88m (standard).
Machinery:
Six oil-fired marine boilers, 16kg/cm².
Two shaft single reduction geared turbines.
One shaft with four MAN seven-cylinder double acting diesels.
60,000shp plus 12,400bhp = 32 knots.
1,235m³ oil-fired plus 348m³ diesel oil = 5,700nm at 19 knots.
Three turbo generators plus three diesel sets = 1,300kW at 220V d.c.
Armament:
Nine 15cm SKC/25 in triple mountings LC/25.
Six 8.8cm SKC/32 in twin mountings LC/32.

Eight 3.7cm SKC/30 in twin mountings LC/30.
Four 2cm MG C/30 in single mountings.
Twelve 50cm torpedo tubes in triple mountings (later replaced by 53.3cm pattern in 1934).
120 mines.
Two aircraft, one catapult.
Protection:
Deck: 20mm (25mm on curved sides).
Belt: 20–50mm.
Conning tower: 100mm.
Turrets: 20–30mm.

NÜRNBERG
Displacement:
Full load: 8,971 tons/9,115 tonnes.
Standard: 6,980 tons/7,091 tonnes.
Length: 181m (oa), 170m (wl).
Beam: 16.4m.
Draught: 6.4m (maximum), 5m (standard).
Machinery:
Six oil-fired marine boilers, 16kg/cm².
Two shaft single reduction Krupp geared turbines.
One shaft with four MAN seven-cylinder double acting diesels.
66,000shp plus 124,000bhp = 32 knots.
1,055m³ oil fuel plus 255m³ diesel fuel = 2,400nm at 13 knots.
Two 350kW turbo generators plus 150kW diesel generators = 1,300kW.
Armament:
Nine 15cm SKC/25 in triple turrets LC/25 (150rpg).
Eight 8.8cm SKC/32 in twin mountings LC/32 (400rpg).
Eight 3.7cm SKC/30 in twin mountings C/30 (1,200rpg).
Four 2cm MG C/30 in single mountings.
Twelve 53.3cm torpedo tubes in triple mountings.
120 mines.
Two aircraft, one catapult.

Protection:
Deck: 20mm (25mm on curvature).
Belt: 18mm–50mm.
Conning tower: 60mm.
Turrets: 20–80mm.

ADMIRAL HIPPER and BLÜCHER

Displacement:
Full load: 18,208 tons/18,500 tonnes.
Standard: 14,247 tons/14,475 tonnes.
Length: 202.8m (oa), (205.9m with 'Atlantic' bow), 194.2m (wl).
Beam: 21.3m.
Draught: 7.74m (maximum), 5.83m (standard).
Machinery:
Twelve oil-fired high-pressure boilers ($70kg/cm^2$ Wagner type in *Blücher*, $80kg/cm^2$ La Mont in *Admiral Hipper*).
Three shaft single reduction geared turbines (Blohm & Voss in *Hipper*, Deschimag in *Blücher*).
133,631shp = 32.5 knots.
$3,050m^3$ oil fuel = 6,500nm at 17 knots (later increased to $3,700m^3$).
Four diesel generators at 150kW each.
Two turbo generators at 230kW, plus four turbo generators at 460kW = 2,900kW.
Armament:
Eight 20.3cm SKC/34 in twin turrets LC/34 (140rpg).
Twelve 10.5cm SKC/33 in 8.8cm twin mountings LC/31 (420rpg).
Twelve 3.7cm SKC/30 in twin mountings LC/30 (1,500rpg).
Eight 2cm MG C/30 in single mountings (7,000rpg).
Twelve 53.3cm torpedo tubes in triple mountings (with ten reload torpedoes).
One catapult, single hangar, three Arado Ar196 float planes.
Protection:
Deck: 12–30mm (upper), 20–50mm (armoured deck).
Belt: 70–80mm.
Conning tower: 50–150mm.
FlaK directors: 14mm.
Turrets: 70–105mm.
(See illustration on page 38 for full details.)

PRINZ EUGEN, SEYDLITZ and LÜTZOW

Displacement:
Full load: *18,700 tons/19,000 tonnes.
Standard: 14,271 tons/14,500 tonnes.
Length: 207.7m (oa), 199.5m (wl).
Beam: 21.9m.
Draught:
7.95m (full load), 6.37m (standard).
Machinery:
As *Admiral Hipper* except La Mont boilers in *Prinz Eugen*, Wagner in *Seydlitz* and *Lützow*.
Brown Boverie turbines in *Prinz Eugen*, Deschimag in other two.
$3,250m^3$ oil fuel later increased to $3,400m^3$ = 6,100nm at 15 knots.

Armament:
As *Admiral Hipper* except that *Seydlitz* and *Lützow* were to ship 10.5 SKC/33 in 10.5cm twin mountings LC/37.
Reserve torpedoes increased to twelve.
Protection: As *Admiral Hipper*.

*See weight breakdown table Chapter 3 for *Seydlitz*. This may also have applied to *Lützow*.

KREUZER 'M'

Displacement:
Full load: 10,400 tons/10,566 tonnes.
Standard: 7,800 tons/7,925 tonnes.
Length: 183m (oa), 178m (wl).
Beam: 17m.
Draught: 7.25m (full load), 5.42m (standard).
Machinery:
Four oil-fired Wagner high-pressure boilers ($70kg/cm^2$).
Two shaft Wagner single reduction geared turbines.
Two shaft with four MAN twelve-cylinder double acting diesels.
100,000shp plus 16,500bhp = 35.5 knots.
$1,080m^3$ oil fuel plus $520m^3$ diesel fuel = 8,000nm at 19 knots.
Armament:
Eight 15cm SKC/28 in twin turrets LC/34 (140rpg).
Four 8.8cm SKC/32 in twin mountings (400rpg).
Eight 3.7cm SKC/30 in twin mountings LC/30.
Eight 53.3cm torpedo tubes in quadruple mountings.
160 mines.
Two aircraft, one catapult.
Protection:
Deck: 20–35mm.
Belt: 30–50mm.
Conning tower: 20–100mm.
Turrets: 20–80mm.

'SPÄHKREUZER 38'

Displacement:
Full load: 5,713 tonnes.
Standard: 4,662 tonnes.
Length: 14.5m.
Beam: 14.62m (later 14.8m).
Draught: 4.66m (standard).
Machinery:
Four two-drum Bauer-Wagner high-pressure ($70kg/cm^2$) boilers.
Two shaft single reduction geared turbines.
One shaft with four double acting two-stroke MAN diesels.
77,500shp (turbines) plus 14,500bhp (diesels) = 35.5 knots.
600 tonnes oil fuel = 7,000nm at 17 knots.
Two diesel generators (180kW each) and one turbo generator of 460kW in each turbine room.
Armament:
Six 15cm Tbts KC/36 T in twin mountings LC/38.

Two 8.8cm SKC/32 in twin mountings LC/32.
Eight 3.7cm SKC/30 in twin mountings LC/30.
Eight 2cm MG C/38.
Ten 53.3cm torpedo tubes (quintuple).
Light flak outfit subsequently modified to ten or twelve 3.7cm and twelve 2cm/38 in vierlings with the deletion of the 8.8cm mounting.
Protection:
Deck: 10mm (main).
Sides: 18mm (inner longitudinal bulkhead).

'SPÄHKREUZER 39'

Displacement:
Full load: 7,550 tonnes.
Standard: 6,050 tonnes.
Length: 160m.
Beam: 16m.
Draught:
4.9m (standard).
Machinery:
Two two-drum Bauer-Wagner high pressure ($70kg/cm^2$) boilers.
One shaft single reduction geared turbine.
Two shafts each with 'V' diesel engine.
50,000shp (turbine) plus 30,000bhp (diesel) = 33 knots.

800 tonnes oil fuel = 11,000nm at 17 knots.
Armament:
Six 15cm Tbts KC/36 T in twin mountings LC/38.
Six 8.8cm SKC/32 in twin mountings LC/32.
Eight 3.7cm SKC/30 in twin mountings LC/30.
Eight 2cm MG C/38 in twin mountings.
One aircraft and one catapult.
Protection:
Deck: 20–25mm, 20mm (upper).
Belt: 50mm.
Inner longitudinal bulkhead: 12mm.

'SPÄHKREUZER 40'

Displacement:
Full load: 7,500 tonnes.
Standard: 6,500 tonnes.
Length: 162m.
Beam: 16m.
Draught: 4.9m (standard).
Machinery:
Four two-drum Bauer-Wagner high-pressure boilers ($70kg/cm^2$).
Two shaft Wagner single reduction geared turbines.
One 'V' diesel motor on centre shaft.
80,000shp (turbines) plus 30,000bhp (diesel) = 36.2 knots.

Four designs were submitted of which 'Trotz Alledem' was an incomplete study.

	'Seeadler'	'Motor Kreuzer'	'Wehr Dich'
Displacement: (standard)	8,400 tonnes	8,959 tonnes	8,128 tonnes
Speed: (based on towing trials)	35.5 (maximum) 34.7 (cont)	35.7 35.1	35.2 34.5
Machinery:	Three shafts 40,000hp turbine on each outer 40,000hp turbine plus 18,000bhp diesels on centre shaft	Two shafts 59,000bhp on each	Three shafts 45,000hp on outers (each) plus 31,000bhp diesel in centre
Boilers:	Deschimag	—	Deschimag
Range:	—	—	8,700nm
Armament:	Four twin 15cm	Three triple 15cm	Four twin 15cm

In the light of wartime experience, and after the evaluation of captured British documents dated 1 September 1940 and 29 June 1940, which gave details of the endurance figures for Royal Navy ships, the Kriegsmarine re-evaluated the data for their own cruisers. The figures were:

Leipzig
3,780nm at 15 knots
2,980nm at 21 knots
2,220nm at 27 knots
940nm at 32 knots
Köln
2,760nm at 15 knots
2,320nm at 21 knots
1,340nm at 27 knots
820nm at 29.9 knots
Nürnberg
2,080nm at 15 knots

2,260nm at 21 knots
1,700nm at 27 knots
922nm at 29.9 knots
Emden
3,400nm at 15 knots
2,320nm at 21 knots
1,160nm at 27 knots
1,060nm at full speed

Admiral Hipper
1,820nm at 32 knots
2,740nm at 27 knots
3,080nm at 21 knots
2,760nm at 15 knots (sic)

Prinz Eugen
2,020nm at 32 knots ($60kg/cm^2$)
3,020nm at 27 knots ($45kg/cm^2$)
4,760nm at 21 knots ($45kg/cm^2$)
5,100nm at 15 knots ($45kg/cm^2$)

800 tonnes oil fuel = 12,000nm at 17 knots.
Armament:
Six 15cm Tbts KC/36 T in LC/38 mountings.
Four 8.8cm SKC/32 in twin mountings LC/32.
Eight 3.7cm SKC/30 in twin mountings LC/30.
Eight 2cm MG C/38.
Ten 53.3cm torpedoes in quintuple mountings.
Protection:
Deck: 20–25mm (main), 12–15mm (upper).
Belt: 50mm.

Inner longitudinal bulkhead: 12mm.
Note:
The *Spähkreuzer* project was in a continual state of flux and it is doubtful if the design was ever 'sealed'. In consequence the data quoted above can only be considered approximate.

POST 'KREUZER M' DESIGNS
General Design Requirements:
Displacement: Under 8,000 tonnes.
Speed: 35/36˙knots with 80% full bunkers.
Bunkers: 2,000 tonnes.
Endurance: 6,000nm at 19 knots.

Boilers:
Air pressure: 250mm WG (maximum).
Cooling water temperature: 20°C (maximum).
Steam temperature at drum: 435°C (maximum).
Hull:
No blister, but double hull alongside engine, boiler and magazine spaces.
Hull Stresses:
1,800kg/cm² (maximum) for longitudinals.
2,100kg/cm² (maximum) lower hull and local loading.
Stability:
Ship fully armed 90° lever arm 90cm.

Ship fully armed (loaded) 90° lever arm 75cm.
Ship fully armed (light) 75–80° lever arm 50cm.
Metacentric height at least 1.2m, 1.91m and 0.7m in above conditions.
Protection:
50mm belt at least 2.5m deep for full length of boilers and magazines, etc.
30mm belt beyond to end bulkheads.
Bow armoured belt 18mm thick, 3.5m deep.
20mm deck with 25mm glacis.
30mm barbettes, 60mm conning tower, 20mm splinter protection.
Crew: 654 (peace), 749 (war).

II. CONSTRUCTION, COMMANDERS AND FATES

EMDEN

Laid down:	Launched:	Completed:	Builder:
8.12.21	7.1.25	15.10.25	Wilhelmshaven Dockyard

Commanding Officers:

Kpt.z.S. Kurt Foerster	15.10.25 to	9.28
K.Kpt./F.Kpt./Kpt.z.S. von Arnauld de la Pierre	9.28 to	10.30
F.Kpt./Kpt.z.S.Witthoeft-Emden	10.30 to	3.32
F.Kpt. Werner Grassmann	3.32 to	4.33
F.Kpt. Karl Dönitz	9.34 to	9.35
Kpt.z.S. Johannes Bachmann	9.35 to	8.36
Kpt.z.S. Walter Lohmann	8.36 to	6.37
F.Kpt./Kpt.z.S. Leopold Bürkner	7.37 to	6.38
Kpt.z.S. Paul Wever	6.38 to	5.39
Kpt.z.S. Werner Lange	5.39 to	26.8.40
Kpt.z.S. Hans Mirow	27.8.40 to	7.42
Kpt.z.S. Friedrich Schmidt	7.42 to	9.43
Kpt.z.S. Hans Henigst	9.43 to	2.44
F.Kpt./Kpt.z.S. Hans-Eberhard Meisner	3.44 to	1.45
Kpt.z.S. Wolfgang Kähler	1.45 to	4.45
F.Kpt. Wickmann (temp)	3.45 to	4.45

Fate:
Damaged by air raid at Deutsche Werke (Kiel) 4.45. Towed to Heinkendorferbucht and scuttled there 3.5.45. Wreck further damaged by depth-charges under engine room by RN 21.5.46. Subsequently broken up in situ.

KÖNIGSBERG

Laid down:	Launched:	Completed:	Builder:
12.4.26	26.3.27	17.4.29	Wilhelmshaven Dockyard

Commanding Officers:

F.Kpt. Wolf von Trotha	17.4.29 to	6.29
F.Kpt. Witthoeft-Emden	6.29 to	9.30
F.Kpt. Hermann Densch	9.30 to	9.32
F.Kpt./Kpt.z.S. Otto von Schrader	9.32 to	9.34
F.Kpt./Kpt.z.S. Hubert Schmundt	9.34 to	9.35
F.Kpt./Kpt.z.S. Theodor Paul	9.35 to	2.37
Kpt.z.S. Robin Schall-Emden	2.37 to	11.38
Kpt.z.S. Ernst Schuerlen	11.38 to	6.39
Kpt.z.S. Kurt Hoffmann	6.39 to	14.9.39
Kpt.z.S. Heinrich Ruhfus	15.9.39 to	10.4.40

Fate:
Bombed and sunk by Skuas of Fleet Air Arm (800 & 803 Squadrons) at Bergen 10.4.40. Wreck raised 1943/44. Later broken up in situ.

KARLSRUHE

Laid down:	Launched:	Completed:	Builder:
27.7.26	20.8.27	6.11.29	Deutsche Werke

Commanding Officers:

F.Kpt./Kpt.z.S. Eugen Lindau	6.11.29 to	9.31
F.Kpt./Kpt.z.S. Erwin Wassner	9.31 to	12.32
F.Kpt. Frhr Harsdorf von Enderndorf	12.32 to	9.34
Kpt.z.S. Gunter Lütjens	9.34 to	9.35
F.Kpt./Kpt.z.S. Leopold Siemens	9.35 to	9.37
Kpt.z.S. Dr Werner Förste	9.37 to	5.38
Kpt.z.S. Friedrich Rieve	13.11.39 to	10.4.40

Fate:
Heavily damaged by torpedoes from HM Submarine *Truant* off Kristiansand (S) 9.4.40. Finally sunk by two torpedoes from *Greif* 10.4.40.

KÖLN

Laid down:	Launched:	Completed:	Builder:
7.8.26	23.5.28	15.1.30	Wilhelmshaven Dockyard

Commanding Officers:

F.Kpt./Kpt.z.S. Ludwig v. Schröder	15.1.30 to	9.32
F.Kpt./Kpt.z.S. Otto Schniewind	9.32 to	3.34
F.Kpt./Kpt.z.S. Werner Fuchs	3.34 to	10.35
F.Kpt./Kpt.z.S. Otto Backenköhler	10.35 to	10.37
Kpt.z.S. Theodor Burchardi	10.37 to	14.1.40
Kpt.z.S. Ernst Kretzenberg	15.1.40 to	5.41
Kpt.z.S. Friedrich Hüffmeier	5.41 to	3.42
K.Kpt. Hellmuth Strobel (temp)	3.42 to	5.42
Kpt.z.S. Martin Baltzer	5.42 to 12.12.42
Kpt.z.S. Hans Meyer	13.2.42 to	2.43
F.Kpt./Kpt.z.S. Hellmuth Strobel	4.44 to	1.45
K.Kpt. Fritz-Henning Brandes	1.45 to	30.4.45

Fate:
Sunk by air raid in Wilhelmshaven dockyard 30.3.45. Paid off 6.4.45. Broken up post war.

LEIPZIG

Laid down:	Launched:	Completed:	Builder:
18.4.28	18.10.29	8.10.31	Wilhelmshaven Dockyard

Commanding Officers:

Kpt.z.S. H-H. Stobwasser	8.10.31 to	9.33
F.Kpt./Kpt.z.S. Otto Hormel	10.33 to	9.35
F.Kpt./Kpt.z.S. Otto Schenk	9.35 to	10.37
Kpt.z.S. Werner Löwisch	10.37 to	4.39
Kpt.z.S. Heinz Nordmann	4.39 to	2.40

Kpt.z.S. Werner Stichling   1.12.40 to 8.42
Kpt.z.S. Friedrich Schmidt (temp)   8.42 to 9.42
Kpt.z.S. Waldemar Winther   25.9.42 to 18.2.43
F.Kpt. Joachim Asmus (temp)   2.43 to 3.43
Kpt.z.S. Walter Hulsemann   1.8.43 to 25.8.44
Kpt.z.S. Heinrich Spörel   26.8.44 to 11.44
K.Kpt. Hagen Küsfer (temp)   11.44 to 1.45
K.Kpt. Walter Bach (temp)   1.45 to 12.45

Fate:
Scuttled in North Sea, loaded with gas shells and redundant ammunition, 11.7.46.

NÜRNBERG

Laid down:	*Launched:*	*Completed:*	*Builder:*
4.11.33	8.12.34	2.11.35	Deutsche Werke Kiel

Commanding Officers:
Kpt.z.S. Hubert Schmundt   2.11.35 to 10.36
Kpt.z.S. Theodore Riedel   10.36 to 10.37
Kpt.z.S. Walter Krastel   10.37 to 11.38
Kpt.z.S. Heinz Degenhardt   11.38
F.Kpt. Walter Hennecke (temp)   11.38
Kpt.z.S. Otto Klüber   11.38 to 7.8.40
Kpt.z.S. Leo Kreisch   8.8.40 to 19.3.41
Kpt.z.S. Ernst v. Studnitz   20.3.41 to 6.43
Kpt.z.S. Gerhardt Böhmig   6.43 to 7.10.44
Kpt.z.S. Helmuth Gressler   8.10.44 to 1.46
(Soviet C.O.s not known)

Fate:
Transferred to USSR 5.1.46 at Libau and renamed *Admiral Makarov*. Discarded and broken up in 1960s.

ADMIRAL HIPPER

Yard No:	*Laid down:*	*Launched:*	*Completed:*	*Builder:*
B501	6.7.35	6.2.37	29.4.39	Blohm & Voss (Hamburg)

Commanding Officers:
Kpt.z.S. Helmuth Heye   29.4.39 to 3.9.40
Kpt.z.S. Wilhelm Meisel   4.9.40 to 10.10.42
Kpt.z.S. Hans Hartmann   11.10.42 to 16.2.43
Kpt.z.S. Hans Henigst   1944 to 1945

Fate:
Badly damaged by RAF air raid while in dock at Deutsche Werke (Kiel) 9/10.4.45. Scuttled by depth-charges 2.5.45. Refloated 1945 and towed to Heinkendorferbucht where she was broken up.

BLÜCHER

Yard No:	*Laid down:*	*Launched:*	*Completed:*	*Builder:*
K246	15.8.35	8.6.37	20.9.39	Deutsche Werke*

*Turbines subcontracted to Blohm & Voss.

Commanding Officer:
Kpt.z.S. Heinrich Woldag   20.9.39 to 9.4.40

Fate:
Torpedoed and sunk by Norwegian shore battery in Drobak Narrows, Oslofjord 9.4.40.

PRINZ EUGEN

Yard No:	*Laid down:*	*Launched:*	*Completed:*	*Builder:*
G564	23.4.36	22.8.38	1.8.40	Krupp (Germania)

Commanding Officers:
Kpt.z.S. Helmuth Brinkmann   1.8.40 to 31.7.42
F.Kpt. Neubauer (temp)   25.6.42 to 30.6.42
K.Kpt. Beck (temp)   1.7.42 to 8.10.42
Kpt.z.S. Hans-Eric Voss   9.10.42 to 28.2.43
Kpt.z.S. Werner Ehrhardt   29.2.43 to 5.1.44
Kpt.z.S. Hans-Jürgen Reinicke   6.1.44 to 7.5.45
Capt. A. H. Graubert, USN   1945 to 1946

Fate:
Taken over by the US Navy and re-named *IX300*. Expended in atom bomb tests (Operation 'Crossroads') July 1946. Paid off at Kwajalein Atoll 29.8.46. Foundered due to leaks 22.12.46.

SEYDLITZ

Yard No:	*Laid down:*	*Launched:*	*Completed:*	*Builder:*
W940	29.12.36	19.1.39	—	Deschimag (Bremen)

Fate:
Projected conversion to aircraft carrier (Project Weser I) never completed. Scuttled at Königsberg 10.4.45. Fell into Soviet hands and probably broken up.

LÜTZOW

Yard No:	*Laid down:*	*Launched:*	*Completed:*	*Builder:*
W941	2.8.37	1.7.39	—	Deschimag (Bremen)

Fate:
Sold to USSR 2.40. Towed to Leningrad 4.40. Re-named *Petropavlovsk*, then *Tallin*. Never completed. Renamed *Dnepr* as training ship 3.53. Scrapped in 1950s at Leningrad.

III. ARMAMENT

20.3cm SKC/34in Drh Tr LC/34

Gun:
Calibre	203mm
Muzzle velocity	925m/sec
Muzzle energy	5,320mt
Barrel length	60 cal/12,500mm
Liner length	56.7 cal/11,518mm
Barrel life	300 rounds
Weight of breech and barrel	20,700kg
Maximum range	33,500m

Ammunition:
Weight of shell	122kg
Weight of charge	8.93kg (HE nose fuze), 6.54kg (HE base fuze), 2.30kg(AP)
Length of shell	953mm (HE nose fuze), 956mm (HE base fuze), 895mm (AP)
Weight of cartridge	20kg (vorkartusche), 48kg (hauptkartusche)
Length of cartridge	900mm (vorkartusche), 875mm (hauptkartusche)

Mounting:
Elevation/ depression	+37°/−10° (−9° 'A' turret)
Training limits	290°
Elevation change rate (power)	8°/sec & 2°/sec
Training change rate (power)	6°/sec & 3°/sec
Weight of cast gun cradle	8,550kg
Weight of pedestal	175,530kg
Weight of sights	2,130kg
Electric power	14,970kg
Total weight of turrets	249,000kg ('A', 'D'), 262,000kg ('B', 'C')
Armour	Front 160mm; top 70mm; sides 70mm; rear 90mm ('A', 'D'), 60mm ('B', 'C')
Armour type	KC

17cm twin turret proposed at various times for new construction

Gun:
Calibre	170mm
Muzzle velocity	850m/sec
Recoil force at 0° elevation	60,000kg
Weight of breech and barrel	23,800kg (per gun)

Ammunition:
Weight of shell	72kg

Mounting:
Elevation/ depression	+45°/−10°
Training limits	±360°

Weight of cast gun cradle	Variously quoted as 2,600kg or 3,200kg per gun
Weight of pedestal	Variously quoted as 53,500kg or 34,000kg per gun
Weight of sighting gear	9,900kg
Electric power	11,000kg or 15,000kg
Weight of armour	27,100kg
Total weight of mounting	140,000kg*

Note: These figures are not thought to represent the definitive design.

*For Kreuzer 'M' & 'N'. For Battleships 'H' & 'J' armour weight increased to 51,500kg for total weight of 164,400kg.

15cm L/45 in MPL C/16

Gun:

Calibre	150mm
Muzzle velocity	835m/sec
Muzzle energy	1,610mt
Barrel length	45cal/6,558mm
Barrel life	1,400 rounds
Length of rifling	5,095mm
Type of rifling	45/30 increasing towards muzzle
Number of grooves	48
Weight of breech and barrel	5,730kg
Maximum range	16,800m

Ammunition:

Weight of shell	45.3kg
Weight of charge	3.90kg (base fuze HE), 4.09kg (nose fuze HE)
HE charge	Fp02
Length of shell	612mm (HE base fuze), 609.2mm (HE nose fuze)
Weight of cartridge	22.7kg
Length of cartridge	865mm
Propellant	RPC12 or RPC38
Fuzes	f2, S/60 or C/27

Mounting:

Elevation/ depression	+27°/−10°
Weight of cast gun cradle	2,345kg
Total weight of mounting	11,386kg

Note: Emden original armament.

15cm TBK C/36 in MPL C/36

Gun:

Calibre	149.1mm
Muzzle velocity	835m/sec
Barrel length	48cal/7,165mm
Liner length	45.7cal/6,815mm
Constructional gas pressure	3,000kg/cm²

Barrel life	1,100 rounds
Recoil force at 0° elevation	58,000kg
Length of rifling	5,587mm
Type of rifling	Cubic parabola 45/30cal
Number of grooves	44
Weight of breech and barrel	8,564kg
Maximum range	21,950m
Construction	Jacket with loose inner tube; cross wedge breech

Ammunition:

	HE	HEmh (mit Haube)
Weight of shell	45.3kg	45.3kg
Weight of charge	6kg,	3.89kg
HE charge	Fp02	Fp02
Length of shell	700mm	678.9mm
Weight of cartridge	23.5kg	24kg
Length of cartridge	865mm	865mm
Fuzes	Time S/30	Inst. Nose C/27

Mounting:

Elevation/ depression	+30°/−10°
Training limits	±360° = 720°
Elevation change per handwheel revolution	1° 52'
Training change per handwheel revolution	3°
Weight of cast gun cradle	1,730kg
Weight of base	2,400kg
Weight of pedestal	3,885kg
Weight of sighting gear	650kg
Electric power	450kg
Weight of shield	3,185kg
Total weight of mounting	16,100kg
Armour	Front 10mm; side and deck 6mm

Note: Emden as re-gunned.

15cm SKC/25

Gun:

Calibre	149.1mm
Muzzle velocity	960m/sec
Barrel length	60cal/9,080mm
Liner length	57.5cal/8,570mm
Constructional gas pressure	3,850kg/cm²
Barrel life	500 rounds
Recoil force at 0° elevation	52,000kg/cm²
Length of rifling	7,067mm
Type of rifling	Parabolic 45/30cal

Number of grooves	44
Weight of breech and barrel	11,970kg
Maximum range	25,700m
Construction	Jacket with loose inner tube. RM thread. Vertical sliding wedge breech

Ammunition:

Weight of shell	45.5kg
Weight of charge	3.892kg (HE head fuze), 3.058kg (HE base fuze), .885kg (AP)
HE charge	Fp02
Length of shell	4.5cal/680mm (HE base fuze), 4.4cal/655mm (HE head fuze), 3.7cal AP
Weight of cartridge	33.4kg
Length of cartridge	1,192mm
Propellant	C/32 or C/38
Fuzes	C/27

Mounting: **Drh TrC/25**

	(Köln)	(Nürnberg)
Elevation/ depression	+40°/−10°,	+40°/−10°
Training limits	±360°=720°	±360°=720°
Elevation change (power)	6°/sec	6° to 8°/sec
Training change (power)	6° to 8°/sec	7.6°/sec
Weight of cast gun cradle	2,440kg	2,457kg
Weight of base	4,230kg	4.230kg
Weight of pedestal	54,260kg	55,450kg
Weight of sighting gear	3,500kg	4,420kg
Electric power	11,120kg	12,500kg
Weight of shield	24,800kg	31,500kg
Total weight of mounting	136,910kg,	147,150kg
Armour	Front 30mm; side 20mm; deck 20mm	Front 80mm; side 20mm; deck 20-35mm; rear 35mm
Armour type	Pz Stahl 420	Whn/A

15cm SKC/28 in Dop.L. C/34

Gun:

Calibre	149.1mm
Muzzle velocity	875m/sec

Muzzle energy	1,770mt
Barrel length	55cal/8,200mm
Liner length	52.4cal/7,816mm
Constructional gas pressure	3,050kg/cm²
Barrel life	1,100 rounds
Recoil force at 0° elevation	52,000kg
Length of rifling	6,588mm
Type of rifling	Cubic parabola 50/30cal
Number of grooves	44
Weight of breech and barrel	9,080kg
Maximum range	23,000m
Construction	Jacket with loose inner sleeve. Rhein-Metall thread. Vertical sliding wedge breech. 2 hydraulic brakes and air recuperator

Ammunition:

Weight of shell	45.3kg
Weight of charge	3.058kg or 3.892kg
HE charge	Fp02
Length of shell	4.5cal/655mm or 4.6cal/678.9mm
Weight of cartridge	23.5kg
Length of cartridge	865mm
Propellant	RPC/32
Fuzes	C/27

Mounting:

Elevation/ depression	+40°/−10°
Training limits	±360° = 720°
Elevation change per handwheel revolution	1.04° (8° Power)
Training change per handwheel revolution	1.09° (9° Power)
Weight of cast gun cradle	2,440kg
Weight of base	2,835kg
Weight of pedestal	41,830kg
Weight of training gear	2,350kg
Electric power	10,300kg
Weight of shield	32,480kg
Total weight of mounting	110,000kg
Armour	Front 100mm; side 40mm; deck 20/35mm; rear 40mm
Armour type	Whn/Au KCn/A

Note: Kreuzer 'M' class.

10.5cm SKC/33

Gun:

Calibre	105mm
Muzzle velocity	900m/sec
Muzzle energy	625mt
Barrel length	65cal/6,840mm

Liner length 60.5cal/6,348mm
Constructional gas pressure 2,850kg/cm²
Barrel life 2,950 rounds
Recoil force at 0° elevation 1,300kg
Length of rifling 5,531mm
Type of rifling Cubic parabola 55/35
Number of grooves 36
Weight of breech and barrel 4,560kg
Maximum range 17,700m (horizontal), 12,500m (80°)
Construction Jacket with loose inner sleeve. Vertical sliding wedge breech

Ammunition:

	HE	tracer
Weight of shell	15.1kg	
Weight of charge	5.2kg	
HE charge	Fp02	Propellant charge (tracer)
Length of shell	459mm (L4.4HE)	438mm (L4.0 tracer)
Weight of cartridge	6kg	6kg
Length of cartridge	769mm	769mm
Propellant	C/32	C/32
Fuzes	Time S/30	Time S/6
Weight of complete round	26.5kg	23.5kg
Length of complete round	1,163mm	1,142mm

Mounting:

	8.8cm Dop.L C/31	10.5cm Dop.L C/3
Elevation/depression	+80°/−8°	+80°/−10°
Training limits	±360°=720°	±360°=720°
Elevation change per handwheel revolution	1.33° (10°/sec power)	1.76° (12°/sec power)
Training change per handwheel revolution	1.5° (8°/sec power)	1.5° (8.5°/sec power)
Weight of cast gun cradle	1,455kg	1,455kg
Weight of base	2,300kg	
Weight of pedestal	7,150kg	7,000kg
Weight of sight	745kg	560kg
Electric power	1,295kg	1,295kg
Weight of shield	6,130kg	5,270kg
Total weight of mounting	27,350kg	26,425kg
Armour	Front 15mm; side and deck 10mm	Front 20mm; side and deck 10mm and 8mm; rear 8mm
Armour type	Whn A	Whn A

10.5cm SKC/32ns in 10.5cm MPL C/32ge

Gun:
Calibre 105mm
Muzzle velocity 780m/sec
Muzzle energy 475mt
Barrel length 45cal/4,740mm
Liner length 42cal/4,400mm
Constructional gas pressure 2,850kg/cm²
Barrel life 4,100 rounds
Recoil force at 0° elevation 22,600kg
Length of rifling 3,694mm
Type of rifling Cubic parabola 45/30cal
Number of grooves 32
Weight of breech and barrel 1,765kg
Maximum range 15,175m
Construction Monobloc jacket with drawn-on vertical sliding wedge breech. Rhein-Metall thread

Ammunition:
Weight of shell (HE) 15.1kg
Weight of charge 3.8kg
HE charge Fp02
Length of shell 459mm
Weight of cartridge 4.6kg
Length of cartridge 657mm
Propellant RPC/32
Fuzes Time S/30, inst C/28
Weight of complete round 24.0kg
Length of complete round 1,050mm

Mounting:
Elevation/depression +70°/−10°
Elevation change per handwheel revolution 3°
Training change per handwheel revolution 3°
Weight of cast gun cradle 655kg
Weight of pedestal 2,100kg
Weight of sight 350kg
Electric power 210kg
Weight of shield 1,670kg

Total weight of mounting 6,750kg
Armour Front 12mm; side and deck 4mm
Armour type Wsh

8.8cm FLAK L/45 in MPL C/13

Gun:
Calibre 88mm
Muzzle velocity 790m/sec
Recoil force at 0° elevation 13,200kg
Weight of breech and barrel 2,500kg

Ammunition:
Weight of shell 9kg
Weight of charge 2.35kg

8.8cm SKC/32 in 8.8cm Dop.L. C/32

Gun:
Calibre 88mm
Muzzle velocity 950m/sec
Barrel length 76cal/6,690mm
Liner length 72cal/6,340mm
Constructional gas pressure 3,150kg/cm²
Barrel life 3,200 rounds
Recoil force at 0° elevation 7,800kg
Weight of breech and barrel 3,640kg
Maximum range 17,200m (horizontal), 12,400m (vertical)

Ammunition:
Weight of shell 9kg
Weight of charge 3.1kg
Length of shell 397mm
Weight of complete round 15kg/932mm

Mounting:
Elevation/depression +80°/−10°
Training limits ±360° = 720°
Elevation change per handwheel revolution 3.6° (10°/sec power)
Training change per handwheel revolution 2.5° (—)
Weight of cast gun cradle 1,775kg
Weight of base 815kg
Weight of pedestal 6,275kg
Weight of sights 745kg
Electric power 1280kg
Weight of shield 5,830kg
Total weight of mounting 23,650kg
Armour Front 12mm; side and deck 10mm
Armour type Whn A

8.8cm SKC/25 in 8.8cm Dop.L.C/25

Gun:
Calibre 88mm
Muzzle velocity 1,060m/s

Barrel length 6,340mm/72 cal
Liner length 6,625mm/75 cal
Constructional gas pressure 3100kg/cm²
Barrel life 600 rounds
Recoil force at 0° elevation 13,000kg
Weight of breech and barrel 5,980kg
Maximum range 17,600m (horizontal), 13,650m (vertical)

Ammunition:
Weight of shell 9kg
Weight of charge 4.53kg
Length of shell 385.5mm
Weight of cartridge 13.5kg
Length of cartridge 1,227mm

Mounting:
Elevation/depression +85°/−10°
Training limits ±360° =720°
Elevation change (power) 10°/sec
Training change (power) 10°/sec
Weight of cast gun cradle 1,030kg
Weight of base 3,900kg
Weight of pedestal 12,155kg
Weight of sights 910kg
Electric power 695kg
Weight of shield 1,170kg
Total weight of mounting 28,950kg
Armour Front, side and deck 8mm
Armour type Panzerstahl

4cm FLAK 28 (BOFORS)

Gun:
Calibre 40mm
Muzzle velocity 854m/sec
Barrel length 2,249mm
Length of rifling 1,932mm

3.7cm SKC/30 in twin mounting C/30

Gun:
Calibre 37mm
Muzzle velocity 1,000m/sec
muzzle energy 38mt
Barrel length 83cal/3,074mm
Bore length 80cal/2,960mm
Constructional gas pressure 3,450kg/cm²
Barrel life 7,500 rounds
Recoil force at 0° elevation 1,000kg
Length of rifling 2,554mm
Type of rifling Cubic parabola 50/35
Number of grooves 16
Weight of breech and barrel 243kg
Maximum horizontal range 8,500m
Maximum vertical range 6,800m (tracer 4,800m)

Construction	Monobloc barrel with drawn on breech ring. Vertical sliding block breech. Hydraulic brake and spring recuperator

Ammunition:

Weight of shell	.742kg
Weight of charge	.365kg
HE charge	Fp02
Length of shell	162mm
Weight of cartridge	.970kg
Length of cartridge	381mm
Propellant	RPC/32
Weight of complete round	2.1kg
Length of complete round	516.5mm
Fuzes	E.nose fuze C/30; nose fuze C/34; Ers St C/34 (tracer)
Duration of tracer	12 secs
Rate of fire	160rpm cyclic, 80rpm practical

Mounting:

Elevation/depression	+85°/−10°
Training limits	±360° = 720°
Elevation change per handwheel revolution	3°
Training change per handwheel revolution	4°
Weight of cradle, brake, etc. (swinging mass)	243kg
Weight of cast gun cradle	152.5kg
Weight of base	71kg
Weight of pedestal	2,162kg
Weight of sight	87kg
Weight of electric power	630kg
Complete mounting	3,670kg

3.7cm MK.42 in 3.7cm A.A.LM42

Gun:

Calibre	37mm
Muzzle velocity	850m/sec (HE)
Muzzle energy	24.4mt
Barrel length	69cal/2,568mm
Barrel life	7,000 rounds
Recoil force at 0°	1,240kg
Length of rifling	2,289mm
Type of rifling	constant r, 7° = 25.6cal
Number of grooves	16
Weight of breech and barrel	109kg
Construction	Monobloc barrel with breech ring connected by bayonet joint. Vertical sliding block breech. Hydraulic brake and spring recuperator

Ammunition:

Weight of shell (HE)	.61kg
Weight of cartridge	.510kg
Weight complete round	1.3kg
Length complete round	355mm
Type of fuze	Nose fuze 40
Fuze filling	Duplex detonator
Supply	8-round linked clips

3.7cm A.A.43

Gun:

Calibre	37mm
Muzzle velocity	870m/sec (HE), 770m/sec (AP), 1,150m/sec (AP40)
Muzzle energy	21.8mt
Barrel length	57cal
Constructional gas pressure	2,900kg/cm²
Barrel life	8,000 rounds
Length of rifling	1,838mm
Type of rifling	Kupa 3°/5°
Number of grooves	20
Weight of breech and barrel	127kg
Maximum vertical range	4,800m
Construction	Modified Rhein Metall 108 MK103 aircraft cannon with gas-operated breech

Ammunition:

Weight of shell	.625kg (HE), .685kg (AP)
Weight complete round	1.5kg
Length complete round	368mm
Fuze	Nose
Fuze filling	Duplex detonator
Supply	8-round linked clips

Mounting:

Elevation/depression	+85°/−10°
Training limits	360°

2cm C/30 in 2cm Pedestal L30

Gun:

Calibre	20mm
Muzzle velocity	835m/sec
Barrel length	65cal/1,300mm
Bore length	65cal/1,300mm
Constructional gas pressure	2,800kg/cm²
Barrel life	22,000 rounds
Recoil force 0° elevation	250kg
Length of rifling	720mm
Weight of breech and barrel	64kg
Maximum horizontal range	4,900m
Maximum vertical range	3,700m

Ammunition:

Weight of shell	134g
Length of shell	78.5mm
Weight of charge	39.5g
Weight of complete round	320g
Length of complete round	203mm
Rate of fire	280rpm cyclic, 120rpm practical 20-round magazine

Mounting:

Elevation/depression	+85°/−11°
Training limits	none
Weight cradle, brake, etc. (swinging mass)	43kg
Weight of mounting without sights	282kg
Weight of complete gun	420kg

2cm C/38 in 2cm Pedestal L30

Gun:

As 2cm C/30, but recoil force at 0°, 290kg; weight of barrel and breech 57.5kg.

Ammunition:

As 2cm C/30, but rate of fire improved to 480rpm cyclic, 220rpm practical.

Mounting:

As 2cm C/30, but weight of complete gun, including spent cartridge net 416kg.

2cm FLAK 35, vierling L38

Guns:

Four 2cm C/38 barrels.

Ammunition:

As 2cm C/38, but rate of fire 1,800rpm cyclic, 880rpm practical.

Mounting:

Weight of cradle and brake	410kg
Weight of mounting less sights	828kg
Weight of sights and training gear	96.6kg
Weight of power training	31.5kg
Weight of armour	500kg
Weight of complete gun	2,150kg

TORPEDOES

Calibre	533mm
Type	G7a
Fuel	Compressed air
Warhead	430kg TNT
Speed/range	30 knots = 15,000m 40 knots = 5,000m 45 knots = 4,500m
Gyro angling	Up to 90° left or right in 1° steps
Depth setting	Up to 52m in 1m steps

SHIPBOARD AIRCRAFT

Heinkel He60C

Power plant	One 660hp BMW VI 6,0 ZU
Performance	225km/hr at 1,000m maximum 190km/hr cruising
Normal range	720km
Service ceiling	5,000m
Dimensions	Wing span 12.9m Length 11.5m Height 4.9m Wing area 53.97m²
Crew	2
Armament	One 7.9mm MG

Arado Ar196 A-3

Power plant	One 960hp BMW 132k radial
Performance	310km/hr at 4,000m maximum 255km/hr cruising
Normal range	1,070km
Service ceiling	7,000m
Dimensions	Wing span 12.4m Length 11.0m Height 4.45m Wing area 28.4m²
Crew	2
Armament	Two fixed MG FF 20mm cannon and one 7.9 fixed MG. Two flexible 7.9mm MG in rear cockpit. Racks for two 50kg bombs

REFERENCES AND BIBLIOGRAPHY

UNPUBLISHED OFFICIAL SOURCES

German-Kriegstagesbücher, (War Diaries)
Flottenkommando
Mar. Gruppe (Nord)
Mar. Gruppe (West)
Marine Oberkommando Ost
Befehlshaber der Kreuzer
Befehlshaber der Aufklärungsstreitkräfte
Ausbildungsverbände
Führer der Zerstörer
Admiral (Nordmeer)
Emden
Königsberg
Karlsruhe
Köln
Leipzig (& Torpedo damage file)
Nürnberg
Admiral Hipper
Blücher (& Associated loss file)
Prinz Eugen
Bismarck
Tirpitz
Scharnhorst
Gneisenau
Lützow
Richard Beitzen
Theodore Riedel
Z29
Z30

British-Ships' Logs
Sheffield
Jamaica
Berwick

British-Submarine Logs and Patrol Reports
Clyde
Graph
Salmon
Swordfish
Tigris
Trident
Triton
Truant
Ursula

British-RAF and FAA Squadron and Station Operational Record Books
801 Sqn. FAA
803 Sqn. FAA
107 Sqn. RAF
110 Sqn. RAF

Technical Documents
German:
The Raeder Files
Der Verlauf der Entwurfsbearbeitung des Kreuzertyps M AV 126/39
Konstruktion Rheinmetall-Borsig: Angeben über Marine-Geschütz
Handbuch der Deutschekriegschiffstypen (Heft 1 M.Dv.401 1944)
Unterlagen und Richtlinien zur Bestimmung der Haupt-kampfentfernung und der Geschosswahl. Heft(a) OKM 1940
Deutsche Minenraumdienstvorschrift Nr.13; Übersicht über Deutsche und fremde Ankertauminen und Sperrschutzmitteln
Vorläufigen Beschreibung der Artillerie-Feuerleit-Anlagen der Kreuzer *Prinz Eugen-Seydlitz-Lützow* Band 1, Oktober 1939
Vorläufige Schiffskunde für Kreuzer *Prinz Eugen*, Band 1, M.Dv Nr. 37197
Plus numerous documents and papers of the period 1930 to 1939 pertaining to the design development of cruisers
British:
German Warships. Details of magazines & ammunition supplies. HMS *Excellent* X1486/48 (ADM1/17978)
Preliminary Inspection of *Prinz Eugen* 27.5.45 (ADM1/17353)
Preliminary Inspection of *Nürnberg* 23.5.45 (ADM1/17353)
German Warship Designs NID/24/T23 (ADM223/51)
World Survey of Naval Machinery Installation Practice. YARD YE47A
British Naval Gunnery Mission to Europe GO 10355 Report No. 3
American:
U.S. Naval Technical Mission to Europe reports TR-137, 138, 159, 393, 442
French:
Croiseur de 10,000 tonnes protégé "C4", Specification No. 2-Protection

PUBLISHED SOURCES

Barker R. *The Ship Busters*. Chatto & Windus, 1957
Bekker, C. *Hitler's Naval War*. Macdonald, 1974
Busch, F. O. *Prinz Eugen*. Futura, 1975
Bradford, E. *The Mighty Hood*. Hodder, 1961
Greger, R. 'Der Kreuzer *Petropavlosk* ex-*Lützow*'. Marine-Rundshau, 12/77 and 12/78
Gröner, E. *Die Deutschen Kriegschiffe, 1815–1936*. Lehmann, 1937
Gröner, E. *Die Deutschen Kriegschiffe, 1815–1945*. Lehmann, 1966
Gröner, E. *Die Schiffe der Deutschen Kriegsmarine und Luftwaffe, 1939–45*. Lehmann, 1954
Jung, D. (et al). *Anstriche und Tarnanstriche der Deutschen Kriegsmarine*. Bernard & Graefe Verlag, 1977
Lacroix, Dr E. 'Development of the 'A' Class cruisers in the IJN'. Warship International, 4/79, 1/81
Lenton, H. T. *German Warships of the Second World War*. Macdonald and Janes, 1975
Le Masson, H. *Navies of the Second World War, The French Navy*, vol. 1. Macdonald, 1969
Macintyre, D. *Fighting Ships and Seamen*. Evans, 1963
Mars, A. *British Submarines at War*. Kimber, 1971
Mullenheim-Rechberg, B. von. *Battleship Bismarck*. Triad, 1982
Potter, J. D. *Fiasco*. Heinemann, 1970
Raven, A. and Roberts, J. *County-Class Cruisers*. RSV Publications, 1978
Raven A. and Roberts, J. *Town-Class Cruisers*. Arms & Armour Press, 1980
Rohwer, J. and Hümmelchen, G. *Chronology of the War at Sea*, vols. I and II. Ian Allan, 1974
Roskill, S. W. *The War at Sea*, vols. I–III. HMSO, 1957
Sturton, J. A. 'HMS *Surrey* and *Northumberland*'. Warship International, 3/77
Whitley, M. J. *Destroyer!*. Arms & Armour Press, 1983
Wright, C. C. 'Comparative Notes on US Treaty Cruiser Design'. Warship International, 4/80
Sieche, E. 'German Naval Radar to 1945'. Warship, 21, 22 and 27

INDEX

Below: 'C' and 'D' turrets of *Admiral Hipper*, in French waters 1941. Points of interest are the painted turret roofs, radar mattress and cluster of diesel exhausts on the tripod mast legs. (Bundesarchiv)

GERMAN CRUISERS
OF WORLD WAR TWO